In this book, Dr Winter gathers all available evidence on the first-century sophistic movement from the two major centres of learning in the East. Together with the writings of Philo and Paul, this provides the first discussion of all the protagonists and antagonists of this movement in Alexandria and Corinth. While both these contemporary Hellenistic Jews responded to the movement on the basis of the Old Testament, Philo was also indebted to Plato for his assessment and Paul filtered important Old Testament texts through the message of the crucified Messiah.

This study provides important insights into the problems this élitist movement created for Diaspora Jews in Alexandria, and for Christians in Corinth. It also fills a crucial gap in our understanding of the rise of the Second Sophistic.

SOCIETY FOR NEW TESTAMENT STUDIES

MONOGRAPH SERIES

General editor: Richard Bauckham

96

PHILO AND PAUL AMONG THE SOPHISTS

Philo and Paul
among the sophists

BRUCE W. WINTER
Tyndale House, Cambridge

PUBLISHED BY THE PRESS SYNDICATE OF
THE UNIVERSITY OF CAMBRIDGE
The Pitt Building, Trumpington Street, Cambridge CB2 1RP, United
Kingdom

CAMBRIDGE UNIVERSITY PRESS
The Edinburgh Building, Cambridge, CB2 2RU, United Kingdom
40 West 20th Street, New York, NY 10011–4211, USA
10 Stamford Road, Oakleigh, Melbourne 3166, Australia

First published 1997

Printed in the United Kingdom at the University Press, Cambridge

Typeset in Times 10/12 pt

A catalogue record for this book is available from the British Library

Library of Congress cataloguing in publication data
Winter, Bruce W.
Philo and Paul among the Sophists / Bruce W. Winter.
 p. cm. – (Monograph series / Society for New Testament Studies: 96)
Revision of the author's thesis (doctoral) – Macquarie University, Sydney,
Australia, 1988.
Includes bibliographical references and indexes.
ISBN 0 521 59108 2 (hardback)
1. Sophists (Greek philosophy). 2. Philo, of Alexandria.
3. Paul, the Apostle, Saint.
4. Alexandria (Egypt) – Intellectual life.
5. Corinth (Greece) – Intellectual life.
6. Rhetoric, Ancient. 7. Rhetoric in the Bible.
8. Bible. N.T. Corinthians – Criticism, interpretation, etc.
9. Bible. N.T. Corinthians – Language, style.
I. Title.
II. Series: Monograph series (Society for New Testament Studies): 96.
B288.W56 1996
183′.1–dc21 96–44600 CIP

ISBN 0 521 59108 2 hardback

CE

CONTENTS

PREFACE

This work had its genesis in a doctoral dissertation as 'Philo and Paul among the Sophists: A Hellenist Jewish and A Christian Response' (1988), with the primary material drawn largely from the first and early second centuries AD. It was undertaken in the very stimulating σχολή of E. A. Judge, Professor of Ancient History, Macquarie University, Sydney. It originally proposed an antithesis to the vibrant thesis of Gnosticism in New Testament studies, especially in relation to Corinthian studies. The publication of the work was not deemed a matter of urgency because W. Schmithals' own thorough outworking of a Gnostic thesis seemed to have been partly responsible for its gradual decline as a possible explanation for the Corinthian situation. Other interests in NT Graeco–Roman background studies also strongly beckoned after the thesis was completed. The recent upsurge of interest in rhetoric in the writings of Philo and Paul provided the major impetus for revising this work for publication and I therefore deleted interactions with Gnosticism except for a general comment in the conclusion. I was also persuaded that the research was highly relevant for studies on an aspect of first-century ancient history, namely the sophistic movement.

Evidence for this movement in the East in the first sixty years of the first century AD comes from two major intellectual centres, namely Alexandria and Corinth, and especially from the works of Philo and Paul. These crucial witnesses have never been fully incorporated, if at all, in recent studies on the highly influential first-century sophistic movement. Their evidence and that from other literary and non-literary sources of the early empire change the perception of the sophistic movement at this time.

From the viewpoint of NT studies, no one could have anticipated the major interest in the late 1980s in rhetoric, in whose spread and esteem the sophists had played such a dominant role throughout the early empire. Yet little or no concern has been given by NT scholars to these leading figures who promoted its study and who played such an influential role in its use in education and politics in cities of the East. These sophists were the media megastars of their day and influenced generations of students of rhetoric and the public generally.

Studies in the application of rhetoric to the NT corpus have not always sufficiently appreciated the stance taken by Paul on the use of oratory for evangelism, or sought to reconcile that stance with rhetorical structures and devices seen to be used in his letters.[1] Furthermore, insufficient note has been taken of the high-profile role its proponents could play in the secular ἐκκλησία of the δῆμος and the paradigm this could create for leadership and teaching positions in associations in general, and the ἐκκλησία of the Christian community in particular.

By asking in what sense were Philo and Paul among these sophists, this book seeks to address the issues of the role and outlook of the latter group in the life of the first century and in particular their impact on Jews and Christians in Alexandria and Corinth respectively. I am extremely grateful for the interest, insights and warm encouragement given by Dr Margaret Thrall, the former series editor; to a long–standing friend, Professor David Runia for his incisive comments on aspects of Philo; to Dr Philip Kern for his own distinctive contribution to the study of rhetoric and the NT and for improving the manuscript, and finally to Mrs Elizabeth Saer, who with her husband, my son-in-law, laboured much in the metamorphosis of the dissertation into a book. This contribution to Philonic, Pauline and sophistic studies is dedicated to my dear wife, who has always willingly shared in the work we have undertaken over the years and has done so well beyond the call of duty. In her own unique way she provided an important perspective for the research that went into this volume.

June, 1996.

---

[1] I regret that R. Dean Anderson's fine treatment of rhetoric in *Ancient Rhetorical Theory and Paul* (Kampen: Kok, 1996) was released at the same time this book was submitted for publication. I was therefore unable to respond to his interpretations of 1 Cor. 2.1–5, 2 Cor. 10.10 and 11.6.

ABBREVIATIONS

PAPYRI

P.Amh.	*The Amherst Papyri*
BGU	*Ägyptische Urkunden aus den Königlichen Museen zu Berline Griechische Unkunden*
P.Coll.Youtie	*Collectanea Papyrologica. Texts published in Honour of H. C. Youtie.*
P.Fam.Tebt.	*A Family Archive from Tebtunis*
P.Flor.	*Papiri fiorentini*
P.Fouad	*Les papyrus Fouad*
P.Giss.	*Griechische Papyri im Museum des oberhessischen Geschichtsvereins zu Giessen*
P.Hamb.	*Griechische Papyrusurkunden aud Hamburger*
P.Harr.	*Rendel Harris Papyri*
P.Lips.	*Griechische Urkunden den Papyrussammlung zer Leipzig*
P. Lit.Lond.	*Literary Papyri in the British Museum*
P.Lond.	*Greek Papyri in the London Museum*
P.Mich.	*Papyri in the University of Michigan Collection*
P.Mil.Volg.	*Papiri della Università degli Studi di Milano*
P.Osl.	*Papyri Osloenses*
P.Oxy.	*The Oxyrhynchus Papyri*
P.Oxy.Hels.	*Fifty Oxyrhynchus Papyri (Helsinki)*
P.Princ.	*Papyri in the Princeton University Collection*
P.Ryl.	*Catalogue of the Greek Papyri in the John Rylands Library*
PSI	*Publicazione della Società Italiana per la ricerca dei Papyri greci e latini*
P. Teb.	*The Tebtunis Papyri*
P.Vindob.	*Papyrologica-Batana*

| P. Yale | Yale Papyri in the Beinecke Rare Book and Manuscript Library |
| SB | Sammelbuch griechischer Urkenden aus Ägypten |

INSCRIPTIONS

IG	Inscriptiones Graecae
OGIS	Orientis Graeci Inscriptiones Selectae
SEG	Supplementum Epigraphicum Graecum
SIG	Sylloge Inscriptionum Graecarum

WORKS OF PHILO

Abr.	De Abrahamo
Aet.	De aeternitate mundi
Agr.	De agricultura
Anim.	De animalibus
Chr.	De Cherubim
Conf.	De confusione linguarum
Congr.	De congressu eruditionis gratia
Contempl.	De vita contemplativa
Decal.	De Decalogo
Det.	Quod deterius potiori insidiari soleat
Deus	Quod Deus sit immutabilis
Ebr.	De ebrietate
Flacc.	In Flaccum
Fug.	De fuga et inventione
Gig.	De gigantibus
Her.	Quis rerum divinarum heres sit
Hyp.	Hypothetica
Ios.	De Iosepho
LA I–III	Legum allegoriae
Legat.	De legatione ad Gaium
Migr.	De migratione Abrahami
Mos. I, II	De vita Moysis
Mut.	De mutatione nominum
Op.	De opificio mundi
Plant.	De plantatione
Post.	De posteritate Caini
Praem.	De praemiis et poenis
Prob.	Quod omnis probus liber sit

Prov. I, II	*De Providentia*
QE I–II	*Quaestiones et solutiones in Exodum*
QG I–IV	*Quaestiones et solutiones in Genesim*
Sacr.	*De sacrificiis Abelis et Caini*
Sobr.	*De sobrietate*
Somn. I–II	*De somniis*
Spec. I–IV	*De specialibus legibus*
Virt.	*De virtutibus*

JOURNALS, SERIES, LEXICAL AIDS

AJP	*American Journal of Papyrology*
ANRW	*Aufstieg und Niedergang der römischen Welt*
ASP	*American Studies in Papyrology*
BAGD	*A Greek–English Lexicon of the New Testament and Other Early Christian Literature* (ed. Blass, Arndt, Gingrich and Danker)
BDF	*A Greek Grammar of the New Testament* (ed. Blass, DeBrunner and Funk)
BJRL	*Bulletin of the John Rylands Library*
BZ	*Biblische Zeitschrift*
CBQ	*Catholic Biblical Quarterly*
CJ	*Classical Journal*
CP	*Classical Philology*
CQ	*Classical Quarterly*
CR	*Classical Review*
CW	*Classical Weekly*
ET	*Expository Times*
GRBS	*Greece, Rome and Byzantine Studies*
HSCP	*Harvard Studies in Classical Philology*
HTR	*Harvard Theological Review*
HUCA	*Hebrew Union College Annual*
JBL	*Journal of Biblical Literature*
JETS	*Journal of Evangelical Theological Studies*
JHS	*Journal of Hellenic Studies*
JRA	*Journal of Roman Archaeology*
JRS	*Journal of Roman Studies*
JSNT	*Journal for the Study of the New Testament*
JSS	*Jewish Social Studies*
JTS	*Journal for Theological Studies*
LCL	*Loeb Classical Library*

LSJ	*A Greek–English Dictionary* (ed. Liddel, Scott and Jones)
New Docs.	*New Documents Illustrating Early Christianity*
NovT	*Novum Testamentum*
NTS	*New Testament Studies*
OCD	*Oxford Classical Dictionary*
RIL	*Rendiconti Istituto Lombardo Academia di Scienze e Lettere*
RSR	*Revue des Sciences Réligieuses*
RTR	*Reformed Theological Review*
SP	*Studia Philonica*
SPA	*Studia Philonica Annual*
TAPA	*Transactions of the American Philological Association*
TDNT	*Theological Dictionary of the New Testament*
Tyn.B.	*Tyndale Bulletin*
ZKG	*Zeitschrift für Kirchengeschichte*
ZNW	*Zeitschrift für die Neutestamentlische Wissenschaft*
ZPE	*Zeitschrift für Papyrologie und Epigraphik*

INTRODUCTION

The purpose of this book

'Is Saul among the prophets?' was the question asked by the Israelites of their king when they saw him engaging in the same public activities as the prophets (1 Samuel 10.11). 'Is Paul among the sophists?' would have been asked of his Latin namesake in his role as a public speaker in the first century. This enquiry would have been thought appropriate of any itinerant speaker in the early Roman Empire, such was the interest in, and status of, the virtuoso orators who dominated much of the public and intellectual life of cities in the East. The question would also have been asked of Philo of Alexandria, Paul's contemporary. He was known to have led an important embassy to the emperor Gaius on behalf of his fellow Alexandrian Jews, for sophists traditionally headed delegations to emperors and governors. The purpose of this book will be to explore in what sense Paul and Philo were 'among the sophists'.

This examination is relevant not only to Jewish and NT scholarship but also to ancient history. There has been a substantial gap in information concerning the sophistic movement in the first seventy years of the first century AD. The received view has been that it is not until the orations of Dio Chrysostom of Prusa in Bithynia that we possess any real witness to its activities in the East.[1] There is, however, evidence to be found in the writing of two Hellenised Jews who preceded the activity of the golden-tongued Dio by at least thirty years. It will be shown in this book just how important those early years were for the understanding of a movement which is generally perceived not to have bloomed until the end of the first century as the Second Sophistic and almost without warning.

---

[1] These date from *c.* AD 68. See C. P. Jones, *The Roman World of Dio Chrysostom* (Cambridge, Mass. and London: Harvard University Press, 1978), pp. 133–40.

That the evidence of Philo has been omitted by those interested in the sophistic movement in the first century was endorsed by the general observation of H. Chadwick in the 1965 T. W. Manson Memorial Lecture on Philo of Alexandria and Paul that 'Philo has not been used half enough'.[2] The neglect of Philo's works on this subject has been long-standing. It goes back at least a century to the time when the first extended semantic investigation of σοφιστής was carried out, based on literary sources.[3] Philo's evidence, which is the only extant witness of the movement in Alexandria, indeed in the East, in the first half of the first century AD, is still either overlooked or scarcely noted by ancient historians in their discussion of the sophistic movement.[4]

The same may also be said of Paul. Much recent discussion of his corpus has been dominated by the study of his indebtedness to ancient rhetoric for an understanding of how he wrote. Yet no real attention has been paid to its witness to those who were the much-admired public performers of rhetoric. Neither has Paul been used to enhance our understanding of the first-century sophistic movement in Corinth prior to references to it in the orations of Dio. According to Philostratus, the 'modern' period of the movement only really began in the reign of Nero.[5] With *Antike und Christentum* the traffic should flow in both directions, for the NT documents can be an important source of information about the social world of the first century for ancient historians. This is especially so for a century which had comparatively few literary sources.[6]

Philo's evidence is also crucial because it has been generally held that there was an absence of rhetorical activity in Alexandria from the late Ptolemaic period through to, and during, the movement called the Second Sophistic in the late first and second centuries AD.[7] This view has arisen largely because an important literary and

---

[2] H. Chadwick, 'St Paul and Philo of Alexandria', *BJRL* 48.2 (1966), 307, quoting from a letter of S. T. Coleridge to Francis Wragham, in E. L. Grigg, *Collected Letters of S. T. Coleridge* (Oxford: Clarendon Press, 1959), vol. IV, p. 803.

[3] C. Brandstätter, 'De notium πολιτικός et σοφιστής usu rhetorico', *Leipzig Stud. z. Class. Phil.* 15 (1894), 215–28.

[4] See pp. 5–7.

[5] Philostratus, *Lives of the Sophists*, 511, begins the 'modern' period from Nero's reign with Nicetes of Smyrna.

[6] For a discussion of this issue see my '*Christentum und Antike*: Acts and Paul's *Corpus* as Ancient History', in T. W. Hillard, R. A. Kearsley, C. E. V. Nixon and A. Nobbs (eds.), *Ancient History in a Modern University* (Grand Rapids: Eerdmans, 1997), Vol. II, pp. 549–59.

[7] So argues P. M. Fraser, *Ptolemaic Alexandria*, 2nd edn (Oxford: Clarendon Press,

a non-literary Alexandrian source have not been incorporated into recent studies on the sophists.[8] These Alexandrian texts are invaluable, sketching as they do aspects of the movement in this important university centre from different perspectives. Five sources on the movement in Corinth are also extremely informative. Together with the Alexandrian witnesses they provide a composite picture of the nature of the sophistic movement as it emerged in the East from the early part of the first century onwards into the early second century AD in two important centres: one the great university city known as the 'second' Athens and the other the foremost Roman colony in the East.[9]

This material also enables us to understand how Paul, the Hellenised Jew and Christian apostle, related to the sophistic tradition both in secular Corinth and in the Christian community which he established in that Roman colony. The same will also be argued of Philo with respect to Alexandria and the Greek and Jewish communities there. The first-century protagonists and antagonists of the sophistic movement noted in the secondary literature have been either Roman or Greek writers. Little or no attention at all has been given to the Alexandrian Jewish and the Christian sources. The intention of this book is to gather together evidence on the sophistic movement in Alexandria and Corinth and to make an assessment of the way in which two contemporaries, the Hellenised Jews Philo and Paul, interacted with it and in part adopted their stance to it on the basis of an ancient source, namely the Old Testament.

The sophists

Who were the sophists? Originally the term σοφιστής described ancient wise men.[10] By the first century AD it was used to designate

1972), vol. I, p. 810. See also E. G. Turner, 'Oxyrhynchus and Rome', *HSCP* 7 (1975), 5, who follows Fraser with the support of G. W. Bowersock, *Greek Sophists in the Roman Empire* (Oxford: Clarendon Press, 1969), pp. 20–1. Bowersock expresses surprise that very few native Alexandrians seem to appear in the records of the Second Sophistic.

[8] See pp. 6–7.

[9] The study made of rhetoric in Alexandria can now also be undertaken for Corinth. See R. W. Smith, *The Art of Rhetoric in Alexandria: its Theory and Practice in the Ancient World* (The Hague: Martinus Nijhoff, 1974).

[10] For a discussion of the origins of the movement see J. S. Morrison, 'An Introductory Chapter in the History of Greek Education', *Durham University Journal* 12 (1949), 55–63, and for the original use of the term applied to 'a wise

those rhetoricians whose ability in oratory was such that they could both secure a public following and attract students to their schools. G. W. Bowersock succinctly defines a sophist as a 'virtuoso rhetor with a big public reputation', a definition endorsed in principle by C. P. Jones, E. L. Bowie and G. Anderson.[11] The phenomenon known as the sophistic movement had its roots in the second half of the fifth century BC.[12] While the history of the growth of the movement from Aristotle's time to the first century AD is somewhat sketchy, in his own day Philo could observe that the sophists were 'winning the admiration of city after city, and . . . drawing well-nigh the whole world to honour them'.[13] It would seem that in the first half of the first century what came to be known in the next as the Second Sophistic was already flowering if not flourishing.[14]

What did the sophists do? This is best seen in the work of the

man' see G. B. Kerferd, 'The First Greek Sophist?', *CR* 64 (1950), 8–10; W. K. C. Guthrie, 'What is a Sophist?', in *The Sophists* (Cambridge: Cambridge University Press, 1971), ch. 3; and D. H. Rankin, *Sophists, Socrates and Cynics* (London: Croom Helm, 1983), pp. 13–15.

[11] Bowersock, *Greek Sophists*, p. 13; C. P. Jones, 'The Reliability of Philostratus', in G. W. Bowersock (ed.), *Approaches to the Second Sophistic* (University Park, Pennsylvania: American Philological Association, 1974), p. 12; E. L. Bowie, 'Greeks and their Past in the Second Sophistic', *Past and Present* 46 (1970), 5; and G. Anderson, *Philostratus: Biography and Belles Lettres in the Third Century A.D.* (London: Croom Helm, 1986), pp. 10, 20, n. 59. Anderson in his article, 'The Pepaideumenos in Action: Sophists and their Outlook in the Early Empire', *ANRW* II.33.1 (1989), 81–2, n. 2, proposes an amendment to Bowersock's definition, adding 'a performing *pepaideumenos* with a big reputation' in order to include some literary figures as well. More recently, in his *The Second Sophistic: A Cultural Phenomenon in the Roman Empire* (London and New York: Routledge, 1993), p. 1, he sees them as 'established public speakers who offered a predominantly rhetorical form of higher education, with distinct emphasis on its more ostentatious forms'. These refinements do not alter in any appreciable way Bowersock's description of the sophists or their role in society. M. W. Gleason, 'Introduction', *Making Men: Sophists and Self-Presentation in Ancient Rome* (Princeton: Princeton University Press, 1995) also follows this basic perception.

[12] For its significance in Plato's time see the careful treatment by R. J. Mortley, 'Plato and the Sophistic Heritage of Protagoras', *Eranos* 67 (1969), 24–32, which was not incorporated into the discussion of this period by G. B. Kerferd, 'The Meaning of the Term Sophist', in *The Sophistic Movement* (Cambridge: Cambridge University Press, 1981), ch. 4.

[13] *Agr.* 143. On Aristotle see C. J. Classen, 'Aristotle's Picture of the Sophists', in *The Sophists and their Legacy: Proceedings of the Fourth International Colloquium on Ancient Philosophy, Hermes* 44 (1978), 7–24; and for a history of the movement H. von Arnim, *Leben und Werke des Dio von Prusa* (Berlin, 1898), ch. 1; and U. von Wilamowitz-Moellendorff, 'Asianismus und Atticismus', *Hermes* 35 (1900), 1–52.

[14] See Bowersock, *Greek Sophists*, pp. 8–14, on the use of the term 'Second Sophistic'.

Epicurean philosopher Philodemus from the first century BC. In his *De Rhetorica* he observes that they dealt with the three branches of rhetoric, namely judicial, deliberative and epideictic oratory. They claimed that their 'art' (τέχνη) was the mother of all other arts and sciences. Consequently, young men were sent to the sophists to be educated by means of model speeches delivered in the classroom and also by observing the public declamations of their teacher. The sophists taught rules on style, and the management of the voice and the body. By the time of Philodemus they no longer claimed to teach all branches of learning but were instructors in oratory.[15] The first and second centuries AD saw the sophists continuing to combine the activities of declaiming in public and teaching students their skills.[16]

How was their training regarded? In the first century AD it was seen as essential preparation for a young man wishing to enter into professional and political life. From the schools of the sophists came senators, forensic rhetoricians and councillors, as well as civic and provincial ambassadors and officials of the imperial government. Parents expected the sophist to make public speakers of their sons, for they judged that this form of education was most useful in producing leaders accomplished in the great art of persuasion whether it be in the legal courts or the council or political assembly of their city.[17]

Philo among the Alexandrian sophists

Three primary sources throw particular light on the sophistic movement in Alexandria in the first century AD. Chronologically, there is first the corpus of Philo reflecting the nature of the movement during the first half of the first century. One of his concerns, among others, was the hindrance that it created for those who sought 'civic virtue' (ἀρετή). Secondly, Dio of Prusa discussed the Alexandrian movement primarily in terms of its relationship to 'public life' (πολιτεία) during his visit to that city in the early seventies.

---

[15] Philodemus, *Rhetorica*, 1.195, xiv; C. Brandstätter, 'De notium πολιτικός et σοφιστής usu rhetorico', 226; J. W. H. Walden, *Universities of Ancient Greece* (London: Routledge, 1912), pp. 72–3, n. 1; and M. Winterbottom, 'Declamation, Greek and Latin', in A. Ceresa-Gastaldo (ed.), *Ars Rhetorica: Antica e Nuova* (Genova: Istituto de Filogia Classica e Medievale, 1983), pp. 67–76.

[16] E. L. Bowie, 'The Importance of the Sophists', *Yale Classical Studies* 27 (1982), 48.

[17] Walden, *Universities of Ancient Greece*, pp. 78–9.

Thirdly, Neilus, a student of rhetoric, wrote home from Alexandria to his father in the reign of Vespasian throwing light on the sophistic movement in the context of 'education' (παιδεία), *P.Oxy.* 2190. R. W. Smith, writing on rhetoric in Alexandria, does not make full use of these important primary sources.[18] G. A. Kennedy, while devoting space to Dio in his extended work on rhetoric in the Roman Empire, ignores the evidence of *P.Oxy.* 2190 and makes only very limited use of the wealth of evidence in the Philo corpus. Although he intended his survey should parallel M. L. Clarke's work *Rhetoric in Rome* by, among other things, 'adding a picture of Greek developments', he devotes only one paragraph to Philo, and that in his chapter 'The Decline of Eloquence', citing *Plant.* 156–8, and commenting, 'The passage tells little about the literary attitudes in Rome for the reference is to Jewish writers and Greek philosophers, but it does show that the association of moral decline and literature among the Greeks in the first century and that discussions of the decline did not always invoke political causes.'[19] G. W. Bowersock in his ground-breaking work on sophists in the Roman

[18] Smith, *The Art of Rhetoric in Alexandria*, p. 130, on the failure of the sophists to communicate with their audience. In the case of Philo, he gives space to the Jewish embassy headed by him, but not to the sophistic movement where he cites only a secondary source, J. Drummond, *Philo Judaeus, or The Jewish Alexandrian Philosophy in its Development and Completion* (London and Edinburgh: Williams & Norgate, 1888), vol. I, p. 5. While Smith makes use of Dio's Alexandrian Oration, *Or.* 32 (cited on pp. 62, 115–22, 130–2), to describe the volatile nature of the audience, he makes no mention in his discussion of Dio's important evidence on the sophists. He notes Dio's comment in *Or.* 32.68a on the behaviour of forensic orators, but the latter's observation about the conduct of the sophists in the lecture room which follows immediately in 32.68b is ignored. Likewise in his discussion of non-literary evidence relating to education, he overlooks the crucial evidence of *P.Oxy.* 2190, while citing a number of papyri, 115–21. Smith's aim, p. vii, is 'to focus on the rhetorical training and practice for some seven hundred years in the Delta city which was renowned for its literary accomplishments, and to subordinate other matters to this one end'. The *terminus ad quem* is *c.* AD 400. His own researches do not appear to have benefited from published works of the late 1960s and early 70s which looked at the broader aspects of the rhetorical movement in the Roman Empire.

[19] G. A. Kennedy, *The Art of Rhetoric in the Roman World* (Princeton: Princeton University Press, 1972) on his intention, p. xv, on Dio, pp. 566–82 and on Philo, pp. 452–3. In a footnote (p. 452, n. 28) he comments on Philo's observations on moral decline, i.e. *Prob.* 62–74. His only other reference to Philo is on the similarity of thought and language to that of Longinus, p. 371. His most recent work, *A New History of Classical Rhetoric* (Princeton: Princeton University Press, 1994), pp. 186–7 repeats his brief comment. From the comprehensive survey in 1872 by R. Volkmann, *Die Rhetorik der Griechen und Römer in systematischer übersicht* (reprinted Hildesheim: Georg Olms Verlag, 1963), to the most recent

Empire expresses surprise about the movement in Alexandria. 'One wonders why hardly anything is heard of sophists from Alexandria. The Museum is there; the men from elsewhere, such as Dionysius and Polemo, belonged to it. But very few native Alexandrians seem to appear in the records of the Second Sophistic.'[20] Although he makes reference to Dio Chrysostom, he does not deal with the evidence from his Alexandrian oration. The Oxyrhynchus papyrus, which was first published in 1941, and Philo's corpus are ignored. C. P. Jones in his discussion of the Roman world of Dio Chrysostom devotes a whole chapter to Alexandria. He, like Bowersock, makes no reference to the two other Alexandrian sources.[21] G. Anderson in his recent book on the Second Sophistic simply provides a lengthy quote from the Embassy to Gaius which demonstrates Philo's 'sophistic panache'. He notes only Philo's 'equivocal acceptance of the traditional Hellenistic demi-gods as benefactors of mankind' and his use of the sophistic technique of amplification in *Ios.* 23ff.[22]

There are, however, forty-two references to 'sophist' (σοφιστής) in Philo, apart from fifty-two references to cognates, and numerous comments on the sophistic movement. His evidence constitutes the single most important witness for the first half of the first century on the Greek side, and nothing comparable exists elsewhere for this period in the empire.

Paul among the Corinthian sophists

Six primary sources throw light on the sophistic movement in Corinth. Firstly, there are the two Diogenes speeches of Dio Chrysostom, *Or.* 6 and 8, which describe sophistic activity in Corinth during the period of his exile from Rome *c.* AD 89–96.

Secondly, there is the Corinthian oration of Favorinus, a noted sophist and pupil of Dio Chrysostom who did not share his teacher's anti-sophistic convictions. Although a Roman, he was the complete Hellenophile. His speech before the citizens of Corinth, which occurs ten years after he first arrived in the Roman colony,

---

works on first-century rhetoric Philo has been omitted, or only referred to in passing.
[20] Bowersock, *Greek Sophists*, pp. 20–1.
[21] Jones, *Roman World of Dio Chrysostom*, ch. 5.
[22] Anderson, *The Second Sophistic*, pp. 203–5. *P.Oxy.* 2190 does not feature in his discussion.

was delivered in the reign of Hadrian on Favorinus' third visit. The value of this oration is that it looks at the Corinthian response to the sophistic movement from the perspective of a very successful sophist, who took not only Corinth but also Rome by storm. He still managed to incur the displeasure of the fickle Corinthians after they had erected statues to him in this Roman colony.

The third source is epigraphic and describes Herodes Atticus, a famous sophist and great benefactor of the city of Corinth, whose magistrates included a dedication to him when he erected a statue to his wife. This demonstrates their adulation of this very significant figure, who was himself a pupil of Favorinus. Herodes Atticus was such a famous sophist that when Philostratus wrote about the Second Sophistic in his *Lives of the Sophists* it centred around him, for he epitomised all that the sophist was meant to be.[23]

Plutarch, who visited Corinth on a number of occasions from the late seventies onwards, is the fourth witness. Although his evidence is slight, it is important for the insight it provides into the status circles in which sophists moved.

Fifthly, the evidence of Epictetus appears to have been bypassed in works on rhetoric. He lived after his exile from Rome (*c.* AD 92–3) in Nicopolis, in the neighbouring province to Achaia, and provides much information on the movement at the turn of the century. He possessed an intimate and detailed knowledge of Corinth, and his discussion with a student of rhetoric from Corinth is extremely informative, as are his general comments on the movement.

Finally, it will be argued that Paul in his Corinthian letters provides an important source of information on the sophistic movement. When all this evidence which has not been assembled to date is collated, it provides a substantial picture of the movement in Corinth.

Recent discussion has overlooked much of the Corinthian evidence. While G. A. Kennedy uses the Pauline letters in his studies on rhetorical criticism, he makes no mention of their witness to the sophistic movement in Corinth during an important period of its development.[24] A. D. Litfin did not make use of all the evidence on

---

[23] There is another sophist, Sceptus of Corinth, but little is known of him except that he was a senior student of and part of the inner circle of Herodes Atticus, according to Philostratus, *Lives of the Sophists*, 573, 585.

[24] G. A. Kennedy, *Classical Rhetoric and its Christian and Secular Tradition from Ancient to Modern Times* (London: Croom Helm, 1980), pp. 130–2, and *New*

Corinth.[25] C. P. Jones, while devoting chapters to various cities in his work on Dio's world, does not deal with Corinth because the oration on Corinth in his corpus is rightly attributed to Favorinus, one of Dio's pupils.[26] J. Murphy-O'Connor has collected extant literary and epigraphic evidence on Corinth. He reproduces the texts on Dio, part of the oration of Favorinus, the comments of Plutarch and an inscription on Herodes Atticus, but makes no mention of Epictetus and provides no comment about the sophistic movement from the sources he cites.[27] The ancient historian, G. Anderson, offers the comment that 'the social context in which such teachings were offered did not presuppose a highly educated audience . . . Christianity harboured a suspicion that anything that could be regarded as worldly wisdom was foolishness in the sight of God'. He cites one of its first 'surviving documents' (1 Cor. 1.21) in support of his contention but makes no reference to the discussion of rhetoric or the sophistic movement in 1 or 2 Corinthians.[28]

Recent sophistic and rhetorical studies

While there has been some discussion of rhetoric in Philo's corpus in recent years, only passing reference has been made to the existence of sophists in Alexandria.[29] Their identity has been the subject of speculation rather than any serious investigation.[30] Philo is a vital witness to the vigour and importance of the movement in that city.

Discussion of a possible rhetorical and/or sophistic background

---

Testament Interpretation through Rhetorical Criticism (Chapel Hill and London: University of North Carolina Press, 1984), esp. ch. 7.

25 A. D. Litfin, *St Paul's Theology of Proclamation: an investigation of 1 Corinthians 1–4 and Greco–Roman Rhetoric*, SNTS Monograph Series 79 (Cambridge: Cambridge University Press, 1994), p. 146, n. 39. The 'Diogenes speeches' of Dio are thought by Litfin to refer to fourth-century BC Corinth and he therefore does not use this evidence. However, Dio uses Diogenes as a mouthpiece for critical comments on first-century AD Roman Corinth, cf. Jones, *Roman World of Dio Chrysostom*, p. 47, in which the latter discusses Dio's use of famous persons from the past, including Diogenes, partly as a literary device to present his views in exile. The evidence of Epictetus was not incorporated in the study.

26 Jones, *Roman World of Dio Chrysostom*, 179.

27 J. Murphy-O'Connor, *St Paul's Corinth: Texts and Archaeology* (Wilmington: Glazier, 1983).

28 Anderson, *The Second Sophistic*, p. 205.　　　29 See p. 60.

30 On the sophists see A. Mendelson, *Secular Education in Philo of Alexandria* (Cincinnati: Hebrew Union College Press, 1982), pp. 8–10, and for the conflicting opinions expressed on Philo's sophists see pp. 61–2.

as the cause of tensions between Paul and the Corinthian church is not new. There have been five recent discussions of note.[31] Two years before W. Schmithals submitted his influential Marburg dissertation on Gnosticism in Corinth, J. Munck argued that problems Paul discusses in 1 Corinthians 1–4, created by bickering and divisive elements, simply reflected the Hellenistic milieu of the sophistic movement. He believed that the Corinthian Christians identified their new faith as 'a kind of wisdom, its leaders teachers of wisdom . . . and themselves – this was the most important thing for them – wise men who had drawn on that wisdom through the Christian leaders'.[32]

There are two difficulties with Munck's thesis. Most of his evidence looked at the first-century movement through the eyes of Philostratus, the early third-century AD sophist, in his *Lives of the Sophists*. However, Philostratus stood on the other side of the peak of the Second Sophistic even though he made reference to sophists in the second half of the first century. What Munck needed to do to secure his case was to detail first-century evidence on the sophistic background, and not to rely so heavily on a late second- and early third-century perception of the movement. While he did cite the first-century witness of Philo, he did so in an all too brief comment, relegating merely ten references from that corpus to a single footnote.[33] His retrojection of later evidence into the first century is not far removed methodologically from the work of Schmithals and others in their use of late Gnostic material to sustain their view that it existed in Corinth in Paul's day.

Munck's work was also written prior to the important work on the Second Sophistic published by G. W. Bowersock in 1969. The latter's book constituted something of a turning point in sophistic studies, for there were some who doubted that the Second Sophistic had ever existed as an important late first- and second-century movement.[34] The nature of the 'strife' (ἔρις) and 'jealousy' (ζῆλος) mentioned in 1 Corinthians 1.11 and 3.3 had to be demonstrated by

---

[31] A. Lynch, 'Pauline Rhetoric: 1 Corinthians 1.10–4.21', MA dissertation, University of North Carolina (1981) is not relevant to the discussion as it is a slender treatment, interested primarily in the rhetorical structure of the passage and not concerned with the sophists.

[32] J. Munck, 'Menigheden uden Partier', *Dansk Teologisk Tidsskrift* 15 (1952), 215–33; English translation: 'The Church without Factions', in *Paul and the Salvation of Mankind* (London: SCM Press, 1959), pp. 135–67, citation on p. 154.

[33] Munck, *Paul and the Salvation of Mankind*, p. 154, n. 1.

[34] Bowersock, *Greek Sophists*.

Munck as being sophistic, and not the theological phenomenon upon which F. C. Baur's extremely influential thesis had been built.[35] Munck's work still remains a substantial piece of scholarship in that it broke new ground. However, it lacked a convincing survey of the sophistic background of the first century and the isolation of established conventions and rhetorical language which clearly related to the language used in the Corinthian letters.[36]

Since Munck's essay, important works have been produced which have specific bearing on the rhetorical but not the sophistic background of the problems of the Corinthian church. In 1980 P. Marshall wrote a thesis on 1 and 2 Corinthians which is an important study of the social institutions of friendship and enmity, the custom of commendation and the use of the figure of the flatterer to engage in invective, all of which Paul drew from literary traditions.[37] He concludes that Paul's opponents in Corinth were not 'gnostic' nor 'pneumatic' but 'hubristic'.[38] Marshall suggested that this accounts for Paul's argument in 1 Corinthians 4.6–13, and also explicates his use of 'the boastful fool' of 2 Corinthians 10–13. While this may well explain the socio-cultural conflict dynamics between some Corinthians and Paul, other background material is needed to understand the primary reason for the way in which the church questioned Paul's leadership after his departure, and the resistance of many to his return. The 'sophistic' language which the Corinthian detractors and Paul used in the controversy must also be accounted for.[39]

A more recent work on rhetoric in 1 Corinthians 1–4 has been undertaken by A. D. Litfin. In *St Paul's Theology of Proclamation:*

---

[35] F. C. Baur, *Paul, the Apostle of Jesus Christ, His Life and Work, His Epistles and His Doctrine*, English translation (London and Edinburgh: Williams & Norgate, 1876), vol. I, pp. 269–95, argued for the contrasting and conflicting Petrine and Pauline theologies surfacing in the Corinthian conflicts, and reflecting the permanent tension between Jewish and Hellenistic Christianity.

[36] His provocative challenge to Baur did not gain widespread acceptance. See however the recent commentary on 1 Corinthians by G. Fee, *The First Epistle to the Corinthians* (Grand Rapids: Eerdmans, 1987), p. 65, n. 79, who accepts Munck's thesis.

[37] PhD dissertation, Macquarie University (1980), published as *Enmity in Corinth: Social Conventions in Paul's Relations with the Corinthians* (Tübingen: J. C. B. Mohr (Paul Siebeck), 1987).

[38] Hubris was a complex ethical notion of 'pride' or 'arrogance' associated with the wealthy and powerful, and carrying with it the notions of superiority and over-confidence.

[39] Marshall, *Enmity in Corinth*, pp. 180–1, questioned the adequacy of Munck's explanation of a sophistic background without exploring that issue further.

1 Corinthians 1–4 and Greco–Roman Rhetoric[40] he first traces the development of rhetoric from the era of Socrates and the rhetoricians through Isocrates and Aristotle to its acculturation by Cicero, Quintilian and lesser lights of the first and second centuries AD with an extensive survey of primary sources. His second section aims to establish the nexus between the rhetorical tradition and 1 Corinthians 1.17–25 and to do so within the context of the Corinthian letters as a whole. His view is that 1 Corinthians 1.17–25 is Paul's *apologia* against the Corinthians' criticism that his preaching failed to measure up to Graeco–Roman eloquence.[41] While Litfin's work is a very important contribution to the discussion of 1 Corinthians 1.17–31, it does not probe the influence of the sophistic movement on the thinking of the Christian community which is the wider issue at stake in the Corinthian letters.

In 1984 H. D. Betz, in a short essay entitled 'The Problem of Rhetoric and Theology According to the Apostle Paul', extended the parameters of his important work based on the term *apologia* in 2 Corinthians 12.[42] In the earlier work he sought to defend the thesis that Paul is consciously following in Socratic footsteps in his refusal to defend himself, having already been tried by the Corinthians *in absentia*. In spite of criticism that has been directed at that monograph,[43] he holds to his original thesis on 2 Corinthians 10–12. In the later essay he seeks to ascertain the nature of the rhetoric which Paul feels is in conflict with the preaching of the cross. The sophists' use of rhetoric is absent from his discussion.

Two more recent works on Corinth have been published, by

---

[40] D.Phil. dissertation, Oxford University, 1983, published in 1994. See n. 25.

[41] Litfin, *St Paul's Theology of Proclamation*, pp. 187–201. If this work does not influence the course of Corinthian studies as it should, it may well be that it does not relate the background material assembled in Part I sufficiently to 1 Corinthians 1.17–31 in order to secure the argument more firmly from the background sources.

[42] In A. Vanhoye (ed.), *L'Apôtre Paul: Personnalité, Style et Conception du Ministère* (Leuven: Leuven University Press, 1986) pp. 16–48, and *Der Apostel Paulus und die sokratische Tradition: eine exegetische Untersuchung zu seiner 'Apologie' 2 Korinther 10–13* (Tübingen: J. C. B. Mohr (Paul Siebeck), 1972).

[43] E. A. Judge, 'St Paul and Socrates', *Interchange* 13 (1973), 106–16, esp. 111–15, where he concludes 'Paul's pseudo-apology is remote from the spirit of Socrates' and observes that H. D. Betz in his *Der Apostel Paulus* has not succeeded in establishing the nexus. See also the criticisms by A. T. Lincoln, 'Paul the Visionary: The Setting and Significance of the Rapture to Paradise in II Corinthians 12.1–10', *NTS* 25 (1979), 204–20, esp. 206.

M. Mitchell[44] and S. M. Pogoloff,[45] which likewise do not deal with the sophistic movement of the first century. They are concerned primarily with rhetoric in Corinth and ignore the first-century sophistic movement. Pogoloff does this because he believes that the sophistic movement post-dates Paul's Corinth by a century – 'we have no evidence that sophists who styled themselves as philosophers were present in Corinth'. He investigates rather what he calls 'the rhetorical situation' of 1 Corinthians.[46]

While much has been also published in scholarly articles on rhetoric,[47] none of these works actually exploits the evidence for the sophistic movement in Corinth. This robs the discussion of that wider perspective which may both control and enhance our interpretation of the Corinthian letters. It could also act as a brake on some of the more extravagant uses of the term 'rhetoric' in recent Pauline and NT studies.

However, even when the extra-biblical evidence of the sophistic movement has been assembled it cannot be assumed *ipso facto* that this provides the actual background to the problems in the church discussed by Paul in 1 Corinthians 1–4, 9, and 2 Corinthians 10–13. What then needs to be established in order to sustain the argument that Paul is 'among the sophists' in Corinth? It has to be demonstrated (1) that the 'strife' (ἔρις) and 'jealousy' (ζῆλος) which are the gravamen of Paul's complaints in 1 Corinthians 1.11, 3.3 are clearly related to the sophistic movement; (2) that Paul's *modus operandi* in Corinth, described in 1 Corinthians 2.1–5, has been formulated in the light of the conventions of sophists 'coming' to a city and operating in it; (3) that he offers a substantial critique of the sophistic movement in 1 Corinthians 1–4; (4) that his own ministry has been critiqued by those trained within the sophistic tradition using its canons in 2 Corinthians 10–13; and (5) that in answering his opponents in 2 Corinthians 10–13 he does so in

---

[44] M. Mitchell, *Paul and the Rhetoric of Reconciliation: An Exegetical Investigation of the Language and Composition of 1 Corinthians* (originally PhD dissertation, University of Chicago Divinity School, 1989); published (Tübingen: J. C. B. Mohr (Paul Siebeck), 1991).

[45] S. M. Pogoloff, *Logos and Sophia: The Rhetorical Situation of 1 Corinthians* (originally PhD dissertation, Yale University, 1990); now published in SBL Dissertation Series 134 (Atlanta: Scholars Press, 1992). For Pogoloff's critique of Mitchell see pp. 89–90.

[46] *Ibid.*, pp. 65, 95.

[47] E.g. D. F. Watson, 'The New Testament and Greco–Roman Rhetoric: A Bibliography', *JETS* 31.4 (1988), 465–72.

categories which show that he is arguing with Christian orators or sophists who are now within the Christian community in Corinth. These questions will occupy the discussion in the latter part of the book.

The structure of this book

This investigation into the sophistic movement will be restricted to two major cities in the East. The first is Alexandria. 'A student among the Alexandrian sophists' is based on *P.Oxy.* 2190, a private letter from a student to his father in the latter part of the first century AD (chapter 1). It will be discussed in the light of educational trends of the sophists of that period.

'Dio and the Alexandrian sophistic leaders' is an evaluation of Dio's discussion of the sophists in the context of his role as the emperor's emissary to Alexandria, their place in *politeia* and his use of the term 'sophist', (chapter 2).

'Who are Philo's sophists?' (chapter 3) is an important foundation chapter because the term 'sophist' has wrongly been read by most recent writers on Philo as a loose, pejorative one, thus clouding the evidence and the issues. 'Philo's critique of the Alexandrian sophistic tradition' and 'Philo among the sophists' (chapters 4 and 5) will survey the nature of the movement in the first half of the first century in this 'second Athens'. Philo critiques the movement from the perspective of one who has had the benefits of a Greek rhetorical education of which he was not unappreciative. His role as a rhetor and debater and his suggestions for defeating the sophists will be explored. His corpus therefore constitutes an invaluable resource.

The second city is Corinth. Evidence from non-biblical sources will be gathered, along parallel lines to that for Alexandria, on 'Epictetus and the Corinthian student of the sophists' and 'Dio and Plutarch among the Corinthian sophists' (chapters 6 and 7).

The last three chapters deal with Paul and Corinth. 'Paul and sophistic conventions' discusses Paul's anti-sophistic *modus operandi* in Corinth and the sophistic perception of Corinthian Christians' relationship with their teachers (chapter 8). Paul's evaluation of the sophistic tradition in 1 Corinthians 1–4 will be examined in 'Paul's critique of the Corinthian sophistic tradition' (chapter 9), while 'Paul among the Christian sophists' deals with two further issues, namely the sophists' assessment of Paul as rhetorician and debater, and Paul's evaluation of those Christians who promoted the importance of the sophistic tradition in the teaching office of the church (chapter 10). These last two chapters parallel chapters 4 and 5 of the discussion of Philo and the issues in the latter chapters are closely related.

This book will conclude with a discussion on the importance of the Jewish and Christian evidence for our understanding of the first-century sophistic movement, together with a comparison of the OT texts and methods used by Philo and Paul in their evaluation of it. The implications of these findings for further understanding Paul's educational background, their further challenge to the almost defunct Gnostic thesis for Corinthian studies and, more importantly, for understanding the use, misuse and the nature of first-century rhetoric in literary discussions of the NT corpus will also be noted.

This is then a sophistic tale of two important cities in the East that were leading centres of commerce and education. It is also about the responses of two Hellenised Jews both of whom resorted to the OT in order to critique a major movement of their day. In the first century it had enchanted, if not seduced, not only the citizens of Alexandria and Corinth, but also some of the members of their respective believing communities.

PART I

The Alexandrian sophists

INTRODUCTION TO PART I

In the following five chapters we will survey evidence of the sophistic movement in Alexandria from the perspective of two of its most important critics, Philo of Alexandria (? – c. AD 50) and Dio of Prusa (c. AD 40–112), and from a student of the sophists named Neilus who wrote early in the Principate of Vespasian.

Neilus, a student of rhetoric, sent a letter to his father from Alexandria about the movement from the perspective of one being educated in Greek *paideia*, *P.Oxy.* 2190. He lived there during a time of great stimulus to the sophistic movement brought about by Vespasian's exemption of teachers of rhetoric from taxes and compulsory liturgies. This papyrus thus provides insight into the world of the sophists.

Dio of Prusa discussed the movement as it existed in Alexandria primarily, but not exclusively, in relation to *politeia* during his visit there in the early seventies. His goal was to mend a rift between Vespasian and the Alexandrians, but, to our benefit, his orations also help to delineate the meaning of the term 'sophist' and its character in one of the leading intellectual centres in the East.

Philo's corpus reflects the nature of the movement during the first half of the first century. He was concerned with, among other things, the hindrance the movement posed for those who sought 'salvation' through 'virtue'.

These three primary sources throw light on the sophistic movement in Alexandria in the first century AD.

1

A STUDENT AMONG THE ALEXANDRIAN SOPHISTS

Through the eyes of a student engaged in the study of rhetoric, unexpected information emerges on the sophistic movement in Alexandria.[1] *P.Oxy.* 2190 is a first-century papyrus, possibly from Vespasian's Principate, which yields vital information on that movement in this 'second Athens' in the East.[2] The primary purpose of this lengthy letter, written by Neilus from Alexandria to his father, Theon, in Oxyrhynchus, was to gain parental approval for alternative educational arrangements which arose because he had been unable to enrol in a reputable sophist's school. His other concerns, including a misdemeanour committed in the theatre, are important for this discussion only as they relate to his education, namely his lack of progress and the shortage of money. He reports on the pressing need for more of the latter, especially with a younger brother due to arrive to 'learn letters' in Alexandria. Apart from food sent by his father, Neilus' other source of income

---

[1] This sixty-five line papyrus was written in Alexandria in two columns. The left-hand margin of column one is damaged but the original editor, C. H. Roberts, has restored the text, *P.Oxy.* 2190, xviii, 145–7. For some alternative reconstructions of the papyrus, see M. David, B. A. van Groningen and E. Kiessling (eds.), *Berichtigungsliste der Griechischen Papyruskunden aus Ägypten* (Leiden: E. J. Brill, 1964) vol. iv, p. 63; E. G. Turner's judicious weighing of those suggestions in 'Oxyrhynchus and Rome', *HSCP* 7 (1975), 7–9, nn. 17–25; and more recently J. Rea, 'A Student's Letter to His Father: P.Oxy. xviii 2190 revised', *ZPE* 99 (1993), 75–88. The original in the Ashmolean Museum, Oxford, has been examined. It was Emeritus Professor E. A. Judge of Macquarie University, Sydney, who first drew my attention to this papyrus.

[2] Roberts' dating of the late first century is supported by Dr R. Coles and Dr J. Rea of the Ashmolean Museum. See the comment of the latter in 'A Student's Letter to His Father', 76 and that of Turner, 'Oxyrhynchus and Rome', 6–7 and n. 15, who suggests a date in the reigns of Vespasian or Domitian based on comparisons with other papyri. See my 'The Messiah as the Tutor: the Meaning of καθηγητής in Matthew 23:10', *Tyn.B.* 42.1 (1991), 153, where I suggest that this serious incident in the theatre can be linked to turmoil in the city in the time of Vespasian which was noted by Dio Chrysostom in his Alexandrian *Or.* 32:72–4. See pp. 40–1. This oration can be dated from internal evidence to the early seventies.

appears to have been a slave who had worked in Alexandria to support him and who had now escaped custody after landing himself in trouble. Neilus was further distressed by the educational difficulties he had encountered in Alexandria. He placed the blame for these on the ineptitude and/or the laziness of teachers, possible interference from a fellow student, Philoxenus, and the worry his slave had caused him. (See Appendix for the full text.)

This interesting letter discusses not only the problems the student encountered with his education in Alexandria, but also important educators in the first-century sophistic tradition, namely the 'sophist' (σοφιστής), the 'tutor' (καθηγητής) and the 'declaimer' (ἐπιδεικνύμενος), including one specifically named Ποσειδώνιος. It also confirms the picture that has recently emerged of first-century *paideia* over against the traditional view of a more structured three-tier education system.[3] This papyrus provides important information on four matters relating to the sophistic movement in the first century: (1) a shortage of sophists' schools in Alexandria; (2) the hiring of a private tutor in rhetoric as an alternative educational route for declamation practice; (3) attendance at public declamations as an additional way of enhancing rhetorical skills; and (4) the social status of the students of the sophists.

The shortage of sophists' schools

Surprisingly, Neilus speaks of 'a shortage of the sophists' (ἡ τῶν σοφιστῶν ἀπορία, lines 18–19) even though other Alexandrian evidence suggests a surplus. Philo speaks of 'the crowd of sophists', *Agr.* 136, and Dio Chrysostom of 'the abundance of them', *Or.* 32.11.[4] Neilus, however, expresses not only his own opinion, but

---

[3] For the standard treatment of the three-tier education system, see H. I. Marrou, *A History of Education in Antiquity*, English translation (London: Sheed and Ward, 1956), pp. 160–205 and M. L. Clarke, *Higher Education in the Ancient World* (London: Routledge and Kegan Paul, 1971), pp. 11–12. For challenges based on terms such as γραμματιστής and γραμματικός, see A. D. Booth, 'The Appearance of the Schola Grammatici', *Hermes* 106 (1978), 117–25; 'Elementary and Secondary Education in the Roman Empire', *Florilegium* 3 (1981), 1–20; 'Litterator', *Hermes* 109 (1981), 371–8; and R. A. Kaster, 'Notes on "Primary" and "Secondary" Schools in Late Antiquity', *TAPA* 113 (1983), 323–46, esp. 346. *P.Oxy.* 2190, although not discussed in the above, provides a first-century example of 'adaptation' based on supply and demand at an important centre of *paideia*, and supports Kaster's general thesis.

[4] Cf. P. M. Fraser, *Ptolemaic Alexandria*, 2nd edn (Oxford: Clarendon Press, 1972),

reports that Philoxenus also agrees with the assessment which in fact had originated with Theon: 'When I informed Philoxenus of your view, he began to be of the same opinion, declaring that it was on account of this shortage of sophists . . .' lines 18–19.[5] Three factors account for this shortage of sophists and places in their schools in the first century. Firstly, recent trends in Alexandrian education played a role, as noted by a first-century rhetorician from that city, Aelius Theon. In the preface to his *Progymnasmata*, Theon contrasts students of ancient times with his contemporaries.[6] The ancients, especially those who studied under famous orators, could not commence studying rhetoric until they had gained some knowledge of philosophy, and more importantly, had been inspired by it. In contrast, most young men of this Theon's day were 'far from the knowledge of philosophy', i.e. presumably they were not interested or had not been trained in it. They had not fully mastered the branches of primary learning. Instead, they had begun to attempt forensic and deliberative themes, and 'worst of all',[7] did so before they had been trained (ἐγγυμνασαμένοι). Theon criticised this trend of beginning

---

vol. I, p. 810, who argues that because of 'the absence of rhetorical studies in the Ptolemaic city [of Alexandria], among the many Greek teachers of rhetoric at Rome, not one of those whom we know was an Alexandrian'. On this basis G. W. Bowersock, *Greek Sophists in the Roman Empire* (Oxford: Clarendon Press, 1969), p. 20, observes that very few native Alexandrians seem to appear in the Second Sophistic. Turner, 'Oxyrhynchus and Rome', 5, endorses this view with his interpretation of Neilus' comment in *P.Oxy.* 2190.

5 Lines 18–19: μόνην τὴν τῶν σοφιστῶν ἀπορίαν.

6 Although *OCD* places Theon in the second century, G. A. Kennedy, *Greek Rhetoric under Christian Emperors* (Princeton: Princeton University Press, 1983), pp. 56–7, defends a first-century date based on Quintilian's reference to one 'Theon' (III.6.48, IX.3.76) who is also an orator. *The Suda* notes that he is author of *Progymnasmata* and that he wrote works on rhetoric and grammar. Kennedy notes similarities with Quintilian's account of *Progymnasmata*. See also D. A. Russell and N. G. Wilson, *Menander Rhetor* (Oxford: Clarendon Press, 1981), p. xxvi and R. W. Smith, *The Art of Rhetoric in Alexandria: its Theory and Practice in the Ancient World* (The Hague: Martinus Nijhoff, 1974), p. 133, for discussion. For a general overview of *Progymnasmata*, see Kennedy, *Greek Rhetoric,* pp. 54–73. For the text see L. Spengel, *Rhetores Graeci* (Leipzig: Teubner, 1854), vol. II, xii, 145, lines 1–11 (Θεῶνος Προγυμνάσματα). R.F. Hock and E. N. O'Neil, *The Chreia in Ancient Rhetoric: The Progymnasmata* (Atlanta: Scholars Press, 1986), vol. I, pp. 64 and 75–6, cite a number of other scholars who accept a first-century dating, but they withhold their own opinions.

7 The phrase 'worst of all', καὶ τὸ πάντων ἀγροικότατον, is meant to convey the worst possible action that students are taking; ἀγροικότατος means 'most countrified' and is obviously a derogatory comment given the division of Egypt into 'the city', i.e. Alexandria, and 'the country' for the rest of the province.

declaiming prior to undertaking any introductory training in it, and before receiving what G. A. Kennedy calls 'a liberal education'.[8] Students undertook actual declamations without the necessary instruction in literature, even before the traditional foundation study of Homer, and without any preliminary theoretical knowledge of the structure of a speech. Theon thus classified and explained in his book the various exercises which one needed to gain the requisite skills for declamation. His *Progymnasmata* on rhetoric represented one attempt to help make good the deficiencies of the present trend of circumventing essential educational foundations and engaging immediately in tertiary activities with the help of a sophist.

This first-century preoccupation with declamation was also the subject of comment by the Latin orator, Quintilian.[9] He refers to students' fathers 'who think their sons are not really studying unless they are declaiming on every possible occasion', II.8.1. He further notes the attitude of the contemporary rhetorician who considers it his responsibility 'merely to declaim and to give instruction in the theory and practice of declamation and confines his activities to deliberative and judicial themes', II.1.2. When teachers met this parental demand, grammarians began to encroach on the field of the orators by teaching declamation. Quintilian recognised that teachers needed to satisfy the demands of parents and so he developed a compromise which aimed to fulfil both the aspirations of parents and the needs and desires of their sons: he proposed that young men should declaim occasionally, but only after having carefully prepared their speech under supervision. This should happen so 'that they may reap the rewards of their labours in the applause of a large audience, that most coveted of all prizes', II.7.5.[10] He further suggested that rather than force rhetoricians to compete with grammarians, a better arrangement would be to allow students to engage in literary education concurrently with

---

[8] Kennedy, *Greek Rhetoric*, p. 57.

[9] Quintilian taught rhetoric in Rome for some twenty years until he retired *c.* AD 90. Vespasian appointed him to a paid chair of rhetoric in the capital and he became the tutor of Domitian's grandnephews while writing his work on oratory. His work shows familiarity with both ancient and contemporary Greek rhetoric from which Latin rhetoric had been hewn: see Kennedy, *The Art of Rhetoric in the Roman World* (Princeton: Princeton University Press, 1972), pp. 487–514.

[10] S. F. Bonner, *Roman Declamation in the Late Republic and Early Empire* (Liverpool: University Press of Liverpool, 1949), p. 49.

training in declamation.[11] As teachers, both Theon and Quintilian recognised the wisdom of responding to the current educational demands of fee-paying parents who required instruction in literature and training in rhetoric at the same time.

Secondly, a number of inducements made training in rhetoric financially attractive for those entering the legal and teaching professions and obtaining posts in the imperial administration. Claudius had revoked the 250-year-old law which proscribed the taking of fees by rhetoricians from clients in court cases. He set the maximum fee at ten thousand *sesterces*.[12]

In addition, on 27 December, AD 75, Vespasian issued a rescript granting immunity from municipal levies to grammarians and rhetoricians.[13] According to Dio's Alexandrian oration, *Or*. 32.60, he sought to promote 'education and rhetoric' (παιδεία καὶ λόγος). Vespasian believed that the role of teachers was 'to train the souls of the young to gentleness and civic virtue'.[14] This financial incentive was intended to attract more young men trained in forensic and political oratory into government service and to recruit more teachers for literary education and rhetoric. So successful was the concession that in AD 93–4 Domitian needed to issue a rescript of his own which threatened to withdraw the privilege from those who used their slaves to engage in the lucrative profession of teaching prospective grammarians and rhetoricians.

---

[11] M. L. Clarke, 'Quintilian and Rhetorical Training', in *Rhetoric at Rome: A Historical Survey* (London: Cohen and West, 1953), ch. 11, esp. p. 121.

[12] Tacitus, *Ann*. 11.7; J. A. Crook, *Legal Advocacy in the Roman World* (London: Duckworth, 1995), pp. 129–31. On the further Claudian reformation of court procedures see Kennedy, *The Art of Rhetoric*, p. 437.

[13] On the text of this rescript as well as that of Domitian, see M. McCrum and A. G. Woodhead, *Select Documents of the Principates of the Flavian Emperors* (Cambridge: Cambridge University Press, 1961), no. 458. On the form of the Vespasian inscription, see M. Benner, *The Emperor Says: Studies in the Rhetorical Style in Edicts of the Early Empire*, Studia Graeca et Latina Gothoburgensia 23 (Göteburg: Acta Universitatis Gothoburgensis, 1975), pp. 139–41.

[14] οἱ τὰς τῶν νέων ψυχὰς πρὸς ἡμερότητα καὶ πολιτικὴν ἀρετὴν παιδεύουσιν. M.St.A. Woodside, 'Vespasian's Patronage of Education and the Arts', *TAPA* 73 (1942), 126, suggests that the emperor saw the importance of training future administrators. See also E. P. Parkes, *The Roman Rhetorical Schools as a Preparation for the Courts under the Early Empire*, Johns Hopkins University Studies in Historical and Political Science 63.2 (Baltimore: Johns Hopkins Press, 1945), p. 104; F. Millar, *The Emperor in the Roman World (31 B.C.–A.D. 337)* (London: Duckworth, 1977), pp. 491–506, 'Empire and City, Augustus to Julian: Obligations, Excuses and Status', *JRS* 73 (1983), 81–2; and Bowersock, *Greek Sophists*, p. 32.

I have judged it necessary to curb by stringent measures the avarice of the physicians and teachers whose profession, which ought to be transmitted only to a limited number of freeborn young men, is being most shamelessly sold to many slave chamberlains, who are admitted to professional training, not out of humane sentiments but in order to augment their teachers' income. Therefore whoever shall derive pay from the instruction of slaves is to be deprived of the immunity granted by my deified father, just as if he were practising his profession in a foreign city.[15]

Vespasian's considerable incentives had been enough to stimulate demand for teachers.

Thirdly, there was a preference for linking a student with a sophist's school, rather than allow a son to train under an orator. If the former was a virtuoso rhetorician with his own school who declaimed to a large public following, why would a rhetorician of lesser reputation not be sufficient? Quintilian comments on a debate in the first century as to whether one ought to seek the best teacher possible for one's son from the beginning of his training, or whether the engagement of a less able rhetorician sufficed for the preliminary stages. He himself counsels parents to seek 'the most eminent teacher' available, even if his expertise would be lost initially on the pupil. Bad habits would develop under an inferior master which would have to be corrected later at no insignificant cost, II.3.1.[16] It is obvious that Theon desired for his son, Neilus, the best possible instructor, namely a sophist.

P.Oxy. 2190 does not simply note a shortage of sophists *per se*, but of suitable schools run by them in which students could enrol and learn to declaim. It was always possible to attend a public declamation by a sophist, as the papyrus notes, lines 34–5. That,

---

15 C. A. Forbes, 'Education and Training of Slaves in Antiquity', *TAPA* 86 (1955), 348–9. The translation of the rescript is Forbes'. For a translation of both see N. Lewis and M. Reinhold, *Roman Civilization. Sourcebook II: The Empire* (New York: Columbia University Press, 1966), pp. 295–6. Forbes argues that Domitian took action because professional teachers resented 'having their ranks swollen by ill-trained and unworthy practitioners' and that the rescript was fundamentally against freedmen, as slaves would not be eligible for the exemption in any case. However, the rescript was intended to penalise the owners of slaves who reaped the financial rewards of their slaves functioning as teachers. For evidence of a slave who taught rhetoric in this period see *P.Erzherzog Rainer*, 11 (AD 72–3).

16 Cf. also Pliny the Younger, *Epistles*, III.3.6.

however, would not satisfy parents. They wanted their sons to learn under the supervision of sophists, lines 33–4, and willingly paid the very considerable sums involved. When this letter was written the great demand for sophists had outstripped the supply, for the reasons outlined above. *P.Oxy.* 2190 thus reflects the known pressures on traditional education in this period.

A private tutor in rhetoric as an alternative

If the Alexandrian schools of the sophists were full, what alternative was open to Neilus? He begins discussing the shortage of sophists with τὰ αὐτὰ μέν before indicating an alternative, τὰ δὲ τὸν Δίδυμον. This 'Didymus' who is described as a καθηγητής 'has a school', lines 20f.[17] He seems to present a viable, if less than ideal, alternative for Neilus' educational needs.

What does 'tutor' (καθηγητής), which appears six times in this papyrus, mean?[18] C. Préaux suggests that perhaps it referred to an itinerant teacher who sought out children of rich parents,[19] while M. H. Ibrahim incorrectly concludes that it was restricted to

[17] The original editor of *P.Oxy.* 2190 has translated σχολὴν ἔχοντα, line 21 as 'has time to spare'. While σχολή did mean 'leisure', by the first century BC εὐκαιρία had supplanted it; and J. Glucker, *Antiochus and the Late Academy*, Hypomnemata 56 (Göttingen: Vandenhoeck & Ruprecht, 1978), pp. 161–2 comments further that 'the most widespread sense of σχολή was that of 'an educational institution' and the second connotation was that of 'an educational activity.' By Quintilian's time it could refer to a school of philosophy, rhetoric or grammar. In this papyrus it seems best to find reference to a school of Didymus for two reasons: firstly, σχολή used with ἔχειν is attested elsewhere in connection with the running of a school (Epictetus, III.21.11) and secondly, Neilus notes that Philoxenus has persuaded others to enrol with Didymus, παραβάλειν ἔπειθεν αὐτῷ. See Plutarch, *Moralia* 846f, παρέβαλεν . . . τῷ ῥήτορι, 'was a pupil of the rhetor'. For παραβάλειν the original editor suggested 'go to', line 23, and in a comment notes that in the transitive it means 'to send someone to school' as in *P.Oxy.* 930, line 21. The aorist in *P.Oxy.* 2190 suggests 'enrolled'. Rea, 'A Student's Letter to His Father', 83, endorses this translation.

[18] Compared with contemporary or near-contemporary literary and non-literary sources only Philodemus uses this term more than *P.Oxy.* 2190. See lines 7–8, 15, 24, 26, 29 (the verb), and 31 *contra* Turner, 'Oxyrhynchus and Rome', 9, n. 26, 'holder of a chair', citing *OGI* 408 (AD 150). This sophist did not hold a chair but ran a school.

[19] C. Préaux, 'Lettres privées grecques d'Egypte relatives à l'éducation', *Revue Belge de Philologie et d'Histoire* 8 (1929), 779–80. Evidence cited in support of this conclusion is *P.Oxy.* 930, *PSI* 94, *P.Lond. Inv.* 1575, now H. I. Bell, *Select Papyri*, *LCL*, vol. I, no. 133. Only in *P.Oxy.* 930 does the term καθηγητής appear, and the fact that he 'sailed away' is not enough to support the contention that he is an itinerant and that the term means this. There is no discussion of *P.Oxy.* 2190 which was not published until 1929.

teachers of students of the 'third' stage of education, namely orators and sophists.[20] The standard lexicographic works overlook significant evidence, as J. Glucker notes.[21] His comprehensive survey of both literary and non-literary sources reveals that the term refers to 'personal tutors' who were 'an extremely common species of teachers in the Hellenistic and Roman world'.[22] It could describe a 'freelance teacher of philosophy', or 'a personal teacher'. Glucker concludes that the term means 'very strictly' a private tutor with no official standing whatsoever.[23] However, he concedes N. E. De Witt's observation that the term was used to describe those in charge of small groups, given the particular attitude taken by the Epicurean school to instructors.[24]

In the early second century AD Pius is described as a rhetorician and the 'tutor' of Acharistus. The term here denotes a private tutor. This is confirmed by the use of instructors for the sons of the imperial household and great families.[25] Two inscriptions from

---

[20] M. H. Ibrahim, Ἡ ἑλληνορωμαικη παιδεία ἐν Αἰγύπτῳ (Athens: Myrtidi, 1972), pp. 265–6, Section 3: καθηγηγταὶ τῆς ἀνωτάτης παιδείας. He cites in support of his distinction between διδάσκαλος for secondary school teachers and καθηγηγτής for tertiary, P.Giss. 80 (early second century AD), P.Oxy. 930 (second or third century AD) and P.Oxy. 2190, 261–2, n. 4. However, the term διδάσκαλος does not occur in any of these texts, καθηγηγτής being used on each occasion. P.Oxy. 930 concerns a boy who still needs a παιδαγωγός and studies Homer. As Glucker, Antiochus and the Late Academy, p. 131, n. 35 notes, Ibrahim reaches his conclusion without evidence or argument.

[21] Glucker, Antiochus and the Late Academy, p. 128.

[22] They could function at various levels, 'from teaching a small girl to read, to teaching Homer to an older boy or teaching rhetoric to a young aspirant to political or forensic glory', ibid., p. 131. Glucker's comment is a summary of the educational levels of students in P.Giss. 80, P.Oxy. 930 and 2190 respectively.

[23] Ibid., 133.

[24] N. E. De Witt, 'Organization and Procedure in Epicurean Groups', CP 31 (1936), 205–11. Glucker, Antiochus and the Late Academy, p. 211, disagrees with De Witt's ranking of the instructors in a hierarchy of σοφός φιλόσοφοι, φιλόλογοι, καθηγηταί, δυνηθείς and κατασκευαζόμενοι. De Witt's conclusion is based on Philodemus, De Ira, xiv.1–14 and he sees the term καθηγητής as 'a synonym of less dignity'. For De Witt 'It is manifest from the contexts that the term denotes teachers, though the latter word is to be avoided as being out of harmony with the spirit of Epicureanism, the adherents of which were not taught but led or guided', 206; hence the appropriateness of the term καθηγητής.

[25] OGIS I. 408, 6–7. The inclusion of a professional designation is testified to in Strabo's comment on Athenodorus, a Stoic philosopher and tutor of Augustus (Καίσαρος καθηγήσατο), and Nestor, an Academic philosopher described as ὁ Μαρκέλλου καθηγησάμενος, the tutor of the nephew of Augustus, Strabo, Geography, xiv.5.14–15. Likewise Isaeus is a rhetorician who leaves the school to become the tutor of Demosthenes, Pseudo-Plutarch, Lives, Isaeus, 340e. In Plutarch, Lives, Cicero, 26.11, Metellus Nepos buries his καθηγητής. For further

Italy and Gaul show that the tutor in a Roman household was a valued residential member of the *familia*.[26] This term was also used of relationships where some development in education had occurred.[27] Thus in the Epicurean school it described the relationship between one who guides but does not teach in the normally accepted use of the term 'teacher', and one who is guided by the tenets of Epicurean philosophy.[28] This pedagogical change was not restricted to the study of philosophy. What happened in Egypt, for example, when students who came from the country to Alexandria were instructed not by a member of the household but by an independent tutor? Feelings of *familia* towards the tutor were strong enough in this situation to motivate the sending of food and warm greetings.[29] In Athens in c. 44 BC Cicero sent his son, Marcus, at the age of twenty-one, to study under orators and philosophers. He declaimed before separate orators in Latin or Greek, whereas at the age of eleven he had declaimed under an orator, Paeonius, who resided in his household. His relationship with Cassius, Bruttius and Cratippus in Athens was identical to the old one with Paeonius but now reflected a more advanced stage of education.[30] These responses to

examples see *Lives, Alexander,* 5.7; *Moralia, De Lib.Ed.* 4a–c; *Prof.Virt.* 85d in the discussion of Glucker, *Antiochus and the Late Academy,* pp. 128–9.

[26] For two excellent examples from imperial Greek inscriptions on tombstones suggesting the close relationship between the tutor and his student, and the custom of burying one's tutor see *IG* 14. 1751, καθηγητὴς ἀγαθὸς καὶ ἄξιος and *IG* 14. 2454, cited in Glucker, *Antiochus and the Late Academy,* p. 128, n. 26.

[27] Kaster, 'Notes on "Primary" and "Secondary" Schools', 346, on the issue of adaptability.

[28] Glucker, *Antiochus and the Late Academy,* pp. 132–3, refers to two Epicurean καθηγηταί who 'teach' and their former student, Philonides, who sets up his own private school in competition and is called καθηγητής. This example seems to undermine the rigid definition Glucker adopts which is crucial to the argument on Ammonius and the Academy.

[29] For example in *P.Osl.* 156 (second century AD, Fajyum) in a letter sent to a καθηγητής, Ammonius begins 'Before all things I pray you and your family are in good health and that you rely on me for the things you need.' There follows a list of food being sent. While the editors suggest the tutor was paid in kind rather than cash, there is no evidence to support this. The tone of the letter suggests a gift expressing φιλία. The food was obviously also meant for the pupil. See also *P.Giss.* 80 and also the large amount of food described in *P.Oxy.* 2190, 58–64.

[30] Cicero declaimed before Cassius in Greek and Brutus in Latin. He studied philosophy under Cratippus and he describes his relationship with him as that of a son to a father and not a pupil to a teacher. Cicero is forced to dismiss Gorgias, a distinguished rhetorician before whom he declaimed, because of his father's objection to the bad influence he was having on his son, *Letters to Friends,* xvi.21.5–6.

educational changes must inform our understanding of the term καθηγητής in *P.Oxy.* 2190, as we seek to read it in the light of the concept's evolution from the *familia* setting to a school context in this 'second Athens'.[31] The term should therefore be regarded as functional rather than hierarchical, for it describes a relationship to a student or students without in any way defining the level of education being provided.[32]

Neilus, in his comments on Didymus, explained what the tutor did. The latter had operated a school in the country, but more recently had opened one in Alexandria, lines 21, 29. He had enrolled pupils, one of whom was Didymus' friend, Philoxenus, who had in turn persuaded the sons of Apollonius to enrol with him, lines 22–3. Substantial fees were charged, which Neilus called 'useless and excessive', line 31. Didymus had promised to take proper care of his students by providing full supervision, and in fact, to do it better than any other sophist in Alexandria, lines 21–2.[33] The sons of Apollonius together with Philoxenus are now looking for a better tutor than Didymus, lines 25–7.[34] Neilus,

---

[31] For a recent survey of the occurrences of καθηγητής see Glucker, *Antiochus and the Late Academy*, pp. 127–33. Because of Glucker's concern to demonstrate the use of the term in the case of Ammonius, his conclusions are a little too rigid. His discussion does not allow for nuances in educational or philosophical development such as education conducted away from one's home or on Epicurean tenets. There is reference to Plutarch as a private tutor but not as an Academic or Platonic philosopher. His survey also throws important light on its only occurrence in the NT in Matt. 23.10: see my 'The Messiah as the Tutor', 152–7.

[32] J. Rea, *The Oxyrhynchus Papyri* (London: Egyptian Exploration Society, 1988), vol. LV, p. 189, points out in a discussion of the recently published papyrus *P.Oxy.* 3808 (first or second century AD) 'The word can apply to teachers of quite advanced pupils, see (*P.Oxy.*) 2190 and this appears to be the former letter, where the young man is old enough to supervise and take part in business if not to manage them [*sic*] quite alone.'

[33] *P.Oxy.* 930 is a good example of the lack of care and concern a καθηγητής might have for his pupil. He had literally 'sailed away' to seek his fortune, leaving his pupil at the sixth book of *The Iliad* after promising the mother that he would do the best he could for her son. She writes telling both her son and his καθηγητής to find a suitable καθηγητής with whom he can enrol (παραβάλλειν), lines 20–1.

[34] The sons of Apollonius 'are searching [present tense] for a better καθηγητής until now', line 24. The phrase μετὰ τούτου, line 23, suggests that after enrolling with Didymus they all realised his limited ability and sought a better καθηγητής. The original editor ignored the phrase μετὰ τούτου and has translated the text to mean that following the death of Philologus until they found Didymus they had been searching for a better καθηγητής. But the text suggests that the sons of Apollonius are not happy in their *present* situation, having enrolled in the school of Didymus, line 24. This comment would support the view that Neilus is seeking to make an *ad hoc* arrangement with Didymus which is preferable to joining the others in enrolling full-time in his school.

however, had made private arrangements with him to gain the benefits of his tuition, but without having to pay the excessive fees demanded of full-time students. Rather than enrol with Didymus, he will learn by himself, but he still 'has Didymus', he informs his father, lines 31–4. In what sense would he be able to help Neilus? 'Having' Didymus is explained by the comment that he is always ready to spend time on him, and that Didymus will do 'everything within his capabilities'. The sentence which follows shows that Neilus will learn by listening to those who declaim,[35] and makes provision for Didymus to help him by criticising his own speeches.[36] Thus he will combine tutorial assistance from this teacher of rhetoric with attendance at public declamations. Presumably this arrangement would assist his own financial situation while also commending itself to his father as a sound educational arrangement.[37] The word 'tutor' (καθηγητής) is thus used here to denote a private tutor in rhetoric who was paid to assist, on an *ad hoc* basis, an individual not enrolled in his school.[38]

In the light of the above investigation into the meaning of καθηγητής, J. Rea's rendering of it as 'teacher' is rejected as is his translation of φιλόλογος in lines 7 and 25 as 'tutor'. He offers no evidence to support these renderings. Certainly, φιλόλογος does not convey the duties understood in the first century of a tutor

---

[35] The editors reconstruct the end of line 34 as ἔτι δέ. This would require five letters and the space is insufficient as the microscopic examination of the traces of ink marks shows. The original editor translated the phrase as 'moreover' and Rea has 'still'. Given the student's frequent use of καί it is possible that the text could read 'I have Didymus . . . and by listening to those who declaim . . . I shall with the help of the gods, do well.' As Epictetus' evidence shows, the listening to orators and declaiming oneself were two separate activities; see following note. The next statement 'I shall do well with the help of the gods' implies that Neilus has made the best possible arrangements under the circumstances, i.e. this *ad hoc* arrangement with Didymus and listening to public declamations by others.

[36] Epictetus observes the dichotomy of 'attending lectures of the orators and declaiming yourself' (τῶν ῥητόρων ἤκουες καὶ αὐτὸς ἐμμελετᾶς), III.9.8. For the reliability of Epictetus' evidence alongside that of Plutarch and Dio Chrysostom see F. Millar, 'Epictetus and the Imperial Court', *JRS* 55 (1965), 147–8.

[37] Quintilian observes that fathers do not regard their sons as learning anything unless they are actually declaiming themselves and not simply listening to professional declamations, II.8.1. Marcus Cicero had declaimed before two separate teachers on a regular basis, see n. 30.

[38] *P.Oxy.* 2190 shows that this arrangement was one which would have made Didymus his καθηγητής, although he does not use the term specifically of him. In lines 7–8 he refers to 'Philologus' (in lines 24–5 this deceased person was a καθηγητής), 'Chaeremon ὁ καθηγητής' and 'Didymus'. However, no inference should be drawn from the term's absence because in lines 25–7 he says 'As for myself, if only I had found a tutor worthy of the name.'

whose *ad hoc* role is explained in part of the letter itself. Rea helpfully points to evidence that φιλόλογος was a term used in funerary inscriptions for brilliant young men who died before they fulfilled their potential, and could be used of members of the Alexandrian Museum.[39] His view that the word is not a personal name 'Philologos' as suggested by the original editor is accepted but not his translation. The word would be best rendered 'scholar', i.e. 'For now in my search for a scholar', line 7, and 'since the scholar whose classes they used to attend has died', line 25. The student is clearly searching for a person whom he can emulate and would see a sophist as such, but has been unable to secure entry into a school run by one. It is misleading to render καθηγητής as 'teacher' and φιλόλογος as 'tutor'.

In *P.Oxy*. 2190 then, the term 'tutor' (καθηγητής) is applied to a person qualified to assist a student in the art of declamation. In Didymus' case he may not have had a sufficient reputation or following to attract an audience to a public performance for he had only recently arrived from 'the country'. He may well have called himself a sophist, for his *synkrisis* must have been with sufficiently qualified orators to warrant the claim that he would care for his pupils better than any other sophist in Alexandria. It seems then that he was a teacher of rhetoric who called himself a σοφιστής and was also ὁ καθηγητής of Neilus. As such he would instruct this student in much the same way that private tutors in the households of the rich had done at a lower level of education. This would be done on an *ad hoc* basis for the purpose of improving his declamation skills.[40]

The public declaimers

Part of Neilus' plan, following his failure to gain entry into a sophist's school of his choice, was 'to listen to the orators declaiming, of whom one was Poseidonius', lines 34–6.[41] His

---

[39]   Rea, 'A Student's Letter to his Father', 80.

[40]   In *P.Oxy*. 2190, line 8 Didymus is designated the son of Aristocles. If he was the son of the forensic orator, Aristocles, mentioned in *P.Oxy*. 37 (49 AD) then he would have followed generally in his father's footsteps. Indeed he may well have changed from a career in forensic rhetoric to that of a teacher, for the Vespasian exemption provided sufficient financial reward for so doing. See p. 23.

[41]   ἀκροώμενος can mean either 'becoming a pupil' or 'listening to' a lecturer. Philostratus illustrates both meanings. In *Lives of the Sophists* it is used of a pupil of Zeno of Athens, of Favorinus and Aristocles, all in the aorist, 527, 576, 615,

proposal is illuminating for a number of reasons. Firstly, it shows that an education was available outside the sophist's classroom, namely listening to those who declaim. He could do this by attending a public display speech for an entrance fee.[42] Secondly, Neilus refers to those who engage in a 'declamation'. Ἐπίδειξις was a practice speech, originally a school exercise[43] intended to train students in *controversia* for a career as a forensic orator, or in *suasoria* for deliberative rhetoric.[44] Forensic practice speeches normally dealt with fictitious legal cases. On the Roman side we possess both summaries and full-length forensic declamations from the first century,[45] while on the Greek side topics for *suasoria* are extant, as are *controversia*. Sources include both

and also to attend lectures, 604–5, or to listen to declamations, 540. Neilus is referring to the latter because he has already told his father he will not enrol in a school but depend upon himself, lines 31–2, and will be listening to numbers of sophists declaim and not any single one in his lecture room.

[42] On the scale of fees charged for public declamations as against those levied for enrolment in schools see the differences in costs, G. B. Kerferd, *The Sophistic Movement* (Cambridge: Cambridge University Press, 1981), pp. 27–8, where they vary greatly between the single declamation or a series and that charged for a pupil of a sophist.

[43] It might be argued that 'those who declaim' could have been involved in philosophical discourse, epideictic rhetoric, lectures on grammatical topics rather than *controversia* and *suasoria*. The help Didymus gives is related to Neilus' need to learn how to declaim and it is unlikely that there is anything but *controversia* or *suasoria* in his mind. Turner, 'Oxyrhynchus and Rome', 7, n. 17, rejects the reconstruction by J. Zuisderduijn at the beginning of line 6, σοφιστῶν ἄξιον, on the grounds that 'it involves sailing down to Alexandria to some centre in search of tutors and his claim to have succeeded is intelligible only if understood ironically'.

[44] For the most recent treatment on declamations on the Greek side, making good the long-felt need for such a treatment since work on the Roman phenomenon by S. F. Bonner, *Roman Declamation*, see D. A. Russell's Gray Lectures, 1981, published as *Greek Declamation* (Cambridge: Cambridge University Press, 1983), especially his excellent ch. 4 on 'Performers and Occasions' and his survey of 'Evidence, Definitions, Origins', ch. 1. Kennedy, *The Art of Rhetoric*, pp. 312–37, concentrates on the Roman side.

[45] Both collections are attributed to Quintilian. On the nineteen declamations, most of which are full-length pieces, see J. Taylor, *The Declamations of Quintilian, Being an Exercitation or Praxis upon His XII Books, Concerning the Institution of the Orator* (London, 1686). It covers 474 pages and deals with imaginary cases, e.g. defending a blind youth accused by his stepmother of her own crime – killing his father. The cases are somewhat exotic and run counter to Quintilian's dictum that the subject chosen for themes should be 'as true to life as possible', II.10.4. There are also the 'minor' declamations of 'Quintilian' of which 145 are extant out of 358. In these declamations the rhetorician gave the class a case and in some instances the law involved, and the theme would then be developed. These are either extracts or full declamations. See M. Winterbottom, *The Minor Declamations Ascribed to Quintilian* (Berlin and New York: de Gruyter, 1984) and *Roman*

literary⁴⁶ and non-literary texts.⁴⁷ Dio Chrysostom's Trojan Oration, *Or.* 11, well illustrates the skill with which a trained orator could declaim on an impossible proposition, namely that 'Troy was not captured' and the corollary that Homer deliberately aimed to mislead his readers.⁴⁸ A number of extant first-century papyri contain not public declamations but classroom exercises. *P.Oxy.* 156 (late first century BC or early first century AD) is a *suasoria* originating possibly from an Alexandrian school.⁴⁹ *P.Lond.* 254 (verso) contains three examples of *controversia*, the first dealing with the question of legitimacy, the second with a charge and counter-charge of dishonesty, and the third on the wrongful assumption of citizenship.⁵⁰ *P.Lit.Lond.* 138 contains two or three forensic speeches with many corrections which, together with the absence of any names, lead to the conclusion that it probably comes from a school of rhetoric.⁵¹ *P.Vindob.* 26747, 29749 likewise recalls a classroom setting with its laboured writing and ortho-

Declamations: Extracts with Commentary (Bristol: Bristol Classical Press, 1980) on Quintilian and others.

⁴⁶ On the Greek side Philostratus notes some forty-five subjects for declamation, thirty-one of which deal with historical subjects, e.g. 'The Lacedaemonians debate whether they should fortify themselves by building a wall', *Lives of the Sophists*, 514. At least four of the themes are judicial. The linguistic distinction observed by the Romans between the two types of declamations was not as clear-cut for the Greeks although the genres were. See G. A. Kennedy, 'The Sophists as Declaimers', in G. W. Bowersock (ed.), *Approaches to the Second Sophistic* (University Park, Pennsylvania: American Philological Association, 1974), pp. 19–20.

⁴⁷ We have fewer declamations from the early empire than the late, although a number are found in Aristides in the mid second century; Russell, *Greek Declamation*, pp. 8–9.

⁴⁸ J. L. Moles, 'The Career and Conversion of Dio Chrysostom', *JHS* 68 (1978), 90; Kennedy, *The Art of Rhetoric*, pp. 571–2.

⁴⁹ On the style of this papyrus see W. M. Edwards, 'ΔΙΑΛΟΓΟΣ, ΔΙΑΤΡΙΒΗ ΜΕΛΕΤΗ', in J. N. Powell and F. A. Barber (eds.), *New Chapters in the History of Greek Literature, Second Series* (Oxford: Clarendon Press, 1929), p. 119: 'The language shows some departure from the classical Attic standard; it is mostly devoid of periods, being composed of short questions and clauses strung together with the minimum of connecting particles.' It is part of a reply by an 'Athenian orator' who argues that a threatening letter, possibly from Philip of Macedon, should be ignored because the city of Athens gives commands and does not receive them.

⁵⁰ Smith, *The Art of Rhetoric in Alexandria*, p. 116, gives the impression that only one case is involved. There are extracts of three speeches. The second provides an example of a forensic case. One person gives another a talent which is hidden in a mutually known place. The former, however, digs it up and when the latter finds out he takes it back, accusing the former person of theft.

⁵¹ R. A. Pack, *The Greek and Latin Literary Texts from Greco–Roman Egypt*, 2nd edn (Ann Arbor: University of Michigan Press, 1972), no. 2515; for such texts covering the period of Pack's collections see nos. 2495–559.

graphic mistakes.[52] *P.Yale* 105 is an important first-century AD declamation in which the orator accuses an admiral of neglecting to pick up or care for his wounded men following a battle (possibly Arginusae, 406 BC, or a similar one). Its vigorous style is more sophisticated than those usually emanating from the classroom, but numerous corrections and abbreviations suggest that it too is the product of a student.[53] If that is the case he was obviously advanced in his studies. These papyri reflect the type of work Neilus would have undertaken.

Thirdly, the movement of this original exercise from the class-room to the public lecture and indeed the lecture tour provided Neilus with an opportunity to learn not only from one declaimer but several.[54] One of these, Poseidonius, may have been known to Theon, the father of Neilus, for he mentions his name without comment.[55] If he was the Poseidonius of Olbiopolis, a city on the

[52] Smith, *The Art of Rhetoric in Alexandria*, p. 117.

[53] *Ibid.*, pp. 117–18, citing D. M. Samuel, 'Rhetorical Papyrus in the Yale Collection', PhD dissertation, Yale University (1964), p. 135. See also discussion of *P.Yale*, 105 by S. A. Stephens, *Yale Papyri in the Beinecke Rare Book and Manuscript Library II*, American Studies in Papyrology 24 (Chico: Scholars Press, 1985), p. 55 and Russell, *Greek Declamation*, p. 4, n. 4.

[54] Clarke, *Higher Education*, pp. 215–6, suggests that the evolution began with the teacher himself declaiming before his students to provide them with a model presentation or a general outline of arguments which could be developed. The students would then write out their own declamation for presentation and criticism by the class and the teacher. He cites Quintilian II.4–6, x.2.39 and postulates that parents were allowed to visit the class and hear their sons or indeed teachers declaiming. The teacher aimed to impress upon the parents that their continued patronage of him was a justified expense. He set aside special days and on those occasions declaimed before 'large and cultivated' audiences. This led to lecture tours with enthusiastic paying audiences as an extension of the custom prevailing in their own city. In his *Rhetoric at Rome*, p. 85, he argues that the 'institution of declamation grew up with the end of the republic and the need to steer clear of contemporary subjects'. He believes oratory survived the decay of the Greek city-state, as it also survived the Roman Republic, but took this new form of declamation. However, it needs to be noted that at least for the East, city-states did not lose their forum and while Clarke's observations about Rome are correct, they do not apply with equal force to the East. See Kennedy, *The Art of Rhetoric*, pp. 430, 553–6.

[55] While Rea, 'A Student's Letter to his Father', 84, suggests that no contemporary rhetorician is known by this name, the Poseidonius mentioned by Neilus may well be the sophist and historian of Olbiopolis, the author of a work on the Dniester region. A. H. McDonald, *OCD*, states that he has been identified with a contemporary of Perseus of Macedon, 179–168 BC, who was noted by Plutarch, *Lives, Aemilius Paulus*, 19.7, but feels this is uncertain. F. Jacoby, *Fragmente der griechischen Historiker*, no. 279 (1940–3) places the same sophist and historian in the second century AD and his dating is cited with approval by H. J. Mette, *P.W.* no. 6 Poseidonios. He is not to be confused with the second-century BC

joint estuary of the Bug and the Dnieper, he may have been in Alexandria on a lecture tour.[56] It could well be that in keeping with sophistic conventions he had come to the city and established himself as a public declaimer.[57] If this is so, then Neilus would have been exposed not only to local sophists but to one of international repute. He may be name-dropping to impress his father.

Neilus believes that if he listens to orators or sophists declaiming publicly, especially Poseidonius, and makes use of Didymus as an *ad hoc* tutor to help him in his own declamations, then he will succeed.[58] It is significant that such an alternative existed for an advanced student of rhetoric. It demonstrates both the central role declamations played in *paideia* in first-century Alexandria, and the prominence that teachers of rhetoric and sophists had secured for themselves through them.

The status of students of the sophists

What light, if any, does *P.Oxy.* 2190 throw upon the first-century rank of the sophists and the social status of their students?[59] G. W. Bowersock has argued, 'The social eminence of the sophists in their cities and provinces brought their families swiftly and inevitably

Alexandrian grammarian of the same name. If the Poseidonius of Olbiopolis is that mentioned in *P.Oxy.* 2190, he may well have been visiting Alexandria and of such reputation to have been known by Neilus' father. He was of sufficient reputation for Neilus to have given no further details to his father. Elsewhere in his letter he cites further details of persons mentioned in his letter not known to his father, e.g. Didymus, son of Aristocles, line 8. *P.W.*, in citing eleven men with this name, does not attempt to identify *P.Oxy.* 2190 with any of their entries.

56 Aristides was an example of a rhetorician who visited Egypt and made his debut as an orator there, *Or.* 36.1, 91.
57 For the coming of a sophist, see pp. 147–51.
58 τάχα θεῶν θελόντων καλῶς πράξομαι. The original editor, C. H. Roberts, rearranged the sentence to read: 'Moreover, with any luck, I shall do well for myself by hearing the lectures', but ἐπιδεικνύμενοι refers to 'those who declaim'. Neilus is presenting a 'package' to his father which involves listening to declaimers in a public context and he cites one in particular. He mentions help from Didymus, lines 32–4, listening to public declamations, lines 34–6 and then adds literally that 'with the help of the gods' he expected to do well. J. L. White, 'Epistolary Formulas and Clichés in Greek Papyrus Letters', *SBL Seminar Papers* 2 (1978), 295, rightly considers phrases such as this clichés.
59 E. A. Judge, *Rank and Status in the World of Caesars and St Paul* (Christchurch: University of Canterbury Publications, 1982), p. 9, has drawn a helpful distinction reflected in non-literary sources between these two terms. By 'rank' he means 'any formally defined position in society', while 'status' refers to 'positions of influence'. See also J. D. Court, 'Some Aspects of Rank and Status in Epictetus: Development of a Methodology', MA dissertation, Macquarie University (1986).

into the Roman upper class.'[60] E. L. Bowie has examined the social origins of sophists and shown that they came from families of high rank who 'had long furnished their cities with magistrates, benefactors and diplomats'.[61] He has further argued that membership of that class was the true key to their success; oratory was not the ladder on which Greek intellectuals scaled the heights of Roman society as Bowersock suggested.[62] There was no swift and inevitable means for advancement. Furthermore, we find in Domitian's rescript the attempt to restrict social climbing with his insistence that instruction 'ought to be transmitted only to a limited number of free-born young men'.[63] In the first century, entry into the Greek aristocracy in the East, and even into positions of rank in one's home city, was through birth; and perhaps just as importantly, it was often only the high-born who could gain access to persons of rank.[64]

We thus can locate Neilus' place on the social ladder if we attend to his access to the powerful. Because of an incident in the theatre in Alexandria, he appears to have sought the help of distinguished officials, lines 4–6.[65] Theon appears to have been unperturbed by

[60] Bowersock, *Greek Sophists*, p. 28. For the long and sometimes uncertain route of free men selling themselves into slavery as stewards of Roman households and on manumission securing Roman citizenship see my 'Social Mobility', in *Seek the Welfare of the City: Christians as Benefactors and Citizens, First–Century Christians in the Graeco–World*, (Grand Rapids and Carlisle: Eerdmans and Paternoster, 1994), ch. 8, esp. pp. 154–9.

[61] E. L. Bowie, 'The Importance of the Sophists', *Yale Classical Studies* 27 (1982), 53, calls them 'a species of the genus Greek aristocrat'. For his survey of origins see 54–9 and his careful analysis of the alleged 'low or middle-class origins' of three sophists in Philostratus, where he shows they were not outside the curial class of the Greek aristocrat. He observes Bowersock's own statement that 'sophists almost always emerged from the notable and wealthy families of their cities', Bowersock, *Greek Sophists*, pp. 21–3. Philostratus' bias in showing the achievements of sophists to support his favourable estimation of their influence must not be overlooked in the way he presents his evidence; see C. P. Jones, 'The Reliability of Philostratus', in Bowersock (ed.), *Approaches to the Second Sophistic*, p. 11.

[62] Bowie, 'Greeks and their Past in the Second Sophistic', *Past and Present* 46 (1970), 23, *contra* Bowersock, *Greek Sophists*, 28.

[63] For a citation of the rescript see p. 24.

[64] For an example see the discussion by Epictetus of the possibilities for the subsequent appointment to positions of rank for a student of rhetoric, and for the use of the term 'well-born', see pp. 119–21 and 189–91.

[65] The original editor of the text has drawn the conclusion that the things which happened in the theatre, line 4, relate to the broken chariots, lines 10–11. The reconstruction of Rea rejects any reference to an accident with chariots. Neilus has certainly been involved in an incident and he says he has already written to his father 'the day before yesterday' presumably about the theatre incident. Dio's

this incident, which was obviously a relief to Neilus, lines 3–4. However, in a subsequent letter to his father, he again mentions the matter because Heraclas, the slave of Neilus, has felt 'no shame in gleefully spreading reports in the city about the incident in the theatre and telling lies such as would not come even from the mouth of an accuser', lines 45–7. Given the proverbial behaviour of the Alexandrians in the theatre, described by Dio as 'uproar, buffoonery and scurrility',[66] it must have been the rumour mongering of his slave that worried Neilus most. This sent him back to Alexandria, 'to the esteemed[. . .]' where he believed himself to have achieved 'something that repaid my eagerness', line 6. Neilus had written to his friend Philoxenus and others 'telling them that they too must leave the matter in the hands of the esteemed[. . .]', lines 12–14.

Another sign that Neilus came from a wealthy background was his possession of his own slave, Heraclas, who was not the person designated to accompany him to school (i.e. his παιδαγωγός) but who worked in Alexandria 'to contribute some obols daily' towards the cost of his master's living expenses, lines 41–2.[67] Neilus expected Heraclas to earn two drachmas a day working under a carpenter and this money would now need to be remitted to him by his father, lines 50–1.[68] When Heraclas was involved in some

speech bears eloquent testimony to the proverbial misbehaviour of citizens in the theatre, *Or.* 32.4. For the seriousness Dio attaches to this well-known Alexandrian trait, see *Or.* 32.73. If Neilus' behaviour in the theatre was such as to provide his slave, Heraclas, with the opportunity to denounce him, lines 45–7, then it must have been a matter of some consequence. Neilus has written to a fellow student, Philoxenus, and his friends, telling them to leave this matter in the hands of a person of distinction, line 12. The distinguished persons of line 5 (plural) appear to be different from the person of lines 13–14, but the text is broken and therefore in neither case are their names known, lines 6–14. The reason for asserting that the theatre incident happened in Alexandria is based on lines 45–6, τὰ περὶ τοῦ θεάτρου ἐν τῇ πόλει. It was customary to refer to Alexandria as 'the city'. For its possible connection to a riot see my 'The Messiah as Tutor', 153.

66 *Or.* 32.4. See E. K. Borthwick, 'Dio Chrysostom on the Mob at Alexandria', *CR* 22 (1972), 1–3; Smith, *The Art of Rhetoric in Alexandria*, pp. 24–8; and W. D. Barry, 'Aristocrats, Orators and the Mob: Dio Chrysostom and the World of the Alexandrians', *Historia* 42 (1993), 82–103.

67 Neilus was too old for a παιδαγωγός. E. A. Judge, 'Cultural Conformity and Innovation in Paul: Some Clues from Contemporary Documents', *Tyn.B.* 35 (1984), 13 calls him 'a university student'.

68 It was apparently the arrangement that Heraclas would provide some income for Neilus and his father would send provisions to his son. Lines 58–64 indicate that in addition to 126lb of salted meat, his father sent lentils and vinegar, as well as thirty baked loaves. The sending of food to students and teachers is attested above, p. 27, n. 29 and examples cited.

misdemeanours, he, unlike his master, was summarily apprehended. Lacking his master's access to men of influence, his solution was to escape the jurisdiction of Alexandria and return to Oxyrhynchus and the security of Theon's household.

Neilus' attitude towards Didymus also reveals a sense of superiority bred by status. He expresses his disgust to his father because, although not competent enough to teach his students properly, Didymus has claimed superiority to all other teachers in Alexandria, lines 21–2.[69] What annoyed Neilus most was not that Didymus dared to involve himself in *synkrisis* with other sophists, but, he adds emphatically, οὗτος ὅς ('he is') 'a country one' at that! (lines 27–9). This is very much a pejorative comment.[70]

Although nothing more can be learned concerning Neilus' status from *P.Oxy.* 2190, the sons of Apollonius mentioned in line 22 may illuminate it further. In *P.Oxy.* 1153 (dated to the first century) a father, Apollonius, writes, from Oxyrhynchus, to his son of the same name, who attends school in Alexandria along with Nicanor, who is apparently his brother. If these are the same students mentioned in *P.Oxy.* 2190, their father reflects the status-consciousness of Greek citizens.[71] Another brother, Pausanias, has sent two variegated wrist bands, one scarlet and the other purple, and the

---

[69] On the use of *synkrisis* in rhetoric see the helpful survey of C. Forbes, 'Comparison, Self-praise and Irony: Paul's Boasting and Conventions of Hellenistic Rhetoric', *NTS* 32 (1986), 7, and its application to the *synkrisis* of Paul's opponents in 2 Cor. 10.12 and the present discussion. Forbes overlooks the content of the *synkrisis* of Didymus with his Alexandrian counterparts in *P.Oxy.* 2190, lines 21–2, citing only lines 23–9. He comments, 'Clearly, part of the unfortunate Didymus' advertising took the form of comparing himself with other teachers, and in Neilus's "humble opinion", he simply didn't measure up.' It was, however, Didymus' promise of better care than anyone else in Alexandria in order to attract pupils that angered Neilus, lines 21–2. This was particularly aggravating when he apparently could not fulfil his promise. This was not only Neilus' opinion, for Philoxenus and the sons of Apollonius seem to have reached the same conclusion. Judge, 'Cultural Conformity', 13, comments that Didymus is 'despised for aspiring to the competition'. The fact is that Didymus advertised his superiority on the grounds that he could offer better supervision to his pupils.

[70] Aelius Theon uses 'country' to express his disgust with recent developments in education – τὸ πάντων ἀγροικότατον ('worst of all'), *Rhetores Graeci*, II, 146. Philostratus, *Lives of the Sophists*, 529, likewise notes that Polemo asks his pupils 'Why do you look to the rustic?', ὁ ἄγροικος, a highly derogatory remark about Marcus, the sophist from Byzantium.

[71] Cf. also Neilus' attitude to the country rhetorician although he himself is obviously from the country and not 'the city'. This letter also mentions a Heraclas as a boatman, line 7, and a Diogas, line 21, the same names as Neilus' slave and his young brother. It may be sheer coincidence that *P.Oxy.* 1153 mentions the sons of Apollonius, Heraclas and Diogas, for they were common names in

letter later mentions cloth made from 'local purple', lines 15–17, 26.[72] Purple was certainly a status symbol in that day, and parents encouraged their sons to wear it.[73]

Conclusion

Can we regard Neilus as a credible witness? It would seem that he accurately reflects the Alexandrian situation, for his father already knows of the difficulties pertaining to entry into the sophists' schools. This view is further confirmed by the references to a fellow student, Philoxenus, whom Theon knows. Too much knowledge is simply assumed throughout the correspondence for it to be based on a false representation. Although Neilus betrays his immaturity in the theatre incident, a certain degree of initiative and self–preservation show through in crises created by his educational needs, his misdemeanour and his slave's rumours. Glucker, over–generously, assesses the character of Neilus positively – 'the style and manner of the letter betray a mature and intelligent young man, living on his own in the great city'. However, there is certainly no reason to doubt the accuracy of Neilus' comments on the educational situation in Alexandria, apart from his pejorative comments on the professional ability of Alexandrian teachers, which may reflect more on his shortage of money for his education – a shortage which may have been caused by his hedonistic life.[74] *P.Oxy.* 2190 is a valuable witness to the sophistic movement in this

Oxyrhynchus and it could be argued it has nothing to do with *P.Oxy.* 2190. However, the possible connection cannot be dismissed.

[72] Apollonius mentions the expense to which Pausanias has gone. M. Reinhold, *The History of Purple as a Status Symbol in Antiquity,* Collection Latomus 116 (Brussels: Revue d'études latines, 1970), p. 51, citing *P.Oxy.* 1153, notes the use of 'local' purple as a private display of status and an increasing phenomenon. For a more recent survey of epigraphic evidence see G. H. R. Horsley, 'The Purple Trade and the Status of Lydia of Thyatira', *New Docs.* 2 (1982), 25–32.

[73] Reinhold, *The History of Purple as a Status Symbol in Antiquity,* p. 72, also notes that the use of this colour as a 'status display' was at its highest intensity in the ancient world in the second century. Apollonius was very keen to have the coat made for his son: 'A pattern of the colour of the dress that is being made is enclosed in this letter, give it to Nicanor to look at, in order that, if he likes it he may write to us, for it has not yet been given out. We are going to use local purple', *P.Oxy.* 1153, lines 22–7.

[74] Glucker, *Antiochus and the Late Academy,* p. 131. Rather his behaviour is hubristic; see P. Marshall's discussion of this in *Enmity in Corinth: Social Conventions in Paul's Relations with the Corinthians* (Tübingen: J. C. B. Mohr (Paul Siebeck), 1987), pp. 182–94, although he makes no reference to *P.Oxy.* 2190.

major educational centre, and constitutes an important perspective for exploring *paideia* and the problems it created in first-century Alexandria, where Philo lived.

This non-literary source has provided a window on the first-century sophistic movement in Alexandria as it touched the life of an advanced student of *paideia*. The sophists emerge from *P.Oxy.* 2190 as an important group in the Alexandrian education system. In an age when declamation was deemed the best method for advanced education, the sophists were in great demand. The acute shortage of such teachers in the city expressed not their unimportance, but that demand outpaced supply.[75]

The exorbitant costs further reflect a seller's market; Neilus' complaint that fees are so high is more than an exaggeration by a financially strapped young man. The sophists had always charged fees, which distinguished them from the philosophers.[76] It mattered little that philosophers denigrated their professional ability: parents who paid substantial amounts to sophists were acknowledging their primacy in *paideia*.

Furthermore, the papyrus demonstrates the high priority placed upon declaiming by students and possibly parents, a preoccupation also noted by Aelius Theon and Quintilian in the first century. The activity of orators who were not recognised by the public as sophists is also reflected in *P.Oxy.* 2190. The competitive desire for such recognition is shown in the *synkrisis* of Didymus, the country orator, who, with his own school and his activity as a tutor (καθηγητής) within an *ad hoc* tutorial system, shows that this level in the educational system was able to adapt to the needs of students. Finally, the tone of the letter with its reference to men of rank in Alexandria shows the circles in which the pupils of the orators and sophists at least hoped to secure influence in times of personal trouble.

[75] The papyrus notes the acute shortage in the country as well as the city, i.e. Alexandria; a well-attested fact that both Neilus' father, Theon, and Philoxenus have noted, lines 16–19.
[76] For discussion see p. 49.

2

DIO AND THE ALEXANDRIAN SOPHISTIC LEADERS

The conflict in Alexandria

Dio of Prusa's oration, delivered to a huge crowd in the Alexandrian theatre, *Or.* 32.2,[1] provides additional information about the city's sophistic movement. In this speech he attempts to persuade Alexandrian citizens to reform their riotous conduct before more serious consequences befall them, noting that a recent confrontation between themselves and the prefect of Egypt (L. Peducaeus

For a survey of recent trends in studies of Dio to 1987 see B. F. Harris, 'Dio of Prusa: A Survey of Recent Works', *ANRW* II.33.5 (1991), 3853–81. Three significant works appeared in 1978 with special bearing on the Alexandrian Oration. C. P. Jones, *The Roman World of Dio Chrysostom* (Cambridge, Mass. and London: Harvard University Press, 1978), devoted ch. 5 to an important discussion of this oration and its setting. Likewise P. Desideri, *Dione di Prusa: un intellettuale greco nell'Impero Romano*, Biblioteca di Cultura Contemporanea, 135 (Messina: Casa Editrice G. d'Anna, 1978), pp. 66–186, produced an extended treatment of the oration. J. L. Moles, 'The Career and Conversion of Dio Chrysostom', *JHS* 68 (1978), 79–100, wrote an important essay on fundamental questions on Dio. In 1970 a short dissertation on the oration was presented to the University of Bonn by E. Wilmes, 'Beiträge zur Alexandrinerede (*Or.* 32) des Dion Chrysostomos', which discussed sections of the oration judged to be significant for an understanding of the whole. Wilmes' treatment of sophists and orators in *Or.* 32.39 should be noted, p. 31. For his understanding of the term 'sophist' see p. 58, n. 77. For a critique of the treatment of the sophists by Jones and Desideri see p. 56, n. 66 and pp. 56–8.

[1] On the dating of the Alexandrian Oration in the seventies see C. P. Jones, 'The Date of Dio of Prusa's Alexandrian Oration', *Historia* 22 (1973), 302–9, accepted by Moles, 'The Career and Conversion of Dio Chrysostom', 84, n. 48. Harris, 'Dio of Prusa', 3860–72, in agreement with Jones, notes Dio's strong links with the Flavian emperors and Alexandria. J. D. Thomas, 'L. Peducaeus Col(nus), Praefectus Aegypti', *ZPE* 21 (1976), 153, likewise agrees and further supports this with a discussion of *S.B.* 676. For the traditional dating *c.* AD 105–12 see H. von Arnim, *Leben und Werke des Dio von Prusa* (Berlin, 1898), pp. 435–6, based on what A. Momigliano called a Hegelian triad, namely rhetoric–thesis, philosophy–antithesis and a harmony between rhetoric and philosophy–synthesis, 'Review and Discussion', *JRS* 40 (1950), 149, citing V. E. Valdenberg, 'The Political Philosophy of Dio Chrysostom', *Izvestia Akad Navk. SSK* (1926), 149.

Colonus) and his forces had attracted the interest of the Roman authorities.[2] Although the prefect had tried to defuse the situation some trouble-makers, described as 'headstrong and unruly spirits who purposely aimed at complete overthrow and utter chaos', brought 'a taste of warfare' on those present, #72. In citing this incident Dio hopes to convince his audience that the confrontation flowed inexorably from the disorderliness which ruled their lives. It was epitomised by their unruly conduct in the theatre (#73–4).[3] They had been played upon by Cynics who deliberately incited thoughtless people to deride philosophers, #10. The problems were also linked to the philosophers' abdication of their roles in *politeia*, creating a gap which orators and poets attempted to fill. In the end none of these groups – which included the many sophists – overcame the problem with Rome that was aggravated by their recent *stasis*, #8,10. Dio's oration provides evidence of the activities of sophists, orators, poets and philosophers within the leadership framework of *politeia* in Alexandria.[4]

[2] For the identification of 'excellent Κόνων' as the prefect, Colonus, see Jones, 'The Date of Dio of Prusa's Alexandrian Oration', 306. He cites F. W. Hall, *A Companion to Classical Texts* (Oxford: Clarendon Press, 1913), p. 159, for uncial confusion of nu and lambda, and R. Reneham, *Greek Textual Criticism: A Reader*, Loeb Classical Monograph (Cambridge, Mass.: Harvard University Press, 1969), p. 67 on the corruption of non-Greek names and the confusion of lesser-known names with well-known ones. In addition to the cognomen on *P.Oxy.* 2349, 2757, see the discussion in support of Jones by Thomas, 'L. Peducaeus Col(nus)', 153–6, citing *SB* 676.38 as further evidence. As the prefect was the commander of the Roman troops stationed in Egypt, the identification with Colonus is further justified. No other prefect bears the same or similar name. On the military role of the prefect of Egypt see P. A. Brunt, 'The Administrators of Egypt', *JRS* 65 (1975), 131, and the list of prefects to AD 236. For a subsequent list see G. Bastianini, 'Lista dei Prefetti d'Egitto dal 30ª al 299ᴾ', *ZPE* 17 (1975), 262–388, where he cites corroborating evidence, although in the case of Colonus, 275, there are deficiencies as Thomas notes, 'L. Peducaeus Col(nus)' 153. Desideri, *Dione di Prusa*, pp. 63, 147 n. 5 rejects Jones' argument, suggesting among other reasons that the argument on the identity is not decisive, but still endorses the delivery during Vespasian's reign as the means of comparison with Alexandria during Nero's reign.

[3] Jones, *Roman World of Dio Chrysostom*, p. 42 suggests that since soldiers were apparently in the theatre during performances, fights between various groups had evidently turned to attacks on the common oppressor, #51. Cassius Dio, *Roman History*, LXV, 8 speaking of the conduct of the Alexandrians during Vespasian's reign, AD 69–70, uses a synonym, ἀσέλγεια, to describe their conduct. He speaks of 'impudent licence which is always working to their detriment'.

[4] On the use here of *politeia* as 'the way of life of the state' see J. Bordes, *Politeia dans la pensée grecque jusqu'à Aristote* (Paris: "Belle Lettres", 1982), p. 116. For an analysis of the structure of the oration see Jones, *Roman World of Dio Chrysostom*, p. 40, with the lengthy preface #1–19, behaviour at public entertainment #20–40,

Dio as Alexandria's counsellor and saviour

The initial discussion of all these groups occurs in #8–11 within the lengthy introduction, #1–29. There Dio seeks to establish his own credentials as counsellor and saviour of Alexandria through his use of comparison with philosophers, sophists, orators and poets. J. L. Moles defines 'counsellor' (σύμβουλος) as 'the typical figure of the external adviser interfering from a higher plane'.[5] Dio may appear in the garb of a philosopher (traditionally 'clad in a mean cloak') but, as he tells his audience, he has been appointed to the task of addressing the Alexandrians 'by the will of some deity', #22,12. The 'deity' in question is Vespasian, to whom Alexandria had recently granted the traditional divine honours immediately on his accession to the Principate.[6] It would seem that Dio came with the knowledge and blessing of Vespasian, as his ambassador.

Dio hoped to heal a rift between the emperor and the Alexandrians. The city's fortunes, robust under Nero, had been sharply reversed under Vespasian even though it was here that the legions first recognised his claim to the Principate in AD 69. Cassius Dio records the city's disappointment at receiving as reward for its acceptance of his claim only a heavier tax burden. Their dashed hopes turned to mocking and questioning of his ability to rule, and soon to open and 'foolhardy' demonstrations at which they abused 'the good nature of the emperor'.[7] It was 'that impudent licence which is always working to their detriment' with which the Alexan-

---

citharody and chariot racing discussed together #41–6, and then separately #46–74, 74–95, and the epilogue #95–101, which brings together introductory themes and relates them to their position with the emperor and their general attitudes to *politeia* #97–100.

[5] Moles sees Dio in this role not only in *Or.* 32 but also in the speech at Rhodes, *Or.* 31, and that delivered to his native city, Prusa, *Or.* 46. He argues that this oration 'foreshadows' Dio's role in 'philosopho–political symbouleutics', 'The Career and Conversion of Dio Chrysostom', 93. Whether 'foreshadows' is the best term is debatable, for Dio seems at home in this role in the orations of this period. On *synkrisis* see #39 and C. Forbes, 'Comparison, Self-praise and Irony: Paul's Boasting and Conventions of Hellenistic Rhetoric', *NTS* 32 (1986), 2–8 for Dio's use of this term.

[6] Dio says he comes as Hermes at the behest of Zeus, #21. The latter was identified with a reigning emperor; Jones, *Roman World of Dio Chrysostom*, pp. 44 and 174, n. 83. See also A. Henrichs, 'Vespasian's Visit to Alexandria', *ZPE* 3 (1968), 58–80, for the Ptolemaic concept of the emperor as the 'living image of Zeus' and the Alexandrians granting divine descent to Vespasian.

[7] Cassius Dio, *Roman History*, LXV.8: 'Six obols more you demand of us' they taunted and in a crowded assembly they all shouted in chorus at Vespasian's son, Titus, 'We forgive him; for he knows not how to play the Caesar.'

drians abused the emperor, Cassius Dio notes;[8] Suetonius adding that they called him a 'fishmonger'.[9]

The conclusion of the oration holds out the possibility of an imperial visit, and even benefactions, if the Alexandrians could prove themselves by their restraint 'worthy of his favour and trust' #95. Dio aims then to convince the citizens that they must heed him, for 'in plain terms and without guile [he] speaks his mind with frankness', #11: he is their 'counsellor and saviour',[10] concerned for the well-being of his audience. Two factors must be constantly before us as we evaluate Dio and his discussion of, and *synkrisis* with philosophers, orators, poets and sophists. First, his speech must be weighed in the light of his overriding ambition to succeed in this difficult imperial mission. Second, any assessment of Dio's role, especially in relation to philosophers and sophists, must be made in the light of recent events in Rome and Dio's response to them.

In AD 71 Vespasian had expelled all philosophers from Rome with the exception of the noted Musonius Rufus.[11] The Cynics he singled out for special mention, perhaps because he, like Seneca, found them to be 'rebellious and fractious persons, over-riding kings and officials and those responsible for the conduct of public affairs'.[12] They taught many doctrines 'inappropriate to the times'

---

8 Vespasian was only dissuaded from taking retaliatory action on 'the obols' issue by his son, Titus. Cassius Dio also notes 'But Vespasian soon ceased to notice them.' The text seems to suggest that matters of higher priority in Rome took precedence in Vespasian's thinking, especially as his imperial claims had not yet been finally secured. The reference to 'soon restoring order to Egypt' may point to further troubles arising out of the spurning of Vespasian, *Roman History*, LXV, 8.

9 Cassius Dio, *Vespasian*, 19.2. 'The Alexandrians persisted in calling him Cybiosacten, the surname of one of their kings who was scandalously stingy.' Cybiosacten is a transliteration of the Greek κυβιοσάκτης, a dealer in square pieces of salt fish, *LCL*, vol. II, p. 312. On the belligerence of the Alexandrians even towards royals, see also Dio Chrysostom, *Or.* 32.22.

10 Dio says at the beginning of his oration that Greeks have the heritage of παιδεία and λόγος which makes them σωτῆρες τῶν πόλεων, #3. On the designation of the prefect as 'saviour of Egypt' and 'saviour' see, e.g. *P.Fouad* 26 (AD 157–9) lines 26, 49–50; of the emperor as 'saviour of the whole human race' see *Select Papyri*, vol II, no. 211 (AD 19) lines 38–40, and on the *sestertius* issued at Rome by Vespasian in AD 71 as 'liberator' or 'saviour' of Rome from slavery see A. Watson, 'Vespasian: Adsertor Libertatis Publicae', *CR* (n.s.) 23 (1973), 127–8.

11 On the expulsion see Cassius Dio, *Roman History*, LXV, 13. On the disappointment of philosophers with Vespasian as emperor and their discussion of the restoration of the republic see Moles, 'The Career and Conversion of Dio Chrysostom', 83, n. 41 and Desideri, *Dione di Prusa*, ch. 2, section 1.

12 Seneca, *Ep. Mor.* 73.

and publicly criticised the relationship of Vespasian's son, Titus, with Berenice.[13] Dio's own lost work attacked philosophers in general and Stoics and Cynics in particular.[14] He is said to have argued that philosophers should 'be expelled from every land and sea in the belief that they are Messengers of Death to state and civil organisations alike'.[15] His comments on the threat of retaliatory measures may therefore be linked with Cynic activity in Alexandria,[16] and his censure of the philosophers there must be coloured to some extent by recent events in the capital, all the more so if he comes as an imperial messenger. These two factors will be considered as we examine his discussion of philosophers, especially with respect to (1) their role in *politeia*, and (2) those who attempted to stand in their place in *politeia*, namely orators, sophists and poets.[17]

Philosophers as former leaders in *politeia*

In apportioning blame for the present instability in Alexandria, Dio tells his audience that they may not have been wholly culpable, #8.[18] Responsibility rests with the one who 'wears the name

13 Cassius Dio, *Roman History*, LXV, 15. For discussion see R. H. Dudley, *A History of Cynicism from Diogenes to the 6th Century A.D.* (London: Methuen, 1937), ch. 7.

14 On his κατὰ τῶν φιλοσόφων, no longer extant, see Synesius, *Dio Chrysostom*, LCL, vol. v, p. 373 and Moles, 'The Career and Conversion of Dio Chrysostom', 85–7, for discussion. Jones, 'The Date of Dio of Prusa's Alexandrian Oration', 305, sees a connection between this lost work and *Or.* 32 on Dio's attitude to philosophers.

15 Cited *Dio Chrysostom*, LCL, vol. v, p. 373.

16 Jones, *Roman World of Dio Chrysostom*, p. 44.

17 Moles, 'The Career and Conversion of Dio Chrysostom', 94, calls Dio's stance in AD 71 'a pose of expediency in a moment of crisis'. However, there seems to be a consistency in attitude on the part of Dio from the time of the expulsion of philosophers from Rome to the delivery of this oration. The Rhodian discourse is dated by Jones prior to the Alexandrian discourse but after the expulsion of the philosophers. Dio's praise of the famous philosopher Musonius Rufus does not deny his consistency. This Stoic philosopher was the only one not expelled by Vespasian in the initial election in AD 71, *Or.* 31.122. According to Fronto, Dio was a pupil of Musonius Rufus. For the discussion of Dio's Πρὸς Μουσώνιον, which is no longer extant, see Moles, 'The Career and Conversion of Dio Chrysostom', 82–3 and 85–8, and for the dating of *Or.* 31, see Jones, *Roman World of Dio Chrysostom*, p. 133.

18 Earlier Dio suggested the problem could have been avoided if the Alexandrians had made use of their heritage, namely 'education and rhetoric' (παιδεία καὶ λόγος). The blessings bestowed on those who have participated in them are that they make 'good men' (ἄνδρες ἀγαθοί) and 'saviours of the cities' (σωτῆρες τῶν πόλεων). The present emperor is devoted to them and they are the remedy of the gods for κακία, #60,61. *Paideia* is meant to produce the opposite of evil, i.e.

philosopher'.[19] Dio divides the philosophers into two groups.[20] There are some 'who do not appear in public' at all because they despair of ever effecting an improvement in 'the masses'.[21] Thus they have 'quit the field and are silent' out of concern for their dignity, #19.

They now serve no more purpose in *politeia* than shadow boxers, the scourge of the wrestling schools and gymnasia who view 'with suspicion the sun's heat and the blows', for they have abdicated their traditional role as admonishers of the citizens, #20. Dio reiterates this charge when he later states, 'In my opening remarks also I laid blame for this [disorder] upon the philosophers who will not appear before the people or even deign to converse with you', #20.

The second group[22] wish to exercise their voices in 'what we call lecture-halls'.[23] Since for Dio the theatre represents 'the organ of hearing of the people', his comment placing the philosophers in lecture-halls rather than in the theatre is critical. He himself addressed the Alexandrian crowd in the theatre, and in so doing fulfilled the traditional role of the philosophers. Contemporary philosophers, however, have now secured an alliance with other audiences, and they and their lecture-hall audience mutually neglect any obligations in the assembly. The philosophers have not simply surrendered their traditional role, but have adopted many of the

virtue. The latter cannot flourish because the former does. Dio lists the vices as 'stupid contention', 'unbridled ambition', 'vain grief', 'senseless joy', 'raillery' and 'extravagance', #5 and the traditional virtues, #5,37,47,55,95,96. He tells them later that their conduct negates these blessings and could make them ἀπαίδευτος, #62.

19 The use of the phrase 'so-called' by Dio is his way of indicating the term is inappropriate to those who use it of themselves because of their unprofessional conduct, e.g. *Or.* 13.11, 34.3, noted by Moles, 'The Career and Conversion of Dio Chrysostom', 91, and for further evidence *Or.* 77/8.34–35, cf. *Or.* 49.3.

20 Cf. Jones, *Roman World of Dio Chrysostom*, p. 172, n. 22.

21 πλῆθος and πολλοί are used in the same sentence in #48. Moles argues that, in Dio, οἱ πολλοί are nearly always mistaken about everything. In *Or.* 32 the context demands that πλῆθος means the people in the theatre #11,20 as it does also in #8 and *LCL*'s translation of εἰς πλῆθος as 'in public' could convey the wrong impression that Dio is stating that they do not go out in the city. His charge is that they will not address the citizens in the theatre, Moles, 'The Career and Conversion of Dio Chrysostom', 89.

22 #97–8. Jones, *Roman World of Dio Chrysostom*, p. 37, suggests (1) that Dio must be referring in part to members of the Museum and (2) that 'the wise Theophilus', who resided in the city and may have been a member of it, never addressed it.

23 See n. 19 above. Dio would seem to imply that the philosophers might call it a lecture-hall but it is not really that because they are not teaching the right people. Their right place is in the theatre among the δῆμος.

sophists' activities. Dio's invective at this point would have aimed to humiliate the Alexandrian philosophers who prided themselves that they were not like the sophists.

Further distinctions are drawn between two types of philosophers: a 'bad' philosopher lacks severity, for 'severity of speech is by nature salutary',[24] while a 'good' one uses persuasion and reason (πειθὸς καὶ λόγος) 'to calm and soften the soul'. They should be the 'saviours and guardians' of all who can be saved, but a dearth exists, for men prefer wealth and power to importance in the *polis*. While 'magistrates, laws and jurymen' have the function of 'cautery and the knife' for the drastic treatment of vice, the philosopher's task resembles 'dieting and drugs'. This treatment is preferable, but in Alexandria they have neglected their practice of it. The bad philosopher then is one who fails to assist in *politeia* or serve as the 'saviour and guardian' through the exercise of his powers of persuasion and reason, #18–19. The good philosopher will do so in spite of abuse, rebuttal and derision from the crowd.[25]

The Cynic philosophers of Alexandria are singled out for special condemnation. He tolerates their fundamental beliefs, for 'they comprise practically nothing spurious or ignoble', #9, but he condemns their eccentricity because of the studiously shameless begging which has brought ridicule upon philosophers in general.[26] In this regard he resembles Epictetus, who endorsed the ideal Cynic philosopher as a type of perfect wise man, but denounced the contemporary Cynic philosophers for their begging with a citation from Homer: 'dogs of the table, guards at the gate'.[27]

In *Or.* 32 comments are related to the majority of Alexandrian Cynics[28] and expose their shortcomings in two areas. Firstly, Dio

---

[24] τὸ δὲ τοῦ λόγου πικρὸν σώζειν, lit. 'the sharpness of speech produces the saving [of the people]', #18. *LCL* has not translated δῆμος to show a continuation of thought within the same paragraph. On the role of the philosopher to censure and rebuke the audience see *Or.* 33.10, 36.38.

[25] Dio says he is empathetic to the philosophers' problem of the awesome and intimidating nature of the Alexandrian crowd. He tells them it is not easy to endure their uproar, #20. He uses a variety of methods to secure and retain the attention of the crowd. It reflects his skill that he uses praise, he evokes *pathos* for himself and attributes the ensuing silence to the supernatural, #2,29,30,33.

[26] The construction ἀλλὰ χρείων τροφῆς expresses his disgust: *LCL* translates 'yet who must make a living – still these Cynics (οὗτοι δέ)'. It would seem Dio is holding them to ridicule before the crowd for they too have to make 'a livelihood'.

[27] Moles, 'The Career and Conversion of Dio Chrysostom', 94, and Epictetus, III.22.80 for the Homeric citation *Iliad*, XXII. 69.

[28] *Contra* Moles, 'The Career and Conversion of Dio Chrysostom', 94.

will be recognised as a man who 'in plain terms and without guile speaks his mind with frankness'; thus he embodies the virtues of the prototypical wise man. His passing reference to, and his basic agreement with, this fundamental Cynic ideal, prepares the way for his own self-praise #11,8.[29]

Secondly, he explains that Cynic begging and constant railing against other philosophers have exacted a high price, because Alexandrians have come to despise all philosophers. The Cynics had betrayed a profession which served to knock insolence out of the people, rather than increase it as they themselves had done. The tragic consequence of this 'arrogance', #9, was the heavy-handed Roman intervention, #71.

The evaluation of the traditional role of the Alexandrian philosopher raises a number of points. Dio refers to the traditional and highly significant role of philosophers in *politeia* and adopts a stance towards their behaviour which is very much in harmony with that of Rome; Vespasian had evicted them because of their opposition to his rule. That this policy would have met with Dio's approval seems clear given his view of the philosopher described in this oration.[30] Dio's charge hits at the Alexandrian philosophers' failure to lead the citizens of their great city, and not at their role as critics of the emperor's performance.[31] Just as Vespasian dealt

[29] On Dio's relationship to Cynic philosophy and what C. P. Jones calls the modern invention of his conversion to Cynicism during his exile at the end of the century, see *Roman World of Dio Chrysostom*, pp. vi, 49 and 175, n. 35. There Jones traces the conversion thesis of 1887 to its adoption by R. Hoistad, *Cynic Hero and Cynic King* (Uppsala: Bloms, 1948). Jones notes that it has never received universal endorsement although it was adopted by the *LCL* editors. Dudley, *A History of Cynicism*, p. 156, in his desire to promote the idea of Dio the Cynic makes no reference to the negative comments in the Alexandrian oration. B. F. Harris, 'Dio of Prusa', notes a recent tendency wrongly to include Dio 'loosely' among the Cynics. Moles, 'The Career and Conversion of Dio Chrysostom', 79 and 94, feels that Dio's Cynicism became more pronounced during his exile, but that comment must be seen in the light of his view of Dio's pragmatism and not as support for a Cynic period. Desideri, *Dione di Prusa*, pp. 537–47, clearly shows that modern scholars made him into a Cynic in order to help in the reconstruction of a history of development of Cynicism. He suggests that there were 'elements of Cynic thinking' but this certainly did not make him into a 'classical' Cynic.

[30] On Dio's call for submission to Roman authority see #95. In *Or.* 32 'Dio's sympathies are with Rome. The Romans are the benevolent guardians of the city, the Alexandrians are unruly "children".' Jones, *Roman World of Dio Chrysostom*, p. 127.

[31] Moles however regards the Rhodian Oration as an 'elegant recantation (at least with regard to Musonius)'. He argues Πρὸς Μουσώνιον was a debate milder than Dio's work κατὰ τῶν φιλοσόφων. In 'The Career and Conversion of Dio Chrysostom', 86–7, Moles suggests Dio's position at that time was one of living

harshly with the Cynics in Rome, so too Dio has censured their behaviour in Alexandria because of the denigration of the philosopher's role as saviour and guardian of the city.[32] As a direct result of this, their leadership role has fallen to others.

Orators, poets and sophists as present leaders in *politeia*

Dio's concern extends beyond the philosophers' activities and motivations to an interest in what happens when they themselves 'quit the field and are silent'. In Alexandria, to nobody's credit, the orators and poets filled the vacuum. There was a heavy demand for forensic orators because there had sprung up 'a multitude of quarrels and lawsuits, harsh cries, tongues that are mischievous and unrestrained, accusers, calumnies, writs, a horde of professional pleaders', #19.[33]

In addition to the forensic orators, two other groups described as 'those who are educated' (πεπαιδευμένοι) emerged in the absence of the philosophers. One group, 'those who declaim speeches for display' (οἱ μὲν ἐπιδεικτικοὺς λόγους κτλ.) are identified in the same paragraph as orators. The others are the poets, #10.

Dio tells the Alexandrians there is nothing terribly shocking in

with 'common notions' rather than philosophy by which issues of political life would be removed from the province of Stoic, Cynic and all philosophers. It is possible to argue that there was a continuity in the stance taken by Dio in Rome and Alexandria, namely the role of the philosopher within the δῆμος. This role is certainly present in *Or.* 32. For a former pupil to be critical of his teachers is not unheard of, as Moles notes. We are not at all certain that Πρὸς Μουσώνιον, now lost, was highly critical. On πρός and κατά see Moles, 'The Career and Conversion of Dio Chrysostom', 85, n. 51. What is clear is that Vespasian did not ban Musonius Rufus from Rome when he banned all others. Therefore any encomium of Musonius such as we have in the Rhodian Oration delivered prior to the Alexandrian, shows no conflict with the emperor's attitude to this distinguished philosopher, nor does the evidence force us to posit such a hypothesis of 'elegant recantation'.

[32] Dio's description of the role of the ideal philosopher in *politeia* is noted in other orations such as *Or.* 36.38, where they 'share in πολιτεία'. In the first Tarsian discourse Dio commended the work of Athenodorus, the Stoic philosopher and former tutor of Augustus, who was sent to reform that city and was subsequently appointed governor, *Or.* 33.48, *LCL*, vol. III, pp. 318–19, n. 1. Also Philostratus tells us that Dio himself was noted as one who 'very often rebuked cities . . . like one who restrains an unruly horse with the bridle rather than the whip', *Lives of the Sophists*, 487. See *Or.* 49 for Dio's discussion of the importance of philosophers in the administration of the affairs of state.

[33] For quarrels Dio uses 'strife' (ἔρις) and combines this elsewhere with civil strife, *Or.* 17.10, 19.8, 34.44, 36.22; enmity 48.6 and jealousy (φιλόνικος) 39.8, 48.6, 53.2; and greed (φθόνος) 77/8.39.

what an orator does, even though in his declamations he shows he is 'unlearned'.[34] However, he takes exception when orators disguise themselves as philosophers for 'deceitful' motives,[35] performing only for personal gain and 'reputation'.

Two important observations about these deliberative orators emerge from Dio's comments. Firstly, we have seen that the rhetorician filled a leadership role in *politeia*, normally associated with the Second Sophistic, and obviously already well established in Alexandria. This is corroborated by the role expected of Nicetes of Smyrna, a first-century sophist of Nero's reign who was skilled in both forensic rhetoric and declamation. He should have addressed the citizens of Smyrna regularly, for they had bestowed upon him their highest honours. Thus when he failed to do so on a regular basis, they accused him of cowardice.[36]

Secondly, Dio accuses the orators of being 'deceitful', for they feign an interest in the welfare of the citizens, but their real concern is for 'gain and glory'. The accusation that orators were primarily interested in their own pecuniary advantage goes back to the first sophist, Protagoras, who charged fees for lectures.[37] This is a charge that the critics of the sophists would find easy to verify, as the evidence of Neilus against Didymus clearly shows.[38] Dio, in linking money and reputation, may be suggesting that a substantial fee was paid to an orator declaiming in the theatre. Alternatively, he could mean that an appearance in the theatre was a form of free advertising by which pupils were attracted to one's school. His words could in some cases mean both, for one established a reputation by appearing there before a large crowd. Philostratus

---

[34] *LCL* translates the phrase as 'and stupid to boot', highlighting καὶ τούτους, which precedes ἀμαθής. The latter word means 'stupid' or 'unlearned' or perhaps in this context 'not calculated to educate'. Dio believes that declaiming on a particular event from the past in the way they do will not bring about the reformation of the Alexandrians.

[35] δεινός means either 'shocking', preferred by *LCL*, or possibly 'deceitful'. Dio notes elsewhere that others have come before the Alexandrians praising them for being σοφός τε καὶ δεινός, 'wise and clever', #2. There Dio uses a non-pejorative meaning, but here the term is pejorative. Dio brings this out clearly for he has just stated that while there is nothing shocking in producing unlearned declamations, there is everything wrong when orators pose as philosophers for gain and glory.

[36] Philostratus, *Lives of the Sophists*, 511–12.

[37] On the issue of fees see Kerferd, *The Sophistic Movement* (Cambridge: Cambridge University Press, 1981), pp. 26–8, and Philostratus' defence of the system in his discussion of Protagoras to the effect that one only values what is paid for and therefore it was not a practice to be despised, *Lives of the Sophists*, 494.

[38] *P.Oxy.* 2190. lines 30–1, a charge he levels at them.

remarks that the path to fame was to present a long oration about one's own renown, for 'this style of speech is likely to win favour for sophists in their public declamations'.[39] Reputation could attract great honours, and there were very famous sophists upon whom such were bestowed as Philostratus records.[40] Dio conceives of the rhetor's mission as addressing the public in place of the philosophers in order to improve the conduct of the body politic. Not only does he indict the philosophers for failing in this responsibility to the citizens, but he condemns the orators who do appear, because they are simply self-seeking.

The poets, as 'those who are educated' (πεπαιδευμένοι) also had a right to centre-stage in *politeia*. Dio had already alluded to their role in Athens where they had confronted not only the individual citizens for misdemeanours, but also the city-state. He counted this to their credit, and regrets that Alexandria had neither this tradition nor the poets 'to reprove you in all friendliness and reveal the weaknesses of your city', #6–7.[41] He laments that Alexandria, 'the second Athens', has not followed the Athenian precedent. They have no chorus, no poets, nor anyone else to admonish them, #7. He reminds them that originally poets were regarded as being possessed by the Muses when they spoke their messages from the gods, but the more recent poets speak of their own wisdom in the assembly. 'Uninitiated addressing uninitiated', he concludes. The poets who have stood before the Alexandrians have adjusted their presentation to suit the foibles of the audience as they 'sing' their poems, *Or.* 36.35–8.

Dio directs his hostility not at the poets' profession *per se* but at the fact that the Alexandrian poets, like the orators, practice deception. They come in the guise of philosophers for their own financial and personal advancement rather than for the improvement of the citizens. He illustrates both groups' lack of professional integrity by revisiting the medical analogy we saw above: a physician would not disregard the treatment and ultimate care of his patient by bringing useless gifts of flowers and perfumes or even

---

[39] That this sophist, Polemo, did not do so when he came to Athens was a sign of his arrogance for 'he conversed with cities as his inferiors, Emperors as not his superiors, and the gods as his equals', *Lives of the Sophists*, 535.

[40] For the imperial honours heaped on Polemo of Laodicea and the city honours bestowed on Nicetes see *Lives of the Sophists*, 512, 532–3.

[41] On the use of this role in Old Comedy see Horace, *Satires*, I.4.1–5.

harmful gifts such as courtesans, #10. Yet orators and poets have done precisely this to the Alexandrians.

Generalisations are tempered with the ironical observation that a few have displayed frankness before the Alexandrian audience. Yet even those have been found wanting. They have merely uttered 'a phrase or two' and, after berating rather than enlightening the audience, they have fled from the theatre lest they should be expelled from the city, #11.

Having denounced those motivated by false motives and the few who panicked and fled, Dio then spells out the qualifications of the person whom Alexandria really needs.

> But to find a man who in plain terms, and without guile speaks his mind with frankness, and neither for the sake of reputation nor for gain makes false pretension, but out of good will and concern for his fellow-men stands ready, if need be, to submit to ridicule, and the disorder and uproar of the mob – to find such a man is not easy, but rather the good fortune of a very lucky city, so great is the dearth of noble, independent souls. (#11)

The Alexandrians, however, are fortunate, for Dio, unlike 'the abundance of flatterers, impostors and sophists', offers himself as that fearless, noble and independent soul.[42]

Dio's self-promotion as the ideal wise leader and adviser at this point is the culmination of his *synkrisis* with orators and poets, but it is by no means the end of it, for he has another criticism of them. He returns to the theme in #39 where he asserts that his aim is not 'to compare' himself, παραβάλλειν, with those 'who habitually sing such strains, whether orators or poets'.[43] While denying that he wishes to engage in *synkrisis* with poets and orators, he very

---

[42] 'Flatterer' (κόλαξ), 'cheat' (γόης). *LCL* translates 'toadies and sophists'. On the meaning of the term 'sophist' in Dio and the linking of the above terms with sophists see Demosthenes, *De Corona*, 276, Plato, *Symposium*, 203d and pp. 56–8. On Philo's use see pp. 91–4.

[43] On Dio's use of παραβολή as a synonym for σύγκρισις see Forbes, 'Comparison, Self-praise and Irony', 4–5, and his discussion of #39 where he suggests Dio is denying the charge of being a flatterer. Jones, *Roman World of Dio Chrysostom*, p. 40, identifies #35–6 as a miniature encomium and argues that Dio is first praising the citizens by commending the city and then jolts them by saying he is not praising them. It would seem that Dio is not answering the charge of 'flattery', *contra* Forbes, for having used the actual word ἐγκώμιον in #37, he is at pains to say he does not want the audience to engage in a *synkrisis* between himself and these others.

skilfully does exactly that by alluding to the superiority of the theme he treats. They praise the Alexandrians by praising their environs: Dio argues that only praise of men's virtue has value, and then spells out three of the traditional four cardinal virtues and a host of subsidiary ones, #39b–40.[44] The gods provide a remedy for the city's ills: παιδεία καὶ λόγος, #16 (cf. #3). Since those who should have administered the medicine failed because they were preoccupied with money and reputation, Dio must serve in their place to ensure that by constant application of the cure of the gods, the Alexandrians can come at last to 'a healthy, happy end', #16. He thus establishes his credentials before the Alexandrians by clearly demonstrating the inadequacy of those who have claimed for themselves leadership roles in the city, namely sophists and poets. He has done so through the skilful use of *synkrisis* and finally through invoking his appointment by a god at whose bidding he speaks.[45]

He also refers to those involved in philosophy and rhetoric in his denunciation of citharody,[46] asserting that 'the people of Alexandria are carried away by song as no other people are, and that if they hear the music of the lyre, however bad, they lose their senses', #65.[47] This mania had a considerable effect on philosophers,

---

[44] Jones, *Roman World of Dio Chrysostom*, p. 40, suggests that Dio has artfully constructed this encomium. There is a similarity between Dio at this point and Paul in 2 Corinthians 10.12, see pp. 222–4. For a discussion of Philo's traditional virtues see my treatment of this, pp. 86–90.

[45] Dio tells them it is the will of a certain god that he should speak to them. He also declares that this god must not only be thought to speak in dreams or through young boys, but 'if one hears words of wisdom, we must believe that they too were sent by god', #12–14. For the identification of this god with Serapis and the famous centre at Alexandria see *LCL*, vol. III, p. 183, n. 3. For some of the added details of its founding by Ptolemy III and its role in the confirmation of Vespasian's imperial claim see Henrichs, 'Vespasian's Visit to Alexandria', 54–65. Although Dio does not identify the god by name, it must be Serapis for the reference reads 'most in honour and to you especially does he display his power through almost daily oracles and dreams', #12.

[46] The cithara was a portable harp often used to accompany singing.

[47] Dio's description of the Alexandrian mania for the lyre and the behaviour in the theatre has been likened to an audience at 'a pop concert' by E. K. Borthwick, 'Dio Chrysostom on the Mob at Alexandria', *CR* 22 (1972), 1. The analogy is not inappropriate for they would hum, jump about and dance during the performance. They even proclaimed a player σωτήρ and θεός. There were instances where people were crushed to death in the excitement; rivalry was rife and streets were alive with supporters, #41, 46, 48–9, 50, 55–6, 69. Dio notes 'these performers here have turned you human beings into savages and made you insensitive to culture', #62. Dio's denunciation of citharody occurs within the context of the recent riot, #59–60. As Jones, *Roman World of Dio Chrysostom*,

including Cynics, as well as orators and sophists, because they adjusted their style to this whim of the Alexandrians, #68.

Dio sees a correlation between, on the one hand, the singing mania of the citizens and their intellectual leaders, and on the other, the subsequent social disorder. He may have drawn this connection from Plato who, in his *Republic*, proposed to ban new music styles because he felt that they promoted social and political unrest.[48] 'Singing' is to Dio's mind a 'disease' which infects not only orators but also philosophers, #68. Some suggest that his claim to being a poor singer contains a sarcastic allusion to declaimers, #22, and that the 'singing' refers to a form of chanting, or even to the delivery of the *peroratio* of a speech in a sing-song fashion.[49] This last suggestion may explain Dio's slur that if you passed a court-room, you could not easily decide whether you heard a drinking party or a trial. Likewise if there was a sophist's lecture room in the neighbourhood, you would not know that a lecture was in progress. Quintilian also complains that this new trend 'outrages the dignity of the courts with noises such as are dear to the Lycians and Carians', a reference to the Asianists' style.[50] Earlier Dio indicates that Alexandria was not alone in this, for he has heard philosophers 'singing' elsewhere, but singing Cynics are an Alexandrian first, #62.[51]

These comments provide clear evidence of a capitulation to

pp. 41–2, says 'He taunts the Alexandrians for "going to war at the sound of a string".' He argues that there is a connection between this mania for the lyre and the riot and believes that it is for this reason the riot occurred in the theatre.

[48] *Republic*, 424c.

[49] See Jones, *Roman World of Dio Chrysostom*, p. 173, n. 56 in which he compares ᾄδω, #22, with ᾠδή in the glossary of rhetorical terms in Philostratus, *Lives of the Sophists*, LCL, p. 575. The latter suggests that the sophists spoke in a sing-song voice suited to the metrical rhythms of the Asianists, especially in the *peroratio* where the use of this term was meant to sway the audience or the jury. Cf. Cicero, *Orator*, XVIII.57; Lucian, *A Professor of Public Speaking*, 19; Quintilian, x.3.57; and Dio, *Or.* 32.68.

[50] On the contrast between the classical style of the Atticists, who looked back to the diction and composition of literary prose found in Athens in the fifth and fourth centuries BC, and the Asianists, the more popular form with its reflection of more contemporary Greek style and adaptability in the early empire, see Kennedy, *The Art of Rhetoric in the Roman World* (Princeton: Princeton University Press, 1972), pp. 241–2.

[51] *LCL* translates 'and yet while I knew there are philosophers called Cynics, harpists of the canine breed have been produced here alone'. Better 'And yet while I knew there were the so-called philosophers' (just described as whining and howling dogs instead of swans and nightingales) 'the singing Cynics are found only here.' The former hardly does justice to text or context.

audience demands, and more importantly, of philosophers necessarily responding to innovation by orators and sophists. The rebuke by Isaeus to his student Dionysius of Miletus, 'Young man from Ionia, I did not train you to sing' seems to have availed nothing. Dio had no greater success with his pupil Favorinus when he attempted to discourage this affectation.[52] Audience response and popular demand were the final arbiter in these matters and thus usurped the power to determine the shape of oratory. Dio, Quintilian and Isaeus witness and oppose, but fail to arrest, this trend. Dio's warning to the unruly Alexandrians and their singing philosophers, poets and orators, and even the threat of further political instability in Alexandria, could not stem the tide.[53] The leaders do not censure, they all sing.

In a further explanation of the functions of orators and sophists in Alexandria, #68, Dio refers to two known facts about these professionals. Firstly, the orators' courtroom activity fulfils a well-established role, which is clearly attested elsewhere in Dio and in other literary, as well as non-literary sources.[54] Secondly, the sophists in their lecture rooms teach students to declaim, as documented in *P.Oxy.* 2190 and in Philostratus.[55] Dio refers to the possibility of having a sophist in one's neighbourhood, suggesting that they were visible in Alexandrian life, #68b. Again he engages in *synkrisis* between himself and such people in terms of his role, for he is noble, while they are 'flatterers and impostors', #10–11,68.

Orators and sophists in Dio's corpus

This picture of Alexandrian orators and sophists in *Or.* 32 is not peculiar to that speech; it occurs also in Dio's Olympian discourse.

---

[52] Philostratus, *Lives of the Sophists*, 513, 490, and a brief description in *LCL*, xxv. Favorinus' *Corinthian Oration* was included in Dio's *Orations*, as was his declamation *On Fortune*, *Or.* 37.64. On his singing literary style see Jones, *Roman World of Dio Chrysostom*, p. 59, n. 47 and p. 179, n. 1.

[53] Jones, *Roman World of Dio Chrysostom*, p. 37, where he describes the history of Alexandria under Roman rule as one of continual unrest.

[54] *Or.* 7.38,39,48,49; 8.9; 18.14; 35.15. For non-literary evidence see, e.g. *BGU* 15, 19, 592, 969; *P.Flor.* 61; *P.Lond.* 354; *P.Mil.Volg.* 25; *PSI* 450; *P.Harr.* 67; *P.Fam.Tebt.* 19, 287; *P.Ryl.* 653; and *P.Oxy.* 37, 472, 707, 2111 for orators and their speeches. For a *peroratio* capable of 'singing' see, e.g. *P.Princ.* 119 and *P.Vindob.Gr.* inv. no. 39757. On the legal profession in Egypt see R. Taubenschlag, 'The Legal Profession in Greco–Roman Egypt', in *Festschrift Fritz Schulz* (Weimar: Hermann Böhlaus Nachfolger, 1951), vol. II, pp. 188–92.

[55] *Lives of the Sophists*, 514,547,604, *P.Oxy.* 2190.20. See discussion on pp. 31–3.

He there describes them as 'able orators, most charming writers of both verse and prose, and finally, like gorgeous peacocks, sophists in great numbers, men who are lifted aloft as on wings by their fame and disciples'. *Or.* 12.5. He expresses 'Socratic' surprise that his audience deigns to listen to him, 'a man who knows nothing and makes no claim of knowing'. In the city of his birth he denies possessing ability as an orator in the market-place and in litigation, and hastens to add that he once appeared in court on behalf of a man whose chance of a fair trial was remote. He claims to seek no patronage or pay from anybody. This *synkrisis* is part of a skilful commendation of his own integrity, especially as he proceeds to hint that his pursuit of the interests of the state led him to neglect his own property, *Or.* 43.61.

One also sees views of the orators at work in Dio's speeches.[56] Some are only concerned with money, 'twisting and warping' unclear laws with eloquence and perverting justice.[57] Some advise the state (συμβουλεύειν) and help legislate on its behalf.[58] In Tarsus 'the orators' alone were allowed to make public speeches, possibly a reference to occasions when an official encomium was required, *Or.* 34.1. Dio envisages the orator 'in the noble and real sense of the word', but recognises that like their counterparts in court, there are good and bad orators. Some stoop to seek bribes, *Or.* 22.2–5.

In discussing sophists, Dio notes that some have schools. While some of these do their task well, others fail their students, 'leaving them to grow old in ignorance'. Their flawed approach to *paideia* robs men of the classical virtues.[59] They are mercenary, engaging in rivalry with other sophists; their pupils, out of loyalty, contribute to the factionalism.[60]

The sophists also have a leadership role in the *polis* with accompanying social status, and are courted by communities and officials as well as pupils.[61] They advise kings though they do not know how to live themselves. Dio states that they are as ineffectual as eunuchs.[62] They love their reputation and so never say anything to offend their audience; thus they simply expound the views of their hearers. He parodies the sort of sophist whose liver swelled

---

[56] *Or.* 21.1; 7.38–9; 48.63; 8.9; 34.15; 43.6; 76.4.   [57] *Or.* 8.9; 21.1; 76.4.
[58] *Or.* 4.108; 13.22–3; 18.14; 21.1–5; 38.5; 43.6.
[59] *Or.* 4.14, 28, 32, 36, 38; 35.10.   [60] *Or.* 6.21; 8.9; 12.13.
[61] *Or.* 6.12; 77/8.27.   [62] *Or.* 4.35; 28.35.

when praised and shrivelled when censured,[63] and complains that they will not debate with him, even claiming that they hate him.[64] His attacks on the ancient sophists are also applied to his contemporaries.[65]

The above views correspond in the main with those expressed in *Or.* 32 as they portray the movement in various parts of the empire. Indeed, this brief review of Dio's opinion of orators and sophists in his corpus explicates the picture of the movement in Alexandria.

One easily gains the impression of a 'blanket condemnation' of sophists, and this may be why the term 'sophist' itself is thought by some to be pejorative. However, Moles demonstrates that this is not the case in Dio, and provides a far more balanced presentation of the evidence than either C. P. Jones or P. Desideri.[66] He notes Dio's pains to reassure his audience that he is not attacking all sophists:[67] 'However my remarks are not levelled at all sophists, for there are some who follow that calling honourably and for the good of others, men to whom we should pour libation and offer incense' (*Or.* 35.10). The term itself, therefore, does not have negative connotations. There are honourable virtuoso orators to contrast with those who are not worthy of the name. In *Or.* 4.35

---

[63] *Or.* 6.21; 8.33; 12.5; 35.8, 81; 55.7; 66.12; 77/8.27.
[64] *Or.* 12.3; 47.16.   [65] *Or.* 54.1,4.
[66] For the treatment by Moles see 'Dio on Sophists and Rhetoric', in 'The Career and Conversion of Dio Chrysostom', 88–93. Jones, *Roman World of Dio Chrysostom*, p. 9, n. 9 surveys Dio's sophists with only three citations out of over forty references to them in his orations. One of those three is acknowledged by him to be tentative. Nevertheless, upon it he seeks to build a case for the term to describe philosophers who 'teach mere words without thought'. In 'The Reliability of Philostratus', in G. W. Bowersock (ed.), *Approaches to the Second Sophistic* (University Park, Pennsylvania: American Philological Association, 1974), pp. 11–16, he endorses Bowersock's definition of the sophist, but his treatment of Dio has been coloured by his own work on Philostratus' evidence where he says it is primarily used of 'inferior' or 'false philosophers'. G. R. Stanton, 'Sophists and Philosophers: Problems of Classification', *AJP* 94.4 (1973), 351–64, whose primary interest was to weigh Dio's use of the terms 'sophist' and 'philosopher' to determine what he and his contemporaries said of themselves, produced three major categories, namely 'neutral', 'derogatory' and 'abusive or derisive'. P. Desideri clearly demonstrates that Stanton's 'neutral' examples belong to the other categories. Desideri says he knows of only one 'neutral' example of Dio's sophists, the reference to Solon and 'the great many of ancient sophists', *Or.* 10.26. Of Stanton's examples and other pejorative passages, Desideri, *Dione di Prusa*, pp. 242–3, suggests that Dio's nuances are simply varying degrees of disgust with the sophist. Stanton does not cite *Or.* 35.10 as a favourable comment, nor does Desideri note it as an important comment on the existence of 'good' sophists.
[67] Moles, 'Dio on Sophists and Rhetoric', 91.

Dio can speak of 'so-called sophists', implying that the term is inappropriate to some who claim it because they do not conform to the standards of their profession.[68] The phrase 'the most ignorant sophist' leaves open the possibility that some are not ignorant, as Dio observes elsewhere.[69] While contemporaries of Dio balked at designating the ancient Seven Sages as 'sophists', Dio did not.[70] *Or.* 71 provides an elaborate *synkrisis* of philosophers and sophists with Hippias. While that philosopher is certainly superior, Dio notes that this well-known ancient sophist had a high degree of skill in both manual and intellectual pursuits.[71] In discussing a case of bribery Dio tells his audience his criticisms are not against the art of rhetoric nor against good exponents but rather against bad ones. Moles maintains that Dio's most revealing comment is found in *Or.* 19.3ff., where he says, 'whenever I attend a sophist's lecture, on account of an uncontrolled craving which possesses me for the spoken word . . . and this is the way I have nearly always been affected when listening to sophists and orators'. Moles rightly adds that this is hardly Dio the aggressive philosopher, scourge of all sophists.[72] Dio's use of the term 'sophist' thus needs to be reviewed.

Jones suggests that the word is used pejoratively, usually of the philosophers, but tentatively cites only one example, *Or.* 32.11.[73] It needs to be noted, however, that Dio does not use either σοφιστής or σοφιστικός when speaking of philosophers. When he critiques the behaviour of those whom he opposes he refers to 'those who are called philosophers'. Of the seventy occurrences of the term 'philosopher' in his orations, it never appears as a collocation with σοφιστής.[74] Had Dio used 'sophist' of charlatan or impostor philosophers, then *Or.* 34.3 would have provided him with the ideal opportunity to do so. In that discourse the philosophers of Tarsus had been guilty of some misdemeanour. But Dio instead encourages the citizens not to curse all philosophers, for no person is

---

[68] On the discussion of the meaning of 'the so-called' see Moles, 'The Career and Conversion of Dio Chrysostom', 32, n. 21.

[69] *Or.* 55.7; 35.10.   [70] *Or.* 10.26, cf. Plutarch, *Moralia*, 385e.

[71] Dio here observes the difference between the ancient sophists and those who are his contemporaries.

[72] On bribery *Or.* 22.5; Moles, 'The Career and Conversion of Dio Chrysostom', 92; cf. Desideri, *Dione di Prusa*, p. 243.

[73] Thus apparently Dio, *Or.* 32.11; Jones, *Roman World of Dio Chrysostom*, p. 162, n. 9.

[74] It is wrong to argue that the term 'philosopher' here means simply a lover of wisdom. Rather Dio is arguing that philosophers are meant to be lovers of wisdom in every sense of the word.

a philosopher who is unjust, wicked, among the Brachmanes, or who harms their country or bands together against their fellow citizens. Just as J. Glucker complains that the later meaning of καθηγητής, namely that of 'professor', has been read back into the earlier period, so too in the case of Dio, our pejorative connotations of 'sophist' have been read into the first-century philosophers.[75] Secondly, even Jones hesitates to cite *Or.* 32.11 in support of his contention that the term is usually used pejoratively of philosophers. There Dio contrasts the dearth of noble, independent souls with the abundance of 'flatterers, impostors and sophists'. Later in the oration he uses these same terms after his encomium, #39, this time while instructing the crowd not to compare him with those who 'habitually sing such strains, whether orators or poets'. His reason is that they are δεινοὶ ἐκεῖνοι καὶ μεγάλοι σοφισταὶ καὶ γόητες, while in comparison he is 'quite ordinary and prosaic', #39. Why does Dio use these terms κόλαξ and γόης with σοφιστής? They were used of sophists by both Plato and Demosthenes, and in his own lifetime, by Philo, to reflect the bewitching effect they had on audiences.[76] Thus 'flatterer' and 'impostor' were used pejoratively of sophists, but the term 'sophist' was not used by Dio to pillory philosophers. *Or.* 32.11 does not support Jones' thesis concerning the identification of sophists with philosophers but instead places them on opposite sides of the scales. The sophists in Dio were a specific group of public orators and poets in Alexandria; hence the term is to be understood in the technical sense of a virtuoso orator with a large public following.[77]

[75] J. Glucker, *Antiochus and the Late Academy*, Hypomnemata 56 (Göttingen: Vandenhoeck and Ruprecht, 1978), p. 127 and Jones, *Roman World of Dio Chrysostom*, p. 9.

[76] Plato, *Symposium*, 203d; Demosthenes, *De Corona*, 276. For subsequent discussion from Aristotle onwards see J. de Romilly, *Magic and Rhetoric in Ancient Greece* (Cambridge, Mass. and London: Harvard University Press, 1975). No reference is made by her to the discussion in Philo, e.g. *Her.* 302, or *The Cynic Epistles*, A. J. Malherbe (ed.), (Missoula: Scholars Press, 1977), 6.30, although the study examines the evidence of Aristides and Philostratus. For the discussion of this issue in Philo see pp. 91–4.

[77] Wilmes, *Beiträge zur Alexandrinerede*, p. 42, suggests that Dio uses the term pejoratively of all who claim to be educated, citing #10, 22, 'ist bei eine . . . Bezeichnung für alle, die mit dem Anspruch gebildet zu sein'. He adds that such persons look upon rhetoric as a means of achieving fame and making money. They have no regard for the moral improvement of their audience. Wilmes cites only four examples from *Or.* 32. He does not relate his conclusions to the remainder of the corpus nor to the definition of the sophists by Bowersock, *Greek Sophists in the Roman Empire* (Oxford: Clarendon Press, 1969), pp. 12–13.

Conclusion

From Dio's evidence we extract important information on the activities of orators and sophists in Alexandria in the first century. The former group were involved in forensic activity and declamations in Alexandria. The latter group ran schools, declaimed publicly and stood in the place of traditional leaders of the *polis*, namely the philosophers. In Dio's opinion, however, they proved to be ineffectual because their chief concerns were fame and wealth. He laments their occupying the place vacated by the philosophers, for they did not seek to improve the citizenry at a time when someone was desperately needed to admonish and persuade the people to a less belligerent frame of mind towards Vespasian and the Roman authorities in Alexandria.

The oration shows that there is a dearth of *willing* philosophers and sophists, that is, willing to come forward and advise the Alexandrians – but not a dearth *per se*. As will be demonstrated in the following chapter, there were 'multitudes of sophists' in this city in the first half of the first century. Dio's evidence is corroborated by Philo, who paints a picture of the same vigorous activity of the sophists.

It is important to note that the term 'sophist' was not used pejoratively by Dio. Invective such as 'flatterer' and 'impostor' was invoked when speaking in a derogatory way against them. Dio's derisive terminology was not peculiar to him, but had a history stretching back to Plato and used by many. This suggests that they were stock-in-trade terms of abuse against the sophists but 'sophist' was never such a term, nor was it used of philosophers.

3

WHO ARE PHILO'S SOPHISTS?

Identifying Philo's sophists

The Hellenised Jew Philo of Alexandria discusses in detail the sophists and the shape of the Alexandrian sophistic movement of the first fifty years AD. The evidence he provides, however, has not been carefully examined.[1] Since he has been shown to be an invaluable source of information on other issues,[2] quarrying his

For recent discussion of Philo see H. L. Goodheart and E. R. Goodenough, *A General Bibliography of Philo* (New Haven: Yale University Press, 1938); P. Borgen, 'Philo of Alexandria. A Critical and Synthetical Survey of Research since World War II', *ANRW* II.21.1 (1984) 98–154; and D. T. Runia, 'Recent Developments in Philonic Studies', in his *Philo of Alexandria and the Timaeus of Plato* (Leiden: E. J. Brill, 1986), ch. 2, and more recently R. Radice and D. T. Runia, *Philo of Alexandria: An Annotated Bibliography 1937–1986* (Leiden: E. J. Brill, 1988).

[1] While Philo's comments on the sophistic movement have been neglected, his use of rhetoric has been discussed. See M. A. Michel, 'Quelques aspects de la rhétorique chez Philon', in R. Arnaldez, C. Mondésert and J. Pouilloux (eds.), *Philon d'Alexandrie* (Paris: Editions du Cerf, 1967) pp. 81–103; J. Leopold, 'Philo's Knowledge of Rhetorical Theory', 'Rhetoric and Allegory', and T. Conley, 'Philo's Use of *topoi*', in D. Winston and J. Dillon (eds.), *Two Treatises of Philo of Alexandria: A Commentary of De Gigantibus* and *Quod Deus Sit Immutabilis*, Brown Judaic Studies 25 (Chico: Scholars Press, 1983), pp. 129–36 and 155–78; B. L. Mack, 'Decoding the Scripture: Philo and the Rules of Rhetoric', in an unpublished paper given at a Philo Seminar, Canterbury, August, 1983, 1–44; T. Conley, *Philo's Rhetoric: Studies in Style, Composition and Exegesis*, Center for Hermeneutical Studies Monograph Series no. 1 (Berkeley: Center for Hermeneutical Studies, 1987); and M. Alexandre, 'The Art of Periodic Composition in Philo of Alexandria', in D. T. Runia, D. M. Hay and D. Winston (eds.) *Heirs of the Septuagint: Philo, Hellenistic Judaism and Early Christianity, Festschrift for Earle Hilgert*, The Studia Philonica Annual 3 (1991), 135–50.

[2] See E. R. Goodenough, *Jurisprudence of the Jewish Courts in Egypt* (New Haven: Yale University Press, 1929) for Philo on Greek, Roman and Egyptian law. See R. Barraclough, 'Philo's Politics: Roman Rule and Hellenistic Judaism', *ANRW* II.21.1 (1983), 417–533 for first-century politics; and H. A. Harris, *Trivium, Greek Athletics and the Jews* (Cardiff: University of Wales Press, 1976) pp. 13, 51–91, for Philo as a source for athletic terms. Harris expresses surprise at the vividness of

corpus for details of the sophistic movement in Alexandria may also prove worthwhile, especially when we recognise his own training in rhetoric.[3] Disagreement surrounds the attempt to identify Philo's sophists, and no survey of the evidence has been undertaken to resolve this dilemma. An assessment of the various opinions concerning his use of the term 'sophist' must therefore precede our investigation of his critique of the sophistic tradition. Lacking this, the insufficiently scrutinised opinions of secondary sources will continue to support the highly questionable premise that for Philo the term 'sophist' has pejorative connotations, and will greatly diminish the value of Philo's evidence for subsequent chapters.

Who then are the sophists Philo describes as his contemporaries in *Contempl.* 31, οἱ ῥήτορες ἢ οἱ νῦν σοφισταί?[4] H. A. Fischel believes that these words function as 'a symbol of notoriously argumentative Epicureanism and occasionally of all "impious" and sophistic (argumentative) philosophies' but do 'not refer to 'a sophist in the technical sense of the word'. He further asserts that the term contains an 'implied anachronism, since he (Philo) speaks of the perennial types and his audience, attuned to him, knew that he castigated simultaneously contemporary situations'.[5] I. Heinemann, alternatively, argues that the term 'sophist' should be taken quite literally.[6]

It is E. Bréhier's opinion that the term 'sophists' includes teachers who give all manner of regular teaching but excludes philosophers.[7] F. H. Colson, however, maintains that teachers of philosophy do fit the group in question.[8] V. Nikiprowetzky concludes that the term

---

Philo's description of athletic activities and describes him not only as 'a keen and well-informed spectator of the Games at Alexandria', but also as a former pupil in the gymnasium.

[3] On the inadequate use of Philo in first-century rhetoric in the Roman empire by G. A. Kennedy and R. W. Smith, on Alexandria see my comments on pp. 2–3, n. 7, and for evidence on his training see pp. 84–5.

[4] For the distinction between orators and sophists, G. W. Bowersock, *Greek Sophists in the Roman Empire* (Oxford: Clarendon Press, 1969), p. 14.

[5] H. A. Fischel, *Rabbinic Literature and Greco–Roman Philosophy: A Study of Epicurea and Rhetoric in early Midrashic Writings*, Studia Post-Biblica 31 (Leiden: E. J. Brill, 1973) p. 131.

[6] I. Heinemann, *Philons griechische und jüdische Bildung* (Breslau: Marcus, 1932), p. 436 and also Michel, 'Quelques aspects de la rhétorique chez Philon', 84.

[7] E. Bréhier, *Les Idées philosophiques et religieuses de Philon d'Alexandrie* (Paris: Boivin et Cie, 1925) pp. 287–9.

[8] F. H. Colson, 'Philo on Education', *JTS* 18 (1917), 161: 'the great mass of "sophists", among whom seem to be included the teachers of philosophy'.

applies in Philo to those whose philosophies differ from Plato's but who stand within the Greek philosophical tradition, especially the Sceptics and Academics.[9] S. Sandmel also associates sophists with philosophers but identifies them as the Peripatetics, Stoics and Epicureans, Eleatics, Sceptics and non-Sceptics.[10]

H. A. Wolfson proposes that the term should include Jewish 'experts' in literal interpretation, and that Philo used it, not in a derogatory sense, but to denote 'sages' and 'experts'. 'Taken in this sense it may reflect the Hebrew term, *ḥakamin* ("sages") which is one of the names by which the Pharisaic interpreters of the law are known.' Wolfson leans heavily on a definition offered by Josephus, namely 'men learned in the law'.[11] He discusses the term with an eye to the literalists/traditionalists of Alexandrian Judaism and includes also the ancient Greek poets. J. Pépin endorses Wolfson's understanding of the term when he writes 'il est donc fondé à flatrir de nom injurieux de sophistes ses adversaires litteralistes'.[12] J. Drummond maintains that the sophists were public speakers who, unlike the philosophers, were 'powerful in saying, but powerless in doing, what was best'.[13]

A. Mendelson, who greatly enhanced our understanding of encyclical education in Philo, states that the term 'cannot be relied upon to designate, consistently, practitioners of sophistry'. The sophist, 'ill-educated in rhetoric', exploits the legitimate arts of speech or methods of persuasion not to defend the truth but to oppose it. Mendelson's caution is evident when he describes 'Alexandrian sophists of whom, if we are to believe Philo, there were many'. He also accepts Wolfson's non-pejorative meaning, 'sages' or 'experts'.[14]

Three important features about the opinions expressed in the past one hundred years call for attention. Firstly, we lack a

---

[9] V. Nikiprowetzky, *Le Commentaire de l'écriture chez Philon d'Alexandrie* (Leiden: E. J. Brill, 1977) pp. 97–8, 110.

[10] S. Sandmel, *Philo's Place in Judaism: A Study of Conceptions of Abraham in Jewish Literature* (New York: Ktav Publishing House, 1971) p. 168, n. 310.

[11] H. A. Wolfson, *Philo: Foundations of Religious Philosophy in Judaism, Christianity and Islam* (Cambridge, Mass.: Harvard University Press, 1962) vol. I, pp. 57–60.

[12] J. Pépin, 'Remarques sur la théorie de l'exégèse allégorique chez Philon', in Arnaldez, Mondésert and Pouilloux (eds.), *Philon d'Alexandrie*, pp. 148–9, n. 6.

[13] J. Drummond, *Philo Judaeus, or the Jewish Alexandrian Philosophy in its Development and Completion* (London and Edinburgh: Williams & Norgate, 1888), vol. I, p. 353 citing *Congr.* 13 and *Migr.* 13.

[14] A. Mendelson, *Secular Education in Philo of Alexandria* (Cincinnati: Hebrew Union College Press, 1982), p. 90, n. 48; pp. 7–10.

thoroughgoing survey of Philo's discussion of the sophists. In fact, some have expressed their opinions in footnotes with few or no actual references to Philo's works. This lacuna is partly responsible for the diverse, even conflicting, opinions relating to the identity of the sophists. Secondly, discussion of Philo's sophists and orators often overlooks recent studies of the sophists of the late first and second centuries AD. Thirdly, Philo's sophists have not generally been discussed within the context of *paideia*, with the exception of Colson's and Mendelson's work, nor have they been measured against the comments by other first-century writers on the sophists in Alexandria. Perhaps modern negative connotations of the term 'sophist' have been read back unconsciously into Philo's use of this term by recent scholarship. The following survey will show that Philo never uses the term pejoratively, although he may castigate the group to which it applies albeit with traditional invective. He furthermore consistently uses it of virtuoso orators, following other first-century writers such as Dio Chrysostom and Plutarch.

Present-day orators and sophists in *Contempl.* 31

He [the Therapeutai Elder] does not make an exhibition of clever rhetoric like the orators or sophist of to-day . . . οἱ ῥήτορες ἢ οἱ νῦν σοφισταί.   (*Contempl.* 31)

Philo declares as he begins his discussion of *De vita contemplativa* that he has not added to the information 'to improve upon the facts as is constantly done by poets and historians', #1.[15] He purports instead to provide a reliable account. A similar criticism of orators and sophists who strive for 'improvement' is found in Philo's 'unadorned' history of the Therapeutai (#31).[16] G. W. Bowersock's definition of the term 'sophist', drawn from first- and second-century sources, also notes that these prominent groups attempted

---

[15] For discussions of the historicity of Philo's account of the Therapeutai and the integrity of *De Vita Contemplativa* see E. Schürer, *The History of the Jewish People in the Age of Jesus Christ*, 2nd edn (Edinburgh: T. & T. Clark, 1979), vol. II, pp. 595–6; and B. M. Bokser, *Philo's Description of Jewish Practices* (Berkeley: The Center for Hermeneutical Studies in Hellenistic and Modern Culture, 1977), pp. 1–12, and pp. 30–40 *contra* the discussion by others at the Bokser seminar which fails to do justice to what has been written before on the question of historicity.

[16] For a recent survey of the literature on this community see Schürer, *History of the Jewish People*, vol. II, p. 591, n. 17.

to enhance the facts, although he does not cite Philo as a source.[17] Philo describes them in contrast both to the ancient sophists, #4, and the Therapeutai elder in #31. The latter individual and his activities he describes in detail while, significantly, he offers no detailed explanation of the activities of the orators and sophists; surely because their methods were well known. Such knowledge, shared by Philo's audience, thus offers him a point of comparison to explain the unknown activities of the Therapeutai elder.

Philo used the sophists as a benchmark to empower five comparisons and contrasts which informed his discussion of the little-known, or perhaps misunderstood, Jewish community of the Therapeutai. Firstly, orators and sophists and the Therapeutai elder all sought to educate. H. I. Marrou observes that 'For the very great majority of students, higher education meant taking lessons from the orator, learning the art of eloquence from him.'[18] Philo similarly describes the Sabbath meeting of the Therapeutai as taking the form of a lecture with the elder resembling the proven teacher who 'has the fullest knowledge of the doctrines which they profess', #31.

Secondly, similar teacher/student relationships characterised both sides. The pupils or members of the community 'sit in order according to their age in the proper attitude . . . and listen, showing their approval merely by their looks or nods . . . with ears pricked up and eyes fixed on him always in exactly the same posture . . . [they praise the speaker] by cheerful change of expression which steals over the face' #30,32,77. Orators and sophists were known to have enjoyed the loyalty of their pupils, and often developed an intimate relationship with them.[19]

Thirdly, and by way of contrast, Philo claims that the elder 'gives a well-reasoned and wise discourse', #31b, while the orators and sophists are said to 'make an exhibition'.[20] He establishes the superiority of the elder's discourse by means of a negative compar-

---

[17] Bowersock, *Greek Sophists*, p. 13 for a summary of views. C. P. Jones, 'The Reliability of Philostratus', in G. W. Bowersock (ed.), *Approaches to the Second Sophistic* (University Park, Pennsylvania: American Philological Association, 1974), p. 12, endorses Bowersock's definition with regard to Philostratus (AD 170–244), although he suggests a pejorative use by earlier authors.

[18] H. I. Marrou, *A History of Education in Antiquity*, English translation (London: Sheed and Ward, 1956), pp. 194–5.

[19] *Ibid.*, p. 197.

[20] παρεπιδείκνυμι, 'declaim'. For this technical term see pp. 31–2 and also *Spec.* 1.56, *Legat.* 94.

ison with sophistic declamation, emphasising in the process that the elder 'does not make an exhibition of clever rhetoric like the orators and sophists of today, but follows careful examination by careful expression of the exact meaning of the thoughts', #31b. Philo's word choice stresses the notion that the elder's concern for precision runs parallel to the affection for 'clever' words shown by orators and sophists in their public declamations.

Fourthly, Philo contrasts the effectiveness of communication between the lecturer and his audience. He says of the elder's message: 'this does not lodge just outside the ears of the audience but passes through the hearing of the soul and then stays securely', #31b. The strong adversative in this sentence indicates that he is still defining the elder by contrasting him with orators and sophists.

Fifthly, Philo notes the motives of the two groups later in the treatise. There he again discusses the elder's methods of addressing his audience on a biblical issue or a matter that has been discussed by another member of the community.[21] These methods betray no thought of giving a display lecture (ἐπίδειξις) for, Philo explains, 'he has no ambition to get a reputation for clever oratory', #75.[22] This contrasts with the ambitious speakers who declaim solely for reputation's sake.[23] The elder speaks for honourable purposes: to 'gain a closer insight into some particular matter and having gained it, not to withhold it selfishly from those who, if not clear-sighted as he is, have a similar desire to learn', #75. Philo may be here alluding to teachers who, for financial gain, refuse to share their knowledge freely but dole out pieces one at a time, thus compelling their pupils to return again and again, *Ios.* 125.

Again Philo contrasts effective communication by the elder with the technique of the orators and sophists. To ensure that the truth is grasped permanently repetition is used, for without this, Philo

---

[21] The president, ὁ πρόεδρος, 'the one who takes the chair', is presumably the elder of *Contempl.* 31.

[22] δεινότης when used of an orator can refer to 'cleverness' or 'shrewdness'. Philo uses it in *Chr.* 105 of the nature of rhetoric 'which seeks out and weighs the materials for shrewd treatment'. This passage describes the encyclical education. Cf. also *Fug.* 84; *Somn.* II.283 (*LCL*, vol. v, pp. 570–1, n. a); *Hyp.* 6.4; *Praem.* 97. For other examples of δεινότης outside Philo see Isocrates, *Orator,* I.4, where it is used to contrast learning that leads to sound character with learning that seeks merely to provide skill in rhetoric; and Demosthenes, *De Corona,* 242, 277; Thucydides also warns against being carried away by this technique, *Histories* III.37; Plutarch, *Lives, Pompey,* 77, 80.

[23] On Bowersock's understanding, both the orators and the sophists desire recognition of their oratorical ability. See *Greek Sophists,* p. 13.

argues, the hearer will not apprehend the lesson. The elder differs in this from the speaker who 'goes on descanting with breathless rapidity'.[24] The audience of the Therapeutai even employ gestures to signal their comprehension: they motion with 'nods and glances if they comprehend and if in difficulty they move their head gently and point with a finger-tip of the right hand', #77. Their lecturer aims to communicate with his audience and so takes time to explain those points not readily understood: the sophists do not share his concern.

The use of orators and sophists and their activities in the Therapeutai discussion was apposite, for they were instructors of rhetoric, which remained at the heart of all Hellenistic and Roman education and culture. They were regarded as specialists in eloquence who both completed a student's higher education and declaimed before an audience.[25] By developing the contrast with these highly specialised professionals – themselves involved in an educative process – Philo successfully demonstrates the superiority of the Therapeutai elder.[26]

In addition to these five comparisons we find that *Contempl.* 31, 75 depends on a number of rhetorical terms. These terms and their import would have been lost on Philo's readers if they were not well versed in rhetoric, for he never explains them.[27] The fact that Philo does explain the activities of the unknown Therapeutai elder in contrast with techniques of known groups of orators and sophists in Alexandria (often referred to with technical language) adds to our impression of a widespread understanding of rhetoric. This familiarity, furthermore, suggests that the sophists under discussion were present and operative in Philo's world.

Contempl. 31 is not, moreover, Philo's only specific reference to contemporary orators and sophists which uses νῦν. In *Post.* 101 he

---

24 εὔτροχος characterises the glib tongue with speech that is so rapid that the speaker does not pause for breath, e. g. Demosthenes, *De Corona*, 308 where the rhetorician strings words together without pausing. Philo levels this charge elsewhere, cf. *Congr.* 64.

25 Marrou, *History of Education,* pp. 194, 196–7.

26 R. Mayer, 'Geschichtserfahrung und Schriftauslegung: Zur Hermeneutik des frühen Judentums', in O. Loretz and W. Strolz (eds.), *Die hermeneutische Frage in der Theologie* (Freiburg: Editiones Herder, 1968) p. 320, argues that Philo's allegorical exegesis 'is formally, even in details the same as the *pesher* methodology of the Essenes and Therapeutai'.

27 Regrettably, rhetorical terms in Philo are not always noted in the *LCL* translations and thus the full import of Philo's lexical choice is not always conveyed by the translation.

refers to 'the sophist group of present day people', denying that their teaching contains true philosophy, namely the utterance and word of God, #102. He supplies three reasons for this. Firstly, they 'practised arts of speech to use against the truth', that is, 'rhetorical art'.[28] Secondly, 'they have given the name of wisdom to rascality'. Thirdly, they have conferred 'on a sorry work a divine name'. Philo notes, with the use of another strong adversative, how present-day sophists differ both from the 'ancient band of aspirants', who pursued with rigour the study of philosophy, #101b, and the followers of Moses.[29] Again we see that Philo speaks not anachronistically but of his own contemporaries.

We can now conclude, in view of (1) the known role of orators and sophists as teachers in first-century Alexandria, (2) the rhetorical terminology Philo used to explain both their work and that of the Therapeutai elder in *Contempl.* 31, 75, and (3) the reference to the sophists as a contemporary, professional group misusing the art of rhetoric in *Post.* 101, that Fischel's assertion of a Philonic use of some 'implied anachronism' or symbol is unsustainable.[30] The evidence suggests that Philo denotes *contemporary*, professional orators and sophists in Alexandria.[31] Other first-century writers such as Plutarch, Epictetus and Dio Chrysostom likewise refer to both groups as a sort of contemporary, identifiable and professional guild.[32]

---

[28] *LCL* adopts a variety of translations for τέχνη λόγων: ('verbal artifices'), *LA* III.232, *Post.* 119, *Aet.* 121; 'oratorical artifices' *Virt.* 206; 'arts of speech' *Det.* 37, *Migr.* 77, *Post.* 101; 'arts that deal with speech' *Det.* 43; 'practice in speech' *Det.* 43; 'practice in rhetoric' *Det.* 43 and 'arts of eloquence' *Det.* 35. In *Det.* 35–43 four alternative renderings are given to the same phrase. The phrase is best translated 'art of rhetoric' or simply 'rhetoric' in Philo, as it is elsewhere.

[29] #101 refers to Moses' followers, and not ancient sophists, for they follow the 'central road' which Philo clearly defines, 'This royal road . . . is called in the Law the utterance and word of God', #102a.

[30] Fischel, *Rabbinic Literature*, p. 130. He takes no account of *Contempl.* 31, nor does he relate the sophist to the wider category of orators. His evidence will not support the necessary nexus which is germane to his thesis on Epicureanism and rhetoric.

[31] It is assumed that the orators in *Contempl.* 31 are not legal advocates because of the educative context in which the Therapeutai discussion is conducted. Only in *Mut.* 198 and *Agr.* 13 is there a reference to the legal advocate. Papyrological references to legal advocates abound, e.g. *P.Teb.* 287.2; 343.75; *P.Amh.* 29.10; *P.Oxy.* 37.4; 151.2; 237 VII.21; 653.9; 707.13; 899.21; *P.Lond.* 188.79; 354.19; 1716.15. There is only one papyrus in the early centuries AD referring to sophists: *P.Oxy.* 2190.

[32] G. R. Stanton, 'Sophists and Philosophers: Problems of Classification', *AJP* 94.4 (1973), 351–7, for references.

The throng of sophists in *Agr*. 136

Who then should we include in the throng[33] of sophists which Philo daily observed everywhere? Is Bréhier justified in including all teachers? 'Les sophistes désignent en général chez Philon, non pas toute une espèce d'enseignement régulier. Ce sont non seulement des chercheurs, mais des grammairiens, des musiciens, des geómètres, ce sont les specialistes dans chaque science.'[34]

He rests his case on the statements made in *Agr*. 136–42, especially #136.[35]

> Day after day the swarm of sophists to be found everywhere wears out the ears of any audience they happen to have with disquisitions on minutiae, unravelling phrases that are ambiguous and can bear two meanings and distinguishing among circumstances such as it is well to bear in mind . . . Or do not some [of them] divide the letters of written speech into consonants and vowels? And do not some [of them] break up language into its three ultimate parts noun, verb and conjunction? Do not geometricians put all lines under two main heads? Do not musicians divide their own science into rhythm, metre, tune? Do not other experts place everything in principal categories?

Bréhier's conclusion, however, falters when one properly assesses the genre used by Philo. The whole treatise, a discussion of Genesis 9.20 ('And Noah began to be a husbandman'), is followed by a lengthy discourse on the virtues of 'distinguishing', #126–68.[36] It indicates how Noah began well, but failed to reach the final stage,

---

[33] *LCL* translates this as 'swarm', which may be unnecessarily pejorative.

[34] The starting point for Bréhier, *Les Idées de Philon*, p. 288, is *Agr*. 136–42. Colson, 'Philo on Education', 161, using the same passage, suggests that teachers of philosophers may be included as well as those included in *paideia*. Because Philo likens them to the pig Colson suggests 'Much of this diatribe is rather unjust.'

[35] A. Mendelson in 'Encyclical Education in Philo of Alexandria', PhD dissertation, University of Chicago (1971), 180, n. 2, rejects Bréhier's identification of the term with the specialist–professor in encyclical education but without explanation, although in his *Secular Education in Philo of Alexandria* (Cincinnati: Hebrew Union College Press, 1982), p. 9, n. 54 he appears to endorse Bréhier's position. Pépin, 'Remarques sur la théorie de l'exégèse allégorique chez Philon', pp. 148–9, n. 46, likewise feels uneasy about Bréhier's conclusion but he does not refute it with evidence.

[36] Philo's use of *diairesis* as a literary genre in #1–124 is succeeded by a discussion of the term; διαίρεσις occurs first in *Agr*. 127.

#181. In #136-41 Philo provides examples of 'distinguishing', *diairesis*, undertaken by various groups, namely sophists, grammarians, musicians, geometricians, any other τεχνίτης, philosophers or dialecticians. Bréhier assumes that this list of professions can be subsumed under the title of 'sophists' who are discussed in #136a, basing this at least partly on the fact that the second group are grammarians but are not referred to by name.

But do grammarians (and the other professions) really form a subset of the class 'sophists'? The difficulties with this view are worth setting out. #136b provides examples of *diairesis* of the grammarians. The use of οἱ μέν and ἔνιοι δέ in #136b indicates the division of grammarians at the levels of primary and secondary education. The first comments refer to primary work: 'Do not some of them divide the letters of written speech [letters of the alphabet] into consonants and vowels?' Children began with reading, first learning the names of the twenty-four letters of the alphabet and then progressing to simple syllables in alphabetical order: βα, βε, βη, βι, βυ, βω.[37] Dionysius Thrax' *Τέχνη γραμματική* observes this division.[38] The second example from #136b refers to a first-century BC innovation, namely instruction in the 'technique' of grammar combined with the study of poets and historians at the secondary level. It comprised the systematic study of the elements of language.[39] 'And do not some of them break up language into three ultimate parts, noun, verb, conjunction?'[40] Bréhier implies that Philo has connected #136b to #136a, subsuming the grammarians under the sophists, but in fact this misses the flow of thought. Philo simply provides two examples of *diairesis* by grammarians, one from each level of grammatical study. Their work was so well

---

[37] Marrou, *History of Education,* pp. 150-1.
[38] For the text see I. Bekker, *Anecdota Graeca* (Berlin, 1819) section III. This was the foundational work for subsequent treatment of formal grammar as we know it. See H. Steinthal, *Geschichte der Sprachwissenschaft bei den Griechen und Römern* (Berlin, 1891), vol. II, pp. 189-209 for a discussion of ἡ γραμματική in Dionysius; and R. H. Robins, *Ancient and Mediaeval Grammatical Theory in Europe* (London: G. Bell & Sons, 1951), p. 39.
[39] Marrou, *History of Education,* pp. 170-2.
[40] ἔνιοι δέ, 'and some' in contrast with the previous group of primary grammarians, τὰ ἀνωτάτω τρία, 'the three ultimate or main parts'. This division of grammatical technique under three headings originates with Aristotle, who added to Plato's twofold division of the noun and the verb, the concept of conjunction to cover all other parts of speech. Philo here follows this division rather than the eight-fold division of Dionysius Thrax which was finally accepted, Robins, *Ancient and Mediaeval Grammatical Theory,* p. 40.

known that he need not name them but only describe their activity in much the same way that mention of 'learning the ABC' would signal a reference to primary education today. Thus Philo's distinction succeeds because of the clear and well-known differences between primary and secondary grammatical studies, as well as clear differences within the levels.

In #136a Philo has provided examples of *diairesis* from sophists who engage in 'unravelling phrases that are ambiguous and can bear two meanings and distinguishing among circumstances such as it is well to bear in mind'.[41] Then comes his illustration based on the two levels of work undertaken by the grammarians, which is then followed by more illustrations of *diairesis* from other professions: musicians, #137; geometricians and other experts, #138; philosophers, #139–40a; and dialecticians, #140–1. Philo then resumes his discussion of those events which stimulate the intellect in #141, that is, beneficial teaching sessions during which the participants are not merely 'chewing the cud', #142. This bovine imagery he then applies to the sophists and adds a further reference to 'their hair-splitting and their clever inventiveness', though not without acknowledging 'their precision in speech and their rhetorical skill in collating material', #143. Thus, in reality Philo speaks of the sophists, turns aside momentarily to provide (non-sophist) examples of *diairesis* (#137–41), and then returns to the sophists. In #136 he does not classify the other professions under the one heading but uses them – through an analogy – to explain *diairesis*.

The Loeb translation contributes to the confusion by translating οἱ μέν and ἔνιοι δέ in #136b as 'some of them' when the description of the activities are of two levels of the grammarians 'Or do not some on the one hand divide . . . And do not others on the other hand . . . ?' Furthermore, it does not translate at all ἤ 'or', which begins the sentence discussing the two levels of the work of grammarians.

Bréhier's mistake is explicable. An initial reading of #136–42 which misconstrues (1) *diairesis* as a literary genre, (2) Philo's use of examples of *diairesis* among professional groups, (3) the background of the differing roles of primary and secondary grammarians and (4) the particle introducing the sentence and the division

---

[41] Philo in *Agr.* 16 attributes a similar function to the key role of logic in philosophy when he affirms that 'it disentangles ambiguous expressions capable of two meanings', M. Alexandre, 'La Culture profane chez Philon', in Arnaldez, Mondésert and Pouilloux (eds.), *Philon d'Alexandrie*, p. 111.

of the labour of the grammarians indicated by οἱ μέν and ἔνιοι δέ, prompts his conclusion that the other professional groups are subsumed under the term 'sophist'. We conclude that the 'throng of the sophists' constitute a specific group in #136, distinguishable from others who specialise in grammar, music, geometry, other sciences, philosophy and dialectics.

Sophists and Sceptics and Academic philosophers in *QG* III.33

Philo in commenting on *Genesis* 16.12, 'He will be a wild man; his hand will be against all, and the hands of all against him', states in *QG* III.33:

> Now this picture clearly represents the sophist whose mother is wise learning and wisdom. But the sophist is wild in thought, while the wise man is civil and is suited to the state and to civilisation; but the man of wild thought is from that very fact a lover of contention. Therefore (Scripture) adds, 'his hands against all, and the hands of all against him', for, being trained in wide learning and much knowledge, he contradicts all men. (He is) like those who are now called Academics and Sceptics . . .

> For they are all kin, in a certain sense, uterine brothers, offspring of the same mother, philosophy. Therefore (Scripture) says, 'over against all his brothers he will dwell'. For in truth the Academics and the Non-committals take opposite stands in their doctrines, and oppose the various opinions which others hold.

Nikiprowetzky suggests that Philo uses 'sophist' in this portion to denigrate the Sceptics and Academics, and that he does not confine it to the followers of the ancient sophist Protagoras.[42] If this is correct we must adjust our understanding of Philo's use of the term to include, at least in this instance, negative connotations.[43] But can we agree that Philo considers Academics and

---

[42] Nikiprowetzky, *Le Commentaire de l'écriture chez Philon d'Alexandrie*, pp. 98 and 97–116, where he has surveyed Philo's comments on philosophy and has classified the term under three headings: Greek philosophy, foreign 'exotic' schools, and the practice or study of the Mosaic Law.

[43] They are therefore no 'virtuoso rhetor' class, Bowersock, *Greek Sophists*, p. 13.

Sceptics actually to be 'sophists', or are we again witness to a metaphor which effectively describes their methods?

Unfortunately, we have only an Armenian translation of the whole of *Quaestiones et solutiones in Genesim* and *Quaestiones et solutiones in Exodum*. Greek fragments of both works exist, but none of *QG* III.33, so that Philo's actual terms remain uncertain.[44] For example, the word 'Sceptics' in #33a means literally 'investigators' in Armenian and *LCL* notes that it evidently reflects the Greek. Of Philo's phrase 'Academics and "Non-committals"' in #33b, we are uncertain that the latter refers only to 'Sceptics'. *LCL* comments, literally 'non-sayers', and notes that 'probably the Sceptics are meant as above'. Now, 'non-committals' *could* refer explicitly to Sceptics, but why then use a different word in #33b from the one introduced in #33a to refer to the same group?[45] Clearly Philo chose a word which encompassed the characteristics of both Sceptics and sophists: both were certainly contentious as Philo notes in #33a. In fact, any doubt that he recognises the differing positions of the two most closely linked members of his analogy, the Academics and the Sceptics, dissolves upon his remark that they 'take opposite stands in their doctrines'.[46] He has already mentioned one common denominator between the Academics and the Sceptics, namely their opposition to other schools of philosophy, a point which he repeats again in describing the Academics and the 'Non-Committals'. Thus, Philo speaks pejoratively of the Sceptics when he uses the term 'Non-Committals' and creates a useful analogy.[47]

---

[44] F. Petit, *Quaestiones in Genesim et in Exodum:Fragmenta graeca* (Paris: Editions du Cerf, 1978).

[45] *QG, LCL*, p. 221, n. 1. It is unlikely that the Armenian translator would substitute another word if σκεπτικοί was used by Philo in both instances. R. Marcus, 'An Armenian–Greek Index to Philo's *Questiones* and *De Vita Contemplativa*', *Journal of the American Oriental Society* 53 (1933), 251, cites with approval the assessment of F. C. Conybeare, *Philo about the Contemplative Life* (Oxford: Clarendon Press, 1895), p. 155, that the translator is 'marvellously faithful, reproducing the Greek original word for word and as a rule without any change of order'.

[46] Cf. Sextus Empiricus I.33, and his whole chapter on 'How Scepticism differs from the Academic Philosophy'.

[47] It has been suggested that Philo adopted as his own the ideas of the Sceptics. *LCL*, vol. III, p. 314, commenting on *Ebr.* 164, states, 'Philo seems to jettison his general dogmatic principles and enrol himself in the school of the Sceptics.' Although he reproduces the arguments of eight of the ten tropes of the Sceptic philosopher, Aenesidemus, Philo does not in fact endorse these views. With respect to *Ebr.* 164–8 it needs to be noted that in the preceding treatise, *De plantatione*, of which *De ebrietate* is the sequel, Philo has been reproducing the

Does Philo, however, identify the Sceptics as sophists? Nikiprowetzky suggests that he does, citing *Mos.* II.212 as supporting evidence:[48] 'wisdom must not be that of the systems hatched by word-catchers and sophists who sell their tenets and arguments like any bit of merchandise in the market, men who for ever pit philosophy against philosophy'. He notes that Philo also uses λογοθῆραι in *Congr.* 53 to describe certain philosophers 'who are merely word-mongers and word-hunters'.[49] That context, however, describes the 'third race', that is, the Sceptics. While Nikiprowetzky correctly identifies the λογοθῆραι of *Mos.* II.212 with the Sceptics of *Congr.* 52–3, it does not follow that the discussion of the false wisdom in the former passage equates the Sceptics and the sophists. οἱ λογοθῆραι καὶ σοφισταί refer to two separate groups, and the καί is not epexegetical.

Congr. 52 is also conscripted as evidence for identifying Sceptics and Academics with sophists.[50] Here Philo speaks of the Sceptics who 'spend themselves on petty quibbles and trifling disputes'. But the use of the term σόφισμα in this passage does not imply that Sceptics are sophists, for it has a wider meaning.[51]

Thus, against Nikiprowetzky's notion that Philo *identifies* the sophists as Academics and Sceptics, we have suggested that 'the wild man', the sophist, is merely *described* as possessing certain characteristics shared also by Academics and Sceptics. Only such a conclusion can adequately account for the words: '(he is) like . . .', #33. We do not argue that no sophist ever held Sceptic or Academic views on particular issues, but that Philo does not say Sceptic and Academic philosophers as a class are sophists. In *QG* III.33 Philo notes that the sophists possess 'wide learning and wisdom'. As men of 'wild thought' they love contention. Thus, like

arguments of other philosophers on drunkenness which he has 'stated to the best of his ability', *Ebr.* 1, and *Plant.* 142–77 follows the model of a θέσις in structure and in the convention of presenting others' arguments in the first person. For a treatment of this convention see D. T. Runia, 'Philo's *De Aeternitate Mundi*: The Problem of Interpretation', *Vigiliae Christianae* 35 (1981), 105–51, esp. 113, and on the structure of *Plant.* 142–77 and for the literary convention and literature cited in support of this, 130. For Philo's refutation of Sceptic ideas elsewhere see *LA* III.206; *Ios.* 125–470; *Op.* 170; *Somn.* II.283.

48 Nikiprowetzky, *Le Commentaire de l'écriture chez Philon d'Alexandre,* 187.

49 The derisive nature of Philo's comment is reflected in the use of 'merely'.

50 Nikiprowetzky, *Le Commentaire de l'écriture chez Philon d'Alexandrie,* p. 108, n. 5.

51 σόφισμα carries a variety of meanings: 'captious argument', 'quibble', 'sophism' or 'sly trick' or 'artifice'.

the Academics and Sceptics, they contradict all men as a result of having been trained in 'wide learning and much knowledge'. The analogy is apposite, although it constitutes no argument for identifying them with these particular philosophers.

Sophists and Peripatetics, Stoics, Epicureans, etc. in *Congr.* 67

Sandmel argues that in *Congr.* 67 Philo identifies as sophists the philosophers of the following schools of thought: 'the Peripatetics, Stoics and Epicureans, Eleatics, Sceptics and non-Sceptics'. He cites in support of his conclusion the editors of *LCL*. While the editors do indeed extract a list of disagreements among the philosophical schools concerning the nature of the cosmos from Philo's comment in *Her.* 247, they do not share Sandmel's conclusion that the philosophers are sophists.[52]

Two difficulties weaken Sandmel's thesis that all who hold the philosophical positions outlined in *Her.* 247 are sophists, and thus the concomitant that this passage can help explain *Congr.* 67. Firstly, this would demand that Philo and Plato are also sophists, for both hold that the cosmos is created and not to be destroyed. As Runia notes: 'The reason that Philo quotes this Platonic text [*The Timaeus,* 41a–b, cited *Aet.* 13] is to prove that according to Plato the cosmos is created (γενητός) but not to be destroyed (ἄφθαρτος). It is moreover clear that there is no difference of view between Plato and Moses [and of course Philo] on this issue, for also Moses affirms this' (Gen. 1.1, 8.22, *Aet.* 19).[53] What Philo has explicated in *Aet.* 13ff. he merely notes in *Her.* 246: 'Thus those who declare the universe to be uncreated are at strife with those who maintain its creation; those who say that it will be destroyed with those who declare that though by nature destructible it will never be destroyed, being held together by a band of superior strength, namely the will of its maker.'

On this second proposition, καὶ πάλιν, the editors of *LCL*

---

52 Sandmel, *Philo of Alexandria: an Introduction* (Oxford and New York: Oxford University Press, 1979), p. 168, n. 310, citing *LCL,* vol. IV, p. 574. For a careful discussion of *Her.* 247 see J. Mansfeld, 'Philosophy in the Service of Scripture: Philo's Exegetical Strategies', in J. M. Dillon and A. A. Long (eds.), *The Question of 'Eclecticism': Studies in Late Greek Philosophy* (Berkeley: University of California Press, 1988), ch. 3, esp. pp. 89–98.

53 Runia, *Philo and the Timaeus,* p. 234 and see pp. 233–8 for the importance of this very substantial debate in the first century.

observe that Philo quotes from *The Timaeus*; but Sandmel ignores this note. He then simply identifies the third proposition as Eleatic, that is, those who subscribe to the notion that 'nothing is, but all things become', in antithesis to Plato's *Theaetetus*. Again Sandmel overlooks the holders of the antithesis even as he cites the holders of the thesis.[54]

Secondly, in *Her.* 246a Philo cites the sophists simply to base an analogy on their conduct, not to identify them, as the context shows. In discussing what 'the man of worth' is like he compares him with a chairman or a president of a council who can arbitrate, *Her.* 243. He comments that some who might be regarded as allies, holding the same position as Philo and Plato, ultimately cause offence when they engage in the conduct of the sophists, namely ἔρις. Philo thus simply notes the similarity between the sophists' conduct and that of allies. He next remarks that some of the proponents of certain views are allies and friends: 'In so far as their minds are fixed on one end to discover the facts of nature they are friends, but when they do not agree, they engage in civil strife.' He thus sees the need of a 'man midwife' who possesses discernment, a chairman who can 'observe', 'throw away', 'save' and 'approve'.[55] In addition, Philo observes that the history of philosophy is 'full of discordance, because truth flees from the credulous mind which deals in conjecture', *Her.* 248.

Hence this portion simply describes the conduct of philosophers of differing viewpoints and insists that allies can hinder one another if their argumentative behaviour begins to resemble the sophists' combativeness.

In addition, Sandmel has linked *Her.* 246–7 with *Congr.* 67 as examples of a negative attitude on the part of Philo compared to a more favourable outlook elsewhere. The latter text, he maintains, supports Philo's identification of the philosophers as sophists.

Again, however, Sandmel neglects certain germane facts. In exegeting Genesis 16.2 in *Congr.* 63–7, where Abraham 'hearkened to the voice of Sarah', Philo comments that hardly a day goes by but lecture-halls and theatres fill with οἱ φιλοσοφοῦντες. Various classes of people listen with different but inadequate responses. But to whom does Philo refer? While οἱ φιλοσοφοῦντες can be

---

[54] This is the one passage where Philo quotes verbatim from *The Timaeus*, 41a–b as Runia notes, *Philo and the Timaeus*, p. 233.

[55] Socrates so designates himself, *Theaetetus*, 151c. Cf. #246 where Philo cites *Theaetetus*, 152.

translated as 'philosophers', it often means sophists in the Philo corpus. In *Post*. 34 Philo mentions that many who have 'professed' philosophy arrive at conclusions belonging to the ancient sophist, Protagoras. *Det*. 74 refers to sophists who have proven to be 'lecturers of the highest order as far as understanding beautiful things and philosophical discourses are concerned', yet they invariably are caught 'indulging in practices that are base'. This clearly refers to those already designated 'sophists' in *Det*. 72. This charge against them, that is, that they teach virtue and yet practise evil, appears elsewhere in Philo. In *Deus* 170 those who commend κακία are said τὸ φιλοσοφεῖν, and their activities to bar 'the heavenly and royal road of virtue'. They are epitomised by the earthly Edomites, referred to elsewhere as 'present day sophists', *Post*. 101. In this same passage Philo alludes to 'the philosophy which is pursued by the present day sophists'. So sophists did debate philosophical subjects,[56] an instance being the thesis, 'The unevenness of the earth would no longer exist if the world were from everlasting', *Aet*. 132.

Congr. 67 seems to authorise translating οἱ φιλοσοφοῦντες not simply as 'philosophers' but as those who discourse on philosophical subjects. Further evidence only reinforces this conclusion: Philo equates their efforts with typical sophistic activity, for they are said to be ἀπνευστὶ συνείροντες τοὺς περὶ ἀρετῆς λόγους;[57] and the subject of their discourse in *Congr*. 67 is one upon which the sophists elsewhere declaimed, for example, *Mut*. 196–7.[58]

Finally, this audience in the lecture-hall responds to the sophist in one of three ways, *Congr*. 65. The minds of some wander to their daily preoccupations. Others hear but do not profit, for they listen 'to please their sense of hearing rather than to gain profit', *Congr*. 66. The third group appear to be students of sophists who learn to reproduce what was said but never bring their lives into conformity with their words.[59] While capable of speaking on the best, that is, about virtue, they fail to live up to what they say, #67. The

---

[56] G. A. Kennedy, *Classical Rhetoric and its Christian and Secular Tradition from Ancient to Modern Times* (London: Croom Helm, 1980), ch. 4.

[57] Philo uses ἀπνευστὶ συνείποντος in the description of declamations of sophists, *Contempl*. 76 and in referring to orators and sophists in *Mut*. 197–8.

[58] Demosthenes, *De Corona*, 64 uses the same clause to describe a rhetorician as Philo does in *Congr*. 67 and *Contempl*. 76.

[59] For an example of students of *paideia* listening to public declamations see *P.Oxy*. 2190 and the discussion on pp. 30–4.

significance of these reactions for our purpose is that these same charges are levelled elsewhere against sophists, *Det.* 72.

Based on both the description of the activities of οἱ φιλοσοφοῦντες and the observation that they affect their audience in ways elsewhere ascribed to the sophists, we conclude that Philo refers to sophists, not philosophers *per se*, in *Congr.* 67.

Sophists and ancient poets, Homer, Hesiod, in *Op.* 157

H. A. Wolfson and P. G. Geoltrain state that Philo uses the term 'sophist' to include the ancient poets, especially Homer and Hesiod.[60] Wolfson finds support for his statement in Diogenes Laertius: 'Sophist was another name for the wise men, and not only philosophers but for the poets also. And so Cratinus when praising Homer and Hesiod in his *Archilochi* gives them the title of sophist', I.12.[61]

Philo does not follow Cratinus in the use of the term 'sophist' but regards the poets, including Homer and Hesiod, as important lifelong educators:[62] 'if we are justified in listening to the poets – and why should we not, since they are our educators through all our days, and as parents in private life teach wisdom to their children, so do they in public life to their cities' (*Prov.* I.143). He elsewhere elevates the poets when he speaks of their importance in the acquisition of 'civic virtue'. 'No doubt, it is profitable, if not for the civic virtue, to feed the mind on ancient and time-honoured thoughts, to trace the venerable tradition of noble deeds, which historians and all the family of poets have handed down to the memory of their own and future generations' (*Sacr.* 78).

In the same section Philo cautions against rejecting ancient learning and argues that 'we should make it our aim to read the writings of the sages', *Sacr.* 79. He acknowledges his own debt to the poets, for he had been exposed to what he called the 'handmaid of philosophy', namely grammar, when at the secondary

---

[60] Wolfson, *Philo*, vol. I, p. 28; P. G. Geoltrain, 'Le Traité de la *Vie Contemplative* de Philon d'Alexandrie', *Semitica* 10 (1960), 51, citing Wolfson.

[61] Cratinus' *Archilochi* was written c. 450 BC but only a fragment exists.

[62] In *Op.* 157, which Wolfson does not cite, Philo speaks of τὸ ποιητικὸν καὶ σοφιστικόν but here γένος is used of two distinct groups, as in *Ios.* 56, where it refers to Greeks and Barbarians. Elsewhere the term is used of poets, *Sacr.* 78, *Agr.* 41, *Spec.* II.164; prophets, *Migr.* 84, *Her.* 249, 265, *Fug.* 247; and the Therapeutai, *Contempl.* 11.

level he 'consorted' with 'the study of the writings of the poets', *Congr.* 74.

Philo attaches importance to the poets – 'For grammar teaches us to study literature in the poets and historians, and will produce intelligence and wealth of knowledge', *Congr.* 15. The task of this level of grammar is 'the elucidation of the writings of the poets and the historians', *Congr.* 148. Elsewhere he commends 'research into poetry . . . and the study of the doings of old times', *Chr.* 105, or 'the diligent search into what wise poets have written', *Agr.* 18. Lovers of wisdom, among whom Philo numbers himself, must have an 'acquaintance with the poets and learning of ancient history', *Somn.* I.205. The index in *LCL* indicates his considerable knowledge and use of literary references.[63] He speaks positively of poets in a way he never does of sophists.[64]

For Philo, Homer[65] is the poet *par excellence*: 'Homer [is] the greatest and most reputed of poets', *Conf.* 4, and 'the poet most highly esteemed among the Greeks' is Homer, *Mut.* 179; 'we give the title "the poet"[66] to Homer in virtue of his pre-eminence', *Abr.* 10. Philo provides twenty direct quotations from Homer.[67] In one instance he cites 'chapter and verse' from memory: 'The same idea is suggested I think by Homer in the *Iliad* at the beginning of the thirteenth book', *Contempl.* 17. *LCL*, responding to the notion that Philo's attempt to locate the quotation is strikingly rare, suggests that it must have been an obscure passage the relevance of which would not have readily occurred to the reader. Philo may, however,

---

[63] Vol. x, pp. 434–86.

[64] On thirteen occasions Philo makes the statement 'as the poets say', or 'to use the poet's term', or 'to use the poet's phrase', when referring to specific words or phrases: *Deus* 60, 169; *Agr.* 24; *Plant.* 151; *Ebr.* 103; *Somn.* II.52, 275; *Spec.* I.74; *Prob.* 42; *Contempl.* 40; *Aet.* 63, 127; *Legat.* 13.

[65] Homer was intensely studied in encyclical education; S. J. Myres, *Homer and His Critics* (London: Routledge and Kegan Paul, 1958) p. 29. For the depth of study, see F. W. Householder Jr., *Literary Quotation and Allusion in Lucian* (New York: King's Crown Press, 1941) p. 57.

[66] Plutarch also calls Homer 'the poet', *Moralia* 667f. For the debate as to precisely who is 'the poet' see A. M. Harmon, 'The Poet κατ᾽ ἐξοχήν, *CP* 18 (1923), 35–47; A. P. Dorjahn, 'Philodemus on Homer', *CJ* 26 (1931), 457–8, and 'Apollonius Dyscolus on Homer', *CP* 25 (1930), 282–4. Certainly Philo makes it quite clear to whom he refers when he speaks of 'the poet'. Dio, *Or.* 55.6, likewise regards Homer as 'a poet without a peer'.

[67] For the use of Homeric quotations by contemporaries of Philo see M. van der Valk, 'The Homeric Quotations or the Indirect Tradition of the Homeric Text', in *Researches on the Text and Scholia of the Iliad* (Leiden: E. J. Brill, 1963), Part 2, ch. 12, esp. p. 285. He makes no reference to Philo.

remember simply because of a deep familiarity with the context: it is the only Homeric quotation that appears at the beginning of a book in either the *Iliad* or the *Odyssey*.[68] In at least one instance Philo knows the context of two lines of Homer, for he notes of *Iliad* II.13.204–5 that the words apply more appropriately to God and the world than to 'cities and men', *Conf.* 170: 'It is not well that many lords should rule ... Multiplicity produces many evils.' Significantly, in this instance he cites Homer over against Genesis l.26, 3.22 to substantiate the monotheism for which he contends, for the text of Genesis says 'Let us make man'. In *Legat.* 149 he uses this same quotation to apply to Augustus, which better fits the Homeric context.

Philo's reapplication of Homeric texts to new situations resembles his approach to other literary sources.[69] For example, *Iliad* II.13.5–6 reads: 'The Mysians fighting hand to hand, and noble mare's milk drinkers – Nought else but milk sustains their life, these men of perfect justice.' Philo's rendering, offered in a discussion of the superiority of the Therapeutai over the Greek philosophers Anaxagoras and Democrates, explains: 'the idea conveyed is that injustice is bred by anxious thought for the means of life and money-making, justice by holding and following the opposite creed', *Contempl.* 17. A survey of Philo's use of Homeric quotations indicates that he, while always accurate with the text, sometimes attends less carefully to the context, a legacy of his literary education and proof of his esteem for this poet.[70]

Philo's debt to Homer is also reflected in his *Quaestiones et solutiones*. R. Marcus suggests that in its form it resembles the Hellenistic commentaries on the Homeric poems.[71] P. Borgen and R. Skarsten's preliminary exploration of the whole Philo corpus would suggest that the influence of such commentaries was even more widespread.[72] Indeed, the influence of Homer on Jewish

---

[68] For the learning of all of Homer by rote see Xenophon, *Symposium*, 3. 5. See also Dio, *Or.* 36. 9.

[69] van der Valk, 'Homeric Quotations', Part 2, p. 266.

[70] Householder, *Literary Quotation,* p. 57 describes how the *Iliad* was studied. Homer was the basic source of illustrations of tropes, figures, barbarisms, solecism, styles, and many other points of grammar and rhetoric. See also M. H. Ibrahim, 'The Study of Homer in Graeco–Roman Education', Ἀθηνα 76 (1976–7) 187–95 for a description of the ongoing use of Homer at all levels of *paideia.*

[71] R. Marcus, *Philo Supplement, LCL,* vol. I, p. xi.

[72] P. Borgen and R. Skarsten, '*Quaestiones et Solutiones*: Some Observations on the Form of Philo's Exegesis', *SP* 4 (1976–7), 1–15.

literature may reach well beyond Philo if F. E. Halleway is correct that *aggadic* works 'resemble Greek and Hellenistic commentaries to the poems of Homer'.[73] H. Dorrie argues that Philo followed the Stoic allegorical exegesis of Homer which regarded the non-literal meaning as superior to the literal.[74] *LCL* also suggests a Homeric allegorising influence on Philo's treatment of the OT.[75] Whatever the outcome of current attempts to measure his indebtedness to Homeric exegesis, Philo's attitude to Homer was consistently positive and his debt considerable. He never calls him a 'sophist'.

Wolfson cites *Contempl.* 4 as his only evidence that other ancient poets were called sophists. There Philo refers to the ancient sophists who gave divine names to the elements: 'air [is called] Hera, because it is lifted up and exalted on high'. But Wolfson neglects the fact that those who gave divine names to the elements *were* sophists, namely Theagenes, Empedokles and Prodikos.[76] While others may have referred to ancient poets as sophists, Philo never so designates them.

Moreover, Wolfson's view that the term designates Jewish 'sages' cannot be substantiated by a single occurrence from the Philo corpus. His only evidence comes from Josephus where, appropriately, a virtuoso forensic rhetorician described as 'learned in the law' was called a sophist. Wolfson's case thus rests on comments from Diogenes Laertius and Josephus, and an unexplored assumption about *Contempl.* 4.

---

[73] F. E. Halleway, 'Biblical Midrash and Homeric Exegesis', *Tarbiz* 31 (1959), 157.

[74] H. Dorrie, 'Zur Methodik antiker Exegese', *ZNW* 65 (1974), 133–4; and also J. C. H. Lebram, 'Eine stoische Auslegung von *Ex.* 3.2 bei Philo', in *Das Institutum Judaicum der Universität Tübingen in der Jahren 1971-2* (Tübingen: J. C. B. Mohr (Paul Siebeck), 1972), p. 31 for the view that Philo's method was based on Stoic Homeric exegesis.

[75] *LCL*, vol. I, p. xvi.

[76] *LCL*, vol. VII, p. 610 believes that this was first suggested by Plato and adopted by the Stoics, citing *Cratylus* 404c. That suggestion is incorrect on two counts. First, it misunderstands the nature of *Cratylus* in believing that the comment by Plato is a serious one, aiming to make fun of the established use of anagrams. See R. K. Sprague, *Plato's Use of Fallacy* (London: Routledge & Kegan Paul, 1962), ch. 3. Second, others were first chronologically. Empedokles, the sophist whom Philo cites elsewhere (*Prov.* 1.23, *Aet.* 5, *Chr.* 25, *Somn.* 1.21) may well be the one to whom he refers, and the others could be Prodikos and Theagenes. For evidence of their use of this or similar anagrams see H. Diels and W. Kranz, *Die Fragmente der Vorsokratiker* (Berlin: Weidmann, 1974) vol. I, Empedokles line 35, p. 286; Prodikos lines 35-6, p. 285, line 44, p. 286; Theagenes lines 9–10, p. 52.

Conclusion

This examination of opinions on Philo's sophists has shown that orators and sophists comprised an identifiable grouping in Alexandrian society similar to those mentioned in *P.Oxy.* 2190 and Dio's *Alexandrian Oration*. Within the educational system of the first century, the term 'sophist' was not a fluid one: it excluded philosophers, dialecticians, grammarians, musicians, geometricians and any other specialised group. Philo's 'sophists' comprised a specific group within *paideia*, *Agr.* 136–42.

Philo does not use the term sophist to stigmatise philosophers such as the Academics and the Sceptics (*QG* III.33), non-Sceptics, Peripatetics, Stoics, Epicureans or Eleatics, *Her.* 246. Nor does he join others in applying it to poets,[77] although he does associate it with those who gave divine names to the elements, *Contempl.* 4.

The term in Philo's corpus is neither a 'symbol' nor a pejorative label applied to Greek or Jewish teachers or Greek philosophers.[78] Heinemann correctly concludes that the word should be read literally.[79] Philo may well speak of the sophists in a pejorative way, but like Dio, he does not use it pejoratively of non-sophists.[80] A distinct vocabulary of invective, drawn from Plato and well suited to its purpose, was used of the actual sophists in the first century.[81]

While this chapter has endeavoured to identify the Alexandrian sophists mentioned by Philo as the virtuoso orators who have public followings, the survey has yielded important information on the sophistic movement which also ought to be noted. Philo records the impact of the sophists on city after city, and describes the great admiration that their technical prowess won for them. They drew the whole world after them, yet were prematurely aged by indulging their lower natures, *Agr.* 142–3. Another complaint is that the sophists bestow no lasting benefit upon their hearers: they only declaim to enhance their own reputations, *Contempl.* 75. In this passage one also finds the allegation that some sophists withhold information for a later lecture merely to inflate profits. Philo notes

---

[77] Unlike Dio, Philo does not call poets 'sophists' because the former group is important for the educated man as this chapter has shown, while the latter is seen as an enemy to the seekers after virtue, as we shall see.

[78] D. I. Sly, *Philo's Alexandria* (London and New York: Routledge, 1996), p. 95, states that Philo looked down on philosophers and called them 'sophists' but she provides no evidence from his corpus to support her conclusion.

[79] See above, n. 6. of this chapter.   [80] On Dio see pp. 57–8.

[81] See p. 58.

that there is a threefold response of the audience to the sophist. Some allow their minds to wander as they hear the declamation. Others derive sensory pleasure from the performance without benefit to the soul: the moment the sophist ceases, so does that pleasure. The students listen to their teacher's display just to learn rhetorical techniques, never to reproduce that over which the sophists proclaimed themselves master, namely ἀρετή, *Congr.* 66–7. The next two chapters will add greater detail to this sketch as they build upon this chapter's conclusions concerning Philo's use of the term 'sophist'.

4

PHILO'S CRITIQUE OF THE ALEXANDRIAN SOPHISTIC TRADITION

> it is strange to find one of the most vexed questions of classical antiquity most fully discussed [in Philo] . . . to find the old issue between the sophists and the philosopher stated to us in terms of the Old Testament.[1]

Although Philo conducts his discussion of the sophistic tradition within a framework of OT characters and texts,[2] we will see that his critique of it depends heavily on Plato's evaluation of the sophists.[3]

Philo did not direct his complaints about the sophistic tradition against the educational ethos which was its source, that is, Greek *paideia*, but rather against its misuse by the orators and sophists of his day. His concerns were threefold. Firstly, the sophistic tradition's use of *paideia* hindered the development of virtue both in its teachers and in its pupils. Since 'all the sophists professed themselves masters of virtue', this failure reflected badly upon their professional ability and integrity.[4] Secondly, the rhetorical skills taught in *paideia* were not used to present the truth, but to seduce the hearers with sophistic 'magic'. Thirdly, sophists involved in *paideia* were often motivated by money rather than by the welfare of students who had to pay handsomely for their education.

---

[1] F. H. Colson, 'Philo on Education', *JTS* 18 (1917), 162.
[2] See T. H. Billings, 'Ethics', in *The Platonism of Philo Judaeus* (Chicago: University of Chicago Press, 1919), ch. 5. For Plato on rhetoric see E. Black, 'Plato's View of Rhetoric', and W. G. Kelly, 'Rhetoric as Seduction', in K. V. Erickson (ed.), *Plato: True and Sophistic Rhetoric* (Amsterdam: Rodopi, 1979), pp. 171–91 and 313–23; C. J. Rowe, 'Poets, Orators and Sophists', in *Plato* (Brighton: Harvester, 1984) ch. 6; and J. de Romilly, 'Plato and the Conjurers', *Magic and Rhetoric in Ancient Greece* (Cambridge, Mass. and London: Harvard University Press, 1975), ch. 2.
[3] See pp. 111–12 for the theoretical justification for such use.
[4] M. Untersteiner, *The Sophists*, English translation (Oxford: Blackwell, 1954), p. xv.

The sophistic misuse of *paideia* for vice

Philo was not opposed to Greek *paideia per se*, for he himself had enjoyed the benefits of this educational system.[5] He was trained in Greek grammar and considered it an art (τέχνη), its teachers τεχνῖται, and thought it of great value for the study of philosophy, *Congr.* 74, *Somn.* I. 205.[6] Grammar itself – consisting of reading, writing and the studying of the poets and the historians – he called the 'younger sister' of philosophy. He praised it for producing both 'intelligence' and 'a wealth of knowledge', *Congr.* 74, *Agr.* 18, *Ebr.* 49, *Congr.* 15,[7] and was convinced of its great importance in the acquisition of virtue, which could employ 'no minor kind of introduction'. In fact, two of the elements which constituted an appropriately 'great introduction' to virtue were Greek grammar and rhetoric, *Congr.* 15, and of the latter he said, 'Rhetoric seeks out and weighs the materials for shrewd treatment in all the subjects which it handles, and welds them to the language that befits them . . . it gives fluency and facility in using our tongues and organs of speech' (*Chr.* 105). Other purposes are described elsewhere: 'Rhetoric, sharpening the mind to the observation of facts, and training and welding thought to expression, will make the man a true master of words and thoughts, thus taking into its charge the peculiar and special gift which nature has not bestowed on any other living creature' (*Congr.* 17). In spelling out the benefits derived from the different branches of *paideia*, Philo recalled that from rhetoric he derived 'conception, expression, arrangement, treatment, memory and delivery' *Somn.* I.205.[8] A. Michel notes

---

5 D. T. Runia, *Philo of Alexandria and the Timaeus of Plato* (Leiden: E. J. Brill, 1986), pp. 35–6.

6 Elsewhere he distinguished between 'elementary' and 'advanced' grammar, *Congr.* 148. The former undertakes to teach reading and writing, and the latter the elucidation of the works of poets and historians. Philo does not consistently maintain the distinction made here between γραμματιστική and γραμματική; H. I. Marrou, *A History of Education in Antiquity*, English translation (London: Sheed and Ward, 1956), p. 160.

7 It had rules or laws which were passed on to succeeding generations, and its specialised vocabulary enabled professionals, but not non-professionals, to communicate with each other, *Det.* 75, *Prob.* 49–50. For the expert grammarian 'no limits can be set in the extensions and enlargements of his subject', but sadly this expertise so often dies with the individual grammarian, *Somn.* I.9, *Mut.* 80.

8 With some minor variations, these are the fundamental divisions of rhetoric and precise terminology found in most works on rhetoric, *LCL*, vol. v, Appendix, p. 604. For terms see J. C. G. Earnesti, *Lexicon technologiae graecorum rhetoricae* (reprinted Hildesheim: Georg Olms Verlag, 1962); A. Mendelson, *Educa-*

'que Philon ne condamne pas la rhétorique lorsqu'elle est segment utilisée; il en préconise au contraire le bon usage'.[9] Philo, like Plato, did not despise rhetoric, 'but only the excesses of the sophists'.[10]

Indeed Philo, following Plato, adopted a recognised dichotomy in *paideia*, and thus used the term to refer both to an intellectual discipline and the training of the will by moral precepts and the control of a superior.[11] In contrasting those trained by the intellectual discipline of *paideia* with the training of the will of others by moral instruction, Philo notes:

> For it is a characteristic mark of the learner that he listens to a voice and to works, since by these only is he taught; whereas he who acquires goodness not through teaching but through practice, fixes his attention not on what is said but on those who say it, and imitates their life as shown in the blamelessness of their successive actions.[12]

Both pedagogical modes are significant, for they represent two of the three means by which one achieves perfection in Philo's schema.[13]

Instead of *paideia* leading to a life of virtue, the sophistic movement too often produced κακία in its proponents and their pupils – φιλαυτία rather than φιλοθεῖα.[14] This stark contrast between the virtuous person, usually the pious Jew, and the sophist colours much of Philo's thought and betrays an animosity towards the

---

tion in Philo of Alexandria (Cincinnati: Hebrew Union College Press, 1982) p. 7; Michel, 'Quelques aspects de la rhétorique chez Philon', in R. Arnaldez, C. Montdésert and J. Pouilloux (eds.), *Philon d'Alexandrie* (Paris: Editions du Cerf, 1967), p. 83 'précisément sur la définiton de la rhétorique et de ses fonctions exactes'.

[9] Michel, 'Quelques aspects de la rhétorique chez Philon', p. 83.

[10] For an excellent discussion of this matter see Black, 'Plato's View of Rhetoric', pp. 171–91, esp. pp. 190–1.

[11] On the former in Plato see *The Republic*, 376e; *Symposium*, 187; *Laws*, 641 and on the latter 656c, 803d, 832c–d. For discussion see Billings, *The Platonism of Philo Judaeus*, pp. 85–7.

[12] *Congr.* 69 and the discussion of Gen. 16. Cf. *Fug.* 172, *Sobr.* 38 and Plato, *Laws*, 653c, 656c, 803d, 832c–d.

[13] On the third, the spontaneously virtuous man, see Plato, *Phaedrus*, 247b and Philo's discussion of this heaven-born man in Mendelson, *Secular Education*, pp. 53–8.

[14] For a discussion of the antithetical character of these terms and the contention that it is the central theme of Philo's thought see W. Warnach, 'Selbtliebe und Gottesliebe im Denken Philons von Alexandrien', in H. Feld and J. Nolte (eds.), *Wort Gottes in der Zeit: Festschrift Hermann Schelkle* (Düsseldorf: Patmos, 1973), pp. 198–214.

sophists which cannot be appreciated until one grasps the vital nexus in his system between *paideia* and virtue and its opposite, κακία.[15] He attached great importance to *paideia* because it was a 'vestibule' to ἀρετή, *Fug*.187, and 'great themes need great introductions, for it deals with the greatest of materials, that is the whole life of man', *Congr*. 11–12.[16] The terms ἀρετή and its antonym κακία are indeed central to an understanding of Philo's anthropology.[17] Virtues and vices are peculiar to man, and distinguish him from the rest of creation, for unlike the heavenly creatures and the rest of creation, man has νοῦς and λόγος which are the dwelling places of ἀρετή and κακία: within man is mixed good and evil, fair and foul, virtue and vice, *Op*. 73.[18]

In fact, like the sophists and philosophers, Philo incorporated into his system the four traditional Greek cardinal virtues with their four corresponding vices.

ἀρετή	κακία
φρόνησις	ἀφροσύνη
σωφροσύνη	ἀκολασία
ἀνδρεία	δειλία
δικαιοσύνη	ἀδικία[19]

[15] He uses this term over nine hundred times in his corpus. For a general discussion of Philo on virtue see Billings, *The Platonism of Philo Judaeus*, ch. 5; H. A. Wolfson, *Philo: Foundations of Religious Philosophy in Judaism, Christianity and Islam* (Cambridge, Mass.: Harvard University Press, 1962), vol. II, pp. 200–25; and also S. Sandmel, 'Confrontation of Greek and Jewish Ethics: Philo, *De Decalogo*', in D. J. Silver (ed.), *Judaism and Ethics* (New York: Ktav Publishing House, 1970), vol. I, pp. 61–76 and 'Virtue and Reward in Philo', in J. L. Crenshaw and J. T. Willis (eds.), *Essays in Old Testament Ethics: J. P. Hyatt In Memoriam* (New York: Ktav Publishing House, 1974), pp. 217–23. For a thorough treatment see A. Bengio, 'La dialectique de Dieu et de l'homme chez Platon et Philon d'Alexandrie: une approche du concept d'ἀρετή chez Philon', PhD dissertation, University of Paris (1971). More recently Philo's views on ethics have been taken up in the context of determinism, e.g. D. Winston, 'Philo's Ethical Theory', *ANRW* II.21.1 (1984), 372–416, who makes no mention of ἀρετή.

[16] W. H. Wagner, 'Philo and Paideia', *Cithera* 10 (1971), 57. 'His general principle is that encyclical studies form only an attractive vestibule.'

[17] See more recently T. H. Tobin, *The Creation of Man: Philo and the History of Interpretation*, CBQ Monograph Series 14 (Washington: Catholic Biblical Association, 1983).

[18] Philo takes this opposing view to his nephew in the dialogue *De animalibus*. For discussion see A. Terian, *Philonus Alexandrini De Animalibus: the Armenian Text with an Introduction, Translation, and Commentary*, Studies in Hellenistic Judaism 1 (Chico: Scholars Press, 1981), p. 45.

[19] Here Philo follows the Platonic ordering of the tetrad of traditional virtues: see

Thus in effect he endorsed the topics upon which the sophists declaimed: 'The social character of righteousness', 'The advantageous nature of moderation', 'The great benefits of piety' and 'The power of every virtue to bring health and safety'. If they discussed aspects of virtue, they also dealt with the opposite vices, namely 'The unsociability of injustice', 'The ill health from a licentious life', 'Irreligion makes one a pariah' and 'The serious harm from all other forms of κακία', *Det.* 72.[20]

Because the sophists were 'the self-proclaimed teachers of ἀρετή'[21] both in Plato's day and in his own, Philo did not criticise the topics upon which they declaimed, but the fact that their lifestyles contradicted their teaching, *Det.* 73.

Topics	*Sophists' Vices*
φρόνησις	ἀφροσύνη
σωφροσύνη	ἀκολασία
δικαιοσύνη	ἀδικία
εὐσέβεια	ἀσεβεία

To the four cardinal Greek virtues Philo added the greatest of all. θεοσέβεια was signified by the tree of immortal life, and was considered 'the consummation of virtue'.[22] Adam and Eve rejected this tree to grasp 'that fleeting and mortal existence which is not an existence but a period of time full of misery', *Op.* 154–6. The penalty for ceding control to irrational pleasures was difficulty in wresting the necessities of life from the earth. In concluding *De opificio mundi* Philo says, 'Such is the life of those who from the

---

The Republic, 419–445e. Listed elsewhere thus in Philo see *LA* I. 63, *Chr.* 5, *Sacr.* 84, *Det.* 75, *Ebr.* 23, *Mos.* II.185, *Spec.* II.62, *Prob.* 67,159, *QG* IV.113, although he does not always follow the order, and note 'piety' also playing an important part. For the ordering and a discussion of these virtues see H. F. North, 'Canons and Hierarchies of the Cardinal Virtues in Greek and Latin Literature', in L. Wallach (ed.), *The Classical Tradition: Literary and Historical Studies in Honor of Harry Caplan* (New York: Cornell University Press, 1966), pp. 166–8. See Wolfson, *Philo*, vol. II, pp. 213, 218–25, for his explanation of the cardinal virtues and their link with others. For a good discussion of their meaning see Terian, *Philonis Alexandrini De Animalibus*, pp. 148, 157–8, 164 and 171.

[20] LCL's translation of this passage does not make it sufficiently clear that these were topics on which the sophists declaimed.

[21] D. Zeyl, 'Socratic Virtue and Happiness', *Archiv für Geschichte der Philosophie* 64 (1982), 227 and n. 10 for evidence, and Rowe, *Plato*, p. 156.

[22] In the exposition of *Genesis* 2.9–14 in *LA* I.56–76 every tree and river stand for virtue flowing from Eden.

outset are in enjoyment of innocence and simplicity of character, but later on prefer vice to virtue', *Op.* 170.

In the hands of the sophists then, *paideia* led to perversion, for even while engaged in teaching the importance of the pursuit of virtue, they lived a contradictory lifestyle. Using the OT figure of Balaam the sophist, Philo argues that they cherish the very things against which they declaim. 'What good have they done?' he asks. Cain, like Balaam has 'done nothing . . . accomplished nothing . . . their souls have died', *Det.* 71–5.[23]

When God inquires of the wise man 'what is in his soul, i.e. his hand?', the answer is 'schooling', *paideia*. This is said to be the bridge over which one crosses to leave behind lethal vices and passions. The disciplined mind makes this crossing by means of *paideia*, and the virtuous man achieves it by leaning on instruction as on a rod. When Moses was instructed to lay hold of the tail of the serpent, God told him to grasp it and quell it so that once again it became a rod instead of a serpent. 'Instead of pleasure, *paideia* shall be in your hand', *LA* II.89–90. W. H. Wagner comments that 'the rod of *paideia* could be transformed into a serpent which bit the soul back to *sophrosyne-arete* when the soul wandered into the wilderness of passion'.[24] Philo maintains that the soul which rejects *paideia* becomes a lover of pleasure rather than of virtue.

Virtue for Philo was thus not a merely theoretical concept; it was also practical: 'clearly, it involves theory, since philosophy is the road that leads to it, involves it through its three parts, logic, ethics, physics; and it involves conduct, for virtue is the art of the whole of life, and life includes all kinds of conduct (πρᾶξις)' (*LA* I. 57). The gravamen of Philo's charge against the sophistic tradition lay in its failure to express virtue in everyday living, a charge which illuminated the gaping discrepancy between the cardinal Greek virtues so strongly endorsed in the sophists' teaching, and the way they themselves lived.[25] The sophistic tradition engaged in 'mis-education in rhetoric', for it used rhetorical techniques against virtue, *Post.* 52.[26] In a word, from their lips 'poured forth the sophist-talk which wars against virtue', (ὁ πόλεμος ἀρετῆς σοφιστοῦ λόγος,

---

23 Balaam was a good choice in this instance: as a foreign seer summoned by Balak, the king of Moab, to curse Israel, he was overthrown.
24 Wagner, 'Philo and Paideia', 57.
25 For discussion see Untersteiner, *Sophists*, p. xv.
26 Mendelson, *Secular Education*, p. 8.

Somn. II. 221).[27] With the sophists virtue had effectively degenerated into 'a kind of amoral "art of success" ' no less than in Plato's day.[28]

Philo further explains that those who proceed through the stages of *paideia* but do not seek virtue, by this very failure, become sophists. Ishmael, the son of Hagar, illustrates this.[29] The mother stood for encyclical studies, μέση *paideia*,[30] and the boy when grown became a sophist, *Post.* 130–1. This theme reappears in *Chr.* 6–10 where Philo presents the expulsion of Hagar and her son as an allegory of the banishing of the sophist and his mother from the presence of wisdom and the wise. She represents μέση καὶ ἐγκύκλιος παιδεία or ἡ τῶν προπαιδευμάτων διδασκαλία, her downfall being her impatience with 'the stern and gloomy life of the virtue-seekers (φιλάρετοι)'. *Sobr.* 8–10 contrasts Isaac, fully grown in virtues, with Ishmael who, although full grown, remains 'a child', 'thus marking the contrast between the sophist and the sage'.[31] Philo intimates that he proposes to demonstrate subsequently that 'wisdom is Isaac's inheritance and Ishmael's sophistry'. Though no

---

[27] Cf. Rowe, *Plato*, pp. 157–8. The sophists in Plato's day treated ἀρετή as merely 'skill in eristic debates, the ability to tie one's opponents in knots by whatever verbal means'.

[28] *Ibid*, p. 158.

[29] For the view that Philo used here the Stoic and Cynic treatment of the Homeric incident of Penelope and her maids, see Colson, 'Philo on Education', 154, and the substantial objections to this raised by T. Conley, *'General Education' in Philo of Alexandria*, Hermeneutical Studies in Hellenistic and Modern Culture 15 (Berkeley: Center for Hermeneutical Studies in Hellenistic and Modern Culture, 1975) 6–7, and Mendelson's response, *Secular Education*, p. 16. Philo can follow other sources closely as in *Plant.* 156; see E. J. Barnes, 'Petronius, Philo and Stoic Rhetoric', *Latomus* 32 (1973), 787–98. He was bound by a source but naturally used it for his own purpose. For discussion of Hagar and Ishmael see Colson, 'Philo on Education', 159–60; Wagner, 'Philo and Paideia', 57; Sandmel, *Philo's Place in Judaism: A Study of Conceptions of Abraham in Jewish Literature* (New York: Ktav Publishing House, 1971), p. 156, Mendelson, 'Encyclical Education in Philo of Alexandria', PhD dissertation, University of Chicago (1971), 107, 148, 178.

[30] *LCL*, I, p. xvii, n.a reports difficulty in translating this phrase because the Stoic use of μέσος implies neither good nor bad. They dismiss the translation 'intermediate' or 'secondary' education because of 'modern connotations' of the word. Mendelson, *Secular Education*, p. 3 supports the view that it has 'a definite value' when not used by Philo in educational contexts. In *Chr.* 3, 6, *Ebr.* 33, *Congr.* 12, 14, 20, 24 and *Fug.* 188 it is a technical term for the second stage of Greek *paideia*. The terms μέση καὶ ἐγκύκλιος παιδεία and ἡ τῶν προπαιδευμάτων διδασκαλία used in *Chr.* 6–10 are synonyms as they both refer to Hagar. *Paideia* was only a stage or prelude to virtue for Philo, and the term is highly apposite for his purpose.

[31] ἀντεξετάζω means 'to measure oneself against another'.

such work is extant, the information cited above allows us to reconstruct the general distinctions he would have drawn.

Defining sophists as virtuoso orators who enjoy a large public following aptly portrays their activities from the perspective of secular Alexandria,[32] but it would not have satisfied Philo because that description lacked a moral judgement. He would have added that because these men's education failed to produce personal virtue, they misused it in the instruction of others.[33] They themselves could declaim on ἀρετή, but could not reproduce it in their own lives.[34] 'This is the way of life of the sophists, for as they spin out their discourses (περὶ φρονήσεως) and endurance they grate on the ears of those most thirsting to listen, but in the choices that they make and the action of their lives we find them going very far wrong', *Post.* 86. Both Plato and Philo saw that these self-appointed teachers of virtue failed in the very thing for which they claimed expertise.[35]

It should be noted in concluding this section that Philo saw a solution to the bleak situation created by the sophistic tradition. The unchecked impulses of men's passions and the infliction of evil on others could be overcome by means of two traditional virtues: self-control and righteousness. These calmed and checked evil; and ἀρετή and the corresponding good works replaced κακία with its fruitless practices, *Op.* 81–2.

> if, in a word, the vices and the fruitless practices to which they prompt were to give place to the virtues and their corresponding activities, the warfare in the soul, of all wars veritably the most dire and most grievous, would have been abolished, and peace would prevail and there would be hope that God, being the Lover of virtue and the Lover of what is good and beautiful and also the Lover of man, would provide for our race good things.   (*Op.* 81)

In conclusion, the successful inculcation of virtue in a pupil's

---

[32] For the definition see Introduction, pp. 3–4.

[33] Dio Chrysostom also complained that the sophists robbed men of the classical virtues. See p. 55, n. 59.

[34] Philo warns that one may be trained in *paideia*, having great ability in expounding themes, yet be a most evil thinker as the sophists are, *Migr.* 72.

[35] As will be seen in the following chapter, the sophists had a philosophical defence for 'the witness' of their lifestyle based on a contemporary exposition of Platonic categories, and were therefore critical of their opponents whom they designated 'the so-called lovers of virtue'.

soul was as crucial for Philo as for Plato. As in the *Protagoras*, so in Philo, one sees the accusation that the sophists jeopardise this important process.[36] Both therefore oppose the sophists' claims to the title 'teachers of virtue', however much the latter pressed their claim upon their contemporaries.[37] The tensions between word and deed which characterised their lives and the lives of their students obviated such claims.

The sophistic misuse of *paideia* for deception

ἀπάτη ('illusion' or 'deception') was the goal of magic, and in Plato's estimation, also characterised rhetoric.[38] The sophist was indeed a magician, 'a kind of juggler (γοής), an imitator of realities . . . in the guild of false-workers and jugglers'.[39] Rhetoricians and sophists were engaged 'in delivering speeches and pouring out words, which have a magical and seductive influence on the audience; here is magic'.[40] Philo leans on this Platonic criticism to inform his second critique of the sophistic tradition. The craft of the sorcerer, σοφιστεία, was for Philo as for Plato, the art of wizardry, *Mos.* I.277.[41]

Philo therefore identified as sophists the Egyptian magicians against whom Moses contended, for they engaged in the tricks (τέχναι) and deceptions (ἀπάται) of sophistry 'like the enchantments of magic', *Det.* 38.[42] This required no exegetical chicanery because 'the sophists and magicians' of Egypt (οἱ σοφισταὶ καὶ

---

[36] *Protagoras*, 313c and the discussion in Zeyl, 'Socratic Virtue', 227–9.
[37] Rowe, *Plato*, p. 156.
[38] Plato was responding to the work of Gorgias, Plato, *Helen*, 10, who used such terms of rhetoric. For a full discussion see de Romilly, 'Gorgias and Magic', *Magic and Rhetoric*, ch. 1.
[39] *The Sophist,* 235a, 241b. Cf. the master of γοητεία καὶ φαρμακεία καὶ σοφιστεία, *The Symposium*, 203d. For a discussion of this issue from Plato onwards see de Romilly, 'Plato and the Conjurers', *Magic and Rhetoric*, ch. 2. Her study covers the second- and third-century AD evidence of Aristides and Philostratus, but she never refers to Philo or *The Cynic Epistles*, 6.30, in this helpful examination of subsequent writers.
[40] Citing de Romilly, *Magic and Rhetoric*, p. 29, and see also Kelly, 'Rhetoric as Seduction', pp. 313–23.
[41] de Romilly, *Magic and Rhetoric*, pp. 31–2.
[42] Cf. *Ios.* 103, 106. J. Leopold, 'Philo's Knowledge of Rhetorical Theory', in D. Winston and J. Dillon (eds.), *Two Treatises of Philo of Alexandria: A Commentary of De Gigantibus and Quod Deus Sit Immutabilis*, Brown Judaic Studies 25 (Chico: Scholars Press, 1983), p. 130, notes in passing that 'Philo's figures of the "Egyptian" sophists and Jethro are strongly reminiscent of Plato's attack on probability and sophistical rhetoric'.

μάγοι) actually did practice deception in their battle with Moses when they cast down their rods which turned to serpents.[43] Just as Socrates overcame the magic of the sophists with his own 'magic', so too, Philo assures us, Moses triumphed with divine power and not with deception of his own, *Mos.* I.92–4.[44]

Deception can only be overcome by a dialectic which 'distinguishes true arguments from false, and convicts the plausibility of sophistry, and will thus heal the great plague of the soul, "deceit"', *Congr.* 18.[45] Philo again leans on Plato in his campaign against sophistic deception: 'The genuine, or nobly born education is that of the dialectic',[46] and the true *paideia* counteracts sophistic deceit.

Philo interprets Moses' plea that he lacks eloquence as a claim 'that he has no gift for oratory'. His opponents engaged in 'specious guesswork at what seems probable' (πιθανῶν εἰκαστικὴ ῥητορεία), which is an interesting phrase, for εἰκαστική refers to 'conjuring', *Det.* 38. The sophist was also a dissembler, 'the trickster' who put on a confident front for popular consumption.[47]

Magic, sophistry and illusion were treated by Plato as virtual synonyms,[48] and Philo also refers to ἀπάτη, γοητεία, and σόφισμα together in *Somn.* II.40 as reprehensible sophistic practices.[49] It often depends on vanity, the 'impostor', which spins 'that web woven of lies and cunningly devised to deceive the beholders . . . along with (σόφισμα) [it] beguiles every city and loses no time in capturing the souls of the young', *Praem.* 25.[50]

Both Plato and Philo also regarded sophistic rhetoric as a form of seduction, for 'while the seducer (the sophist) pretends to the greatest good (love), they perpetuate the greatest evil (deceit) on his victim' as W. G. Kelly notes of Plato's critique.[51] ἀπάτη and

---

[43] *LCL*'s translation renders the term οἱ σοφισταί as 'wizards' without warrant.
[44] de Romilly, *Magic and Rhetoric*, pp. 32–7, citing *Meno*, 80b and *Symposium*, 215c, *The Republic*, 358d, *et al.*, and concludes, 'Whereas the magic of the sophists aimed at producing illusion, Socrates' magic rests on the obstinate destruction of all illusions. It is the magic of implacable truth . . . The new magic was the answer to the first', *Magic and Rhetoric*, pp. 36–7.
[45] See also *Agr.* 13.
[46] R. J. Mortley, 'Plato and the Sophistic Heritage of Protagoras', *Eranos* 67 (1969), 28, on the importance of dialectic in Plato. For a brief discussion of dialectic in Philo as the means of opposing errors see Mendelson, *Secular Education*, pp. 10–12.
[47] Mortley, 'Plato and the Sophistic Heritage of Protagoras', 31.
[48] de Romilly, *Magic and Rhetoric*, p. 32.
[49] For a discussion in Dio and others see p. 58.
[50] The 'delusive arguments' of the sophists are referred to in *Aet.* 132.
[51] Kelly, 'Rhetoric as Seduction', p. 323 discusses this theme in Plato's *Symposium*

σόφισμα elsewhere work deception and illusion through the eyes of souls which are willingly seduced, *Gig.* 59. The serpent 'played the sophist with innocent ways' (ἐνσοφιστεύων ἀκακωτάτοις ἤθεσι) and 'deceived the woman with seductive plausibility' (πιθανότης), *Agr.* 96.[52] Sophists engage in rhetorical arguments by which they seek to 'seduce us with their plausibility, while their enticements make us powerless to turn away'. Philo argues that even if all the plausible fallacies are refuted by true beliefs, one should still sail away from the land of falsehood and sophistry to the most secure anchorage, the haven of truth, *Her.* 304–5.

Philo calls the sophists 'impostors, flatterers, inventors of cunning plausibilities (οἱ πιθανῶν σοφισμάτων εὑρεταί), who know well how to cheat and mislead, but that only, and have no thought for honest truth', *Her.* 302. They are interested in 'the sophistries of deceitful word and thought', *Her.* 85; and by 'fallacies of any kind and verbal ambiguities', the sophists of Plato's day sought to achieve or appear to achieve 'victory in argument'. However, 'concern for truth is not a necessary part of the art – victory in argument can be secured without it, sometimes more easily so'. Philo, like Plato, also used ἐριστικός of the sophists who loved wrangling in debates,[53] and he argued that it epitomised the sophists' way with their 'excessive open-mindedness' and 'love of arguing for arguing's sake', *Det.* 36, 45.

The role of the sophists in the political life of the city also drew criticism from Philo, for the deception of the sophistic tradition inevitably spilt over into that arena. 'All the sophists of Egypt' were said to have sprung up in the area of *politeia* from 'a meagre mixture' of truth and 'many large portions of false, probable, plausible, conjectural matter'. They became experts 'in decoying, charming, and bewitching' their hearers, *Somn.* I.220. Plato's view was that among the sophists, those who attempted to direct the

---

and *Phaedrus*. Philo considers it possible for a sophist who wishes to pass from vanity to truth to become a sage by instruction, διδασκαλία, *Praem.* 58.

52 In Plato πιθανότης refers to an argument based on probabilities as against an argument based on demonstration, ἀπόδειξις, *Ebr.* 70–1: 'the sophist implants the specious, the probable and the persuasive for the destruction of our noblest possession, truth.'

53 The term can refer to the art which cultivates and provides appropriate means and devices for so doing. See G. B. Kerferd, *The Sophistic Movement* (Cambridge: Cambridge University Press, 1981), pp. 62–3 for discussion. Philo uses ἔρις to describe the wrangling among the sophists, *Mut.* 10 and *Her.* 246, and in *Congr.* 129 he refers to the quarrelsome sophist.

polis through deliberative oratory were the greatest sorcerers and most practised in charlatanism. For him they were 'the sophists of the sophists . . . the greatest imitators and cheats . . . the so-called statesmen'.[54] Furthermore, Philo and Dio Chrysostom were concerned, just as Plato had been, that the sophists had won the admiration of city after city and the honour of nearly the entire world. Philo objected to their 'hair-splitting' and their clever inventiveness, *Agr.* 143,[55] and yet consoled himself with the thought that though the world misjudge the sophists, God would not, *Ebr.* 71.

Philo also denounced forensic orators for similar reasons: 'the kind of oratory practised by the hired advocate is concerned not to find out the rights of the case, but to influence the hearers by falsehood', *Agr.* 13. A similar concern, noted by Philodemus, was that the use of deception by forensic orators had cost them their credibility, that a jury often found 'even stammering' by a layman more persuasive than the fluid speech of the orator. The classical virtues of δικαιοσύνη, ἀνδρεία and σώφροσύνη were preferred by juries to the forms of rhetorical speech;[56] and the judges also needed to evaluate truth without σοφιστεία, *Spec.* III.53.[57] Sihon the sophist illustrates the perils of playing the game. He indulged in sophistic riddles in forensic cases, loved to engage in probabilities and plausible arguments without concern for the truth, and relished trials, disputations, eristic contests and victory; yet he perished because he was the corrupter of the healthy rule of truth, *LA* III.233.[58]

---

[54] *The Statesman*, 291c, 303c.

[55] δεινότης referred to the 'cleverness' or 'shrewdness' of an orator, in contrast to a person who spoke ἀλήθεια. It was regarded as one of the three high qualities needed to govern a country, *Praem.* 97, and referred to the requisite skill needed in attaining political power, *Fug.* 82. *Somn.* II.283 is a possible reference to Epicureans and Sceptics who were clever at words, *LCL*, vol. v, pp. 570–1, n.a and *Hyp.* 6.4 a reference to eloquence. On the honouring of sophists see the discussion of the Corinthian council and people in the honouring of Favorinus and Herodes Atticus on pp. 132–7, 137–43.

[56] For a discussion see p. 214.

[57] Barraclough, 'Philo's Politics: Roman Rule and Hellenistic Judaism', *ANRW* II.21.1 (1983), 515 where he notes that the judge was 'to possess those virtues which made him alert to deceit'.

[58] He is clever at searching out verbal artifices and transgressing the boundaries of truth by the exercising of his sophistic techniques, *LA* III.232.

The sophistic misuse of *paideia* for personal gain

Philo levelled three criticisms against the sophists who used *paideia* to make money. Firstly, he was critical because they 'sell their tenets and arguments like any bit of merchandise in the market', *Mos.* II.212. This statement summarises Plato's critique: 'Can it be ... that the sophist is really a sort of merchant or dealer in provisions on which the soul is nourished ... hawking them about to any old purchaser who desires them'.[59] Neilus remarked that Didymus advertised himself by promising better care than any other of the city's sophists.[60] Dio Chrysostom detested the way that sophists viewed their pupils as 'their catch', concerned only for 'gain and glory'.[61] In *The Cynic Epistles*, 'Socrates' excoriates them because they 'have little regard for education, but concern themselves with making money'; in contrast he states that he does not fear for his 'own things' as the sophists do.[62] The sophists' defence against this charge was that poets, artists and doctors charged fees, and merchants also charged for their goods.[63]

Secondly, Philo detested those 'teachers of the lower subjects' who arrogantly claimed credit for a pupil's attainments. Such claims allowed them to demand huge fees from those who attended their courses, a fault compounded by their refusal to enrol the poor regardless of their thirst for *paideia*, *Congr.* 127.[64] In contrast, the Cynic 'Socrates' states 'I give my philosophic instruction in public, and equally allow the one who has much and the one who does not to hear me'.[65] Not only were excellent pupils of the sophists a reason for boasting but they also generated substantial income.

Thirdly and most seriously, he accused the sophists of actually stunting the growth of their pupils by withholding 'much that they ought to tell them, carefully reserving for themselves against another day the opportunity of making money', *Post.* 150. 'They zealously pursue wealth' and 'the luxurious life'.[66] Given that the sophists were from the wealthy ruling class, and were benefactors of the cities where they settled and taught, their use of *paideia* for

---

[59] *Protagoras*, 313c–d.   [60] *P.Oxy.* 2190, lines 21–2.
[61] *Or.* 32.10 and discussion on pp. 48–9.
[62] *The Cynic Epistles*, 'Of Socrates', 1.4 and 6.10. These are from either the first century AD or slightly earlier.
[63] Kerferd, *The Sophistic Movement*, p. 25.
[64] G. W. Bowersock, *Greek Sophists in the Roman Empire* (Oxford, Clarendon Press, 1969), p. 21 and Philostratus, *Lives of the Sophists*, 519, 527, 591, 600.
[65] *The Cynic Epistles*, 1.2.   [66] *The Cynic Epistles*, 6.1–2.

the purpose of obtaining more money by stringing out instruction rightly evoked disdain. Wealthy parents were, of course, willing to pay.[67]

G. B. Kerferd has argued that the real objection to sophists charging fees for *paideia* was that they sold their 'wisdom to *all comers* without discrimination – by charging fees they have deprived themselves of the right to pick and choose among their pupils'.[68] Philo was not alone in objecting to sophistic greed; Plato voiced similar criticisms, and they even lay behind Domitian's rescript.[69] Certainly by the first century, if not already in Plato's time, the fees charged to pupils put *paideia* beyond the reach of all but the wealthy, so it was not available to all comers.[70] Alongside Dio Chrysostom's objections that the sophists did not care for the welfare of the city but only for glory and greed,[71] the Cynics had another reason for their objections: they sought to highlight and commend their particular philosophy by teaching for free.[72] Thus, given the important role of *paideia* in establishing virtue, the Platonic charge of merchandising was still repugnant to some in Philo's day.

Some Jews pursued *paideia* not for virtue but 'with no higher motive than parading their superiority, or from desire of office under our rulers', *LA* iii.167.[73] That such civic ministrations were open to Jews possessing Greek *paideia* even before the letter of Claudius to the Alexandrians is no longer contested.[74] Philo clearly

---

[67] For the comments of Neilus, see p. 28.

[68] Kerferd, *The Sophistic Movement*, pp. 25–6.

[69] For Domitian's concerns, see p. 49–50.

[70] Mendelson, *Secular Education*, pp. 26–7. On the size of the fees in Plato's day see Kerferd, *The Sophistic Movement*, pp. 26–8.

[71] On the comments in *Or.* 32 see pp. 55–6.

[72] 'And it is not surprising that other people consider one who is thus inclined (to take no money for teaching) to be insane. Yet one must consider not only this feature, but also the rest of our way of life, and if we appear different from others in regard to bodily practices, one must not be surprised if we also stand apart in our attitude to material gain', *The Cynic Epistles*, 6.2.

[73] This definitely included Jews, for Philo refers to 'our race' in *LA* iii.166. See P. Borgen, *Bread from Heaven: An Exegetical Study of the Concept of Manna in the Gospel of John and the Writings of Philo* (Leiden: E. J. Brill, 1965), p. 125, and Mendelson, *Secular Education*, p. 29.

[74] For evidence of Jews among the list of *ephebi* see V. A. Tcherikover and A. Fuks (eds.), *Corpus Papyrorum Judaicarum* (Cambridge, Mass.: Harvard University Press, 1957), vol. i, p. 39, n. 99; pp. 41, 75–6. On the letter of Claudius relating to Jewish participation see *P.Lond.* 1912, lines 52–4, 92–3. For the view that Jews were excluded see Wolfson, *Philo*, vol. i, p. 79; and that some did participate see L. H. Feldman, 'The Orthodoxy of the Jews in Hellenistic Egypt', *JSS* 22 (1960),

attests that wealth and rank together with status were gained by sophists, *Det.* 33–4.[75] Philo fears that those who have received *paideia* in a crooked and distorted form have transformed the stamp of wisdom's beauty into the ugliness of σοφιστεία, *Prob.* 4.[76] Clearly one such distorted form is the sophistic tradition; the sophists mimicked and debased the authentic coin, and like Balaam, mocked wisdom with σοφιστεία μαντική, *Mut.* 203, 208.[77] As we have seen, Philo's was no lone voice crying out against the sophistic tradition in the first century, nor was he the only critic to pattern his responses after Plato's. *The Cynic Epistles* yield a similar if much briefer contemporary discussion. They too attack the sophists who have lost the true fame that derives from virtue and 'have sold themselves for the sake of profit'.[78]

Conclusion

If it is strange (as F. H. Colson maintains[79]), it is also highly informative that Philo evaluated the Alexandrian sophistic tradition by means of OT incidents imported into the structure of

---

223; V. A. Tcherikover, *Hellenistic Civilization and the Jews* (Philadelphia: Jewish Publication Society of America, 1961), p. 350; P. Borgen, *Bread from Heaven*, pp. 124–6; M. Hengel, *Jews, Greeks and Barbarians: Aspects of the Hellenization of Judaism in the Pre-Christian Period*, English translation (London: SCM Press, 1988), p. 101; and Mendelson, *Secular Education*, pp. 28–33. Jews were involved in trade guilds in Alexandria during the Roman period: see M. Wischnitzer, 'Notes to a History of the Jewish Guilds', *HUCA* 23.2 (1952), 252–3. For the positive response of some Jews to Hellenism, in contrast to the early Roman reaction recorded by Suetonius, *On Rhetoricians*, 1, see J. Goldstein, 'Jewish Acceptance and Rejection of Hellenism' in E. P. Sanders (ed.), *Jewish and Christian Self-Definition: Aspects of Judaism in the Graeco–Roman Period* (London: SCM Press, 1981), vol. II, p. 70. For evidence of a Jew who was 'a Greek not only in his language but also in his soul' see M. Hengel, *Judaism and Hellenism: Studies in their Encounter during the Early Hellenistic Period*, English translation (London: SCM Press, 1974), vol. I, p. 59.

75 On their status see also pp. 34–8.
76 This statement follows a comment relating to those who have not experienced education, Mendelson, *Secular Education*, pp. 1–2. Those not exposed to education he elsewhere calls *Barbaroi*, *Spec.* III.163, and identifies them with those who have been miseducated by the sophists, who claimed to make a person wise.
77 Cf. Plato, *The Sophist*, 267b, 'an ignorant mimic of knowledge'.
78 *The Cynic Epistles* 1.2,4; 6.1,3,6; *P.Oxy.* 2190 and Dio Chrysostom also criticise the preoccupation with pecuniary interests of the sophists; in Dio's case he also expresses concern about ἀρετή. See p. 55.
79 Colson, 'Philo on Education', 162.

Plato's critique. For the latter there were a number of basic 'forms in which the sophist appeared':

> he was found to be a paid hunter after the young and wealthy . . . a kind of merchant in articles of knowledge for the soul . . . a retailer of those same articles of knowledge . . . a seller of his own productions of knowledge . . . an athlete in contests of words who has taken for his own the art of disputations . . . a purger of the soul who removes opinions that obstruct learning . . . a trickster . . . a kind of juggler, an imitator of realities . . . a conjurer.[80]

Since they clearly remained relevant to the movement of his own day there was no need for Philo to move the discussion beyond these parameters. This in no way devalues his assessment, for to find in Plato an abiding critique of the movement was advantageous in an age which notionally esteemed the ancients. However, in listening to Philo's critique of the Alexandrian tradition one must remember that, despite all their perceived deficiencies, it was the sophists and not the philosophers who won the argument, which enabled them to occupy centre stage in the educational and political arena of first-century Alexandria.

---

[80] Plato, *The Sophist*, 231d–e, 232e, 233b, 235a–b. See P. Coby, 'The Education of a Sophist: Aspects of Plato's *Protagoras*', *Interpretation* 10 (1982), 154–6.

5

PHILO AMONG THE SOPHISTS

Philo's own experiences among the sophists are important for two reasons. Firstly, his rhetorical ability is made abundantly clear by his presentation of a case for the Alexandrian Jews before the emperor, Gaius, together with his debate with his famous apostate nephew, Tiberius Julius Alexander, the future Prefect of Egypt. Secondly, he subsequently would provide the 'lovers of virtue' with his guidelines for debating: rules which grew out of these two experiences.

Philo as orator and debater

Orator

Philo participated in the Jewish embassy from Alexandria to the emperor, Gaius in the aftermath of the carnage of the anti-Semitic *stasis* by Alexandrian Greeks.[1] That a person with his training in *paideia* was selected conformed to custom, for it was normally able orators such as sophists who undertook such important embassies to provincial governors, prefects, or indeed to the emperor himself to seek redress or concessions on behalf of a city.[2] It is evident that he was conscious of fulfilling this role from his reference to his own qualifications – namely training which

---

[1] For a discussion see E. M. Smallwood, *Philonis Alexandrini: Legatio ad Gaium* (Leiden: E. J. Brill, 1961), pp. 19–27.

[2] On the use of the term 'orator' for an envoy see C. Phillipson, *The International Law and Custom of Ancient Greece and Rome* (London: MacMillan, 1911), vol. I, p. 305. On the role of sophists in embassies see R. W. Smith, *The Art of Rhetoric in Alexandria: its Theory and Practice in the Ancient World* (The Hague: Martinus Nijhoff, 1974), pp. 50–9; G. W. Bowersock, *Greek Sophists in the Roman Empire* (Oxford: Clarendon Press, 1969), pp. 44–58; and E. L. Bowie, 'The Importance of the Sophists', *Yale Classical Studies* 27 (1982), 53, 55–7, with a list of some embassies.

distinguished him from the remainder of the Jewish delegation.[3]
This appears in Philo's response to the brief word from the
emperor to the Alexandrian Jewish delegation: 'But as I believe
myself in virtue of my age and my good education, what gave joy
to others rather alarmed me', *Legat.* 182. The Greek delegation
contained Isidorus, one of the three leaders of the anti-Semitic
party in Alexandria and later holder of the important post of
gymnasiarch; Apion the anti-Semitic writer; and possibly
Lampon.[4] The Greeks were well represented by these men who,
needless to say, possessed the rhetorical training needed to present
their case.

The considerable rhetorical ability of Philo was put to good use
in his extant *captatio benevolentiae*, recorded in *De legatione ad
Gaium.*[5] He incorporates into his discussion this customary section
of the *exordium*, which was an important element in an official
petition, #8–22a.[6] This *captatio benevolentiae* would have been
perspicuous to a first-century educated reader as would other
aspects of the speech.[7]

He follows form by referring to a universal feeling of *providentia*[8]
inspired by the accession of the emperor:

---

[3] We do not know who comprised the Jewish delegation. The numbers tended to be
five: Phillipson, *International Law and Custom*, vol. I, p. 322, and Smallwood,
Philonis Alexandrini, p. 24.

[4] *Flacc.* 20 and discussion *LCL*, vol. IX, p. 532.

[5] For other examples of *captatio benevolentiae* and their significant function see my
'The Importance of the *Captatio Benevolentiae* in the Speeches of Tertullus and
Paul in Acts 24:1–21', *JTS* ns 42 (1991), 505–31, and *P.Coll.Youtie* 66 A and C
published, *New Docs. 1976* no. 26.

[6] He refers elsewhere to a document presented to Gaius which summarised their
'sufferings' and their 'claims'. It was the petition sent through King Agrippa,
#178–9.

[7] On the question of the structure of the *Legatio ad Gaium* see *LCL*, vol. X,
pp. xxiv–v. Smith, *The Art of Rhetoric in Alexandria*, pp. 54–6, suggests that Philo
was indebted to Isocrates' division of a judicial speech within the *proemium*,
narration, proof and epilogue, 'though the speaker was probably not aware of it'.
It would seem that Philo has used a petition with the *exordium*, perhaps expanding
it. The *captatio benevolentiae* is interspersed with relevant comment, and the
narrative would have shown readers that the Jewish delegation clearly observed
the proper form in presenting an imperial petition, and rightly addressed the
emperor as 'Emperor Augustus' and 'Lord Gaius', #352, 356. On the structure of
#53–6 see M. Alexandre, 'The Art of Periodic Composition in Philo of Alexan-
dria', in D. T. Runia, D. M. Hay and D. Winston (eds.) *Heirs of the Septuagint:
Philo, Hellenistic Judaism and Early Christianity, Festschrift for Earle Hilgert*, The
Studia Philonica Annual 3 (1991), 149.

[8] M. P. Charlesworth, 'Providentia and Aeternitas', *HTR* 29 (1936) 107–32.

by Greek and Barbarian, the civil with the military with
the accession of Gaius over a dominion not confined to the
really vital parts which make up most of the inhabited
world . . . and all the more brutish nations . . . but a
dominion extending, as I said above from the rising to the
setting of the sun both within the ocean and beyond it . . .
a joy to the Roman people and all . . .   (#8–11)

This portion continues by noting that the recovery of the emperor
from illness was accompanied by an empire-wide feeling of great
relief, #15, and

> every continent, every island, returned once more to its
> former happiness, for they felt that they personally shared
> in his preservation . . . to take their place under a guar-
> dian, a shepherd of the civilised flock . . . ὁ σωτὴρ καὶ
> εὐεργέτης, who would pour new blessings on Asia and
> Europe, giving happiness indestructible to each singly and
> all in common.   (#18–22)[9]

The *captatio benevolentiae* also remarked upon the competence of
the judge to hear a particular case, for it referred to qualities
exhibited by the recipient of the petition which had a direct bearing
on the matter under adjudication.[10] Here Philo pays homage to
that great ideal, the continuation of the *Pax Romana*, made sure by
Roman law and order. The peace had already been established
early in the Principate of Gaius:

> In these days [that is, the opening months of his Principate]
> the rich had no precedence over the poor, nor the distin-
> guished over the obscure, the creditors were not above the
> debtors, nor masters above slaves, the times giving equality
> before the law . . . [there was] the freedom from grief and
> fear, the joy which pervaded households and people, night
> and day.   (#13)

Philo states all this within the conventions of the *captatio benevolentiae* in order to contrast the Roman pursuit of justice with the

---

[9] Philo repeats this sentiment in a refutation of the charge of Jewish impiety
towards Gaius alleged by the Greeks. He indicates that a sacrifice had been
offered up in Jerusalem 'when you escaped the severe sickness which all the
habitable world suffered with you', #356.

[10] Winter, 'The Importance of the *Captatio Benevolentiae*', 507–15.

Alexandrian injustices manifested in the attack on Jewish synagogues. His words tactfully imply an erosion of order, and are first supplemented with statements concerning the loss of civic rights in the *narratio*, and then supported by evidence and argument in the *confirmatio*.[11]

The presence of the *narratio* or the *refutatio*[12] and *confirmatio* can be seen from the account.[13] Though the emperor said, 'We want to hear what claims you make about your citizenship', he soon cut short their preliminary 'arguments' in the *confirmatio*.[14] He did this after getting 'a taste of our pleadings and recognised that it was by no means contemptible', but before the Jews could produce their 'stronger' arguments, #363–4. Because he rushed into another room to instruct his workmen they could not introduce the points which came next 'in the thread of the argument' (τὰ ἀκόλουθα), #365. 'So with the statement of our case thus mangled and disjointed . . . we gave up . . .' After a short statement by Gaius about the 'unfortunate, rather than wicked' Jews, he dismissed the case, #366–7.[15]

De legatione ad Gaium never concedes that the Jews argued an inferior case. On the contrary, only the Greek delegation's appeal to Gaius' anti-Semitism, which perhaps inevitably drew a response from an emperor determined to erect a statue in the temple in Jerusalem, resulted in the case's dismissal.

Although our evidence for the body of the forensic presentation of the Jewish case is fragmentary – the petition to the emperor is no longer extant – the preserved *captatio benevolentiae* stands as a monument to Philo's rhetorical skills.[16] He argued his case so

---

[11] *Legat.* 191 περὶ προσευχῶν which raised the issue of religious liberty for Jews; Smallwood, *Philonis Alexandrini*, p. 25.

[12] The opponents also appear to have introduced earlier charges of impiety by the Jews against the emperor during the proceedings. The Jews roundly denied making these accusations and produced confirmatory evidence, although it did not satisfy the emperor, #335–6.

[13] The emperor conducted the case while issuing instructions to workmen concerning his redecoration programme and moving from room to room as he did so, which greatly dislocated the proceedings and did not help the Jews.

[14] δικαιολογία, a reference to 'a plea in justification' in court which alludes to part of the *confirmatio*, Aristotle, *Rhetorica ad Alexandrum*, 1438a.25.

[15] See *Legat.* 356, 358, esp. 363, 365–7.

[16] Smallwood, *Philonis Alexandrini*, p. 24. In addition there is his skilled use of forms elsewhere in his corpus. See D. T. Runia, 'Philo's *De Aeternitate Mundi*: The Problem of its Interpretation', *Vigiliae Christianae* 35 (1981), 101–51; and on his composition skills generally, Alexandre, 'The Art of Periodic Composition in Philo of Alexandria'.

effectively that at least at one point he caught the elusive attention of Gaius 'who recognised it was by no means contemptible', #363.

Debater

We possess portions of Philo's debate with his nephew, namely *De Providentia* i and ii and *De animalibus*.[17] They record the interactions of two Jews who were well trained in Greek rhetoric. In *De Providentia* i the topic and the syllogistic methods are laid out, #1–5, three issues are discussed, (namely the creation of the world, its governance and destruction, #6–36; the problem of natural catastrophes, divine protection and retribution, #37–76; and the foolishness of the fatalism of astrology, #77–88), and a summary of the arguments concludes the dialogue, #89–92. The debate resumes the following day to explore further the issue of #6–76. The problems of retribution, #3–44, the creation of the cosmos, #45–58, its governance, #59–84, and natural phenomena, #85–112, are also probed. From the epilogue one sees that Philo believed himself to have answered the difficulties raised by his nephew. He invited further questions, but the offer was declined.[18]

Much of *De animalibus* presents Alexander's written discourse defending the rationality of animals as well as men, #10–71, and Philo's refutation of it, #77–100. It also contains the comments of an interlocutor, Lysimachus, in #1–9, 72–6.[19] The debate was sophisticated, with Philo calling upon Platonism and Stoicism,[20] and reflects the ethos which drove him to argue elsewhere that the ἰδιώτης had no business being 'on the plain', *Det.* 1.

It has been suggested recently that the dialogues of Philo represent a later apologetic interest, rather than the exegetical approach which characterises the remainder of the corpus.[21] This

---

[17] For the translation of these Armenian texts of Philo's debates see M. Hadas-Lebel, *De Providentia I et II: Les oeuvres de Philon d'Alexandrie*, 35, (Paris: Editions du Cerf, 1973). *LCL*, vol. ix have only a Greek fragment of Eusebius for i and a fuller text of ii; and *De animalibus*, in A. Terian, *Philonis Alexandrini De Animalibus: the Armenian Text with an Introduction, Translation, and Commentary*, Studies in Hellenistic Judaism 1 (Chico: Scholars Press, 1981).

[18] A. Terian, 'A Critical Introduction to Philo's Dialogues', *ANRW* ii.21.1 (1984), especially 276–7, for a synopsis.

[19] Terian, *Philonis Alexandrini De Animalibus*, pp. 62–3.

[20] Terian, 'A Critical Introduction to Philo's Dialogues', 277–81, and the relationship between *De Animalibus* and Plato, *Phaedrus*, 285–9.

[21] *Ibid.*, 294.

opinion attempts to correct the earlier view that these dialogues, together with *De aeternitate mundi* and *Quod omnis probus liber sit,* belong to his 'youthful' period,[22] but it merely begs the important question of the relationship between his exegesis and his Greek philosophy. A better suggestion comes from D. T. Runia who, after a careful analysis of the genre of a θέσις in relationship to *De aeternitate mundi,* demonstrates Philo's sophisticated adaptation of it for his own purposes. He suggests that the philosophical treatises were serious works written for Alexandrian intellectuals, proselytes or fellow Jews such as Philo's nephew.[23]

The philosophical treatises, the dialogues and his rhetorical ability as demonstrated in *De legatione ad Gaium,* clearly reveal Philo's educational and intellectual milieu. *Quod deterius potiori insidiari soleat* shows that those whom he considered competent to argue with the sophists, amongst whom he himself operated with apparent ease and effectiveness, were 'ready and equipped . . . with the means of withstanding their enemies' with λόγους ταῖς περὶ αὐτοὺς τέχναις, *Det.* 35–6.

Debating with and defeating the sophists

In *Quod deterius potiori insidiari soleat,* Philo deals more fully than anywhere else in his corpus with the subject of debating (συζήτησις) with the sophists.[24] He distinguishes 'shadow' debates from genuine ones. Choosing Cain and Abel, because of their conflict, to epitomise the sophist and the layman[25] he warns his fellow Jews, 'the friends of Moses',[26] who were 'laymen' in rhetoric, not to accept a challenge from the sophists to a debate. He then discusses who should in fact engage the sophists, which affords him yet another opportunity to reinforce the importance of virtue for those who love God, be they laymen or orators.

---

[22] *Ibid.,* 275–6 and authors cited n. 12.
[23] Runia, 'Philo's *De aeternitate mundi*', 139–40.
[24] In only one other instance does he use this term for debating, *LA* III.131.
[25] They also represent a central theme in Philo's thought, namely the stark contrast between the φιλόθεος and the φίλαυτος. For a discussion of the antithetical character of these terms and the contention it is *the* central theme of Philo's thought see W. Warnach, 'Selbtliebe und Gottesliebe im Denken Philons von Alexandrien', in H. Feld and J. Nolte (eds.), *Wort Gottes in der Zeit: Festschrift Hermann Schelke* (Düsseldorf: Patmos, 1973), pp. 198–214.
[26] οἱ γνώριμοι refers to 'friends' rather than 'pupils' as *LCL* translates the term.

Debating and not declaiming

Philo asserts from the beginning of this work that Cain's invitation to Abel to come 'to the plain' was an invitation to a disputation, not simply to a declamation given by the sophists, *Det.* 1. Philo later differentiates between these distinct events by comparing a disputation with the activity of a boxer engaged in actual combat, and a 'declamation' (ἐπίδειξις) with another who is engaged in shadow boxing.[27] The images are apposite because σκιαμάχειν means 'to fight in the shade' and is applied figuratively to activity 'in the school', #41.[28] Declamations were not only carried out in public, but, as we have already seen, were also important school exercises.[29]

The real abilities of the contestants, however, are needed not for declaiming, but for debating. Thus Philo considered debate no showpiece but a 'contest and desperate battle', #1,[30] the danger of which he stresses by treating 'the plain' as the location of this debate in the opening section of *Det.* 1–31.

Qualifications for debating

If debating is such a serious activity, who should accept the challenge to a disputation? In Philo's judgement, Abel should certainly never have done so, for he had 'never learnt the art of rhetoric' (τεχναὶ λόγων), #37.[31] Elsewhere he discusses those who should not engage 'in the war waged by the sophist', designating them ἰδιῶται, *Agr.* 159–65. They include not only those who have never been instructed in rhetoric, but even 'those who are beginning to learn, those making progress and "those who have reached perfection"'. Experience had shown they were defeated for different

---

27 *LCL* translates ἐπιδείκνυσθαι δόξουσι δύναμιν as 'they will be seen to be exhibiting the prowess of men sparring for practice'. ἐπίδειξις refers to declaiming and δύναμις to rhetorical power or ability.
28 See Plutarch, *Moralia*, 514d.   29 See pp. 22–3.
30 *LA* III.131. Philo uses the term συζήτησις to denote a debate among those who love to contend and in which anger arises from the wrangling.
31 Philo reaffirms this in *Migr.* 75 where Abel is said to be untrained (περὶ λόγους) and thus is defeated by Cain. In spite of his many natural endowments, fault is found with Abel because he actually accepted the challenge instead of remaining silent. He ought to have ignored his quarrelsome brother, for Philo adds 'the village sages usually get the worst of it when they encounter those who acquire the cleverness of the town'. See A. Mendelson, *Secular Education in Philo of Alexandria* (Cincinnati: Hebrew Union College Press, 1982), p. 7.

reasons: the beginner [was overthrown] because of his lack of experience, the man who was progressing because he was incomplete, the man who had reached completeness, because he was unpractised in virtue', *Agr.* 160.[32] Philo later in *Agr.* 143 distinguishes these three groups from sophists, and both from men in general.[33] The 'unlearned' thus include not only students of rhetoric, but also those who have graduated from such schools. The graduates often fail, however, because they lack training in virtue.

Philo suggests that no shame derives from declining to debate with the sophists; indeed friends will consider 'shrinking back' from the challenge of 'the enemy' prudent, not cowardly, *Det.* 37. Moses did precisely this because he was not 'eloquent', which Philo argues is the equivalent to saying he had no gift, literally, 'he did not have the defences against the rhetoric of eloquence and plausible arguments based on specious guess-work', #38. He thus imputes to Moses the notion that to engage in conflicts with the sophists before undergoing a thorough training in all ἰδέαι would have been wrong, #39.[34] It is important for the unprepared not to join the fray with the sophists, but to keep quiet and so win the prize which involves no risks. Such is the task of the man who has been equipped with all virtues, #42.

Philo praises those who pursue virtue, calling them 'experts' not in rhetoric,[35] but in praiseworthy deeds. They alone make the soul the treasure house of the good without even a thought for the 'juggling tricks of rhetoric', #35a.[36]

Another group, however, also seeks virtue; thus they too may enter into disputations with the sophists. Their strength is twofold: they fortify themselves by 'wisdom in counsel' and good works, and their speech with the art of rhetoric, #35b. All who possess good works and words are thus equipped to successfully counter the

---

[32] It has been suggested that Philo may be reproducing Seneca's threefold classification of learners, D. Winston and J. Dillon, (eds.), *Two Treatises of Philo of Alexandria: A Commentary of De Gigantibus and Quod Deus Sit Immutabilis*, Brown Judaic Studies 25 (Chico: Scholars Press, 1983), p. 260. In Seneca's *Epistles*, 75.9–15, the three categories relate to passion and vice and the extent to which men escape them. The third group is beyond their reach. Philo may have been influenced by this particular division among philosophers whose teaching Seneca is citing, whilst adapting it to his own purpose.

[33] *LCL* translates ἰδιώτης pejoratively in *Agr.* 146 as 'a nobody' and *Agr.* 160 as 'a mere professional'. However, in the latter citation Philo refers to them as 'friends' and contrasts them with 'trained and seasoned fighters'.

[34] A technical word in rhetoric referring to various qualities of ἑρμηνεία ('style').

[35] ἀσκητής is the antonym for ἰδιώτης.   [36] See pp. 91–4.

wranglings of the sophists, #36. They can then expose the sophists as mere 'shadow boxers' and not real combatants. While shadow boxers may win the admiration of fellow boxers, they 'are thought very little of when they engage in a real match', #42.

The sophists' debating

Philo then cites *in toto* an argument the sophists present to defend their lifestyle.[37] They contend that because 'the body is the soul's house', the physical senses that surround the soul are indeed its 'allies and friends'. The senses thus have value equal to that of the soul. Since nature intended that 'pleasures and enjoyment and the delights that meet us all the way through life' should appeal to our senses, they must be legitimate. It follows then that 'the πλοῦτος, δόξα, τιμή, ἀρχή and "everything else of that sort" exist not only for our security, but also for our happiness', #33. Thus in the sophists' hands ἀρετή had effectively degenerated into 'a kind of amoral "art of success"'.[38]

The sophists' argument is extremely interesting, for it shows how the imagery associated with Plato's trilocation of the soul was developed and interpreted in the first century AD not only by the sophists but by others as well.[39] It allowed them to insist that their status, privileges and pleasures were the quite legitimate result of treating the senses as 'friends and allies'. They further added that nature did not create enjoyable sense experiences for the dead and the unborn, but for the living. Hence the enjoyment of their lifestyle was not wrong; indeed their 'success' proved that they were right while their opponents – the so-called seekers after virtue – were wrong.

'The mode of life of these two classes is a witness of the truth of what I say (μάρτυς ὁ βίος τούτων)', #33.[40]

---

37 *LCL* rightly places *Det.* 33–45 in quotation marks. #33 consists of a series of questions, as Philo notes: 'They leave no stone unturned, as the saying is, while they ply their questions.' The six questions are sequential in thought and connected with particles. Then follows supporting evidence, #34a, in which the lifestyle and status of the sophists is contrasted with that of their opponents, #34b.

38 C. J. Rowe, *Plato* (Brighton: Harvester, 1984), p. 158.

39 These sophists argued, 'Are not eyes and ears and the band of other senses guards and courtiers of the soul?' D. T. Runia, *Philo of Alexandria and the Timaeus of Plato* (Leiden: E. J. Brill, 1986), pp. 306–8, shows that this was an accepted canon of interpretation.

40 Cf. Epictetus, III.22, 86–9, ἰδοὺ καὶ τούτου μάρτυς εἰμὶ ἐγὼ καὶ τὸ σῶμα τὸ ἐμόν.

Sophists' μάρτυς	Opponents' μάρτυς
ἔνδοξοι	ἄδοξοι
πλούσιοι	εὐκαταφρόνητοι
ἡγεμόνες	ταπεινοί
ἐπαινούμενοι	τῶν ἀναγκαίων ἐνδεεῖς
τιμώμενοι	ὑπηκόων καὶ δούλων ἀτιμότεροι
ὑγιεινοί	ῥυπόωντες
πίονες	ὠχροί
ἐρρωμένοι	κατεσκελευμένοι
ἁβροδίαιτοι	λιμόν ὑπ᾽ ἀστρίας ἐμβλέποντι
θρυπτόμενοι	νοσερώτατοι
πόνον οὐκ εἰδότες	
ἡδοναῖς συζῶντες	μελετῶντες ἀποθνῄσκειν (#34)

The sophists expounded thus on the witness of their wealth, glory, honour and authority, proclaiming themselves to be 'men of mark and wealth, holding leading positions, praised on all hands, recipients of honours, portly, healthy and robust, revelling in luxurious and riotous living, knowing nothing of labour, conversant with pleasures which carry the sweets of life to the all-welcoming soul by every channel of sense' (#34b).[41] With a series of antonyms they argued that their opponents were 'almost without exception obscure people, looked down upon, of mean estate, destitute of the necessities of life, not enjoying the privileges of subject peoples or even of slaves, filthy, sallow, reduced to skeletons, with a hungry look from want of food, the prey of disease, in training for dying' (#34a).[42]

It is unclear whether the detractors are referring to the Jews in general or specifically to the Therapeutai community.[43] If the former, then the 'almost without exception' acknowledges only a few notables, and may refer to Philo's family, who enjoyed wealth and influence in Alexandria.[44] Certainly, when taken as a whole,

---

[41] Cf. Aristides, *Or.* 33.19, where the benefits of engaging in oratory are outlined, namely 'wealth, reputation, honour, marriage, or any acquisition'.

[42] This last reference to 'training for dying' has been seen as an equivalent statement for ἐπιτηδεύει ἀποθνῄσκειν used of the philosopher in Plato, *Phaedo* 64a. See *LCL*, vol. II, pp. 493–4 and Simmias' response that 'this is exactly what my unphilosophical countrymen would say of the philosophers'.

[43] *Contempl.* 14–17 where the Therapeutai gave away their possessions.

[44] On the question of the wealth and status of his wider family see J. Schwartz, 'Note sur la famille de Philon d'Alexandrie', *Annuaire de l'Institut de Philologie et d'Histoire Orientales et Slaves, Université Libre de Bruxelles,* 13 (1953), 591–602,

the derogatory comments of the sophists describe a group without status.

If, alternatively, these words refer to the Therapeutai, then the transfer of property to their children upon joining the community and the general renunciation of material possessions could explain the language. Philo does speak of 'their longing for the deathless and blessed life', *Contempl.* 13. The fact that he discusses the activities of this community by means of a *synkrisis* with orators and sophists need not imply that his readers only knew of the activities of those he opposed. In fact, Philo may be engaged in a counter *synkrisis* in *De vita contemplativa* in response to the sophists' pillorying of the Therapeutai as the seekers of virtue as described in *Det.* 32–4. Self-control was the foundation of life for those whom Philo endorsed, and upon it they 'built other virtues', pressing on 'to reach the summit of virtue' which 'procured for them God's friendship', *Contempl.* 34, 72, 90.

Defeating the sophists

Philo maintained that those with a thorough training in 'the styles of rhetoric' (περὶ τὰς τῶν λόγων ἴδεας) will conquer the sophists, *Det.* 41. He as much as repeats this when he insists that one wins sophistic debates (ἀγὼν σοφιστικός) by carefully attending to λόγοι, not only for the purpose of eluding an opponent's grip, but for taking the offensive and proving one's own superiority in artistry and power, *Migr.* 82.

While Moses initially excused himself from 'the well-worded and specious arguments' of the sophists, he did become acquainted with them 'with a view to getting the better of the sophists of Egypt', *Migr.* 76. He could never have defeated them if he had not been armed with λόγος; and it is by Aaron his mouthpiece, and by Aaron's rod, that 'all the arguments of the sophists are devoured and done away with by the "finger of God" '. This narrative functions as a divine rescript which declares that 'sophistry is ever defeated by wisdom'. So the sorcerers can no longer withstand Moses, 'but fall as in a wrestling-bout vanquished by the sturdy strength of the opponent', *Migr.* 85. Like Moses, Philo affirms, 'we shall no more

and 'L'Egypte de Philon', in R. Arnaldez, C. Mondésert and J. Pouilloux (eds.), *Philon d'Alexandrie* (Paris: Editions du Cerf, 1967), pp. 35–45. But note also the reservations of S. Foster, 'A Note on the "Note" of J. Schwartz', *SP* 4 (1976–7), 25–32.

sink to the ground through inexperience of the tricks of rhetoric, but we shall spring up and carry on the struggle and disentangle ourselves with ease from the grips which their art has taught them' (*Det.* 41). So the better can overcome the worse and not, as the title *quod deterius potiori insidiari soleat* implies, the reverse.

The 'ancient band' of Moses' disciples pursued 'a hard-fought contest', eschewing the paths of 'the present day sophists who have practised arts of speech against the truth', for a royal road, 'true and genuine philosophy' paved with ῥῆμα καὶ λόγος θεοῦ. They despised 'the soft enchantments of pleasure' and 'engaged with a fine severity in the study of what is good and fair', *Post.* 101–2. Philo knew that the sophists of Egypt could only be overcome by those who had adequately prepared for such combat; hence in his own day, only those versed in rhetoric should ever do battle with the sophists.

His advice, then, as outlined in this chapter surely reflects his own methods of engaging the sophists. The manner in which he joined the fray, be it against the Alexandrian Greek delegation in Rome or in his philosophical works and his debates with his nephew, demonstrates both his careful approach to debating and his opinion on who is qualified for such an undertaking.

General conclusions

In concluding this survey of Philo and the sophists it may prove helpful to consider the work of another Hellenised Jew, Caecilius of Calacte.[45] A contemporary of Philo, he was a rhetorician during the reign of Augustus. His writings include *How the Attic Style Differs from the Asian; A Comparison of Demosthenes and Cicero; Essay on Lysias; On the Character of the Ten Orators*; and a history of the Servile Wars in Sicily. This list of known works provides clues to his interests. The first essay attempts to overthrow the Asianic style in favour of the pure Attic to which he ardently adhered. The second work drew sharp criticism from Plutarch who likened him to 'a dolphin on dry land [who] . . . never knew when to stop' in his criticism of the Latin style. His essay on Lysias sought to demonstrate that orator's superiority over Plato. His *magnum opus* described the ten Attic orators, and while we cannot

[45] E. Schürer, *The History of the Jewish People in the Age of Jesus Christ*, 2nd edn (Edinburgh: T. & T. Clark, 1986), vol. III.1, pp. 701–3; and G. A. Kennedy, *The Art of Rhetoric in the Roman World* (Princeton: Princeton University Press, 1972), pp. 364–9, for a discussion of his works.

be certain, he may well have been responsible for establishing the members of that canon.[46]

According to W. Rhys Roberts, Caecilius was one of 'the two leading critics in the literary world of Greece and Rome'.[47] Many rhetoricians from the Greek tradition flocked to Rome at the invitation of Augustus and attached themselves to the great Roman houses, as Caecilius did.[48] He, however, left a greater mark than most on the literary circles of Rome, being cited by Quintilian and Plutarch. Longinus' work on literary criticism, *On the Sublime*, clearly owes a debt to Caecilius.

The Suda records that 'in faith he was a Jew' (τὴν δόξαν Ἰουδαῖος), not an apostate like Philo's nephew. He stands then on the same ground as Philo, both in his training in rhetoric and in his faith. Yet there is no hint that he ever sought to integrate his training as a rhetorician and literary critic with his Judaism.

Philo, by contrast, went to Rome only briefly, and not to establish any reputation for himself. In terms of his literary output we have his extended exegetical work on the Pentateuch, his important philosophical treatises and his apologetic works. These were born of a desire to gather together such philosophical insights as he judged to be closest to the thought world of Moses so that he could, having 'discovered' the philosophy embedded in the Pentateuch, offer a sophisticated reading to a new generation.[49] The contrast with Caecilius could not be sharper.

Moses was for Philo *the* wise man (πάνσοφος), exceeding in age and wisdom even the Seven Wise Men of the Greeks who flourished as the pillars of civilisation in the seventh and sixth centuries BC.[50] While Caecilius thought in terms of a canon of orators, Philo placed Moses at the head of a canon of wise men. As R. Mortley notes 'the idea of antiquity implies superiority: once a culture has

[46] W. Rhys Roberts, 'Caecilius of Calacte: A Contribution to the History of Greek Literary Criticism', *AJP* 18 (1897), 302–12. Although we know little about his historical work, his interest in that subject may have been sparked by his own servile origins and the fact that his home town, Calacte, had been founded by the rebel leader Ducetius.

[47] W. Rhys Roberts, 'The Literary Circle of Dionysius of Halicarnassus', *CR* 14 (1900), 44.

[48] See Kennedy, *The Art of Rhetoric*, p. 337, for a description.

[49] Runia, *Plato and the Timaeus*, pp. 446–7. This methodological tool helped Philo to make 'a pivotal point in the history of thought'.

[50] Philo, *Det.* 126; *Post.* 28, 169; *Gig.* 24, 56; *Agr.* 20, 43; *Plant.* 27, *et al.* For a similar argument see Eupolemus in V. B. C. Wacholder, *Eupolemus: A Study of Judaeo-Greek Literature* (New York: Hebrew Union College, 1974), pp. 76–7.

been demonstrated to be the most ancient, it has also been demonstrated to be the source of all others'.[51] Clement of Alexandria, echoing Numenius the Pythagorean philosopher, asks: 'What else is Plato, but Moses speaking Attic Greek (Μωυσῆς ἀττικίζων)?'[52] The same notion vivifies Philo's overall enterprise.

Philo's war against contemporary sophistic activity was an outworking of this perspective. He believed that conflicts in which noted OT characters engaged provided the paradigm for his evaluation of the sophists, with Plato's critique of them and their 'magic' presenting the key which enabled him to identify the magicians of Egypt with the sophists of Alexandria. Philo thus did not unthinkingly 'borrow' the ideas simply because he found them helpful.

Our chapters on Philo derive from his writings a description of the sophistic tradition which shows little variation in their activities from Philodemus' era to Philo's day and that reflected in Philostratus' *Lives*. Philostratus does not distinguish between the activities of first-century sophists during the Principate of Nero onward and those of great second-century representatives such as Herodes Atticus. The evidence from Philo's corpus surely challenges the view of Philostratus that the Second Sophistic began in earnest in Nero's Principate. The same characteristics and trends which characterised the Second Sophistic are in fact to be found a century before Philo, if the evidence of Philodemus is accepted, and we have no reason to doubt its veracity when he discusses the sophists of his own day.

Philo has proved to be an important but largely neglected commentator on the social world of the first half of the first century,[53] and a significant witness to, and critic of, the sophistic tradition in the East. In the second half of this book we will turn to Paul's interaction with, and assessment of, the sophistic tradition as he experienced it, before comparing and contrasting the ways in which both men confronted this exceedingly powerful movement in their day.

---

[51] R. J. Mortley, 'The Past in Clement of Alexandria: A Study of an Attempt to Define Christianity in Socio-Cultural Terms', in E. P. Sanders (ed.), *The Shaping of Christianity in the Second and Third Centuries: Jewish and Christian Self-Definition* (Philadelphia: Fortress Press, 1980), vol. I, p. 193.

[52] Clement of Alexandria, *Str.*, I.150, cited in Mortley, 'The Past in Clement of Alexandria', p. 146.

[53] For the most recent treatment see D. I. Sly, *Philo's Alexandria* (London and New York: Routledge, 1996), although there are substantial gaps in her treatment of Philo's evidence, including the sophists.

PART II

The Corinthian sophists

INTRODUCTION TO PART II

These next five chapters survey evidence of the sophistic movement in Corinth from the perspectives of both critics and protagonists. The movement's opponents were Epictetus of Hierapolis in Phrygia, Dio of Prusa, Plutarch of Chaeronea, Greece, and, we will argue, Saul of Tarsus. The protagonists were well-known sophists: Favorinus of Arles and Herodes Atticus of Athens, and, it will be suggested, a group of Jewish Christian teachers.

None were citizens of Corinth, although all visited or interacted closely with the city. In the case of Dio it is known that he was there *c.* AD 97–101 and possibly also AD 89–96 because of his relegation from Rome and Bithynia by Domitian.[1]

Epictetus' dissertations were written after his exile from Rome to Nicopolis in Epirus (which bordered on Achaia) *c.* AD 92–3, and his works were recorded and dedicated by his pupil to a prominent Corinthian citizen, L. Gellius Menander.[2] Epictetus' discussion with a student of rhetoric reveals an extensive knowledge of Corinth, especially its leading offices.[3]

Plutarch first saw Corinth as a young man while on a mission to the proconsul. He later visited Rome via Corinth at the end of the seventies and again at the beginning of the nineties. He was also present in the city during the Isthmian games of the first decade of the second century.[4]

---

[1] See ch. 7, n. 5 for his presence in Corinth and the dating of *Or.* 12. The 'Diogenes speeches' where he discusses the sophists, *Or.* 6–10, are dated *c.* AD 100 in C. P. Jones, *The Roman World of Dio Chrysostom* (Cambridge, Mass. and London: Harvard University Press, 1978), p. 136. On exile during Domitian's reign see *ibid.*, pp. 45–55 and esp. p. 46, where the milder form of banishment called 'relegation' is discussed. This enabled him to visit Corinth.

[2] See the epigraphic evidence in J. H. Kent, *Corinth: Inscriptions 1926–1960* (Princeton: The American School of Classical Studies at Athens, 1966) vol. VIII, part iii, nos. 124, 125, 135, 137, 223, 263.

[3] III.1.34–5. F. Millar, 'Epictetus and the Imperial Court', *JRS* 55 (1965), 142.

[4] C. P. Jones, *Plutarch and Rome* (Oxford: Clarendon Press, 1971), pp. 32–3 and

Favorinus, although born west of Rome, travelled to the East and visited Corinth on three occasions. The statue and inscription erected by the city's magistrates indicate his enormous impact as a sophist on the people of Corinth. His third visit followed his first by ten years, all three placing him in the city during the first decade of the second century.[5]

Herodes Atticus often visited Corinth and was a great benefactor of both that city and Athens. Plutarch records this famous sophist's presence at a dinner during the Isthmian games, an incident also dated *c.* 101–10.[6]

Paul visited and taught in Corinth for eighteen months in the fifties. Unnamed Jewish Christian 'orators' were connected with the same congregation(s) for an unknown period during that decade.[7]

Three preliminary observations need to be made. Firstly, with the exception of Paul and his opponents, all were prominent literary men in their day, friends and sometimes intimates of one emperor and sometimes enemies of another. They are not insignificant witnesses. Secondly, and again apart from Paul and his detractors, their lives were intertwined. Plutarch's discussion and speech at Olympia was entitled Πρὸς Δίωνα, and he dined with Herodes Atticus.[8] Favorinus was a pupil of Dio and friend of Plutarch. Epictetus received eminent friends of Plutarch and Dio. Thirdly, except for Epictetus, all were trained in Greek rhetoric. We will argue that this was also true of Paul and his adversaries. Plutarch, Dio and Favorinus, according to C.P. Jones, all stood 'on the threshold of a major historical movement, the Second Sophistic'.[9] One could add Epictetus to this list and then move forward secure in the knowledge that these men left enough material for us to construct an accurate picture of sophistic activity in first- and early second-century Corinth.

J. Murphy-O'Connor, *St Paul's Corinth: Texts and Archaeology* (Wilmington: Glazier, 1983), pp. 98–9.

[5] See pp. 132–7 and *Or.* 37.   [6] See pp. 141–3 and Plutarch, *Moralia,* 723a.

[7] 2 Corinthians 11.22–3 and see also pp. 220–1.

[8] Jones, *Plutarch and Rome*, pp. 35–6.

[9] On their relationship to the Second Sophistic and to one another see Jones, *ibid.,* pp. 35–7. On education see his *Roman World of Dio Chrysostom*, p. 8 and *Plutarch and Rome*, pp. 13–6. For Epictetus' education as a pupil of the famous philosopher, Musonius Rufus, see Favorinus, *P.W.* VI, 2078, and for Herodes Atticus as a pupil of Favorinus, see Philostratus, *Lives of the Sophists*, 564.

6

EPICTETUS AND THE CORINTHIAN STUDENT OF THE SOPHISTS

Epictetus and the sophists

Epictetus (AD 55–c. 135) in his discussion, 'On personal adornment' (Περὶ καλλωπισμοῦ), III.1, deals with issues relating to the personal appearance or public 'presence' and career expectations of a young student of rhetoric, a citizen of Corinth who visited the noted Stoic philosopher in Nicopolis. This discourse is relevant to our study in that it includes a lengthy discussion of sophistic and declamatory activities.[1] The very dedication of his discourses by his pupil, Flavius Arrianus, to the well-known aristocrat of Corinth, L. Gellius Menander, would suggest that, at the very least, the reputation of Epictetus had reached that city.[2] His knowledge of liturgies indicates the familiarity of one who had done more than simply visit the city. These speeches, reconstructed from shorthand notes made c. AD 108 by his pupil, aim accurately to portray Epictetus.[3] F. Millar, in assessing the reliability of his witness, acknowledges 'the considerable quantity of factual range of topics, from the workings of the Court to the life of the Greek cities. He should thus take his place as a historical source alongside his two direct contemporaries, Plutarch and Dio of Prusa.'[4]

When Epictetus was visited by a student of rhetoric (ὁ νεανίσκος ῥητορικός) from Corinth, he described the young man as 'some-

---

[1] His value as a commentator on rhetoric and declamation has not been noted in recent works, e.g. G. A. Kennedy, *The Art of Rhetoric in the Roman World* (Princeton: Princeton University Press, 1972), and D. A. Russell, *Greek Declamation*, (Cambridge: Cambridge University Press, 1983) nor are his comments on Corinth included by J. Murphy-O'Connor in his documents on Corinth, *St Paul's Corinth: Texts and Archaeology* (Wilmington: Glazier, 1983).

[2] See G. B. Bowersock, 'A New Inscription of Arrian', *GRBS* 8 (1967), 279–80.

[3] F. Millar, 'Epictetus and the Imperial Court', *JRS* 55 (1965), 142. For the evidence cited in support of an AD 115 date see F. H. Sandbach, *The Stoics* (London: Chatto & Windus, 1975) p. 164.

[4] Millar, 'Epictetus and the Imperial Court', 147–8.

what too elaborately dressed' and as someone 'whose attire in general was highly embellished', III.1.1. We know that this was not atypical, for elsewhere remarks allude to the elaborate dress of sophists and their followers who imitated them even in this detail. Philostratus notes that the sophist Hadrian, a former pupil of Herodes Atticus, who held the chair of rhetoric at Athens, wore very expensive clothes. His followers not only imitated his accent and his walk, but also 'the elegance of his attire'.[5]

This young Corinthian not only 'set' his hair and wore jewellery, but also plucked the hair from his body to enhance his appeal to the audience. This latter practice drew strong censure from Epictetus, #14,26–7,32.[6] Again, Philostratus records how Scopelian, the sophist, regularly used pitch-plaster to remove hair from his body.[7] Sophists and their pupils were concerned with personal adornment, hence the title of this discourse 'On personal adornment'.

These idiosyncrasies were only part of the wider issue of personal appearance or image, a matter discussed by Epictetus, #7. Sophists and their pupils, as well as the former's audiences, paid attention to the physical attributes of those who declaimed, as noted by Philostratus: when Alexander of Seleucia came to Athens his 'perfect elegance' sent an 'appreciative murmur' through the audience and he was described as 'godlike'.[8] This preoccupation with natural attributes was not only a feature of the Second Sophistic but was likewise discussed by Philodemus before the first century AD.[9]

To help the student understand the true beauty of man Epictetus asks a series of questions to which the student replies.

---

[5] *Lives of the Sophists*, 586–8. He also notes that Aristides of Pergamon, when he converted from being a philosopher to a sophist, began to be fastidious whereas previously he was 'slovenly in appearance, unkempt and squalid in his dress', #567.

[6] Epictetus regards this practice as highly effeminate, #32. He does not promote neglect of appearance, for elsewhere he expresses preference for young students of philosophy to have their hair 'carefully dressed', IV.2.25. The Corinthian student had overdone it.

[7] *Lives of the Sophists*, 536.

[8] 'For his beard was curly and of moderate length, his eyes large and melting, his nose well shaped, his teeth very white, his fingers long and slender, and well fitted to hold the reigns of eloquence', *Lives of the Sophists*, 572, 570, discussed by Russell, *Greek Declamation*, p. 85, n. 52 as a comment on the audience's positive response.

[9] *c.* 110 BC–*c.* 40/35 BC. For evidence and for discussion in relation to 2 Corinthians 10.10 see pp. 208–13.

'What, then makes a man beautiful other than just that which makes a dog or a horse beautiful in its kind?' 'Just that,' he said. 'What is it, then, that makes a dog beautiful?' 'The presence of a dog's excellence (ἡ ἀρετὴ ἡ κυνὸς παροῦσα).' 'What, then, makes a man beautiful? Is it not the presence of a man's excellence?' 'Very well, then, young man, do you too, if you wish to be beautiful, labour to achieve this, the excellence that characterises a man (ἡ ἀρετὴ ἡ ἀνθρώπου παροῦσα).'   (#6–7)

The next step in this argument is not difficult as Epictetus seeks to help the young man see what 'supreme excellence' means for some men, #1,3. The student is asked whether people praise injustice, intemperance or lack of control, that is, the cardinal Greek vices. Epictetus argued that the possession of their opposites, namely the cardinal virtues, would make the student beautiful. Their neglect would of course make him ugly regardless of any cosmetic attempts to look beautiful, #9.[10] He thus in effect argued that these virtues make the bodily presence of a man beautiful, while elaborate hair styles, jewellery, expensive clothing, and even natural attributes such as smooth skin do not.

To downgrade further any preoccupation with his appearance, Epictetus refers contemptuously to 'the paltry body', #31, 43. He confesses to the student that he almost lacks the courage to tell him he is 'ugly', a slander which reinforces the whole discussion about the unimportance of personal adornment, #41. He also contrasts his own grey beard and rough philosopher's cloak with the cultivated appearance of the student and notes that people still, regardless of his lack of finery, seek his advice, even as this Corinthian has done, #24.

A Socratic path is recommended. The student must 'know himself', adorn himself with reason, and leave his hair 'to Him who fashioned it as He willed', #16, 42, 24–6.[11] 'Make beautiful moral purpose, eradicate worthless opinions', #43.

[10] The emphasis on cardinal virtues is conventional. Philo stated that the sophists themselves taught their importance *ad nauseam*, and also notes the failure of these teachers and their students to possess these virtues, *Det.* 72. For discussion see pp. 85–8. The irony in the comments of both men is that the sophists were regarded as masters of ἀρετή and claimed to impart virtues to their disciples, M. Untersteiner, *The Sophists*, English translation (Oxford: Blackwell, 1954), p. xv.

[11] Epictetus followed his teacher, Musonius, who said that hair should be trimmed solely to avoid discomfort and inconvenience, Sandbach, *Stoics*, 163.

Epictetus thus reveals how far at least one student of rhetoric in the first century had extended the concept of ὑπόκρισις to personal adornment.

He also conveys the way sophists pandered to the wishes of the audience, even to the point of attempting to look 'smooth'; for the student acknowledges that the practice of removing hair is a sign of effeminacy but adds, 'Yes, but they like smooth men', #42.[12]

This same encounter also provides an insight into the rank and status that a Corinthian student of rhetoric might expect to achieve later in life, #34–6.[13] A citizen trained in rhetoric could be elected to the following positions in the city: 'administrator of the city' (ἀστυνόμος), 'the superintendent of the *ephebi*' (ἐφήβαρχος), 'a magistrate' (στρατηγός), or 'superintendent of the games' (ἀγωνοθέτης). Epictetus also reminds him that his son could become 'a fine citizen' (καλὸς πολίτης), 'a senator' (βουλευτής) and 'an orator' (ῥήτωρ).

Extant evidence corroborates the positions outlined by Epictetus

---

[12] See p. 208–11 for a discussion of ὑπόκρισις. Epictetus' comments in this discourse more adequately demonstrate what he means by 'bodily presence' than the evidence H. D. Betz draws from this corpus to support the meaning of σχῆμα as a synonym for the term. In his *Der Apostel Paulus und die sokratische Tradition: eine exegetische Untersuchung zu seiner 'Apologie' 2 korinther 10–13* (Tübingen: J. C. B. Mohr (Paul Siebeck), 1972), pp. 53–4, H. D. Betz ignores this discourse 'On personal adornment' and wrongly parallels III.22.86–9 with 2 Corinthians 10.10. S. K. Stowers, 'Social Status, Public Speaking and Private Teaching: The Circumstances of Paul's Preaching Activity', *NovT* 26 (1984), 75, n. 92, mentions III.1 as evidence of 'showy costumes' and 'elaborate hairdos' and wishes to use it to support his argument of clear distinguishing marks between philosophers and sophists *contra* G. P. Stanton, 'Sophists and Philosophers: Problems of Classification', *AJP* 94.4 (1973). Epictetus, as subsequent discussion will show, sees an overlapping between philosophers and sophists in their use of oratory. Stowers cites evidence from Dio Chrysostom who 'makes it clear how crucial dress and life-style were for the distinction of the two'. However, the evidence from Dio does not support his conclusion. In *Or.* 12.15 Dio refers not to dress or hair style when he refers to a sophist who is 'handsome in appearance and strong'. Καλοῦ τὸ εἶδος clearly refers to physical attributes. While Dio mentions the sophists in *Or.* 35 engaging in a comparison on rhetorical presentation, he is not contrasting lifestyle or dress when he refers to the wearing of 'long hair' as a sign *per se* that one is really a philosopher. Likewise in *Or.* 72 which is specifically about 'personal appearance', σχῆμα, Dio makes no mention of sophists, only philosophers. Stowers cites *Or.* 70.7–9 as a specific example of the contrast, but Dio clearly states the contrast is between the philosopher and the layman (ἰδιώτης).

[13] On rank and status see pp. 34–8. 'Making a citizen of Corinth' refers to the procedure by which citizenship is recognised and does not mean the conferring of Corinthian citizenship upon a foreigner. Otherwise πολιτεύειν, which means to be made a citizen, would have been used. W. A. Oldfather, *LCL*, vol. II, p. 16, n. 2 rightly concludes that the interlocutor must have been a citizen.

and indicates that the list presents an ascending hierarchy of status positions.[14] The superintendent of the games occupied a position of great prestige because, along with a board of ten *Hellanodikai,* he was responsible for 'the biennial Isthmian games, the quadrennial Caesarean, and a third series of imperial contests named after the reigning emperor. As president of the games he was responsible for most of the expenses and was expected to provide the extensive hospitality himself.'[15] The reference by Epictetus reflects an intimate knowledge of the political structures of the city, especially that of the *aedile* (ἀστυνόμος) who in other circumstances would have also run the Games. However the importance of the Isthmian Games and the enormous cost incurred by the holders of this office in running them saw the creation in Corinth of a separate office of President whose status superseded that of the magistrates.

The στρατηγός convened the council and the assembly, and presided over meetings and elections. Until AD 69 his name appeared on the Corinthian bronze coins.[16] This magistrate held the highest rank, though the great importance of the Isthmian Games during the first century meant that the status of the ἀγωνοθέτης outweighed the rank of the στρατηγός. The liturgy attached to this position demanded great wealth and was rewarded with correspondingly great honours.[17] Wiseman remarks that 'The honour was considered the highest that the city could bestow, to judge from its prime place in most of the texts preserving a *cursus honorum* in ascending order.'[18]

The ἐφήβαρχος was responsible for the *ephebeia* whom they trained in the gymnasium. Least important of the four offices, the ἀστυνόμος (the *aedile*) was responsible for the upkeep and welfare

[14] See J. Wiseman, 'Corinth and Rome I', *ANRW* II.7.1 (1979), 498–515 and epigraphic evidence cited. See also G. Theissen, 'Social Stratification in the Corinthian Community', in *The Social Setting of Pauline Christianity: Essays on Corinth* (Philadelphia: Fortress Press, 1982) pp. 79–80.

[15] Wiseman, 'Corinth and Rome I', 499–500. Plutarch notes that 'he entertained a great many foreign visitors at once, and several times entertained all the citizens' and in addition to men of learning who were his close friends as was the case with Antonius Sospis, *Moralia,* 723.

[16] Wiseman, 'Corinth and Rome I', 498 and Theissen, *Social Setting,* p. 79. *LCL*'s translation of the term as 'general' is inadequate.

[17] Sospis was president three times during Trajan's reign, J. H. Kent, *Corinth: Inscriptions 1926–1960* (Princeton: The American School of Classical Studies at Athens, 1966), pp. 78–9.

[18] Wiseman, 'Corinth and Rome I', 519. See also D. J. Geagan, 'Notes on the Agonistic Institutions of Roman Corinth', *GRBS* 9 (1968), 69–80.

of city property, the collection of public revenue, and financial and judicial jurisdiction.[19] Epictetus also mentions that the son of a respected citizen could become a council member (βουλευτής), which required citizenship, and experience in a number of public offices. The mention of 'orator' suggests a role in the assembly or council addressing civic concerns.[20] It would seem that the final three positions – good citizen, senator, that is, member of the council, and orator – are arranged in ascending order of importance, #35. Epictetus wishes to confront the student with the notion that one's appearance, especially a 'smooth' body, could prove a liability should one pursue public office as was expected of this young man from the elite circles of Corinth. This appeal to rank and status supports E. L. Bowie's contention that sophists emerged from the powerful and wealthy families of their cities.[21]

Epictetus and sophistic declamations

Epictetus devotes a discourse to the subject of declamations entitled 'To those who read and discuss for the purpose of display' (Πρὸς τοὺς ἀναγιγνώσκοντας καὶ διαλεγομένους ἐπιδεικτικῶς)' III.23. This speech yields much to supplement our picture of sophistic activity on the Greek mainland at the turn of the century, but it has been largely overlooked in standard treatments of rhetoric. This is because, firstly, it is not immediately obvious that Epictetus refers to declamations by sophists, for he never mentions any by name, even though he does cite philosophers and orators.[22]

Secondly, the Loeb translation by W.A. Oldfather obscures the thrust of this discourse by rendering ἐπιδεικτικός as 'display' rather than the more technical term 'declamation', and 'discussion'

---

[19] F. E. Peters, *The Harvest of Hellenism* (New York: Simon and Schuster, 1970) pp. 197–8 and for a full discussion of the duties of ἀστυνόμοι see my *Seek the Welfare of the City: Christians as Benefactors and Citizens, Early Christians in the Graeco–World*) Grand Rapids and Carlisle: Eerdmans and Paternostes, 1994), pp. 185–93.

[20] ἀγοραῖοι ῥήτορες such as Dio refers to in *Or.* 34.1 where in Tarsus they may also have delivered an encomium on official occasions.

[21] E. L. Bowie, 'The Importance of the Sophists', *Yale Classical Studies* 27 (1982), 30; E. W. Bowersock, *Greek Sophists in the Roman Empire* (Oxford: Clarendon Press, 1969), pp. 21–3.

[22] #5, 20, 27, 30, 38. Stanton, 'Sophists and Philosophers', 358, notes that in the first two centuries AD epigraphic and literary evidence shows that philosophers may also be referred to as 'orators' but not as 'sophists'.

instead of 'discourse' – or, even better, 'lecture' – for it is to these activities that Epictetus refers.[23]

Thirdly, because of the deliberate distancing of the philosophers from the sophists, one easily overlooks the fact that philosophers did not disparage rhetoric even if they did criticise its misuse by their opponents. Epictetus reflects this dichotomy, II.23.46. Cicero encourages the philosopher to derive all the benefit he could from oratory and orators/sophists from philosophy. Seneca the Elder advances this same position especially with respect to the value of declamation, arguing that audiences had grown accustomed to ornate rhetoric in Rome.[24] This undoubtedly arose from the influence of Greek sophists who had gravitated to the capital with imperial blessing during the age of Augustus. Even philosophers were forced to respond to audience demands.

It has to be said that Epictetus, in this work, accurately depicts the sophists' activities, in particular declamation. Epictetus is either laying down the parameters for declamation by philosophers or this discourse constitutes an anti-sophistic attack aimed at convincing philosophers of the inappropriateness of the sophists' methods for their discourse. If it is the latter issue then the rhetorical questions Epictetus directs at the activities of the philosophers will also unlock important information (#27,38).

In referring to four 'styles' (χαρακτήρ) Epictetus discusses alongside 'exhortation', 'refutation' and 'instruction', a fourth style: ἐπιδεικτικός, 'display', or better, 'declamation', #33–4.[25] After defining 'exhortation', he notes that both the individual and the crowd pay little attention, for they seek happiness 'in the wrong place', and then he moves on to discuss public declamations by asking: 'To achieve that [happiness] must a thousand benches be placed, and the prospective audience be invited, and you put on a fancy cloak, or a dainty mantle, and mount the speaker's stand, and paint a word-picture of how Achilles died?' (#35). If the

---

23 For example Epictetus uses διαλέγειν 'to discuss', see #23, when it is explained in the following section as ἐπιδείκνυμι. Philostratus uses διαλέγειν with reference to the delivery of a formal διάλεξις, *Lives of the Sophists*, 604.

24 J. Fairweather, *Seneca the Elder* (Cambridge: Cambridge University Press, 1981), pp. 118–9, 320–3.

25 ὁ προτρεπτικός χαρακτήρ, ὁ ἐλεγκτικός, ὁ διδασκαλικός and ἐπιδεικτικός. For discussion see S. K. Stowers, *The Diatribe and Paul's Letter to the Romans*, SBL Dissertation Series 57 (Chico: Scholars Press, 1981), p. 57. Stowers however does not discuss the context of the declamation in this passage from Epictetus, and his conclusion that the reference is to 'philosophical method' is incorrect.

declaimer makes 'an unusually fine impression' one listener may say, 'That was beautiful diction in the passage about Xerxes' and the other answers, 'No, I preferred the one about the battle of Thermopylae.' Epictetus concludes his discourse by asking: 'Is this what listening to a philosopher amounts to?' #38.

Several factors again suggest that Epictetus envisages sophists rather than philosophers, and that 'the wrong place' refers to the declaimer's large lecture-hall.[26] Philosophers did not send out invitations (as Epictetus observes, #27) but the sophists did.[27] Elaborate clothing was characteristic of sophists, as we have seen.[28] And the performance did not result in the audience resolving to change their conduct: they simply measured the relative merits of the declaimer in handling this or that section. The question which concludes the discourse confirms the view that this is an anti-sophistic discourse. 'Is this what listening to a philosopher amounts to?' asks Epictetus. The whole of his discussion demands the answer 'No!' However, the discourse clearly shows that this was the sum total of what listening to a sophist declaim meant!

If our interpretation is correct, then this discourse is a highly anti-sophistic polemic. Does this reading find other corroborative evidence? There is the invitation to the house of Quadratus to 'deliver' a discourse which is described as ἐπίδειξις. When Epictetus asks why he should listen to the declaimer, for 'What good will it do?', the question receives no answer. All that is said is 'but praise me' (ἀλλ᾽ ἐπαινεσόν με). When Epictetus asks what 'praise' means, the response is: 'Cry to me "Bravo!" ' or 'Marvellous!', #23–4. Pupils described as 'young men' who have left home, family, friends and relatives likewise listen simply to cry 'Bravo!', #32. This implies that the disciples or pupils of the sophists are being discussed. The solicitation of praise after a declamation is described in a telling manner:

> The other day, when your audience gathered rather coolly, and did not shout applause, you walked out of the hall in low spirits. And again the other day, when you were received with applause, you walked around and asked

---

26 Russell, *Greek Declamation*, p. 76, n. 14 draws attention to audiences of one thousand or more seated in large and splendid halls, citing Lucian, *De domo*, I. 58. See also Dio, *Or.* 32.8–9.
27 Aristides, *Or.* 51.29.   28 See pp. 116–17.

> everybody, 'What did you think of me? . . . How did I
> render that particular passage? Which one? When I drew a
> picture of Pan and the Nymphs?'   (#10–11)

Epictetus has already mentioned this preoccupation with 'praise', #7. In contrasting declamatory activity with forensic activity by an orator, he notes the anxiety orators feel in spite of having composed a good speech, memorising it and having a pleasing voice. The anxiety arises from the rhetor's dissatisfaction with the mere practice of quality oratory, for 'he wants to be praised by his audience'. He notes that in spite of all his training, the rhetorician has not learned to handle 'praise and blame', ii.16.4ff. In the discourse on declamation there is a graphic description of declaimers who 'grasp for men to praise' them.[29] This clamouring for the praise of the audience and pupils became a constant refrain in critiques of the sophistic movement, #9.[30]

Closely linked with the audience's response is a discussion of its size. After declaiming the speaker notes, 'Today I had a much larger audience', with five hundred suggested as the number attending. 'Nonsense,' the speaker replies, 'make it a thousand.' 'Dio never had so large an audience.' 'How could you expect him to?' There is also a comparison of abilities. Of one declaimer it was said, 'This fellow has a most artistic style; it is much finer than Dio's', #17–19.[31]

Epictetus adds the audience's lack of interest in self-examination to his criticisms, for the hearers gather to learn to deliver a speech and not 'how one ought to live' (πῶς δεῖ φράζειν); and not as the philosophers urge, #17. The audience's ability to 'catch the points' is what is noted in the post-mortem conducted on the declamation of the day, #19. The desired response – 'I must not act like this any longer' – is not forthcoming. Instead one finds an exchange of views on the declaimer's diction and handling of stock subjects such as Xerxes or the battle of Thermopylae.[32]

As activities such as grasping for praise from audience and pupils and discussing audience size stand alongside the lack of concern for

---

[29] He cites his teacher, Musonius Rufus, who said 'If you have nothing better to do than to praise me, then I am speaking to no purpose', # 29.
[30] See p. 130 on Dio.
[31] The reference is apparently to Dio of Prusa, *LCL*, vol. ii, p. 174.
[32] W. A. Oldfather, *LCL*, vol. ii, p. 183, n. 3 notes that this is what Cicero called a typical *rhetorum campus, De officiis* i.61.

genuine virtue,[33] they conspire to demonstrate that Epictetus clearly engages in an anti-sophistic polemic which attacks this form of hollow oratory. He appears to be intent on steering philosophers away from it, for his questions suggest that he strongly opposes the inroads made by declamation into his profession. He is not, moreover, the first to criticise the art.[34]

In conclusion, evidence from this discourse and from that on personal adornment throws further light on what Millar calls 'life in the Greek city',[35] and as a result of this discussion the nature of sophistic activity in a city in the East. Epictetus highlights the rank and status expectations of those sufficiently wealthy, especially within the life of the Corinthian *polis*. For this reason, we agree with Millar that Epictetus should take his place as a source alongside Dio and Plutarch. Nowhere is his usefulness better demonstrated than in the case of this lively critique of the sophists' preoccupation and those of their pupils, with personal adornment, and of the sophists engaged in declamation.[36]

[33] Untersteiner, *Sophists,* xv on the sophists as specialists in teaching ἀρετή and the discussion pp. 86–9.

[34] Kennedy, *The Art of Rhetoric*, pp. 330–7. Like Seneca and Quintilian, Epictetus was critical of declamation not as a classroom exercise but rather in its failure to persuade. It had become an art form by which the declaimer promoted his ability, see especially p. 337.

[35] Elsewhere Epictetos mentions aspects of the movement. In III.8.1 he speaks of 'exercising ourselves to meet sophistic interrogations'. For a discourse involving a forensic rhetorician passing through on his way to Rome and a reference to attending lectures and declaiming, see III.9.8. Another concerns 'those who enter light-heartedly (ἐπὶ τὸ σοφιστεύειν)', III.21. He certainly sides with the philosophers against the sophists, Stanton, 'Sophists and Philosophers', 357. For derogatory connotations given by him to the sophists see III.2.11 where he notes Diogenes' insult to the sophists, and I.27.6, I.7.11, II.25.2, I.27.2, II.16.3, II.18.18, III.26.16, for use of cognates.

[36] Millar, 'Epictetus and the Imperial Court', 148.

7

DIO AND PLUTARCH AMONG THE CORINTHIAN SOPHISTS

Dio among the Corinthian sophists[1]

The eighth oration of Dio of Prusa (*c.* AD 40–112) focuses on the sophistic movement in Corinth. Together with the sixth (which also mentions the Corinthian sophists) it belongs to the corpus known as his 'Diogenes speeches', a cluster purporting to be verbatim speeches by the founder of the Cynic sect, Diogenes of Sinope, who lived *c.* 400–*c.* 325 BC. Using Diogenes allows Dio to hide behind a great person of the past 'because exile made it unwise to speak freely'. Dio chose well, for Diogenes, like Dio under Domitian, had manifested his disdain for power and suffered exile as a result.[2] The

---

For the discussion by A. D. Litfin of the rhetorical movement in Corinth see *St Paul's Theology of Proclamation: an Investigation of 1 Corinthians 1–4 and Greco–Roman Rhetoric*, SNTS Monograph Series 79 (Cambridge: Cambridge University Press, 1994), pp. 140–6. He argues that no specific corroboration is required because of the prevalence of public speaking in the mid first century, rightly supposing 'that Corinth generally mirrored the broad values of the Greco–Roman culture of which it was clearly a part', p. 143. He notes however that such corroboration does exist. In addition to obvious evidence of the βῆμα in the South Stoa of Corinth, there is the witness of Favorinus *c.* AD 80–150. He alludes to Herodes Atticus and his benefaction of the theatre in Corinth.

[1] For secondary literature on Dio, see B. F. Harris, 'Dio of Prusa: A Survey of Recent Works', *ANRW* II.33.5 (1991).

[2] The use of this device by Dio was not restricted to Diogenes, but was used with Socrates and Odysseus as well, C. P. Jones, *The Roman World of Dio Chrysostom* (Cambridge, Mass. and London: Harvard University Press, 1978), pp. 47, 49. He argues that Dio's choice of Diogenes was apt because of the latter's apparent conversation with Alexander of Macedon, and he was the chief hero of Trajan. *LCL*, vol. I, p. 249 likewise feels the speeches 'fit better the experience of Dio himself'. P. Desideri, *Dione di Prusa: un intellettuale greco nell' Impero Romano*, Biblioteca di Cultura Contemporanea, 135 (Messina: Casa Editrice G. d'Anna, 1978) p. 201, also argues that Diogenes was a 'cover' *contra* Litfin, *St Paul's Theology of Proclamation*, p. 146, n. 39, who comments 'Cf. the interesting picture of the Corinth of Diogenes' day in Dio Chrysostom, Discourse 8'. Diogenes was widely admired by the Cynics and Stoics of Dio's day. Cf. also the Cynic Epistles of the Augustan age especially 'the Epistles of Diogenes', as well as those by

information garnered from these orations can thus be regarded as Dio's assessment of the sophistic movement in Corinth during his exile, which extended from *c.* AD 89 to 96, although the recording of these orations was a little later and that is usually dated *c.* AD 100.[3] His description of Corinth is surely firsthand, for he notes the summer breezes, the Acrocorinth, the harbour and the aristocratic suburb of Craneion.[4] The sophistic activity during the Isthmian games held at Corinth is described in *Or.* 8. The speech is set in the large *temenos* of the temple of Poseidon in whose honour the games were held and were now in progress.[5]

The title of *Or.* 8, 'Diogenes' or 'On Virtue', hints at the purpose of the visit to Corinth. The city was chosen partly because of the great numbers living at what Dio calls 'the cross roads of Greece', and partly because of the great need of its many inhabitants. As ὁ φρόνιμος ἀνήρ, he compares himself to a physician who goes where he will find the greatest number of sick people. However, unlike the physician whose services arc eagerly accepted, his are not sought after, even though he can cure that which is far more important than diseases of the body, namely diseases of the soul. He offers treatment for 'folly, wickedness and intemperance', ἄγνοια, πονηρία καὶ ἀκολασία, but, he laments, 'not a man would listen to him nor seek to be cured by him, no matter how much richer he might become thereby', #8. Even non-Corinthians attending the Isthmian games would only listen briefly, 'fearing his refutation of their views', #10. He describes the sophists within a

---

Socrates and the Socratics, A. J. Malherbe (ed.), *The Cynic Epistles* (Missoula: Scholars Press, 1977).

[3] On the dating of Diogenes' speeches see H. von Arnim, *Leben und Werke des Dio von Prusa* (Berlin: 1898), p. 260; M. Szarmach, 'Les Discours Diogeniens de Dion', *Eos* (1977), 77–90; and Jones, *Roman World of Dio Chrysostom*, p. 136.

[4] *Or.* 6.3–4. It 'betrays an eyewitness', J. Murphy-O'Connor, *St Paul's Corinth Texts and Archaeology* (Wilmington: Glazier, 1983), pp. 94–5. Dio was exiled from Rome and Bithynia, but wandered in Greek-speaking lands. He was certainly in Greece at the turn of the century. See *Or.* 12, the Olympian Discourse which he delivered at the time of the games. This oration was dated by *LCL*, vol. ii, p. 1 and Murphy-O'Connor as AD 97, *St Paul's Corinth*, p. 92, but the more likely date of the visit was AD 101. See Jones' argument in *Roman World of Dio Chrysostom*, p. 53.

[5] καὶ δὴ καὶ τότε = when the games were being held. On the date of the return of the games to Corinth, see J. Wiseman, 'Corinth and Rome I', *ANRW* II.7.1 (1979), 533, and more recently E. R. Gebhard, 'The Isthmian Games and the Sanctuary of Poseidon in the Early Empire', in T. E. Gregory (ed.), *The Corinthia in the Roman Period, JRA Supp.* 8 (1994), 78–94, who argues that the games did not move immediately to Isthmia but to Corinth proper and only later to its special site.

discussion of the aims of the philosopher Diogenes, and contrasts their activities with his. Dio strives to steer men towards virtue, hence the title of the oration.[6]

> That was the time, too, when one could hear crowds of wretched sophists around Poseidon's temple shouting and reviling one another, and their disciples, as they were called, fighting with one another, many writers reading aloud their stupid works, many poets reciting their poems while others applauded them, many jugglers showing their tricks, many fortune-tellers interpreting fortunes, lawyers innumerable perverting judgement, and peddlers not a few peddling whatever they happened to have. (*Or.* 8.9)

Dio's evidence, though brief, offers significant insights into the sophists' activities. He mocks the rivalries that existed among the many 'wretched' sophists,[7] observing that they are antagonistic towards each other. Such quarrels were common, and some are well documented. G. W. Bowersock, who devotes a chapter of *Greek Sophists* to 'Professional Quarrels', notes that they can be classified as either factional and political divisions, or inter-city rivalries.[8] An example of the former is Herodes Atticus' quarrel with Polemo.[9] The latter is well demonstrated in the quarrel between Ephesus and Smyrna, which were championed by the sophists Favorinus and Polemo respectively, neither of whom was native born.[10] Such strife could sometimes lead to official or even to imperial intervention because of 'the very eminence of the sophists'.[11]

Dio also denounces the conduct of the sophists' pupils. He

---

[6] The oration begins with Diogenes' arrival in Corinth, #5–8. #9 deals with aspects of the sophistic movement and #10 sums up the response of the crowd to Diogenes beginning with εὐθὺς οὖν καὶ αὐτῷ τινές.

[7] Dio uses this term elsewhere to describe the sophists, *Or.* 11.8.

[8] G. W. Bowersock, *Greek Sophists in the Roman Empire* (Oxford: Clarendon Press, 1969), ch. 7, and p. 100, where he discusses Philostratus' evidence.

[9] For a discussion of the quarrel in Athens with Polemo see G. Anderson, *Philostratus: Biography and Belles Lettres in the Third Century A.D.* (London: Croom Helm, 1986), p. 65.

[10] *Ibid.*, p. 65. On Favorinus in Corinth see pp. 159–63.

[11] Bowersock, *Greek Sophists*, p. 100. For the discussion of social status see pp. 32–6 and especially Bowie's careful analysis of sophists, 'The Importance of the Sophists', *Yale Classical Studies* 27 (1982), which verifies and amends Bowersock's work.

describes them as 'so-called μαθηταί',[12] a phrase frequently applied to unworthy pupils of philosophers, orators and sophists.[13] They too, inevitably, engaged in intense rivalry.[14] Once pupils of a sophist were so incensed by the ridicule heaped upon their teacher that they ordered their slaves to thrash the competitor, which led to his death.[15] Though Dio's concern in this instance is with verbal abuse, #9, being the 'disciple' of a sophist instilled such loyalty and spirit of rivalry that one group often took up cudgels against another.

His discussion of disciples elsewhere further illuminates relationships between students and mentors, especially among the sophists. He communicates the degree of commitment involved in being a disciple by the use of an accompanying term, namely ζηλωτής. In *Or.* 55.3 it is asked: of which wise man was Socrates a μαθητής. Dio answers, 'Homer', and is asked, 'How would it be possible to be a zealous follower (ζηλωτής) of a person long since dead?' Dio responds 'If a ζηλωτής, then he would also be a μαθητής.'

> For whoever really follows anyone surely knows what that person was like, and by imitating his acts and words he tries as best he can to make himself like him. But that is precisely, it seems, what the pupil (ὁ μαθητής) does – by imitating his teacher and paying heed to him he tries to acquire his art . . . However, if you shrink from calling Socrates a μαθητής of Homer but call him just a ζηλωτής, it will make no difference to me.[16]

In the first discourse on kingship, Dio speaks of the ideal ruler as one who is μαθητής τε καὶ ζηλωτής τοῦ θεοῦ τούτου, that is Zeus. His success is certain because he is 'Zeus nurtured' and 'like Zeus in counsel' (cf. 'the admirer and henchman', ζηλωτής τε καὶ

---

12 *LCL* gives the wrong impression by translating οἱ λεγόμενοι μαθηταί as 'disciples as they were called'. Dio refers elsewhere to those who hold a title but behave unprofessionally and thereby deny it as 'so-called', see p. 45, n. 19 and literature cited. Their unworthy behaviour is seen here in their fighting.
13 For a survey of the term in the Greek world see K. H. Rengstorf, μαθητής *TWNT*, vol. IV, pp. 415–26 and literature cited, especially the reference to disciples of Protagoras the sophist.
14 The use of μάχομαι covers not only physical combat but also 'wrangling', 'disputing' and 'arguing' and is thus used by Plato, *Republic* 342d.
15 Bowersock, *Greek Sophists*, pp. 91–2 citing Philostratus, *Lives of the Sophists*, 588.
16 *Or.* 55.1, 3, 5.

ὑπηρέτης).[17] Here Dio combines μαθητής and ζηλωτής to claim that commitment to Zeus and zealousness for him characterise the ideal king.

This form of 'discipleship' means great personal δόξα for sophists who, like 'gorgeous peacocks' are 'lifted aloft on the wings of their fame (δόξα) and their disciples'.[18] Dio, however, is different, for he refuses to recruit any disciples, a point he reiterates in Socratic fashion. To do so would imply that he had something to teach, which he denies. He suggests ironically that he could instead help by gathering a crowd so that the sophists can 'dispose of the catch just as they wish', that is, to gain further disciples or perhaps declaim for money, but for 'some reason or other' they never accept his offer, Or. 12.13. Thus, while crowds and disciples adhere to sophists, Diogenes and Dio have neither, which is proof of their shortcomings as sophists, orators and flatterers. Diogenes has only 'long hair', notes Dio ironically. Recruiting disciples is one of the prime objectives of sophists, who love to be among 'the would-be great' in the theatre, in the camps in order to deliver an oration, or among their pupils in various communities.[19]

Having described the sophists and their disciples, Dio discusses six other groups who congregate in the temple precincts. Of these, three are directly connected with the sophistic movement.[20] First, he speaks of the forensic orators who by argument pervert justice.[21] Their presence in the temple precincts during the games, Dio explains, owes not to their soliciting business by advising the wronged of the merits of their case but to their desire to present *controversia*, such as are extant in 'Quintilian' and in the

---

17 *Or.* 1.38; 4.122.
18 Dio, *Or.* 12.5. Plutarch also notes that Theophrastus was admired because of his many disciples, *Moralia*, 78a. Cf. Anderson, *Philostratus*, p. 48, 'the prestige of the sophist began with his pupils'.
19 *Or.* 12.15; 4.14; 66.12; 77/8.27.
20 πολλοὶ μέν refers to the sophists and their disciples whose activity is subsumed under their teachers' because of the similarity of competitive conduct. πολλοὶ δέ is used five times to introduce other categories of people. μύριαι δέ refers to orators and οὐκ ὀλίγοι δέ 'peddlers of whatsoever they have'. In addition to those connected specifically with the sophistic movement, Dio comments on 'the historian' or 'prose writer' who reads aloud his 'stupid works', and the poet, who attracts no pejorative comment. Dio simply notes that others applauded his reading. There are also those who divine signs and portents whom *LCL* translates as 'fortune tellers'.
21 στρέφειν used of a wrestler trying to avoid an adversary and metaphorically of arguments; hence Dio's reference to the wrestling with justice by the many forensic orators.

papyri.[22] A second group of orators engage in *suasoria* or epideictic oratory, although this fact is not clear from *LCL*'s translation of the term as 'jugglers'.[23] They too declaim[24] and engage in θαῦμα, that is, 'rhetorical tricks'.[25] Dio's description conjures up a picture of virtuoso orators who declaim to capture the attention of the crowd.[26] The third group are poets who read their works in the temple precincts.[27]

A further reference to sophists appears in #33–6. Dio makes use of the myth of Prometheus, whose liver was consumed every day by an eagle but grew again at night until Heracles slew the bird and released him. Prometheus represents the sophists who are destroyed by the very fame they crave,[28] for their liver swells and grows when they are praised but shrivels again when censured. He attests elsewhere the response of listeners to sophists: they could applaud with great enthusiasm or shout the speaker down; they could pelt him with stones, being incensed by what was said, or listen with rapt attention; and they could jeer and hiss.[29] It was not only in Alexandria that the audience's response could make or break the performance of an orator. In Corinth too, those who sought the acclaim of the crowd could be devastated by a negative response.[30] Diogenes himself at the end of his oration drew the disapproval of the crowd and, as Dio notes, 'again the crowd of sophists raised their din, like frogs in a pond when they do not see the water snake', #36.[31]

---

[22] For discussion see pp. 31–3.

[23] θαυματοποιεῖν is used of orators who 'strain for the marvellous'.

[24] ἐπιδείκνυμι. For a discussion of this activity see pp. 31–3.

[25] Plato, *The Sophists*, 233a, τὸ τῆς σοφιστικῆς δυνάμεως θαῦμα.

[26] This interpretation of the clause is more defensible, because of the use of three rhetorical terms, than that of *LCL*, which assumes the reference is to jugglers.

[27] For the relationship of poets and orators to the sophistic movement in Alexandria see pp. 48–51. In this instance his comments are not pejorative. In the Alexandrian oration he accuses them of being motivated by the desire for personal aggrandisement and pecuniary advantage, *Or.* 32.

[28] Dio notes this elsewhere, *Or.* 32.10.

[29] *Or.* 40.6; 7.25, 39; 38.6–7; 32.11; 48.3; 34.6; 33.5; 43.3; 32.11.

[30] The solution, if indeed Dio produces one, is uncertain because of a possible lacuna after this statement. Prometheus was released and it is possible that 'being taught wisdom' was what Dio has in mind, see *LCL*, vol. I, p. 396, n. 1. Diogenes may here be likened to Heracles. Certainly there is the decision to fight unrelentingly against δόξα as much as one needs to fight against wild beasts and wicked men, #35. *LCL*, vol. I, p. 397 suggests δόξα means 'the false opinion of the crowd'.

[31] This may be a veiled reference to the singing of the sophists or a reference back to the din created by their shouting and reviling one another in #9. On 'singing' see pp. 53–4.

Dio, like Diogenes before him, derides the sophists of Corinth who crave the esteem of the crowd, and despises their arrogance, which is born of the conviction that they are intellectually superior – they 'wanted to be looked up to and thought they knew more than other men'.[32]

Thus from Dio's brief comments a helpful description of the sophistic movement in Corinth emerges. Corinth was flush with sophists, orators and poets, and the intense rivalry which seemed to arise wherever two or three were gathered together. We have seen that these quarrels did not depend only on the sophists, for the 'disciples' were also quite adept at giving and taking offence, especially when the master was not shown the deference deemed appropriate. The sophists, because of their educational prowess, believed that they knew more than others. While their activities are seen most clearly in connection with the Isthmian games, *Or.* 8.9, Dio also provides information showing that they were part of the fabric of normal activity in Corinth, *Or.* 6.21.

Favorinus, the sophist, in Corinth[33]

Favorinus of Arles (*c.* AD 80–150), a Roman of the equestrian order and an eminent pupil of Dio Chrysostom, visited Corinth three times.[34] His Corinthian oration (*Or.* 37), the text of which we will explore in an effort to supplement our understanding of sophists in Corinth, is not his first address to its citizens but was in fact delivered on his final visit. He had, on his first visit ten years earlier, impressed the δῆμος and the magistrates with his eloquence (λόγος), and established a friendly and intimate relationship with them, #1, 9.

---

[32] *Or.* 6.21. On the meaning of the term ὑβρίζω see Marshall's treatment, *Enmity in Corinth: Social Conventions in Paul's Relations with the Corinthians* (Tübingen: J. C. B. Mohr (Paul Siebeck), 1987), pp. 182–94.

[33] For literature see A. Barigazzi, *Favorino di Arelate: Opera* (Florence: Lelice Le Monnier, 1966), pp. 298–302 and discussion of his authorship of *Or.* 37 and *Or.* 64. See also my 'Favorinus', in B. W. Winter and A. D. Clarke (eds.), *The Book of Acts in its Ancient Literary Setting*, *The Book of Acts in its First-Century Setting* (Grand Rapids and Carlisle: Eerdmans and Paternoster, 1993), pp. 196–205; and M. W. Gleason, 'Favorinus and his Statue', in *Making Men: Sophists and Self-Presentation in Ancient Rome* (Princeton: Princeton University Press, 1995), ch. 1. For details of his life see Philostratus, *Lives of the Sophists*, 489–92, and Anderson, *Philostratus*, pp. 102–4. On his friendship with Plutarch see C. P. Jones, *Plutarch and Rome* (Oxford: Clarendon Press, 1971), p. 35.

[34] Jones, *Roman World of Dio Chrysostom*, pp. 58, 78. On his status see *Or.* 37.25–6 and his visits *Or.* 37.1, 8, 9.

On his second visit they were so glad to see him again that the Corinthians did everything in their power to encourage him to stay, but to no avail. However, they did erect a statue of him in the most prominent place in their library[35] in order to inspire the youth of the city to persevere in the pursuits which won such fame for Favorinus. He was greatly honoured by this gesture and took it as a token of true friendship, #8. The statue, of much-prized Corinthian bronze, spoke volumes even apart from the title which appears to have been bestowed upon him in the inscription, #10. He says he was 'set up' as 'the noblest among the Greeks' (ἄριστος Ἑλλήνων), high praise indeed for a Roman, #22.[36] He proudly accepted the title, for, as he himself reminded them, he was 'of the equestrian order' and had become a complete Hellenophile who adopted the language, thought, manner and dress of the Greeks with such mastery that no Roman past or present, or indeed any Greek, had achieved all that he had, #25.[37]

While 'the best of the Greeks' had been inclining to Rome, Favorinus favoured the rich heritage and glories of Greece at enormous political and economic cost to himself. In fact, to his

[35] He says, 'it was given a front-row seat as it were', i.e. a place of permanent and conspicuous honour. For a discussion of the seat of honour, προεδρία, and statues see A. S. Henry, 'Seats in Theatre and Stadium, Statues and Painted Portraits', in *Honours and Privileges in Athenian Decrees: The Principle Formulae of Athenian Honorary Decrees* (Hildesheim and New York: G. Olms, 1983), ch. X.

[36] On Corinthian bronzes see the comments from antiquity cited in Murphy-O'Connor, *St Paul's Corinth*, pp. 103–4. It is possible that 'the benefit of the city and all Greece' or equivalent phrases were also part of the inscription. On the title on the inscription see the importance of 'primary' and the use of superlatives, R. Ansoul, 'The Self-Estimate of the Apostle Paul Contained in II Corinthians 10 and 11', PhD dissertation, Macquarie University (1978), pp. 100–8, 123–30.

[37] His emphasis is clear, 'not . . . ἀλλά of the equestrian order'. Philostratus says of him 'though he was a Gaul he led the life of a Hellene', *Lives of the Sophists*, 489. Cf. the Greek-educated Palestinian Jew of the third century BC of whom it was said 'he was a Greek not only in his language but also in his soul', M. Hengel, *Judaism and Hellenism: Studies in their Encounter during the Early Hellenistic Period*, English translation (London: SCM Press, 1974), p. 59. For the disdain by early conservative Romans of things Greek during Cicero's time see E. S. Gruen, 'Philosophy, Rhetoric and Roman Anxieties', in *Studies in Greek Culture and Roman Policy* (Leiden: E. J. Brill, 1990), ch. V; and also J. Goldstein, 'Jewish Acceptance and Rejection of Hellenism', in E. P. Sanders (ed.), *Jewish and Christian Self-Definition: Aspects of Judaism in the Graeco–Roman Period* (London: SCM Press, 1981), pp. 69–70 where he contrasts the Jewish and Roman responses. For the wide acceptance of Hellenism in Rome during the first century AD and the encouragement of Greek scholars to come to Rome see D. A. Russell, *Greek Declamation* (Cambridge: Cambridge University Press, 1983), pp. 8–9, and G. A. Kennedy, *The Art of Rhetoric in the Roman World* (Princeton: Princeton University Press, 1972), pp. 336–77.

mind it had cost him everything, for he did not want merely to appear a Greek, but actually to be one. He had devoted himself to oratory in Athens and athletics in Sparta. Because he had pursued the study of wisdom in all the cities he visited, he had been instrumental in encouraging many Greeks to follow this pursuit. Indeed, he persuaded many barbarians to do the same, #26. He thus felt that the gods had equipped him to be a paradigm

> for the Greeks, so that the natives of that land may have an example (παράδειγμα) before them to show that culture is no whit inferior to birth with respect to renown; for the Romans, so that not even those who are wrapped up in their own self-esteem may disregard culture with respect to real esteem; for the Celts, so that no one even of the barbarians may despair of attaining the culture of Greece when he looks upon this man. #27

But despite such accomplishments, some had thrown his statue down! With such achievements to his credit he had thought it only right that Corinth should honour him. Now he wished to know who, in the light of all that he had done for Hellenism, could have perpetrated such a deed, #20. The reason for the action escaped him, and any charges against him, he suggests, were unspecified.[38]

The value of this Corinthian oration is manifold. Firstly, it provides evidence for the degree to which an orator could be admired, and the reasons for the people's praise. The citizens honour this foreigner for mastering Greek rhetoric to the point where he inspires them and their offspring to pursue it too. All Corinthian youth should emulate him, #26.[39] Favorinus believes that his case demonstrates to the Greeks that in terms of public 'renown', he is in no way inferior to those native-born Greeks.[40]

Secondly, Favorinus refers to his serving as a model for the

---

[38] According to Philostratus, the Athenians likewise threw down a statue because of his conflict with the emperor, Hadrian, *Lives of the Sophists*, 490. On the throwing down of statues see Jones, *Roman World of Dio Chrysostom*, p. 169, n. 27. On the claiming of exemption from the liturgy which is said to have caused the Athenian incident and for a discussion of his possible exile as the grounds for the removal of his statue see Bowersock, *Greek Sophists*, pp. 35–6, 41–2, 51–2.

[39] It provides an interesting parallel to the Corinthian Christians' response to the Alexandrian Jew, Apollos, see pp. 174–6.

[40] 'Renown' (τὸ δοκεῖν) refers to the decision of the Corinthians, both the Council and the People, to erect a statue of him because of his distinguished ability. τὸ παιδευθῆναι must refer to Greek *paideia* in this context.

Romans. He says that even though they are taken up with their own self-esteem (τὸ ἴδιον ἀξίωμα), they cannot disregard the traditional Greek education when it comes to real acclaim.[41] Philostratus records that Favorinus took Rome by storm when he delivered his discourses there in Greek, and it was said that even those who could not understand were captivated by 'the tone of his voice, by his expressive glances and the rhythm of his speech'. They called the *peroratio* of his oration 'The Ode', a reference to his 'singing' style.[42] So we need not discount Favorinus' self-aggrandising words as he attempts, with his comments on Roman interest in Greek *paideia*, to persuade his audience to restore his statue to its place: Roman enchantment with his delivery was well attested.

Thirdly, he says that he is also a paradigm for the Celts and the barbarians in general, who need never despair of attaining Greek *paideia*. The aspiration for and the availability of Greek *paideia* is within the grasp of the barbarians according to Favorinus, #27.[43]

Fourthly, Favorinus bears witness to the Corinthians' enthusiastic response to the sophistic movement. He 'gave [samples] of speeches' (τῶν λόγων μετέδωκα), that is, delivered an encomium and declaimed to the δῆμος and the magistrates which, he reminds them, elicited a response more indicative of 'true friendship' than that accorded by their Corinthian forebears to Arion, who composed and taught them the dithyramb, a choral song in honour of Dionysus. He speaks of his 'friendly, yes intimate terms' with them, and these he attributes directly to his speeches given on his first visit, #1.[44] He recalls the enthusiasm of the populace on his second visit and their attempts to persuade him to stay. Their affection for him and appreciation of his rhetorical gifts were such that his full-length statue was given 'pride of place' in the library as an incentive to young men to follow in Favorinus' footsteps, #8–9.[45] The

---

[41] *Paideia* refers to Roman rhetorical education which was indebted to that of the Greeks. In #27c with regard to the education of the barbarians, Favorinus uses the term ἡ Ἑλληνικὴ παιδεία, thereby specifying the nature of *paideia* open to them. This would distinguish this education from Roman *paideia*.

[42] Philostratus, *Lives of the Sophists*, 491. For the discussion of this particular trend noted by Dio in the Alexandrian orations see pp. 53–4. Philostratus also refers to another sophist, Hadrian, whose reputation was such that when it was announced he would declaim in the Athenaeum in Rome, even the members of the senate would rise from their sitting to hear him, *Lives of the Sophists*, 589.

[43] This is also attested by Philostratus, *Lives of the Sophists*, 553.

[44] For the procedures involved in 'entry' by the sophists see pp. 149–51.

[45] He calls the statue 'a mute semblance of my eloquence', #46.

'charm of his eloquence' captivated not only the men in his audience, but also 'women and children', all of whom, it is expressly stated, approved of the gift of eloquence, #33.[46]

However, the Corinthians were as fickle as they were enthusiastic. Favorinus saw the removal of his statue as an affront to 'the Greeks' and their sense of right, which was something he could not bear from a city renowned for justice. While other cities sought his services for embassies and were honouring him 'by actually erecting statues of him', the Corinthians had now in effect banished him by the removal of his statue, #16, 37. This turn of events left him baffled, for he knew of no charge against him: if he had led 'a decent life in Greece, in the midst of greater licence and indulgence', he would hardly misbehave in Rome in the presence of the emperor and 'the laws'.[47] Favorinus grudgingly suggests that all who 'lived distinguished lives' were unable to escape some censure, #33. A. D. Litfin concludes that the Corinthians 'had not the slightest compunction about standing in judgement on the orators who came before them'.[48]

Philostratus illuminates another matter related to Favorinus, namely his prolonged professional quarrels with the sophist, Polemo of Laodicea. They appear to have arisen out of inter-city rivalry between Ephesus, who favoured the former, and Smyrna, who idolised the latter, a contest Bowersock calls 'cultural'.[49] The strife continued when both men went to Rome, where it intensified. Their speeches were so saturated with invective that, according to Philostratus, even the truth of their statements could not diminish the guilt incurred by those who engaged in such disgraceful behaviour.

But Philostratus does not censure the spirit of rivalry *per se*, for,

---

[46] Litfin, *St Paul's Theology of Proclamation*, pp. 144–5, commenting on this evidence argues that the Corinthians 'loved eloquence, lionised its practitioners, and were concerned that their own youth excel in it. Moreover, this attitude was broadly based among the Corinthian populace.'

[47] *LCL*, vol. IV, p. 1, 33, n. 7 suggests, on the basis of his reference to Aphrodite, that the charge made by the Corinthians related to immorality. Philostratus notes that he was charged with adultery with the wife of a consul. He also quarrelled with the latter but the latter event is said to have been over his liturgy, *Lives of the Sophists*, 489–90.

[48] Litfin, *St Paul's Theology of Proclamation*, p. 146. However, their action was not based on Favorinus' rhetorical performance as a sophist but rather on his personal conduct and his relationship with the emperor, Hadrian.

[49] These two cities were rivals for pre-eminence in Asia Minor, Bowersock, *Greek Sophists*, p. 90 and Philostratus, *Lives of the Sophists*, 490–1.

he argues, it can be forgiven 'since human nature holds that the love of glory never grows old'. It is interesting that Philostratus should epitomise the sophists by the spirit of rivalry for he contended that 'when people called Favorinus a sophist, the mere fact that he had quarrelled with a sophist was evidence enough'.[50] He expounds further on this with an observation from Hesiod that one always competes with others engaged in the same craft.[51] Philostratus does not oppose rivalry itself, but the invective which in this case it has engendered.

Not only does Philostratus throw light on the quarrel, but he also shows how the followers of rival sophists fan the controversy. He notes that in Rome 'consulars and sons of consulars' applauded either one or the other. The status of the audience who took sides was significant. As Bowersock notes, 'Neither side could have the slightest doubt that the quarrel increased the reputations of both', and it might be added, the importance of their followers. The result was that there started between Favorinus and Polemo, 'a rivalry such as kindles the keenest envy and malice in the hearts of wise men'.[52]

Our discussion demonstrates that Favorinus confirms and supplements Dio's picture of the sophistic movement in Corinth. The former, moreover, does it not as a critic, but as a participant, and therefore is on the opposite side to Dio. Philostratus says of him that 'he is as different from Dio as any who never were his pupils', *Lives of the Sophists*, 492.

Herodes Atticus, the sophist and benefactor of Corinth[53]

The most eminent of Favorinus' pupils was Herodes Atticus of Athens (*c.* AD 101–77), a sophist who, like his mentor, spent time

---

[50] *Lives of the Sophists*, 491.   [51] Hesiod, *Works and Days*, 25.
[52] Bowersock, *Greek Sophists*, p. 91.
[53] Herodes Atticus, an Athenian, was a sophist and a great benefactor in Athens, Corinth and other Greek cities. He dedicated the theatre in Athens to the memory of his wife, Regilla, and gave the roofed theatre at Corinth, Philostratus, *Lives of the Sophists*, 551. Apart from the inscription to his wife, two other inscriptions exist, G. Kaibel, *Epigrammata Graeca ex lapidibus collecta* (Berlin, 1878), nos. 1046–7. On his visits and activities in Corinth see P. Graindor, *Un milliardaire antique: Herodes Atticus et sa famille* (Cairo: MISR, 1930), pp. 52–4, 66, 88, 121, 131–2; and J. R. Marten, 'Inscriptions at Corinth', *Hesperia* 46 (1977), 178–98. On his career see Bowersock, *Greek Sophists*, esp. pp. 22–3, 78–91, 92–100, and Anderson, *Philostratus*, pp. 108–15.

in Corinth. His reputation was such that 'For Philostratus, the Second Sophistic revolves around Herodes Atticus.'[54] Plutarch records an evening dinner spent with the intimate friends of Sospis, the president (ἀγωνοθέτης) of the Isthmian games, which Herodes Atticus, whom Plutarch described as ὁ ῥήτωρ, attended.[55] As Herodes Atticus' career unfolded he proved to be a power-wielding sophist and a great benefactor of Corinth. In March 1935 a statue base was found in the western area of Corinth near the foundations of what may have been the temple of Tyche. It contains a second-century inscription erected by the βουλή in honour of Regilla, Herodes Atticus' wife. The value of this inscription lies apart from the information it provides on Regilla, for though the statue honoured her during her lifetime, the inscription was certainly what is called an 'accolade profile' on her famous sophist husband by the Corinthian council.[56]

> [Ῥηγίλλας τ]όδ᾽ ἄγαλμα. φυὴν δ᾽ ἐχάραξε τεχνείτης
> [πᾶσαν σ]ωφροσύνην ἐς λίθον ἀραμένην.
> [Ἀττικ]ὸς Ἡρώδης μέγας ὤπασεν, ἔξοχος ἄλλων,
> [παντ]οίης ἀρετῆς εἰς ἄκρον εἰκόμενος
> [ὃν π]όσιν Ἑλλήνων ἔλαχεν περίβωτον ἁπάντων   5
> [κρέσ]σονα δ᾽ αὐτεπ<ά>ῒν ἄνθος Ἀχαιϊάδος
> [Ῥηγίλ]λα, ἡ βουλή σε Τύχην ὡς εἰλάσκουσα,
> [εἰκόνα π]ρ<ὸς> τεμένι στήσατο λαϊνέην.

This is statue of Regilla. An artist carved the figure which has translated all her prudent moderation into stone. It was given by great Herodes Atticus, pre-eminent above others, who had attained the peak of every kind of virtue, whom she took as her husband, Herodes famous among the Hellenes and furthermore a son [of Greece] greater than them all, the flower of Achaia. O Regilla, the City Council, as if hailing you, 'Tyche', has set up the marble statue before Tyche's sanctuary.[57]

We are told that this statue of Regilla, which captured all her prudent moderation (σωφροσύνη), was given by her husband who

---

54 Anderson, *Philostratus*, p. 108. It is certainly the longest discussion by Philostratus of any sophist, *Lives of the Sophists*, 545–66.
55 Plutarch, *Moralia*, 723.
56 Ansoul, 'Self-Estimate of the Apostle Paul', p. 117.
57 J. H. Kent, *Corinth: Inscriptions 1926–1960* (Princeton: The American School of Classical Studies at Athens, 1966), no. 128.

himself is described there as μέγας and 'pre-eminent above others, who had attained the peak of every kind of virtue'. He is 'pre-eminent above the Hellenes', literally 'he was destined for fame among all the Hellenes', 'greater (than them all)', 'and furthermore a son [of Greece] . . . the flower of Achaia'.[58] Such accolades were prompted by Herodes' numerous benefactions to the city of Corinth and his achievements as a sophist.[59] No other extant Corinthian inscriptions of the first half or middle of the second century surpass the superlatives heaped upon Herodes.[60] Although it is not explicitly mentioned, his rhetorical ability can be inferred from the statements concerning his fame among the Hellenes. In addition, Philostratus notes, 'And youths from all parts of the world hung on his lips, and they flocked to Athens in their desire to hear his eloquence.'[61] The inscription also demonstrates the influence and status of this famous sophist.[62]

The very existence of such testimonials to orators and sophists indicates their status in the minds of the Corinthians. Herodes Atticus' inscription belongs to a genre which is well attested especially from agonistic inscriptions.[63] This reflects the fame of this sophist upon whom the Corinthian council showered such honours.

Philostratus portrays Herodes as unabashed by the long applause of 'all Greece'; certainly he enjoyed being called 'one of the Ten', that is, Attic Orators of the canon. Rather than being embarrassed by the compliment, he replied that he was at any rate better than

---

[58] Kent's translation reads 'pre-eminent above others', which does not quite convey the city council's view that he 'was destined' (ἔλαχεν) 'to be noised abroad', i.e. famous, above all the Greeks. παῖν = παίδα = υἱόν, translated 'son (of Greece)', Regilla had one traditional virtue, Herodes excelled at them all. For a discussion of the traditional virtues, see pp. 86–7.

[59] Bowersock, *Greek Sophists*, p. 27, comments 'no sophist could match the lavish expenditure of Herodes'. For his building achievements which included the theatre at Corinth see Graindor, *Un milliardaire antique,* pp. 179–230.

[60] See Kent, *Corinth*, no. 226: Publius Aelius Sospinus, grandson of the host of Plutarch who was honoured as 'rhetor'; no. 264: (Lucius?) Maecius Faustinus, *strategos*, member of the *panhellenion* and a good orator erected in 'honour of his upright character'; no. 268: Marcus Valerius Taurinus who is described as 'a good orator erected because of his fine virtues', and no. 269: Peducaeus Cestianus, the Apollian orator for whom Corinth erected a monument.

[61] *Lives of the Sophists*, 562. On the style of his oratory see #564–5.

[62] On his imperial influence see Bowie, 'The Importance of Sophists', 52; on his famous family, see Bowersock, *Greek Sophists*, p. 27 and Philostratus, *Lives of the Sophists*, 545; and on his wife's family, #555.

[63] For a collection of such inscriptions and their relevance to 2 Corinthians 10–13 see Ansoul, 'Self-Estimate of the Apostle Paul', ch. 3, esp. p. 232, n. 78.

Andocides, the Attic orator whom Greek and Roman critics accused of stylistic faults.[64] He may have considered the praise inscribed by the Council and People inadequate.[65] The *synkrisis* of himself with Andocides was done with the greatest skill and refinement, and Philostratus describes it with the superlative, ἀστειότατος.[66]

Herodes' life was characterised by rivalries at least as much as Favorinus': his battles with a number of sophists make their way into Philostratus' account, Bowersock noting that his life was 'full of quarrels'.[67] His students, ever loyal, followed in his steps, as is demonstrated in an incident related by Philostratus concerning Herodes' most distinguished pupil, Amphicles. Philagrus of Cilicia, a sophist, was walking 'with four men of the sort that at Athens chase after the sophists', when Amphicles with other youths made a jest at his expense. In the heated exchange which followed, a barbarism fell from the lips of Philagrus and was pounced upon by Herodes' pupils, who exploited the sophistic abhorrence of such terms.[68] Philagrus shortly thereafter wrote to Herodes and accused him of failing to teach manners to his pupils, to which Herodes retorted: 'It seems to me you are not very successful with your *proemium*.' Philostratus understood this as a rebuke of Philagrus' failure 'to win the good-will of his hearers . . . a true *proemium* of a declamation'.[69]

The pupils of Herodes further humiliated Philagrus when he fell into their trap and declaimed on a subject which they themselves proposed. He accepted the topic, shouted to him by members of an audience at a public gathering, because he thought them unaware that he had elsewhere declaimed, and then published, on it. What he thought was advantage soon turned to embarrassment, however, for when he 'pretended to be improvising, they retaliated by reading the declamation aloud', exposing his use of 'stale argu-

---

[64] *OCD*, p. 63 on the Ten Attic Orators, Philostratus, *Lives of the Sophists*, 564–5. Philostratus describes Herodes' style of eloquence as being 'like gold dust shining beneath the waters of a silvery eddying river', *Lives of the Sophists*, 564.

[65] He may have wished for an explication of the inscription on his tombstone which read 'Here lies all that remains of Herodes . . . but his glory is world wide', *ibid.*, 552, 566.

[66] *Ibid.*, 564. For 'refinement', 'town-bred', cf. with the use of 'countrified', see p. 37, n. 70.

[67] Bowersock, *Greek Sophists*, pp. 93–100, for a full discussion of his quarrels.

[68] *Lives of the Sophists*, 208, n. 1. See Anderson, *Philostratus*, 44 on barbarisms as the chief enemy.

[69] *Lives of the Sophists*, 578–9. For further attempts to 'set up' a sophist see #579.

ments'. The uproar and laughter that ensued threw him into a rage, though he must have known that this recycling represented a breach of the rules governing declamation in Athens, and that the audience's response only reflected the attitude towards those who declaimed from a manuscript.[70] These incidents involving the pupils of Herodes aimed to humiliate and drive out other sophists. They show how strife and jealousy were fanned among sophists and illustrate the lengths to which followers would go to gain victory through the permanent humiliation of rival sophists.[71]

In conclusion, Herodes Atticus epitomises all that a virtuoso rhetorician should be, and was deemed worthy of the longest treatment in Philostratus' *Lives*.[72] Of his success as a declaimer there is no doubt. Furthermore he was well born and had vast financial resources[73] which he used to erect fine buildings in a city not his own, namely Corinth. The accolades bestowed upon him were meant to secure further benefactions for this city.[74] E. L. Bowie's discussion of the status of sophists surely finds its focus in this man who may rightly be called wise, powerful, and well-born.[75]

Plutarch among the Corinthian sophists[76]

Corroborating evidence for Dio's observations about the presence of orators and sophists at the Isthmian games is found in Plutarch of Chaeronea, Greece (*c.* AD 50–120) in *Quaestiones Conviviales*, a work dated between AD 99 and 116, *Moralia* 676c, 723–4f.[77]

[70] *Lives of the Sophists*, 580; Anderson, *Philostratus*, p. 45. Bowersock, *Greek Sophists*, p. 93, notes in his discussion of this passage the bad relations between these two sophists, and the rank of Amphicles, the most eminent pupil, who was of the consular class.

[71] Philostratus notes that Philagrus, although promoted to the chair of rhetoric in Rome, was nevertheless deprived of the recognition that was his due in Athens because of these incidents, *Lives of the Sophists*, 580, Anderson, *Philostratus*, p. 45. On written v. extempore speeches see pp. 205–7.

[72] In fact, he was the one around whom Philostratus wrote his *Lives of the Sophists*; see *Lives of the Sophists*, 545b–66.

[73] Bowersock, *Greek Sophists*, p. 27: 'No sophist could match the lavish expenditures of Herodes', and on his family, *ibid.*, pp. 22–3.

[74] *Ibid.*, p. 27.   [75] Bowie, 'The Importance of the Sophists', 50.

[76] For the most recent treatment of Plutarch see Jones, *Plutarch and Rome*, and D. A. Russell, *Plutarch* (London: Duckworth, 1972), and for a careful assessment of his place in the literary world of the sophists along with Dio of Prusa, see Bowersock, *Greek Sophists*, pp. 110–17, and G. R. Stanton, 'Sophists and Philosophers: Problems of Classification', *AJP* 94 (1973), 351–4.

[77] See C. P. Jones, 'Towards a Chronology of Plutarch', *JRS* 65 (1966), 72–3, for a justification of the dating.

Plutarch appears to have visited Corinth often, especially during the games. He counted among his friends Antonius Sospis, thrice president of the games during Trajan's reign,[78] who, in fulfilment of official duties, entertained 'a great many foreign visitors at once' and all the citizens several times. In addition to these 'official' commitments, Sospis gathered his closest friends, all of whom were 'scholars' (φιλόλογοι).[79] Plutarch's social interaction is also seen in his dedication of *De capienda ex inimicis utilitate* to a notable and wealthy magistrate who served Corinth for many years during Trajan's reign,[80] and in his introducing the wealthy clique with whom he mixed in Corinth during the games, which included Herodes Atticus.[81] Certainly he impresses the reader with the social status of his acquaintances in Corinth. He also informs us that on both visits orators dined at the tables of leading officials of Corinth and moved in the company of men of rank and status.[82]

In addition to evidence concerning the leading men of Corinth, Plutarch offers a glimpse of a lively circle of literary men, one of whom is said to 'have a wider acquaintance with polite literature than anyone else'. That this unnamed rhetorician was a teacher is clear from his wide knowledge of literature and, more importantly, his accompanying reputation. Designating him a 'rhetor' does not imply an inferiority to sophists, for Plutarch appears not to distinguish readily between the two.[83] Here the term 'rhetor' has a non-pejorative sense, as elsewhere in his corpus.[84]

Plutarch also briefly mentions the presentation of a palm frond

---

[78] Kent, *Corinth*, no. 97. No. 226 is an inscription to his grandson, who was an orator, in which mention is made of the status of Sospis as *agonothete* three times. See also no. 170 for an earlier inscription mentioning the holding of the office on two occasions.

[79] For a discussion of 'table talk' and the list of professions recorded see R. H. Barrow, *Plutarch and his Times* (London: Chatto & Windus, 1967), p. 20.

[80] Wiseman, 'Corinth and Rome I', 507 and epigraphic evidence n. 272.

[81] This raises the question of the date of birth of Herodes Atticus, which is usually given as *c.* AD 101. However, as Plutarch mentions his presence at a dinner and also one of Herodes' pupils having won a contest with an encomiastic oration, it would seem his date of birth should be brought forward, see *Moralia*, 723b.

[82] In both instances when recording his visit he mentions a dinner given by officials of the games. In *Moralia*, 675d he mentions Lucanius, 'the chief priest' who gives the dinner, and Praxiteles, 'the official guide', *Moralia*, 723. See Bowie, 'The Importance of the Sophists', 30.

[83] Plutarch, *Moralia*, e.g. 59f, 235e, 447e, 788d, 1000d, 1087b.

[84] Plutarch does refer to orators and sophists elsewhere who are motivated by repute and ambition (δόξα and φιλοτιμία), others by money (μισθός) and others still by political rivalries, e.g. *Moralia* 131a, but the terms are not used pejoratively of other groups.

and plaited wreath by a pupil to his teacher, Herodes Atticus, as 'a special honour' at the dinner. It was won at a competition in an encomiastic oration at the games.[85] The 'special honour' may not refer to the winning of the prize by the pupil, but rather to its presentation to his teacher as a sign of recognition that the teacher was responsible for the prize. Having accepted the compliment, Herodes returned it to its proud owner. Dio's comment that the sophists are 'like gorgeous peacocks . . . lifted aloft on the wings of their fame and their disciples' is perhaps illustrated in this incident. The passage also reflects something of the relationship between the sophist and his disciple, for, as Anderson notes, 'The prestige of a sophist began with his pupils.'[86]

Plutarch often criticises the sophists.[87] Like Dio and Philo he notes that some orators and sophists are led by 'repute and ambition' (δόξα καὶ φιλοτιμία), others by 'pecuniary interests' (μισθός), and still others engage in rivalries for political supremacy.[88] In contrast with philosophers, sophists are shown to be motivated by selfish ambition and to care little for their audience or their disciples' welfare.[89]

Bowersock notes that Dio and Plutarch flourished 'on the eve of the most colourful period of the Second Sophistic; and although not a part of it, their lives adumbrated many of its pronounced characteristics'.[90] He refers to their imperial service, which included a procuratorship in Achaia for Plutarch.[91] In addition, both men addressed the magistrates and citizens of the cities, and the elite of the East and emperors of Rome.

Conclusion

The sources discussed in these two chapters round out our understanding of the sophistic movement in Corinth as they present it from the viewpoint of its opponents and its chief protagonists.

Epictetus reveals the preoccupations of a student of rhetoric in Corinth and of the sophists of his day. Dio and Plutarch place

---

[85] *Moralia* 723a. For this form of oratory see D. A. Russell and N. G. Wilson, *Menander Rhetor* (Oxford: Clarendon Press, 1981), pp. xiii–xv.
[86] Dio, *Or.* 12.5. Anderson, *Philostratus*, p. 48.
[87] Stanton, 'Sophists and Philosophers', 351–3, for a survey of the term.
[88] *Moralia*, 131a.
[89] Stanton, 'Sophists and Philosophers', 351–3, and Jones, *Plutarch and Rome*, p. 14.
[90] Bowersock, *Greek Sophists*, p. 112.   [91] *Ibid.*, p. 111.

orators alongside athletes as major public figures, though orators hold greater influence. Dio also provides an image of orators and their disciples as they participate in daily life in the city.

The esteem afforded orators shines through the words of those who visited Corinth. Favorinus describes the enthusiastic response he received from all levels of society: they were taken by his eloquence and concluded that this foreign orator, a complete Hellenophile, was the paradigm for the Greeks, Romans and barbarians living there. He also recounts how the council and the people erected a full-length statue of him which bore an inscription in the agonistic genre that he was 'the noblest among the Greeks'. What that inscription only implied became explicit in the one where Herodes Atticus, the great sophist and benefactor of Corinth, was praised. The self-estimate of both Favorinus and Herodes is thus clearly attested and probably accords with the opinion of the city fathers and the magistrates of Corinth.

What Dio merely notes about the professional jealousy of sophists and their disciples Philostratus documents in some detail in the cases of Favorinus and Herodes Atticus. The 'table talk' of Plutarch also indicates the access of orators and sophists to the upper strata of Corinthian society.

There can be no doubt, then, that sophists and their students were prominent in Corinth and played an important role in the life of the city. This survey does not, however, establish that the dislocation reflected in Paul's Corinthian correspondence was caused by the sophistic tradition and Christian sophists. That proposition needs to be demonstrated from a discussion of the text itself in the following chapters, but we have at least provided a foundation for such a task by showing that sophists were a major force in first-century Corinth.

8

PAUL AND SOPHISTIC CONVENTIONS

Introduction

The next three chapters will explore the relationship between the sophistic movement and Paul's Corinthian correspondence.[1] This chapter will examine Paul's description of his initial coming to Corinth and an explanation for his conduct while based there (1 Cor. 2.1–5 and 1 Cor. 9). The latter presumes his readers' awareness of conventions observed by orators and sophists at work in the cities of the East. It will be argued that Paul deliberately adopts an anti-sophistic stance and thus defends his church-planting activities in Corinth against a backdrop of sophistic conventions, perceptions and categories. The reaction of the Corinthians to the Christian evangelists and teachers will then be examined, revealing that Paul's converts formulated a sophistic conception of 'discipleship', which in turn exposed the churches to the inevitable problems of dissension and jealousy associated with that secular movement. This problem was aggravated to some extent by the *modus operandi* of Apollos who arrived in Corinth subsequent to Paul's departure (1 Cor. 1.12, 3.1–5). Paul's critique of the sophistic tradition as presented in 1 Corinthians 1–4 is then discussed in chapter 9.

In chapter 10, 'Paul among the Christian sophists', it will be argued that Paul's critique of the sophistic tradition angered at least some in the congregation, namely those wise by the world's

---

[1] Paul's first visit, with his *apologia* and the nexus between his preaching and an appropriate lifestyle, are discussed in 1 Cor. 1–4 and 9, and a subsequent development in the history of the church after Apollos declined the invitation to return (1 Cor. 16.12) in 2 Cor. 10–13. Debate over the number and presence of Corinthian letters within that corpus does not affect the overall discussion which focuses on 1 Cor. 1–4, 9 and 2 Cor. 10–13. For the most radical division see W. Schmithals, 'Die Korintherbriefe als Briefsammlung', *ZNW* 63 (1972), 263–88, and cf. the measured comments of J. C. Hurd Jr., *The Origin of 1 Corinthians* (London: SPCK, 1965), pp. 43–7, which applies equally to 2 Cor.

standards (1 Cor. 3.18). Along with other anti-Paulinists in the church, they had become 'puffed up' in the face of his inability to return to Corinth at that point (1 Cor. 4.18–19). In fact, the congregation as a whole had been persuaded to solicit Apollos' return despite their loyalty to different teachers – an invitation which Apollos was to reject for the present (1 Cor. 16.12). Subsequently the church appointed men with Greek rhetorical training to teach the congregation. Did these teachers have access to Paul's critique of the sophistic tradition? It seems so, for they ridiculed his performance as a public speaker by drawing on categories from his own *apologia* and critique of the sophistic tradition found in 1 Corinthians 1–4 and 9. Their criticisms can be recovered from 2 Corinthians 10.10 and 11.6, and are supplemented by an allusion to his 'sophistic' attitude towards money (2 Cor. 12.16–18).

The opening discussion of chapter 10, 'The assessment of Paul as orator and debater', is then followed by an analysis of Paul's assessment of the Christian sophists. In 2 Corinthians 10–13 Paul engages in an extensive critique, not this time of the sophistic tradition as it had been imbibed by the Corinthian congregation, but of that same tradition as possessed and promoted by the new teachers in the church.

Chapters 8–10 will thus discuss Paul's interaction with oratory in so far as it sheds light on the situation in the Corinthian church. These chapters do not address the wider issue of Paul's rhetorical style[2] (although there are implications for it). Such concerns do not come within the purview of this book which deals with a more specific topic: the impact of the sophists on the Corinthian church.

Was J. Munck correct when he described the situation which Paul faced in Corinth as follows? 'The apostle . . . suddenly sees himself compared with a professional sophist . . . [with] a theme on which to improvise . . . Christianity [as] a kind of wisdom, its leaders teachers of wisdom [sophists], and themselves [the Cor-

---

[2] For a summary of the history of discussion on Paul's use of rhetoric from the Church Fathers onwards through Erasmus, Melanchthon, Luther and Calvin, see H. D. Betz, 'Rhetoric and Theology', in A. Vanhoye (ed.), *L'Apôtre Paul: Personnalité, Style et Conception du Ministère* (Leuven: Leuven University Press, 1986), pp. 16–21, although he gives more attention to recent discussion, namely J. Weiss and R. Bultmann. His interests are restricted to Galatians and/or Romans. See also the helpful survey in F. W. Hughes, 'The Rhetoric of Letters', in *Early Christian Rhetoric and 2 Thessalonians* (Sheffield: Sheffield Academic Press, 1989) ch. 2.

inthians as] . . . wise men who had drawn on that wisdom through the Christian leaders.'[3] To this question, and to the more important matter of how Paul dealt with the problems of 'sophistic' Christianity, we now turn.

Paul's anti-sophistic coming and conduct: 1 Corinthians 2.1–5; 9

In 1 Corinthians 2.1–5 and 1 Corinthians 9 Paul defends his *modus operandi* in coming to Corinth to establish a Christian community. The *apologia* of these sections depends heavily on rhetorical language and allusions. It shows that his approach has been shaped by his message and that he rejects the conventions associated with public orators in that city.

Paul's anti-sophistic 'coming': 1 Corinthians 2.1–5

1 Corinthians 2.1–5 has been variously assessed as 'a digression' in the argument,[4] a 'simple testimony',[5] and 'the clearest and most detailed statement – both positive and negative – of the Apostle's manner of preaching to be found anywhere in his writings'.[6] Munck argues that the Corinthians did not receive Paul's wisdom or man's wisdom and hence should not boast in their leaders.[7] Others have designated this passage 'anti-rhetorical',[8] or as indicative of the following: 'the commencement of Paul's theme of personal shame in socio-cultural terms';[9] the renunciation of 'the

---

[3] J. Munck, 'The Church without Factions', in *Paul and the Salvation of Mankind* (London: SCM Press, 1959), p. 154.

[4] W. Wuellner, 'Haggadic Homily Genre in 1 Corinthians 1–3', *JBL* 89 (1970) 201. Because this passage does not fit into his thesis of the homily he sees it as Paul's digression from the *haphtarah* from the prophets (1.20–5), a Torah *seder* (1.26–31), and *haphtarot* from the Prophets and the Writings (2.6–16). He notes the legitimacy of this digression which he labels a stylistic feature in his *halakic* discussion.

[5] C. K. Barrett, *The First Epistle to the Corinthians* (London: A. & C. Black, 1971), p. 64, suggests that because of Paul's inability to match the eloquence and wisdom of the Greek world, he wisely fixes his attention on one theme.

[6] A. D. Litfin, *St Paul's Theology of Proclamation: an investigation of 1 Corinthians 1–4 and Greco-Roman Rhetoric*, SNTS 79 (Cambridge: Cambridge University Press, 1994), p. 204.

[7] J. Munck, '1 Thess. 1. 9–10 and the Missionary Preaching of Paul: Textual Exegesis and Hermeneutic Reflexions', *NTS*, 9 (1962-3), 106.

[8] C. M. Horne, 'The Power of Paul's Preaching', *Bulletin of the Evangelical Society* 8 (1965) 112, 115.

[9] P. Marshall, *Enmity in Corinth: Social Conventions in Paul's Relations with the Corinthians* (Tübingen: J. C. B. Mohr (Paul Siebeck), 1987), p. 389.

grand style' of rhetoric[10] or of the epideictic branch of oratory;[11] his refusal to adopt the rhetorical practices of other Christian preachers in Corinth;[12] his renunciation of all technical rhetorical devices in his gospel presentation;[13] the use of a Socratic–Cynic *topos* to establish the consistency of his method with a theology of a crucified Messiah;[14] and the Pauline defence of conduct which placed him in a powerless position in relation to the status structure of Corinth.[15]

In order to establish that this explanation is framed in anti-sophistic language three issues need to be addressed. Firstly, what do we know about sophistic conventions regarding the initial visit to a city by an orator seeking to establish a reputation as a professional speaker? Secondly, is Paul alone in his concern for the appropriate correlation of message and method? Thirdly, is Paul not ultimately endeavouring to establish πίστις in his hearers as he insists in verse 5? Rhetorical handbooks have much to say about this technical term as well as the other rhetorical language Paul uses or alludes to in these verses. That such technical language dominates the passage has been recognised even by those who reject a sophistic background to 1 Corinthians 1–4.[16] An appreciation of these terms will help elucidate the nature of Paul's defence before both friends and critics in the Corinthian church.

[10] E. A. Judge, 'Paul's Boasting in Relation to Contemporary Professional Practice', *Australian Biblical Review* 16 (1968), 38.

[11] J. Weiss, *Der erste Korintherbriefe* (reprinted Göttingen: Vandenhoeck & Ruprecht, 1977), p. 51.

[12] T. H. Lim, 'Not in Persuasive Words of Wisdom, but in Demonstration of the Spirit and Power', *NovT* 29.2 (1987), 147–8.

[13] L. Hartman, 'Some Remarks on 1 Cor. 2.1–5', *Svensk Exegetisk Årsbok* 39 (1974), 117.

[14] H. D. Betz, *Der Apostel Paulus und die sokratische Tradition: eine exegetische Untersuchung zu seiner 'Apologie' 2 Korinther 10–13* (Tübingen: J. C. B. Mohr (Paul Siebeck), 1972), pp. 55–7.

[15] R. F. Hock, *The Social Context of Paul's Ministry: Tentmaking and Apostleship* (Philadelphia: Fortress Press, 1980) pp. 59–60. See also F. S. Darrow, 'The History of Corinth from Mummius to Herodes Atticus', PhD dissertation, Harvard University (1906), p. 167, who concludes from this passage that Paul's preaching was emotional rather than predominantly rational.

[16] W. Schmithals, *Gnosticism in Corinth*, English translation (Nashville, Abingdon Press, 1971), p. 142. 'Paul sets himself against the rhetorically elaborated eloquence which the Hellenist treasured in the highest manner and regarded as a necessary precondition for any genuine education.' Yet his subsequent discussion ignores this and proceeds with the treatment of *gnosis*.

The coming of a sophist

Extant sources allow us to reconstruct the conventions which surrounded the initial arrival of a sophist in a city. In the first and second centuries AD there were high honours to be obtained by the sophist if he could successfully establish himself in both *politeia* and *paideia*. Naturally the citizenry expected the sophist to reciprocate by contributing to the welfare of the city; for example he might provide benefactions and make himself politically useful by serving as a spokesman of an embassy to a proconsul or the emperor for obtaining concessions or resolving inter-city rivalry. Thus it was mutually beneficial for a city to grant citizenship to a sophist. The entire process, however, began with an initial visit during which the sophist gave a sample of his eloquence and, if he passed this preliminary test, ended when he received endorsement to the advantage of both sides. At the commencement of an oration Favorinus reminds the Corinthians of his initial visit to the city when he 'gave a sample' of his eloquence by which he established friendly, indeed intimate, terms with the δῆμος and the magistrates.[17]

D. A. Russell cites Aristides' initial visit to Smyrna in AD 176 to illustrate the conventions followed by sophists upon entering a city.[18] The people came out to greet the orator, to whom 'the most distinguished' of young men offered themselves as students. A lecture was planned and an invitation to attend was issued which was 'exactly fulfilled in every detail'.[19] However, before all these arrangements could be finalised, Aristides had 'a dream' telling him to declaim at the council chamber at ten o'clock on that very day. 'An advertisement was put out' and this 'impromptu' appearance was hastily arranged. Although 'most people knew nothing about it', the council chamber was tightly packed. The preliminary speech, delivered sitting down, was followed by the declamation, presented standing up. It was received by an enthusiastic audience held spellbound throughout. His concern that a rival sophist, 'an Egyptian' who happened to be declaiming in the Odeion on that day at two days' notice, might steal his thunder, may account for his sudden decision to declaim the same day. The result was an

---

[17] See *Or.* 37.1 and p. 135.
[18] D. A. Russell, *Greek Declamation* (Cambridge: Cambridge University Press, 1983), pp. 76–7 citing *Or.* 51.29–34.
[19] *Discourse* 51.29. Russell, *Greek Declamation*, pp. 76–7.

overwhelming victory by Aristides.[20] Of interest are (1) the advance publicity for the performance and (2) the proceedings which began with the introductory speech and were followed by the declamation. The sophists, always competitive, were anxious to impress. They wished to attract not only young men of the elite but also an invited audience, and ultimately an even wider group who might wish to hear the sophist declaim in a larger meeting, for which they would pay.

Philostratus records initial visits by three sophists intent on establishing their reputations in Athens. When Polemo first visited Athens, Philostratus notes with surprise, he broke with convention in that he did not give an encomium when 'there are so many things that one might say in honour of the Athenians'. He also 'did not make a long oration about his own renown', called the διάλεξις, which was customary and was intended 'to win favour for sophists in their public declamations'.[21] This neglect was attributed to his arrogance, an assessment corroborated by the fact that he declaimed immediately after the topic had been agreed upon – by no means a universal practice.[22] The thrust of Philostratus' account is that Polemo succeeded despite violating established conventions.

On the other hand, Philagrus of Cilicia, a sophist of considerable reputation, failed to impress because of his quarrel with Herodes Atticus. The audience became ill disposed towards him when he digressed to lament his late wife during his encomium to the citizens. Convention was further breached with humiliating results when his oration, which had been published elsewhere, was read aloud by the disciples of Herodes as he delivered it, as noted in chapter 7. Philagrus had dared repeat what custom decreed must be an original creation which would test his prowess in extempore oration. He subsequently declaimed in the theatre of Agrippa and the council chamber of the powerful theatrical artisans, but by then his reputation was irreversibly tarnished. Philostratus further observed his unbecoming appearance and a weakness of voice which

---

[20] *Discourse* 51.34. The Egyptian managed to attract only seventeen, which was the traditionally derisory number, as Russell, *Greek Declamation*, p. 77, n. 16 argues.

[21] *Lives of the Sophists*, 535; Russell, *Greek Declamation*, p. 79. E. Anderson, *Philostratus: Biography and Belles Lettres in the Third Century A.D.* (London: Croom Helm, 1986), p. 45 comments on Polemo's action 'this was simply not professional behaviour'.

[22] The conventions also allowed for one day to prepare the speech, *Lives of the Sophists*, 535, Russell, *Greek Declamation*, p. 80.

was the 'result of his choleric disposition'.[23] This surely contributed to his failure before the Athenians, for to them 'presence' (ὑπόκρισις) was an essential criterion of a good sophist. Philagrus later held the chair of rhetoric in Rome, but even that glory could not erase the memory of his professional 'misconduct' and great humiliation in Athens.[24]

If Philagrus failed in part because of his encomium, Alexander of Seleucia, the third newcomer to Athens, succeeded. This was because his διάλεξις was a panegyric of the city, and his ἀπολογία flatteringly explained why he had not visited even earlier. It was of 'the appropriate length, for it was like the epitome of a Panathenaic oration'.[25]

Finally, Dio in an oration delivered at the turn of the first century, gives a glimpse of the reception a famous speaker could expect when he visited 'the greatest cities' of the empire. He writes that he was 'escorted with much enthusiasm and éclat (φιλοτιμία), the recipients of my visits being grateful for my presence and begging me to address them and advise them (λέγειν καὶ συμβουλεύειν) and flocking about my doors from early dawn, all without my having incurred any expense or having made any contribution.'[26]

Our brief survey reveals that upon a sophist's first 'coming' to a city he was expected to observe certain conventions and by such means establish his reputation as a speaker. There was the introduction – often an encomium to the city – which could colour the audience's response to the declamation as a whole. The performances, not restricted by custom to any one place, could be delivered in a large lecture room or a theatre. They could be initiated by a personal invitation to attend a private lecture or a general invitation to a public performance. In reality the sophist was on trial, for the citizens who heard him determined his success or failure in that city, the possibility of the latter being high. But those who met with success reaped its fruit: an enhanced reputation and pecuniary gain. Paul, on the other hand and for reasons to be explained below, rejected these conventions when he came to Corinth.

---

[23] *Lives of the Sophists*, 579, and discussion pp. 140–1.
[24] *Lives of the Sophists*, 580.   [25] *Lives of the Sophists*, 572.
[26] *Or*. 47.22, where the last reference is to the promise of benefactions for the city by the sophists. See Epictetus III.23.23 for the convention of inviting a popular speaker into a private house to hear a distinguished speaker.

The relationship between method and message

There are parallels between Dio's *apologia* (*Or.* 47) and Paul's defence (1 Cor. 2.1–5) which help explain why the apostle might have adopted an unconventional stance. In an address to his native Prusa *c.* AD 102, Dio begins by warning his audience not to expect, when he rises to speak, a discourse which is 'extraordinary' or 'remarkable'.[27] The words 'when I rise' indicate that Dio refers to declaiming, an observation further supported by the following statement in which he explains the type of discourse he will not be offering: 'one composed to produce a kind of pleasure or to exhibit beauty or σοφία'. He suggests ironically that this is beyond his capacity, indeed he has 'forgotten' how to declaim at this moment; he is not now equal to 'that sort of thing' and his past efforts are to be attributed purely to good luck. He had been able to deceive 'the public and all the cities' – but no longer.[28] Later in the oration he returns to this use of irony, instructing the audience not to expect any 'high-minded' (μεγαλόφρων) or 'sage' address, but an 'amateurish and commonplace' one which was appropriate to the concerns of the speech.[29]

The issues to which Dio refers are by no means insignificant, for they relate to a scheme dear to his heart: the beautification of his home city. The project in the beginning had commended itself to the citizens who had promised to help defray its cost.[30] He had canvassed the support of the assembly, the council and the proconsul, and subsequently addressed the citizens in the theatre in order to secure their backing for this important civic undertaking. But now opponents had persuaded certain benefactors to withhold promised support from the project, so Dio had to engage in 'a powerful *apologia*'.[31]

The purpose of this *apologia* determined the λόγοι that Dio would employ: 'For a man's words must needs be coloured by the nature of what he is doing and in which he is engaging.'[32] His

---

[27] *Or.* 47. 1.
[28] For an excellent treatment of Dio's problem and its background see C. P. Jones, *The Roman World of Dio Chrysostom* (Cambridge, Mass. and London: Harvard University Press, 1978), ch. 12.
[29] *Or.* 47. 8.   [30] *Or.* 45.13, 40. 6.
[31] B. F. Harris, 'Bithynia: Roman Sovereignty and the Survival of Hellenism', *ANRW* II. 7. 1 (1980), 892. See also Jones, *Roman World of Dio Chrysostom*, p. 113.
[32] παραπλήσις ('nearly resembling', 'coming alongside') used by Plato of sophists and orators. Cf. *Gorgias*, 520a.

modus operandi could be defended in contrast to the 'pettiness' of his opponents and their inglorious behaviour. He says that his response will be commensurate with the actions and criticisms of his opponents and will therefore be 'amateurish' and 'commonplace'. It could not take the form of an eloquent declamation. Thus Dio's feigned loss of memory concerning declamation was a vital part of his invective, drawing attention to his adversaries' misconduct and denying the audience what they most desired from this golden-tongued orator: a declamation.[33] As will be shown, Paul's *modus operandi* likewise provided reasons for not dressing his message in rhetorical finery.[34]

Rhetorical terms and allusions

Important rhetorical terms and allusions appear in 1 Corinthians 2.1–5. They must be understood in their own right before we can assess Paul's use of them. In his extended treatment of rhetoric Aristotle connected πίστις, 'confidence' or 'conviction', with the combined and simultaneous application of three proofs: τὸ ἦθος τοῦ λέγοντος, τὰ πάθη, and ἀπόδειξις.[35] He argued: 'The orator persuades by ἦθος, when his speech is delivered in such a manner as to render him worthy of confidence . . . [it] constitutes the most effective means of proof.'[36] ἦθος has been summarised as 'establishing the persuader's good character and hence credibility'.[37] The speaker had 'to project a sympathetic image of himself' as a likeable and trustworthy person. To make the necessary impression he had to 'identify and study the specific qualities of his audience' and be able to anticipate their response.[38] This par-

---

[33] Cf. the oration of Aristides, 'To those who criticise him because he does not declaim' esp. *Or.* 33.24–5, where he refuses to declaim because of the ingratitude of the young men of the city who gave lip-service to his greatness as an orator but neglected his lectures.

[34] See pp. 155–61.

[35] *Rhetoric*, I.I.1356a, discussed by F. Solmsen, 'Aristotle and Cicero on the Orator's Playing on Feelings', *CP* 33 (1938) 393–4. See also his 'The Aristotelian Tradition in Ancient Rhetoric', *AJP* 62 (1941), 35–50, and its later influence *ibid.*, 169–190.

[36] *Rhetoric*, I.II. 4.

[37] R. A. Lanham, *A Handlist of Rhetorical Terms* (Berkeley and London: University of California Press, 1968). See also G. A. Kennedy, *New Testament Interpretation through Rhetorical Criticism* (Chapel Hill: University of North Carolina Press, 1984), p. 15.

[38] Russell, *Greek Declamation*, p. 8, and esp. p. 87. In declamations, ἦθος was of great importance because a speaker had to project himself into the character of an

ticular πίστις, 'character', was thus an important means of swaying an audience.

The second πίστις, πάθος, refers to 'playing on the feelings' of an audience. Aristotle discusses the ten πάθη at length, first defining each one, then elaborating on the definition and outlining the circumstances under which they could be evoked, the type of person in whom they will be aroused, and against whom they could be directed.[39] Cicero endorsed Aristotle's view that one of the prime objectives of the rhetorician's activity was τό εἰς πάθη ἄγειν τὸν ἀκροατήν.[40]

The term ἀπόδειξις, used by Paul in verse 5, means, according to Quintilian, 'a clear proof', 'a method of proving what is not certain by means of what is certain'. Cicero defines it as 'a process of reasoning that leads from things perceived to something not previously perceived'.[41] J. Wisse observed that in broad terms *ethos* was bound up with the sender, *pathos* with the effect of the message on the receiver, and arguments with the contents of the message itself.[42] These three πίστεις constituted the proofs or techniques by which an orator sought to persuade his audience.

Other rhetorical terms are used by Paul in verses 1 and 5, for example the 'power' (δύναμις) of verse 5. Aristotle adopts Isocrates' definition of rhetoric as the 'power' (δύναμις) of discovering the possible means of persuasion, and 'eloquence' as the 'power of speaking' (δύναμις τοῦ λέγειν). Quintilian notes that a standard definition of rhetoric in his day was 'the power of persuasion', *vis persuadendi*. Standing behind 'power', as his text makes clear, is the Greek term δύναμις. Dio Chrysostom refers to the gift of eloquence

---

ancient person and sound authentic. See also W. Süss, *Ethos* (Leipzig: Teubner, 1910), W. Kroll, ''Εν ἤθει', in R. Stark and P. Steinmetz (eds.), *Rhetorika: Schriften zur aristotelischen und hellenistischen Rhetorik* (Hildesheim: Georg Olms Verlag, 1968), ch. 13; and J. Wisse, *Ethos and Pathos from Aristotle to Cicero*, (Amsterdam: Hakkert, 1989).

39 *Rhetoric*, I. 2.2–11.
40 Solmsen, 'Aristotle and Cicero', 390–404, esp. 401. He also discusses the important evidence of Quintilian, 395–6. See also G. A. Kennedy, *The Art of Rhetoric in the Roman World* (Princeton: Princeton University Press, 1972), pp. 221–4 on Aristotle's influence on Cicero's placing ἦθος on a par with πάθος and ἀπόδειξις and more recently Wisse, *Ethos and Pathos*.
41 J. Martin, *Antike Rhetorik: Technik und Methode*, (Munich: C. H. Beck'sche Verlag, 1974), p. 102; Quintilian, v.10.7, Cicero, *Academica*, II. 8. For further discussion see pp. 159–60.
42 Wisse, *Ethos and Pathos*, p. 6. The concepts are more complex and he himself notes that further work on post–Ciceronian authors needs to be done to clarify later treatment, *ibid.*, 315–6.

simply as δύναμις.[43] The noun πειθώ (verse 5), an appellative which means 'persuasiveness', likewise often appears in definitions of 'rhetoric', for rhetoric is the art of persuasion.[44] The term ὑπεροχή which also appears in verse 1 Aristotle uses to describe the superiority men feel based on γένος, δύναμις and ἀρετή, and he also observes the superiority of the eloquent over against the incompetent speaker in the matter of oratory.[45]

1 Corinthians 2.1–5 reveals a distinct constellation of rhetorical terms and allusions, a point conceded even by those who ultimately neglect the sophistic background of the Corinthian situation.[46]

Paul and his coming

The survey has shown that standardised conventions controlled the initial arrival of sophists who sought recognition by a city's elite.[47] Is Paul in 1 Corinthians 2.1–5 contrasting his coming to Corinth with established sophistic conventions? If he is, does his choice of rhetorical terms and allusions show that his *modus operandi* was a calculated anti-sophistic stance adopted to replace conviction derived from sophistic rhetorical wisdom with confidence in the power of God? A number of observations suggest an affirmative answer.

1 Corinthians 2.1–5, in referring back to Paul's 'coming' to Corinth,[48] divides into two sub-sections, each introduced by κἀγώ (verses 1, 3). The autobiographical κἀγώ, 'I for instance' or 'I also' introduces the evangelistic method which he adopted upon his arrival and used throughout his visit (verses 1–4), and points to his overall purpose as stated in the final clause (verse 5). It is an autobiographical account of why he will not preach the message of the cross using 'the wisdom of words' (cf. 1 Cor. 1.17) and why the

---

[43] Aristotle, *Rhetoric*, I.II.2.1; Quintilian, II.15.2–4; Dio Chrysostom, *Or.* 33. 3.
[44] For a discussion of this word's etymology see R. G. A. Buxton, *Persuasion in Greek Tragedy: A Study of peitho* (Cambridge: Cambridge University Press, 1982), pp. 10–20, 48–53.
[45] *Rhetoric*, II. 2.7.
[46] Schmithals, *Gnosticism in Corinth*, p. 142. Cf. U. Wilkens, *Weisheit und Torheit*, (Tübingen: J. C. B. Mohr (Paul Siebeck), 1979) p. 505.
[47] See pp. 149–51.
[48] κἀγὼ ἐλθὼν πρὸς ὑμας . . . ἦλθον (verses 1–2), κἀγὼ . . . ἐγενόμην πρὸς ὑμας (verse 3) with a final clause ἵνα (verse 5). On the highlighting by Paul of his 'coming' in verses 3–4, see Weiss, *Der erste Korintherbriefe*, p. 47; H. Conzelmann, *The First Epistle to the Corinthians*, English translation (Philadelphia: Fortress Press, 1975), p. 54.

one who glories should only glory in the Lord, citing Jeremiah 9.23–4.[49] Verse 1 is constructed in such a way as to focus not on the fact of his physical arrival but on the stance he adopted when he arrived. κἀγὼ ἐλθὼν πρὸς ὑμᾶς, ἀδελφοί, ἦλθον οὐ καθ' ὑπεροχὴν λόγου ἢ σοφίας καταγγέλλων ὑμῖν τὸ μυστήριον τοῦ θεοῦ. He wishes to inform the Corinthians that he did not come καθ' ὑπεροχὴν λόγου ἢ σοφίας.[50] The sentence has been translated either, 'I did not come proclaiming to you the testimony[51] of God in lofty words or wisdom', or as 'When I came to you I did not come in such a way as to distinguish myself in eloquence or wisdom.'[52] In the latter rendering καθ' ὑπεροχὴν is connected with ἦλθον and not καταγγέλλων. The preposition κατά is taken as a reference to the manner of Paul's coming, that is, 'not with the superiority of eloquence or wisdom'.[53] It was Aristotle who drew attention to the superiority felt by those trained in oratory because of their eloquence.[54] With the stress on ἐλθών/ἦλθον and the use of κατά to describe his manner, it appears that the emphasis rests on Paul's conscious rejection of the superiority of rhetoric in the *modus operandi* of his gospel and not the fact that he simply arrived in Corinth. Dio

49 Barrett, *The First Epistle to the Corinthians*, p. 62, translates κἀγὼ as 'it was in line with this principle'.
50 The terms λόγος and σοφία in verse 1, which are also used by Dio, can refer to 'eloquence' and 'cleverness' in rhetoric, *Or.* 47. Cf. Barrett, *The First Epistle to the Corinthians*, p. 63.
51 μαρτύριον is to be preferred as a variant reading if Paul has in mind the sophist's μάρτυς as a sign of the truth of his method. See pp. 107–8 for a discussion in Philo and also G. D. Fee, *The First Epistle to the Corinthians* (Grand Rapids: Eerdmans, 1987), p. 91, who favours this reading on textual grounds.
52 Conzelmann, *Corinthians*, p. 53, n. 2; Weiss, *Der erste Korintherbriefe*, p. 45 *contra* A. Plummer and A. Robertson, *A Critical and Exegetical Commentary on the First Epistle of St Paul to the Corinthians* (Edinburgh: T. & T. Clark, 1914), p. 29; and Barrett, *The First Epistle to the Corinthians*, 62.
53 *BAGD* #5. b. b.
54 Aristotle, *Rhetoric* II. 2. 7. It is suggested that Paul is not simply rejecting the 'grand style' of oratory but rhetoric as a means of gospel presentation. See A. Deissmann, *Light from the Ancient East: The New Testament Illustrated by Recently Discovered Texts of the Graeco–Roman World*, English translation (reprinted Grand Rapids: Baker Book House, 1978), p. 70, who comments, 'It is never disciplined, say, by the canon of the Atticists, never tuned to the Asian rhythm.' Judge, 'Paul's Boasting', 40, notes Paul 'is ostensibly in conscious reaction against all rhetoric', although he wonders whether Paul's forceful rejection of it reflects his ability to use it against itself. In a later discussion of 1 Cor. 2.1 he translates ὑπεροχὴν as 'excessive' rather than 'superior', 'The Reaction against Classical Education in the New Testament', *Journal of Christian Education, Paper* 77 (1983), 11.

comments that Corinthian orators 'wanted to be looked up to and thought they knew more than other men' and he derides the deference they sought and the self-importance they exhibited.[55] Paul has no interest in winning adulation for himself.

The use of καταγγέλειν together with the content of his proclamations as stated in verse 2 explains why Paul adopted the stance he did: his task was to proclaim Jesus the Messiah[56] and, he adds with an epexegetical καί, a crucified Messiah at that.[57] The message Paul brought did not require a διάλεξις concerning himself or an encomium on the greatness of Corinth. He needed no topic to be suggested by a critical audience on which to declaim in order to gain the Corinthians' approval. Indeed, he found no reason to alter his message when he contemplated his visit (verse 2) for the 'topic' had been determined long before his arrival;[58] and no other subject would distract him. All grounds for a sophistic attitude of superiority were removed by the predetermined topic, for he had not come to establish his own reputation but to declare Jesus, the crucified Messiah.

If verses 1–2 explain why Paul repudiated the sophistic method of 'presenting himself' when he came to Corinth, verses 3–5 reveal that he also rejected the three traditional means (that is, rhetorical proofs) of persuading his hearers that his message was true. The Corinthian audience were accustomed to public speakers who treated their own trustworthiness as a preliminary to conviction. The orator laboured at projecting (or manufacturing) an image of himself as likeable and trustworthy – someone who could identify with their feelings – thus putting them in a receptive state.[59] Philostratus describes the late first-century sophist Scopelian as one who argued 'with great skill' in his διάλεξις, and then was 'even more impressive and vigorous' when he stood to declaim. He did not need time to compose the suggested topic but began immediately in an 'extremely melodious voice' with 'charming pronuncia-

---

55 *Or.* 6.21. For discussion see p. 132.
56 Paul uses the perfect passive participle.
57 See Fee, *The First Epistle to the Corinthians*, p. 92 who suggests the contrast is not because of an alleged change of strategy on Paul's part, but 'if any contrast is implied . . . it would be with the wandering sophists and orators'.
58 ἔκρινα – 'I resolved'. Cf. 2 Cor. 5.14, κρίναντος τοῦτο, when Paul reached a decision about the significance of the death of the Messiah on behalf of all – a reference taken to refer to a reassessment of his initial conclusion about the death of Jesus.
59 Cf. the initial warm reception of Favorinus from the Corinthians, *Or.* 37. 1.

tion' and excelled in 'covert allusions'. He did not have the bearing of 'a timid speaker' but 'entered the lists to win glory for himself'.[60] In contrast Paul describes himself in Corinth as κἀγὼ ἐν ἀσθενείᾳ καὶ ἐν φόβῳ καὶ ἐν τρόμῳ ἐγενόμην πρὸς ὑμᾶς ('and I myself was with you in weakness and fear and trembling'), verse 3. Numerous attempts have been made to explain this verse. Some have argued that it concerns a lack of resources for the task, others that it implies a physical or psychological disability, others that it describes a socially disadvantaged and humiliated person.[61] Still others suggest that Paul refers to being struck by the awe of God.[62] P. Marshall sees these terms as a 'trilogy of shame' and the antithesis of the persuasive, forceful and eloquent orator. He aligns these terms with those used of Paul by his opponents in 2 Corinthians 10.1 and 10 where the apostle is described as 'servile', 'weak' and 'contemptible'.[63] While A. D. Litfin states that we lack a basis for precisely defining these three terms, he suggests that the weakness is of a sort which may be juxtaposed against rhetorical skills and power.[64] It seems that Paul portrays himself as one who is anti-ἦθος and anti-πάθος by describing himself as 'weak', 'fearful' and one who 'trembled much'.[65] He did not project 'the character' or 'characteristics' expected of an orator. From his description of himself he certainly would not have enticed the audience by playing on their feelings, nor would his preaching have evoked shouts of 'Bravo' or 'Marvellous'.[66]

If verse 3 represents Paul's failure to be the persuasive orator because he did not use ἦθος and πάθος, how did he fare with the remaining proof, that is, ἀπόδειξις? In verse 4a he continues his

---

[60] *Lives of the Sophists*, 519.
[61] Litfin, *St Paul's Theology of Proclamation*, p. 209, n. 1; C. Forbes, 'Comparison, Self-praise and Irony: Paul's Boasting and Conventions of Hellenistic Rhetoric', *NTS* 32 (1986), 14; Hock, *The Social Context of Paul's Ministry*, p. 95, n. 15.
[62] T. B. Savage, *Power through Weakness: Paul's Understanding of the Christian Ministry in 2 Corinthians*, SNTS 86 (Cambridge: Cambridge University Press, 1996), pp. 72–3.
[63] Marshall, *Enmity in Corinth*, p. 389. It is uncertain whether the terms used in 2 Cor. 10.1 should be taken as those used against Paul. They do constitute the grounds of his appeal – 'the meekness and gentleness of Christ'.
[64] *St Paul's Theology of Proclamation*, p. 302, n. 1. Certainly Philo describes the ἰσχύς of the sophists and contrasts this with the ἀσθένεια 'at this sort of thing' of their opponents, i. e. those without rhetorical training, Philo, *Det*. 35.
[65] Plummer and Robertson, *1 Corinthians*, p. 31: 'I not only eschewed all affectation of cleverness or grandiloquence, but I went to the opposite extreme of diffidence and nervous self-effacement.'
[66] See Epictetus III.23.23–4 and for discussion see p. 123.

autobiographical account – καὶ ὁ λόγος μου καὶ τὸ κήρυγμά μου οὐκ ἐν πειθοῖ σοφίας ἀλλ᾽ ἐν ἀποδείξει πνεύματος καὶ δυνάμεως ('and my "rhetoric" and my preaching was not in the "persuasiveness of rhetoric" but in "clear proof" of the Spirit and "power" ').[67] The terms πειθώ, ἀπόδειξις and δύναμις have, as was noted previously, rhetorical connotations, namely, respectively, 'the persuasiveness of rhetoric', 'clear proof' and 'powerful eloquence'. Paul's selection of these terms is important, for they serve a crucial function in driving home his point. His preaching did not achieve results through the persuasiveness of wisdom, that is, the art of persuasion, which was rhetoric.[68] There was an ἀπόδειξις but it was not that πίστις recommended by the works on rhetoric. Instead, the Corinthians had witnessed incontrovertible evidence of the Spirit's work and power. Paul indicates subsequently in 2 Corinthians 12.12 that the signs of apostolic ministry were manifest in Corinth ἐν ὑμῖν. C. K. Barrett, commenting on 1 Corinthians 2.4, states: 'the supernatural conviction and force that accompanied the preaching furnished a better proof of its truth than any logical process'.[69] Weiss wrongly suggests that in proscribing ἀπόδειξις in its rhetorical context, Paul simply rejects 'epideictic style' – that he prefers the Stoic and Cynic diatribe. But Paul does not merely substitute one form of oratory for another:[70] the concluding ἵνα clause shows that where preaching was concerned, his overall strategy left no room for confidence in technical rhetorical devices.

Paul states in verse 5b his motivation for adopting a method of preaching which would have been unacceptable to those Corinthians who delighted in public declamations and orations. He says it was so that their πίστις would be in God's power rather than man's wisdom (σοφία). Paul's anti-ἦθος, anti-ἀπόδειξις and anti-πάθος argument, as well as his unconventional 'coming' to Corinth, it will be argued in the following chapter, illustrate his anti-sophistic thesis of 1 Corinthians 1.26–31 concerning God's calling

[67] J. Héring, *The First Epistle of Saint Paul to the Corinthians*, English translation (London: Epworth Press, 1962), p. 15, provides a convincing argument for the acceptance of this textual reading, rejecting πειθοί as an adjective which does not exist.
[68] Conzelmann, *Corinthians*, p. 54 *et al.* rightly do not seek to draw any significant distinction between λόγος and κήρυγμα.
[69] Barrett, *The First Epistle to the Corinthians*, p. 65. See also Darrow, 'History of Corinth', p. 167, who identified this with Paul's actual preaching and juxtaposed it with 'for the satisfaction of the mind'.
[70] Weiss, *Der erste Korintherbriefe*, pp. 49–50.

of his people, 1.31. Thus once again Paul is seen to repudiate ingratiation, a favourite strategy of the sophists, so that the church's πίστις might have a firm foundation. How should we understand πίστις in this context? Does Paul use the term in the rhetorical sense of 'proof'?[71] This meaning would have occurred to the educated first-century reader given its use in rhetorical handbooks, the cluster of rhetorical terms already encountered in verses 1–5 and the preceding context of the sophistic tradition in 1 Corinthians 1. While such a use of πίστις would be unique in the Pauline letters, that does not constitute sufficient grounds for rejecting it. The semantic field of rhetoric from which a particular meaning is attached to this term is the setting in which Paul discusses his entry and method of operating.

In support of rendering πίστις as 'proof', the term ἀπόδειξις implies for Aristotle that an argument's premises are known to be true and the conclusion is not only logical but certain. This he compares with the syllogism where the premise may be untrue. Aristotle held that demanding 'rigid demonstration', ἀπόδειξις, of a rhetorician is as unreasonable as allowing a mathematician to deal in 'mere plausibilities'.[72] Paul's use of ἀπόδειξις in verse 5 refers to a demonstration by the Spirit and power that gives absolute certainty, thereby involving an important change in significance of the word. If Paul adopts this term to indicate what is certainly true, then it is possible that he also uses the rhetorical πίστις to indicate the 'proof' God gave to the Corinthian converts.[73]

E. A. Judge observes that Paul in 1 Corinthians 2.1–5 'was not willing to concede terms to his opponents. He stigmatises what is invalid.' He suggests that Paul 'plunders the Egyptians', using important terms and proofs but evacuating them of their rhetorical meaning,[74] and in so doing, re-enforcing the importance of trusting the gospel rather than persuasive wisdom.

---

[71] See Acts 17.31 where πίστις or 'proof' of final judgement is the resurrection of Jesus from the dead in Paul's Athenian speech.

[72] *Nicomachean Ethics*, I.iii. 4. See Plummer and Robertson, *1 Corinthians*, p. 33, for discussion *contra* C. C. Oke, 'Paul's Method not a Demonstration but an Exhibition of the Spirit', *ET* 47 (1955–6), 35–6.

[73] H. Ljungman in his *Pistis: A Study of its Presuppositions and its Meaning in Pauline Use*, Acta 64 (Lund: Gleerup, 1964) neither discusses this possible meaning nor does he make any reference to this text in his study.

[74] Judge, 'The Reaction against Classical Education', 11. In 'Paul's Boasting', 40, Judge notes the phrase 'the plundering of the Egyptians' was used by the early Church Fathers to describe such an activity.

L. Hartman in a discussion of 1 Corinthians 2.1–5 comments that this passage 'provides a theological interpretation of his behaviour when defending himself in the first chapters of 1 Corinthians he became a kind of "anti-rhetorician" in order that it might be evident from whence came the power and the effect'.[75] By flouting accepted sophistic conventions and with the skilful use of terms wrenched from the semantic field of rhetoric, Paul aimed to further his central thesis, disclosed in 1 Corinthians 1.18, that the sophistic means of persuasion are unsuitable for securing belief in the gospel – a matter which we examine in detail in the following chapter.

The recent proposal that Paul opposed other preachers who had adopted rhetorical devices does not fit well with the text of 1 Corinthians. In fact, it seems a more plausible scenario for 2 Corinthians, though the description of the ministry of Apollos in Acts 18.24–8 must be taken into account.[76] Indeed, Paul's *apologia* explained his adoption of an anti-sophistic stance the first time he came to Corinth. He refused to anchor the confidence of the Corinthian converts in the persuasiveness of rhetorical argumentation; therefore he adopted an anti-sophistic posture to eliminate any confusion of his message with that of the sophists. The Corinthian response to his person did not concern him as it did the orators. Thus he would not modify his 'plain' style to elicit praise, instead striving to highlight the message rather than the messenger.

Similarities between Paul's and Dio's attitude towards their audience have already been noted.[77] There were however marked differences in intention. Dio withheld what his audience desired most – an 'extraordinary' or 'remarkable' discourse – to punish them. Paul on the other hand sought not to punish his audience but to adopt a method appropriate to his message of the humiliated crucified God in order to bring the blessings of the gospel to them.[78]

---

[75] 'Some Remarks on 1 Cor. 2.1–5', 120.
[76] Lim, 'Not in Persuasive Words of Wisdom', 148, who affirms this without producing evidence. For a discussion of the ministry of Apollos see pp. 174–6.
[77] See pp. 152–3.
[78] *Or.* 47. 1. For a discussion of his concern not to evacuate the cross of its effectiveness by rhetorical methods referred to in 1 Cor. 1.17–18 see pp. 186–7.

Paul's work in Corinth: 1 Corinthians 9

Sophists were meant to observe yet another convention when they settled in a city: the promise to undertake public benefactions.[79] Corinth greatly benefited from the coming of Herodes Atticus in the following century. Archaeological evidence from Corinth indicates that benefactors undertook major building projects during the reigns of all the first-century emperors.[80] In the second century Aristides commented that an Egyptian sophist visiting Smyrna led some councillors and ordinary people to believe not only that he would participate in civic affairs, but that he would also 'with his money exercise his wonderfully great ambition', presumably to beautify the city.[81]

In contrast, when Paul arrived in Corinth, not only was there no rush of young men eager to be his disciples as there was for Aristides, but he offered no promise of material benefactions for their city. He thereby deprived himself of the *entrée* which such promises would have won for him.[82] Instead he indicates in 1 Corinthians 9 that he *worked* at his craft! Plutarch well expressed the indignation felt by citizens of social status towards craftsmen:

> while we delight in the work [of craftsmen artisans], we despise the workman ... Labour with one's hands on lowly tasks gives witness, in the toil thus expended on useless things, to one's own indifference to higher things ... it does not necessarily follow that, if the work delights you with its graces, the one who wrought it is worthy of your esteem.[83]

---

[79] On the role of benefactors in cities in the Graeco–Roman world see Jones, *Roman World of Dio Chrysostom*, ch. 12; for some epigraphic evidence see F. W. Danker, *Benefactor: Epigraphic Study of a Graeco–Roman and New Testament Semantic Field* (St Louis: Clayton Publishing House, 1982); and also my 'The Public Honouring of Christian Benefactors: Romans 13.3 and 1 Peter 2.14–15', *JSNT* 33 (1988), 88–95, and more recently my *Seek the Welfare of the City: Christians as Benefactors and Citizens, Early Christians in the Graeco-World* (Grand Rapids and Carlisle: Eerdmans and Paternoster, 1994), pp. 26-36.

[80] J. H. Kent, *Corinth: Inscriptions 1926–1960* (Princeton: American School of Classical Studies at Athens, 1966), pp. 20–1 for discussion and pp. 123–37 for inscriptions.

[81] Aristides, *Or*, 51.30 and for Dio Chrysostom's benefactions to his native city see *Or*. 47.

[82] A. R. Hands, *Charities and Social Aid in Greece and Rome* (London: Thames and Hudson, 1968), p. 36.

[83] *Lives, Pericles*, I.4 – II. 1. 2.

Manual labour would cost Paul credibility with many, presumably at least with those converted subsequent to his departure who did not wish to have a 'working-class' apostle back in their midst. Furthermore, it may be that Apollos, in contrast, had exercised his right to financial support, for only Barnabas is mentioned with Paul as not having used it (1 Cor. 9.5). The prospect of Paul, not Apollos, returning would be seen as a social step backwards and a source of acute embarrassment for members of the social elite in the church (1 Cor. 1.26, 3.18, 16.12).

1 Corinthians 9 helps explain the enigma of why Paul undertook the drastic step of working in Corinth. It is clearly his *apologia* in the face of criticism for so doing, for he states emphatically: 'my ἀπολογία to those who accuse me is this' (verse 3).[84] From verses 1–11 he poses a series of fifteen questions proving the right of an apostle to derive financial support from his hearers. The climax to these questions comes in verse 12b: 'but (ἀλλά) we did not exercise this right over you'. With another strong adversative he then affirms, 'but we have endured everything' and explains why he endured the extra self-imposed burden: so that (ἵνα) nothing would hinder his preaching Christ. On the basis of this purpose clause we must ask: how could making use of apostolic rights to financial support hinder the furtherance of the gospel in Corinth? In the light of our conclusions concerning 1 Corinthians 2.1–5 we might also ask: if Paul entered Corinth and conducted his ministry there as an 'anti-sophist', did he take a further anti-sophistic step by earning his living in order not to impede the progress of the gospel? The two issues are interrelated, for the nexus between the reception of a speaker and financial gain would have been clear to the sophists.

The financial precedent

Our portraits of sophists in both Alexandria and Corinth reveal their insatiable appetite for wealth. Indeed, their credibility as teachers of civic virtue was all too often undermined by this

---

[84] There is no evidence that Paul, in refusing money offered by converts, thereby refused friendship, *contra* Marshall, *Enmity in Corinth*, pp. 245–50, 284, who interprets Paul's *apologia* on this assumption. K. F. Nickle, 'A Parenthetical Apologia: 1 Cor. 9.1–3', *Currents in Theology and Mission* 1.2 (1974), 68–70, wrongly argues that the demonstrative, αὕτη, refers to what he calls the parenthetical *apologia* located in verses 1b–2 and not verses 1–27, but it cannot be confined to verses 1b–2 as Nickel would argue. The whole chapter is obviously a defence.

preoccupation. Neilus complained to his father that the untried and boastful 'country sophist' Didymus had established a school charging exorbitant fees. He thus was forced to pay for his private tuition as well as for the public declamations of other sophists whom he heard perform.[85] Dio, we have seen, laments the Alexandrian orators' and sophists' consuming interest in 'gain and glory'.[86] Philo presents a more detailed criticism of greed, exposing the strategy of extending their lecture series in order to acquire more fees.[87] All testify to the sophists' potential for wealth; and what was said of the sophists in Alexandria was certainly true elsewhere. Dio's reference to 'disposing of their catch' lampoons their proverbial greed in the eyes of philosophers and others.[88]

This hallmark of the sophists was not simply a first-century phenomenon. From the second half of the fifth century BC onwards the distinguishing mark of the sophists was their 'professionalism', reflected in fees charged for instruction. G.B. Kerferd's analysis of evidence from that period shows that the income of sophists was derived primarily from the high fees charged in their schools, with public display lectures (ἐπίδειξεις) providing a secondary source of revenue.[89] Philostratus mentions the charging of fees for lectures, a custom which he believed was introduced by Protagoras. The sophists whom he discusses from the mid-first century AD onwards charged fees, and his defence of the practice surely responds to ongoing criticism.[90] This issue formed the crux of the complaints against them from Plato's time to the end of the second century and early third century AD.

The objection to the sophists by the philosophers of Plato's day was that they 'sold' the truth to all paying customers – which was seen as abhorrent. 'Can it be . . . that the sophist is really a sort of merchant or dealer in provisions on which the soul is nourished . . . ? And in the same way, those who take their doctrines the round of the cities, hawking them about to any odd purchaser who desires them . . .'[91] Two widely-held perceptions circulated by the first

---

[85] *P.Oxy.* 2190 and discussion on pp. 28–31.

[86] *Or.* 32.10 and discussion on pp. 49–50.   [87] See discussion on p. 95.

[88] *Or.* 12.13

[89] G. B. Kerferd, *The Sophistic Movement* (Cambridge: Cambridge University Press, 1981), pp. 27–30. See also Hock, *The Social Context of Paul's Ministry*, p. 52 and Marshall, *Enmity in Corinth*, p. 230, n. 215.

[90] *Lives of the Sophists*, 495: 'the pursuits on which we spend money we prize more than those for which no money is charged'.

[91] *Protagoras*, 313 c–d. Kerferd, *The Sophistic Movement*, pp. 25–6, argues that

century AD. Firstly, only the wealthy could afford instruction in the sophists' schools. Secondly, the sophists were impostors and flatterers motivated by love of glory and money.[92]

Paul's financial strategy: 1 Corinthians 9.1–23

Did Paul fear that 'living off' the gospel would have led to his identification in the eyes of a potential audience with the commercialism of the sophists – an identification he had already anticipated in his anti-sophistic stance when he came to Corinth (1 Cor.2.1–5)? 1 Corinthians 9 provides the answer to this question, but before it discloses its message we must determine how the Corinthians' financial provisions could have created a 'hindrance' or 'obstacle' (ἐλκοπή) to his message (9.12).

A cognate of καπηλεύω appears in the passage already cited from Plato concerning the sophists, as well as Dio Chrysostom's discussion of the sophists and orators at the Isthmian Games.[93] In 2 Corinthians 2.17, Paul, in a comment on his Corinthian mission and money, explains: 'for we are not among the many who "hawk around" the word of God'.[94] According to R. P. Martin, Paul actively strives to distance himself from his opponents' activity, the group in question he sees as the evangelists and teachers of 9.12.[95] Paul's Corinthian audience might identify him with the sophists and orators who charged willing students for the truth. To correct this misconception of his ministry Paul replaces the sophists' boast that they 'knew nothing of labour' with his own: he charges

both the selling *and* the indiscriminate teaching of all comers offended, for they put the art of statesmanship in the hands of any who could afford it.

[92] On those who could afford the fees see E. L. Bowie, 'The Importance of the Sophists', *Yale Classical Studies* 27 (1982), 21; and G. W. Bowersock, *Greek Sophists in the Roman Empire* (Oxford: Clarendon Press, 1969), p. 21. On the comments of Dio and Philo, see 49–50 and 95–7.

[93] Plato, *Protagoras*, 313, and also Philostratus, *The Life of Apollonius*, 1.13. R. P. Martin, *2 Corinthians* (Waco: Word, 1986), p. 50 to 'pseudo-sophists and mock philosophers'. On Dio see *Or.* 8. 9. For a discussion of καπηλεύω see Lim, 'Not in Persuasive Words of Wisdom', 142–4.

[94] Cf. Aristides, *Or.* 33.19 'we did not engage in oratory for wealth'.

[95] Martin, *2 Corinthians*, p. 49. For a discussion of Paul's twin concerns of not being a burden on the church (2 Cor. 11.9, 12.14, 1 Thess. 2.6,9), and the possibility of turning people away (2 Cor. 2.17), see D. L. Dungan, *The Sayings of Jesus in the Churches of Paul* (Philadelphia: Fortress Press, 1971), pp. 30–1. For a discussion of Paul's attitude towards work in Thessalonica see my '"If a man does not wish to work . . . " A Cultural and Historical Setting for 2 Thessalonians 3:6–16' *Tyn. B.* 40.2 (1989), 303–15.

nothing for his message (9.15) so as 'not to use to the full my right in the gospel' (9.18).[96]

Paul carries into verses 19–23 the argument of verse 18 as he seeks to justify this course of action. His adaptability to a variety of ethnic, religious and perhaps economic groups sprang from a desire to remove any obstacles which might hinder others from listening and responding to his message. He refused to have his message rejected out of hand because of an inflexibility on his part towards financial support in cross-cultural situations.[97] On the contrary, 1 Corinthians 2.1–5 reveals that he was constrained to choose methods of communication appropriate to his message, for he did not wish 'to become all things to all men' to gain honour and wealth, but in order 'to save some', verse 22.[98]

To summarise thus far: the sophists boasted that they 'did not know hard work', while Paul boasted that he renounced his right not to work, thus 'enduring all things' for the good of his hearers. Messengers and money were synonymous in the sophistic tradition. Thus 1 Corinthians 9.1–23 suggests another expression of Paul's anti-sophistic stance – this time bound up with his desire to support himself in order to avoid any identification with the sophists in the crucial issue of money.

Paul's self-discipline and the sophists: 1 Corinthians 9.24–7

Can the issue of self-discipline discussed in 1 Corinthians 9.24–7 be related in any way to this ongoing anti-sophistic portrayal of Paul's conduct? It has been argued that verses 24–7 fit well with 1 Corinthians 10.1–23 and 6.1–20, tolerably with 9.1–18 but very

---

[96] Philo, *Det.* 33. On the latter point Paul uses himself as a paradigm for those Corinthians who wished to exercise what they saw as 'their rights' even though their conduct was a stumbling block to Christians possessed of a weak conscience (1 Cor. 8). See 'Civic Rights', in my *Seek the Welfare of the City*, ch. 9.

[97] For a recent discussion see D. A. Carson, 'Pauline Inconsistency', *The Churchman* 100 (1986), 6–45, for literature cited and esp. 9–16 on the limits of Paul's accommodation. G. Bornkamm, 'The Missionary Stance of Paul in 1 Corinthians 9 and in Acts', in L. E. Keck and J. L. Martin (eds.), *Studies in Luke–Acts: Essays Presented in Honour of Paul Schubert* (Nashville, NY: Abingdon Press, 1966), p. 196 concludes that Paul was free to change his stance given the particular circumstances of the location and the individuals involved.

[98] The informative essay by H. Chadwick 'All things to all men (I Cor. xi.22)', *NTS* 1 (1954–5), 261–75, may wrongly give the impression that Paul's evangelistic method was necessarily also his pastoral and ecclesiological *modus operandi*.

badly with 9.19–22.[99] Although H. Conzelmann feels that it 'stands out' of its context, he notes the ties with 9.1–23 created by the correspondence between verses 23 and 27.[100] Verses 23–7 appear to be a continuation of Paul's anti-sophistic stance. The sophists boasted that they were those 'who take care of themselves . . . [and are] stout, sleek, robust, living luxuriously, proud, knowing nothing of labour, conversant with pleasures which carry the sweets of life to the all-welcoming soul by every channel of sense'.[101] Furthermore, they despised their opponents – the 'so-called' lovers of virtue – and applied contrasting terms to them. Their adversaries they described as 'destitute of the necessities of life . . . sallow, reduced to skeletons, with a hungry look for want of food, the prey of disease',[102] engaged in 'training for dying' and 'from first to last' studying 'to die to the life in the body'.[103]

The adversaries of the sophists in Alexandria, on the other hand, counter that they only fight 'in the shade', that is, the school, 'beating the air', declaiming powerfully (ἐπιδείκνυσθαι δύναμιν), winning admiration in their mock encounter, but accomplishing little of consequence when engaged in real combat.[104] Philo's notion of 'real combat', as we have seen, is debating.[105] But Paul does not box 'in the air'. He controls his body lest having preached to others he be rejected because of lack of control over his appetites (verse 27).[106] Surely this passage amounts to more than simply 'an injunction to self-discipline'.[107] Although Paul relates it to what follows, it also functions as part of his *apologia*. The sophists boast

[99] Weiss, *Der erste Korintherbriefe*, p. 246. Schmithals, 'Die Korintherbriefe als Briefsammlung', 288, n. 70 suggests that it belongs with 10.1–22 as part of the *Vorbrief*.

[100] Conzelmann, *Corinthians*, pp. 161–2. Marshall, *Enmity in Corinth*, pp. 282–3, does not address verses 23–7 in his discussion.

[101] Philo, *Det.* 33 and discussion on pp. 107–9.   [102] Philo, *Det.* 34.

[103] Philo, *Gig.* 14, and on his reference there to Plato's *Phaedo* 64a see 108 n. 42.

[104] See p. 105 and Philo, *Det.* 1, 41. Cf. also Dio, *Or.* 32.20, which asserts that Alexandrian philosophers who refuse to appear before the people are like 'degenerate athletes who are a nuisance to the wrestling–schools and gymnasia with their make–believe sparring and wrestling, but refuse to enter the stadium, viewing with suspicion the sun's heat and the blows'. See p. 45.

[105] Philo, *Det.* 42.

[106] E. Käsemann, 'A Pauline Version of the "Amor Fati"', in *New Testament Questions of Today*, English translation (London: SCM Press, 1969), p. 218.

[107] See B. B. Warfield, 'Paul's Buffeting of His Body', *ET* 31 (1919–20), 520–2, where he notes the statement's relationship to Paul's role as a teacher and suggests that the subordination refers to comforts which, if one yields to them, become evil.

about their lifestyle, justifying it philosophically as a logical consequence of the senses as the allies and friends of the soul.[108] Paul, as the anti-sophist, describes his own conduct as a buffeting of the body, a term not dissimilar to that used by genuine philosophers in Plato's time and also reflected by 'the lovers of virtue' in their anti-sophistic stance in Philo's Alexandria.[109]

The discipline and self-control which Paul exercises over his own appetites in verses 24–7 contrast starkly with the self-indulgence of the sophists, whose own lifestyle they attempt to defend on philosophical grounds. As noted previously, Philo calls them 'lovers of themselves' and likens them to pigs. They lecture *ad nauseam* as experts on the classical virtues and the self-defeating nature of the corresponding vices but their behaviour denies the very virtues they espouse.[110] Thus Paul goes beyond manual labour to a thoroughly anti-sophistic lifestyle in order to decrease further any possible connection with the sophists. He likens himself to a well-disciplined athlete (verses 24–6a): he is not what Philo calls a 'shadow boxer'.[111]

Paul's defence: conclusion

Paul's *apologia* in 1 Corinthians 9 views his apostolic ministry in terms of his rights as part of his criticism of those who are determined to exercise 'this right of yours' (ἐξουσία), 8.9.[112] It supplements the discussion of 1 Corinthians 2.1–5, for in both passages Paul confronts the matter of his coming to Corinth as an anti-sophist. He adopts this *modus operandi* in order to remove any obstacle to his message which might arise from his being identified – by his preaching or his lifestyle – with the sophists. The theological reasons for this choice revolve around the need to adopt methods, however costly to Paul, which further his message and protect him and his gospel from any suggestion that he is simply like the sophists. This is not the first instance of Paul resorting to working for theological reasons. Writing from Corinth to the Thessalonians he reiterates aspects of his coming (εἴσοδος), the fact that he did not depend on guile (δόλος), flattering words (λόγος

---

[108] For discussion see p. 107.
[109] For the argument see Plato, *Phaedo*, 67–9, Philo, *Gig.* 14, *Det.* 32–4.
[110] For Philo's complaints, see 87–8.   [111] Philo, *Det.* 4.
[112] For an explanation of the Corinthians' right, see my *Seek the Welfare of the City*, pp. 166-77.

κολακείας) or a cloak of covetousness (πρόφασις πλεονεξίας), nor did he seek glory from men (δόξαν ἐξ ἀνθρώπων), but he worked day and night to avoid burdening them.[113] This reading of 1 Corinthians 9 does not endorse R. F. Hock's suggestion that the paradigm for Paul's ministry is the Cynic tradition and its working philosopher,[114] though it agrees with his conclusion that Paul's labour policy was not related *per se* to the rabbinic tradition, for the text reveals much more than that behind the intense self-defence. Hock does not satisfactorily explain how Paul avoided ἑλκοπή in 1 Corinthians 9.12 by working, and says, 'The argument at this point [verses 15b–18] becomes difficult to follow, but its conclusion is clear. By not accepting support Paul could affirm he was free.'[115] He does not allow verses 23–7 their full impact within the argument of chapter 9. He himself acknowledges the preliminary and tentative nature of his conclusions, which were an attempt to work out a possible Cynic precedent for understanding Paul and his intellectual milieu.[116] If Paul is anti-sophist, why would a pro-Cynic stance be any less a stumbling block in the light of the argument of 1 Corinthians 1–4 and 9? The sophistic background is far more convincing as the explanation for Paul's *apologia*. S. K. Stowers' view that Paul resembled the Cynics 'in stressing the continuity between his preaching activity and everyday life' likewise does not adequately account for the intensity of the language of 1 Corinthians 2.1–5 and 9.[117] It is certainly not the case that Paul unthinkingly followed the Cynics. Instead Paul took great pains to emphasise he supported himself, for this was crucial to his message although costly to himself – a cost felt immediately in terms of the distraction of daily work in Corinth.[118] As 1 Corinthians 9 shows, the labour he undertook meant anguish for Paul in the form of the resulting strain on his relationship with the church after his departure (1 Cor. 9.3). It may even have occasioned the resistance of some

---

[113] For a look at Paul's treatment of the issues dealt with in 1 Cor. 2.1–5 and 1 Cor. 9 in a Thessalonian context, see my 'The Entries and Ethics of Orators and Paul (1 Thessalonians 2:1–12)', *Tyn. B.* 44.1 (1993), 55–74.

[114] Hock, *The Social Context of Paul's Ministry,* 18–9, a suggestion which he attributes to A. J. Malherbe, 'Gentle as a Nurse: The Cynic Background of 1 Thess 2', *NovT* 12 (1970), 203–17 and Betz, *Der Apostel Paulus.*

[115] Hock, *The Social Context of Paul's Ministry,* p. 61.   [116] *Ibid.*

[117] S. K. Stowers, 'Social Status, Public Speaking and Private Teaching: The Circumstances of Paul's Preaching Activity', *NovT* 26 (1984), 81.

[118] See Acts 20.33–4, which indicates the cost of following the same policy in Ephesus.

Corinthians to the thought of his return (1 Cor. 4.18–19) – hence the request for Apollos instead (1 Cor. 16.12).

The Corinthians' sophistic response: 1 Corinthians 1.12, 3.4

When the sophist Aristides arrived in Smyrna the response was overwhelming. He boasted that people came out to meet him even before he came to the city gates, and proudly recalled that 'the most distinguished young men offered themselves [as students].'[119] This was no isolated incident, for Dio Chrysostom records that in the great cities of the empire famous orators were guaranteed an enthusiastic reception and a loyal personal following.[120] It has already been noted that young men who enrolled in sophists' schools were called μαθηταί.[121] They were also described as ζηλωταί, because they gave exclusive loyalty to their teacher and were zealous for his reputation.[122] Such loyalty often resulted in strong competition between the disciples of different sophists in the cities of the East.[123] This rivalry was described as ἔρις or ἐριστός.[124]

Does our evidence suggest that some Corinthian converts had begun to perceive themselves as μαθηταί/ζηλωταί of their Christian teachers according to the sophistic understanding of the term? Had Paul begun to fear that their attitude to Apollos and himself was not all that different from that of disciples to their sophists? He describes their conduct in sophistic terms, that is, as ἔρις and ζῆλος. Does this explain their behaviour as recorded in 1 Corinthians 1.11 and 3.3?

The Corinthian perception of their relationship to Paul and others is recorded in two instances. 'I say this because each of you is saying' ('Ἐγὼ μέν εἰμι Παύλου, Ἐγὼ δὲ . . . , Ἐγὼ δὲ . . .) (1 Cor.1.12). Later Paul asks, 'When anyone says Ἐγὼ μέν εἰμι Παύλου and another says Ἐγὼ Ἀπολλῶ, are you not ἄνθρωποι?' (1 Cor. 3.4). Ἐγὼ εἰμι should be translated 'I myself belong to', for elsewhere in 1 Corinthians Paul uses the copula followed by the

---

119 *Or.* 51.29. δοῦναι ('give oneself up to', 'devote oneself') is normally used of pleasure but is used here by Aristides to indicate the measure of whole-hearted commitment.
120 *Or.* 47.22, when one was greeted with ζῆλος καὶ φιλοτιμία.
121 See pp. 129–30.
122 Philostratus, *Lives of the Sophists*, 504 notes of Demosthenes that he was μαθητής of Isaeus but ζηλωτής of Isocrates, i. e. he gave his loyalty to the latter.
123 See p. 129 and the literature cited there.   124 See p. 93 for Philo's evidence.

genitive to indicate origin or relationship. In 3.21 he states πάντα ὑμῶν ἐστιν, and in 6.19 οὐκ ἐστέ ἑαυτῶν. Therefore it is best translated 'belong to'.[125] Thus the polarity of loyalties is suggested by Paul's use of ἐγὼ μέν . . . ἐγὼ δέ . . . ἐγὼ δέ which is preceded by the report from those of Chloe's household that ἕκαστος ὑμῶν λέγει (1.12) and repeated in 3.4: ἐγὼ μέν . . . ἕτερος δέ.[126] The sentiments behind the comment of Aristides that the young men 'gave themselves' to him resemble those expressed in these two passages in 1 Corinthians. Perhaps Christians considered themselves exclusively committed to one of the 'itinerant' teachers who had visited Corinth, following the sophistic precedent.[127]

Can we place alongside this verbatim report of the Corinthians' perception of their relationship to their evangelists other evidence that their attitude corresponded to that of the sophists' μαθηταί and ζηλωταί? Paul describes them as κατὰ ἄνθρωπον περιπατεῖν, and in the following verse as ἄνθρωποι (1 Cor. 3.3,4). When Paul so characterises Corinthian behaviour, he means that they are behaving in a thoroughly secular fashion. The preposition κατά, here meaning 'after the fashion', denotes the measure or standard by which their conduct is to be assessed[128] – in keeping with Paul's use of κατά with περιπατεῖν to categorise behaviour.[129] That he here refers to 'secular' behaviour is confirmed by his explanation:

---

[125] *BDF* #162(7). Cf. Acts 27.23 , ὁ θεὸς, οὐ εἰμι ἐγώ. Also cf. τὰς 'Αφροδίτας ἐμί, Kent, *Corinth*, VIII/III, no. 3 and 'Απέλλονος C. Roebuck, *The Asklepieion and Lerna*, Corinth XIV (Princeton: American School of Classical Studies at Athens, 1951), no. 1, fig. 4 . For the discussion of these texts see p. 186.

[126] Conzelmann, *Corinthians*, p, 31, n. 4 states that the construction in 1.12 shows that Paul 'is writing from the standpoint of a reporter'.

[127] Cf. teachers of rhetoric in Egypt who had a tendency to 'sail away' from their pupils after a period of time, *P.Oxy.* 930 and discussion p. 28 n. 3.

[128] *BAGD* #5, κατά. J. B. Lightfoot, *Notes on the Epistles of St Paul from Unpublished Commentaries*, (London: MacMillan, 1895), p. 186. Paul uses the phrase κατὰ ἄνθρωπον elsewhere to refer to an established rule in society and always in the singular to denote (1 Cor. 9.8); to illustrate a social convention (Gal. 3.15: see C. H. Cosgrove, 'Arguing like a Mere Human Being: Galatians 3.15-18 in Rhetorical Perspective', *NTS* 34.4 (1988), 536-49); to refer to a human way of speaking (Rom. 3.5); to indicate that a message has its origins in man's thinking (Gal. 1.11); and that the phrase means as popularly or commonly understood (1 Cor. 15.32).

[129] Eph. 2.2; 2 Cor. 10.2; Rom. 8.7. For a discussion of περιπατεῖν see R. Banks, ' "Walking" as a Metaphor of the Christian Life: The Origins of a Significant Pauline Usage', in E. W. Conrad and E. G. Newing (eds.), *Perspectives on Language and Text: Essays and Poems in Honour of Francis I. Andersen on his Sixtieth Birthday July 28, 1985* (Winona Lake: Eisenbrauns, 1987), pp. 303–13.

ὅταν γὰρ λέγῃ τις ἐγὼ μέν κτλ; and the question which follows οὐκ ἄνθρωποι ἐστε; (verse 4). The constellation of terms in 1 Corinthians 3.1–3 further supports the view that Paul accuses the Corinthians of operating in a secular fashion, for it links σάρκινος, νήπιος, and σαρκικός with κατὰ ἄνθρωπον and ἄνθρωποι to charge that they are not πνευματικοί. In 3.3 they are said to be σαρκικοί and to behave in a 'secular' fashion. Paul uses the term σάρκινος in a comparable way elsewhere with respect to his own ministry. He declares that he has acted 'by the grace of God' and not by the σοφία σαρκική of the world (2 Cor. 1.12). Later he contends that the methods, that is, weapons (τὰ ὅπλα) of his ministry are not σαρκικὰ ἀλλὰ δυνατά, contrasting his methods with those of his sophistic opponents (2 Cor. 10.4). The first reference to sophistic preachers is implicit, while the second is explicit, as subsequent discussion will show.[130] In 1 Corinthians 3.1, 3 Paul uses both σαρκικός and σάρκινος to describe the Corinthians' past and present condition: 'It was not possible to speak to you as spiritual but as σάρκινοι, and it is not yet possible, for you are still σαρκικοί.' verses 1–3. In fact, σάρκινοι in verse 1 combines with ὡς νηπίοις to express their ongoing immaturity toward himself and Apollos, an attitude evident from the very beginning of their relationship with Paul.[131] These two terms serve as antonyms to πνευματικός. Within the context of 1 Corinthians 3. 1–4 the former are to be understood as the reason for the existence of ἔρις and ζῆλος. The presence of contention and emulation is seen in the explanatory statement in

---

[130] See pp. 208, 220–1.

[131] σάρκινος = made of flesh i. e. babies; cf. 2 Cor. 3.3, σάρκικος, behaving like children. -ινος indicates a material relationship and -ικος an ethical relationship, Plummer and Robertson, *1 Corinthians*, p. 52. On the meaning of the term 'babes in Christ' various suggestions have been made. J. J. Grundman, 'Die nepioi in der urchristlichen Parenese', *NTS* 5 (1958–9), 190–205 concludes that the reference is to those who fail to grow up spiritually and are not τέλειοι. W. Thusing, '"Milch" und "feste Speise"' (1 Kor. 3.1ff und Hebr. 5.11–6.3) Elementarkatechese und theologische Vertifung in neutestamentlicher Sicht', *Triere Theologische Zeitschrift*, 76 (1976), 233–46 argues that the difference rests in the ability to assimilate the doctrine of the cross. Cf. R. Schnackenburg, 'Christian Adulthood according to the Apostle Paul', *CBQ* 25 (1965), 335–6; and M. D. Hooker, 'Hard Sayings', *Theology* 69 (1966), 19–22. The term σάρκικος is best seen in this context as an explication of σάρκινος and an antonym of πνευματικός. Paul is searching for words to show the immaturity of their outlook, and when all the terms are considered together the implication is that they are still behaving as babies even though their spiritual birth happened some time ago.

verse 4, 'For when one says, "I belong to Paul" and another says, "I belong to Apollos", are you not ἄνθρωποι?' Paul has therefore used a set of categories as antonyms for the spiritually mature, πνευματικός, in order to explain his accusing them of operating κατὰ ἄνθρωπον and being nothing more than ἄνθρωποι.[132] In conclusion, the essence of the charge levelled against the Corinthians is that they behave in a secular fashion, that is, they measure their instructors by the same canon as secular Corinthians.

It remains for us to investigate whether chapters 1–4 as a whole support the contention that sophistic perceptions lurk behind Paul's indictment of secular attitudes towards himself and Apollos (1. Cor. 3.1–4). Paul uses two sophistic terms, ζῆλος καὶ ἔρις, to describe the Corinthians' conduct. Philo in like fashion applies the latter term to sophists who love wrangling in debates, and the cognate ἐριστός to those who are 'seeking victory in argument',[133] thereby with one stroke epitomising the sophist's 'excessive open-mindedness' and 'love of arguing for arguing's sake'.[134]

Dio Chrysostom describes the μαθηταί of the sophists as

132 On the progression of ideas see J. A. T. Robinson's succinct summary, *The Body: A Study in Pauline Theology* (London: SCM Press, 1952), p. 24, n. 4. The literature on πνευματικός in Paul is considerable. J. Painter summarises the interpretations argued for in 'Paul and the πνευματικοί at Corinth', in M. D. Hooker and S. G. Wilson (eds.), *Paul and Paulinism: Essays in Honour of C. K. Barrett* (London: SPCK, 1982) ch. 19, esp. 238–40. Painter himself suggests that πνευματικοί and σοφία are terms used by Paul's opponents, who were influenced by pagan ecstatic religion, and by Paul but in a different way. The position taken is unnecessarily complicated as Litfin, *St Paul's Theology of Proclamation*, p. 221 points out, 'The common assumption [that the Corinthians claimed the term for themselves] is the primary weakness of, e. g. Painter, who refers repeatedly to the "self-styled πνευματικοί" without ever defending from the text the validity of such a term. He [Painter] also assumes without warrant that πνευματικόν in 12.1 is masculine, and glosses over much of the substance of 1 Cor. 1–4 so as to be able to claim they are dealing with the same topic – Paul's response to "pneumatic wisdom at Corinth".' The observation of Conzelmann, *Corinthians*, p. 71, is correct when he states that the terms are Pauline and are to be understood within the context of the divisions and not related to theological differences.
133 *Det.* 36, 45 on ἐριστικός. For the use by more ancient authors, e.g. Plato, see Kerferd, 'Dialectic, antilogic and eristic', in *The Sophistic Movement*, ch. 6, esp. pp. 62–3. For discussion see p. 93. Philo uses ἔρις to describe the wrangling among the sophists, *Mut.* 10, *Her.* 246 pace L. L. Welborn, 'On the Discord in Corinth: 1 Corinthians 1–4 and Ancient Politics', *JBL* 106.1 (1987), 87, where he argues that both terms are political. He cites Plutarch, *Lives, Caesar,* 33 and Philo, *Flacc.* 41 but in the latter case bypasses the sophistic references. It is upon this that he builds his case that it is solely political and not sophistic.
134 Philo, *Fug.* 209.

ζηλωταί, as already seen. The importance of this discussion is that it delineates a disciple's responsibilities: by imitating his teacher's actions and his λόγοι the student could acquire the sophist's art, τέχνη. While Dio does not endorse the verbal sparring among disciples of competing sophists with their 'wrangling', 'disputing' and 'arguing', he does recognise an appropriate commitment by a disciple to his sophist.[135]

Aristotle in his *Rhetoric* treats ζῆλος as a positive virtue and contrasts it with φθόνος (envy). For him it means 'emulation' and he notes that the young and high-minded are 'emulous', as are also those who possess such advantages as wealth, numerous friends and positions of office. The 'objects of emulations' in Aristotle are those who possess courage, wisdom and authority, and of those in authority, he specifically mentions orators and 'those who desire to be like [them]'.[136]

Paul sometimes uses ζῆλος positively, but when combined with ἔρις, negative connotations predominate.[137] He denounces any improper 'emulation' of himself by which anyone on his behalf is 'puffed up' against a supporter of Apollos (1 Cor. 4.6c).[138] The terms thus connote 'strife' (between contending groups) and 'emulation' in the sophistic sense of the word. Philo's choice of ἐριστός and ἔρις and Dio's use of ζηλωτής convey a concern remarkably similar to Paul's.[139]

Furthermore, it should be noted that in 1 Corinthians 3.4 the focus is on Paul and Apollos. There ζῆλος καὶ ἔρις clearly relate to matters of loyalty, μὲν . . . ἕτερος, and ἕτερος appear again in 4.6 as the discussion turns to present disturbances in Corinth specifically linked to these two teachers. The classical use of ἕτερος in the sense of 'a division into two parts' supports this reading.[140] In 1 Corinthians 1.12 Paul uses ἕκαστος to describe the groupings, but his choice of ἕτερος δέ in 3.4 and his inclusion of the additional term ζῆλος could suggest that the allegiance of members of the church is now in effect divided between two former teachers,

---

[135] *Or.* 55.1, 3–4, 5. For discussion see p. 129.   [136] *Rhetoric*, II.9.5–11.7.
[137] Positive: 2 Cor. 7.7; 11; 9.2; 11.2; negative: Rom. 13.13; 2 Cor. 12.20; Gal. 5.20.
[138] Conzelmann, *Corinthians*, p. 86, n. 17 on φύσιν ('puffed up'). 'Not to be high and mighty toward *one* teacher in favour of another teacher.'
[139] Cf. Athenaeus, *The Deipnosophists*, VI.380–2 esp. 'an excellent poet, made it his first boast that he was able to take part in these civic rivalries' (πρῶτον ἀκαυχήσατο τῷ δύνασθαι μετέχειν τῶν ἀγώνων πολιτικῶν).
[140] J. K. Elliott, 'The Use of ἕτερος in the New Testament', *ZNW* 70 (1969), 140–1, although he does not cite 1 Cor. 3. 4. See also *BDF* #306.

himself and Apollos. The church's request 'concerning Apollos' (Περὶ δὲ 'Απολλῶ) and his return to minister to the congregation (1 Cor. 16.12b), and the obvious relief and subsequent assertiveness on the part of some in the church because Paul's promised return had not eventuated would support this (1 Cor. 4.18).

Is there evidence from the background and the *modus operandi* of Apollos to confirm that the congregational party spirit and desire to emulate former teachers had been culturally determined by the sophistic movement in that city? Acts 18.24–8 contains important biographical information concerning Apollos.[141] First, he was a Jew described as 'Alexandrian by birth'. While Luke's wording does not demand that he was a full citizen of the Greek πόλις,[142]

---

[141] Apollos' social and educational background has received inadequate attention. R. Schümacher, *Der Alexandriner Apollos, Eine exegetische Studie* (Munich:, 1916), pp. 5–20, is the longest discussion but only speculates with little factual information. He refers to ἀνὴρ λόγιος as 'natural eloquence' but explores none of the Alexandrian evidence. For more recent discussion on Apollos with little or no reference to his background see A. T. Robinson, 'Apollos the Gifted', *Biblical Review* 6 (1921) 381; G. A. Barton, 'Some Influences of Apollos in the New Testament', *JBL* 43 (1924), 207–9; D. H. Prelaker, 'Apollos und die Johannesjunger in Act 18.24–19.6', *ZNW* 30 (1931), 301; A. Dittberner, 'Who is Apollos and Who is Paul?', *The Bible Today* 71 (1974), 1550; A. M. Hunter, 'Apollos the Alexandrian', in J. R. McKay and J. F. Miller (eds.), *Biblical Studies: Essays in Honour of William Barclay* (London: Collins, 1976), p. 151; L. Herrmann, 'Apollos', *RSR* 50 (1976), 330; N. Hyldahl, 'Den korintiske situation – en skitse', *Dansk Teologisk Tidsskrift* 40 (1977), 19; F. F. Bruce, 'Stephen and Other Hellenists', in *Men and Movements in the Primitive Church* (Exeter: Paternoster, 1979), pp. 65–70; W. Ollrog, *Paulus und seine Mitarbeiter: Untersuchungen zu Theorie und Praxis der paulinschen Mission,* Wissenschaftliche Monographien zum Alten und Neuen Testament 20 (Neukirchen-Vlwyn: Neukirchener Verlag, 1979), p. 40; C. K. Barrett, 'Christianity at Corinth', in *Essays on Paul* (London: SCM Press, 1982), ch. 1; W. A. Meeks, *The First Urban Christians: The Social World of the Apostle Paul* (New Haven and London: Yale University Press, 1983), p. 61. The Alexandrian background is discussed in the author's unpublished paper 'Apollos as *aner logios*: A Problem for the Corinthian Church and Paul', read at a conference at Macquarie University, Sydney on the Graeco-Roman Cultural Setting of the Corinthian Correspondence in July, 1982. This paragraph and the two following notes represent a brief summary of relevant parts of that paper.

[142] Elsewhere in Acts Barnabas was 'a Cypriot by birth' 4.36, 'Aquila, a man of Pontus by birth', 18. 2. All three occurrences use τῷ γένει. See A. Kasher, *The Jews in Hellenistic and Roman Egypt: The Struggle for Equal Rights* (Tübingen: J. C. B. Mohr (Paul Siebeck), 1985), pp. 197–207, 260, 356, and on Roman citizenship for Jews see pp. 77–8 for literary and non-literary evidence that the term 'Alexandrian' denotes provenance and not *ipso facto* full citizenship; Philo's nephew, Tiberius Julius Alexander, inherited Greek citizenship from his father. E. M. Smallwood, *Philonis Alexandrini*: Legatio ad Gaium (Leiden: E. J. Brill, 1961), p. 13, and E. G. Turner, 'TIBERIVS IVLIVS ALEXANDER', *JRS* 44 (1954), 54 argue he was an Alexandrian citizen in the fullest sense regardless of the general

Jews did occasionally hold multiple citizenship at that time. More important for our purposes, he is described as ἀνὴρ λόγιος in verse 24, a collocation clearly connected with rhetoric.[143] Philo uses the identical phrase to refer to those with rhetorical training.[144] Regarding Apollos, still other sophistic terms are used of his *modus operandi* which throw light on his background. In his handling of the OT scriptures his method is described as δυνατός (18.24), and he also powerfully refuted the Jews in public, 'demonstrating' (ἐπιδείκνυμι) by means of the Old Testament, that Jesus was the Messiah (Acts 18.28).[145] The three terms have rhetorical connotations, so that the Acts account of Apollos would have conveyed to the readers that this Christian Jew from Alexandria depended on his rhetorical skills in his open συζήτησις with the Jews (verse 28).[146] Thus the rivalry in the congregation – which pitted Paul against Apollos – and Apollos' rejecting the request for his own return (καὶ πάντως οὐκ ἦν θέλημα, 1 Cor. 16.12b) become clearer when seen against the latter's background.

status of the Jews. That Apollos was an Alexandrian citizen cannot be determined from the particular comment of Luke, although his status with regards to education by no means rules out the possibility. Well-to-do Jews, at least up until the letter of Claudius to the Alexandrians, participated in Greek education. See L. H. Feldman, 'The Orthodoxy of Jews in Hellenistic Egypt', *JSS* 22 (1960), 223.

143 For a full discussion of examples see E. Orth, *Logios* (Leipzig: Norske, 1926). The evidence cited above is drawn from the first century BC to the second century AD. In Orth's comments on Acts 18.24 he connects λόγιος with δυνατὸς ἐν ταῖς γραφαῖς and says that it also means a scholar with rhetorical ability, *Logios*, p. 46. He does not draw attention to the rhetorical terminology used in verse 28. It would seem that Luke intends the reader to understand that Apollos is trained in rhetoric and makes use of it during his ministry in Corinth.

144 Philo, *Post.* 53 uses λόγιος ἀνήρ of men engaged in σοφιστικαὶ τέχναί, and uses λόγιος in connection with παιδεία elsewhere in his *corpus*, *Legat.* 142. On the attributes of Tiberius, who was trained in rhetoric, see B. Levick, *Tiberius the Politician* (London: Thames and Hudson, 1976), pp. 15–18; *Legat.* 310 of Augustus who had intercourse with λόγιοι who are identified with those educated in *paideia*; *Mos.* I, 2 of Greek λογίοι, who abuse the power παιδεία bestowed upon them; *Mos.* I, 23 of Moses' education, which was at the hands of οἱ λόγιοι of Egypt and others in specific areas of education, cf. Plato's description of Egyptian *paideia Laws*, 656d, 799a, 819a; *Mut.* 220 of eloquence related to ἐν λόγῳ; *Chr.* 116 of the lips of the most eloquent; *Post.* 162 of ancient learned men; *Legat.* 237 of the most learned men of Greece; and *Virt.* 174 of superiority in eloquence.

145 On δυνατός see pp. 154–5.

146 On συζήτησις see Philo, *Det.* 1 and discussion pp. 104, 187–9.

Conclusion

It is therefore concluded that not only does Paul decry the secular conduct of the Corinthians, but we can be more specific and state that it was sophistic in its nature. The Corinthian Christians' perception of a μαθητής and a ζηλωτής has been contaminated by a culturally determined understanding of the terms drawn from the sophistic movement in Corinth. It was Isocrates who commented, 'I suppose all men are aware that a sophist reaps his finest and largest reward when his pupils prove to be honourable and intelligent and highly esteemed by their fellow-citizens, since pupils of that sort inspire many with the desire to enjoy his teaching.'[147] Certain Corinthians enjoyed the ministry of Apollos and persuaded the church, in spite of a commitment on the part of some to Cephas, to invite Apollos to return even though some had supported Paul (1 Cor. 3.18, 16.12).

Despite the financial hardships which Paul endured in order to avoid misconceptions about ministry, some in the church continued to misconstrue either the theological motivation behind his Corinthian activity or the nature of Christian discipleship. He had seen, to be sure, storm clouds on the horizon during his initial ministry in Corinth, for he says that even then he needed to treat them as infants (1 Cor. 3.1–2). There was a whole-hearted commitment by the Corinthian converts to Paul which he found disturbing but which remained uncurbed whilst he was among them. The subsequent preaching by one trained in rhetoric only heightened their predilection for secular perceptions of teachers. Even the discussion of the problem in 1 Corinthians 1–4 and 9 did not result in the eradication of this culturally conditioned response to teachers, as will be argued in the final chapter. The proposal of the congregation to invite Apollos back provided the opportunity to signal to Paul that he was not welcome. This appears to have been the catalyst which brought the divisions into the open, although they had existed in nascent form from the beginning of Paul's ministry.

Finally we note the wild enthusiasm with which the orators of Corinth responded to the oration of another visitor to that city, Favorinus. Recording that even 'the women and children' listened to him, Favorinus affords us a glimpse into the zealousness and commitment which the Christians had characterised in response to

---

[147] *Antidosis*, 220.

their religious teachers.[148] Favorinus, like Paul, also illustrates how easily the same Corinthian enthusiasm could wax and wane and even turn to opposition after he 'sailed away', for he discerned on a return visit that 'his statue' had been 'thrown down' as a sign of their rejection of him.

[148] *Or.* 37.33 and for discussion see p. 136.

9

PAUL'S CRITIQUE OF THE CORINTHIAN SOPHISTIC TRADITION

1 Corinthians 1–4 presents a radical critique of the cultural mores which Paul encountered in Corinth. His need to discuss such matters arises from the Corinthians' incorporation of certain secular values into their Christian self-perception.[1] It will be argued, again largely from Paul's terminology, that Corinthian identity was influenced by sophistic tradition.

Paul deals with three crucial issues raised by the sophistic tradition, namely status, imitation and boasting. Firstly, the Corinthians' self-perception, aggravated by the rhetorical movement, is discussed in the light of their status 'in Christ' (1 Cor. 1.4–7, 30, 4.8–13). Secondly, Paul redirects the loyalty inherent in this tradition both by proposing that the teachers 'belong' to the congregation, not vice versa, and by redefining 'following' in soteriological and not sophistic terms (1 Cor. 1.10–16, 3.18–23, 4.10–17). Thirdly, Paul assaults sophistic boasting with the help of certain OT passages which find their fulfilment in the work of God in Christ (1 Cor. 1.17–31, 3.18–23, 4.6–21).

These three issues concerning the sophistic tradition as it impinged on the life of the Corinthian church will unfold as we examine: (1) the so-called *'apologia'*, (2) inferiority and sophistic status, (3) the idolatry of sophistic imitation and (4) sophistic boasting. These themes then receive further treatment in Paul's discussion as we consider (5) the sophists/disciples – the boasting and imitation reversed, and (6) the irony of Paul's 'covert allusion' – boasting, status and true imitation.

---

[1] For Paul's *modus operandi* and their response see pp. 155–6 and 170–5.

The so-called 'apologia': 1 Corinthians 1–4

1 Corinthians 1–4 has long been regarded as an *apologia* for Paul's ministry. This label is, however, misleading because of the presence of hortatory sections which clearly build upon Paul's argument within the *apologia*. For example, in 1.10 Paul exhorts the Corinthian congregation to hold the same views. The statements ἵνα τὸ αὐτὸ λέγητε πάντες (verse 10a), and ἐν τῷ αὐτῷ νοῒ καὶ τῇ αὐτῇ γνώμῃ (verse 10c) point to an agreed judgement.[2] The former statement has clear parallels in Thucydides, 'holding the same view' (τὸ αὐτὸ λέγοντες), and Polybius, 'speaking with one heart and mind' (λέγοντες ἓν καὶ τὸ αὐτὸ πάντες), refers to forming an identical view or judgement.[3] 1.10c has parallels in Pollux, μίαν γνώμην ἔχειν, and Dionysius of Halicarnassus where αὐτοί τε οὐκέτι μίαν γνώμην ἔχοντες.[4] The lack of a common mind in the Corinthian church lies behind the strife-creating σχίσματα (verses 10–11) caused by, it has been argued, their perception of themselves as μαθηταί and ζηλωταί of certain Christian teachers in Corinth.[5]

Paul subsequently specifies in 4.1 precisely how they ought to think about the function of Apollos and himself, οὕτως ἡμᾶς ἄνθρωπος κτλ. It is therefore important not to find in 1.10 a mere call to consensus, for Paul instead wants to restore them to 'the same mind and the same judgement' as himself on this matter, hence his use of καταρτίζειν.[6] The following verses do not imply that the church lacks unity. Indeed on the contrary, the majority, if not all, seem undisturbed by the attitude reported to Paul by members of Chloe's household, and seem to have reached agreement on the invitation to Apollos to return in 16.12.[7] They have

---

[2] H. Conzelmann, *The First Epistle to the Corinthians*, English translation (Philadelphia: Fortress Press, 1975), p. 30.

[3] See, for example, Thucydides, v.31; Polybius, v.104.

[4] Pollux, *Onomasticon*, 151; Dionysius of Halicarnassus, 1.85. Cf. also the *Scholion of Thucydides* v.31, τὴν αὐτὴν γνώμην ἔχοντες, and Isocrates, *Archidamus*, 37, πάντες τὴν αὐτὴν γνώμην ἔχομεν. First-century literature called this 'concord' and 'discord' in *politeia*. For discussion of this in relation to Phil. 1.27–2.18 see my *Seek the Welfare of the City: Christians as Benefactors and Citizens, Early Christians in the Graeco–World* (Grand Rapids and Carlisle: Eerdmans and Paternoster, 1994), pp. 86–93.

[5] See pp. 170–5.

[6] See Plutarch, *Lives*, Cato Minor, 65.5 'It is your duty to reduce this man's swollen pride and restore him to conformity with his best interests' (καταρτίζειν τίνα εἰς τὸ συμφερτόν).

[7] δηλοῦν denotes 'a rationally intelligible communication', Conzelmann, *Corinthians*, p. 32, n. 17.

conceptualised the role of Apollos and Paul and others according to a culturally determined perception of secular teachers. Paul must push them outside this cultural sphere and invite them to follow him not as μαθηταί but μιμηταί.[8] The apostle applies OT citations (in verses 1.19, 1.31, 3.19–20) to the issue which threatens the unity and hence future ministry of the church.[9] As E. Best has rightly noted, 'He [Paul] is more concerned to refute what he believes to be a serious error on the part of the Corinthians than to reinforce his own position over against them.'[10] His *apologia* must be seen as his critique of the Corinthians and not simply a justification of his *modus operandi*. Like Aristides, who concluded his apologetic oration to a friend with 'Call these remarks a defence (ἀπολογία), or if you wish, a well intentioned censure (ἐπιτίμησις), or even a combination of the two',[11] Paul in 1 Corinthians 1–4 clearly combines both.

Paul's critique commences not with the verses normally designated *apologia* (1.10–4.21), but rather with the thanksgiving (1.4–9). This would certainly be consistent with the literary convention he adopts in the opening sections of his letters, for it has been amply demonstrated that Paul often introduces with a preliminary comment in his thanksgiving portion issues which receive fuller development in the body of the letter.[12] But though it has been argued from literary precedent that 1.4–9 connects with 1.10–4.21, the exact nature of that nexus has not been finally established.[13] P. T. O'Brien therefore maintains that though other

---

[8] E. Earle Ellis, 'Paul and His Co-workers', in *Prophecy and Hermeneutic in Early Christianity* (Tübingen: J. C. B. Mohr (Paul Siebeck), 1978), p. 3 rightly notes that Paul had no 'disciples'.

[9] See 2 Cor. 2.9 for the response Paul expected, and also his strong warning in 1 Cor. 4.21 about the choices they faced.

[10] E. Best, 'The Power and the Wisdom of God', in L. de Lorenzi (ed.), *Paolo: A Una Chiesa Divisa (1 Co 1-4)* (Rome: Abbazia di S. Paolo, 1980), p. 14.

[11] Aristides, *Or.* 33.34.

[12] For the fullest treatment see P. T. O'Brien, *Introductory Thanksgivings in the Letters of Paul*, Supp. *NovT* 44 (Leiden: E. J. Brill, 1977).

[13] N. A. Dahl, 'Paul and the Church in Corinth in 1 Cor. 1.10–4.21', in W. F. Farmer et al. (eds.), *Christian History and Interpretation: Studies Presented to John Knox* (Cambridge: Cambridge University Press, 1967), p. 326, where he simply notes that what follows the very short introductory thanksgiving is the exhortation. C. J. Bjerkelund, *Parakalō: Form, Funktion und Sinn der parakalō-Sätze in den paulinischen Briefen* (Oslo: Universitetsforlaget, 1967), pp. 141–4, 152–3, cites non-literary evidence which shows a clear connection between thanksgiving and exhortation. He does not establish the actual nature of this connection in 1 Cor. but sees a 'formal' relationship.

elements in 1 Corinthians were introduced in 1.4–9, 'Paul's apostolic authority [discussed in 1.10–4.21] [was] not prefigured in the introductory thanksgiving.'[14] But T. Y. Mullins, correctly as we shall see, observes that at least in relation to 1 Corinthians 1, too rigid a boundary should not be drawn between the thanksgiving and what he designates the 'disclosure' section which follows.[15] W. Wuellner's rhetorical analysis of 1 Corinthians 1–4 also suggests that verses 4–9 lead to the main theme in 1.10.[16] The following section seeks to clarify the nature of this connection.

Inferiority and sophistic status: 1 Corinthians 1.4–9

In 1 Corinthians 1.4–9 Paul attends to a danger engendered by the sophistic movement: the debilitating sense of inadequacy felt by many who lacked a rhetorical education. This is well demonstrated in Dio Chrysostom's discourse, 'On Training for Public Speaking', in which a man of wealth and influence seeks Dio's help to overcome his lack of *paideia* and public speaking skills. The enquirer and Dio agree that a public figure needs experience and training both in public speaking and eloquence, for such abilities cause their possessor to be 'loved, influential and honoured' instead of 'looked down on' (καταφρονεῖσθαι). So Dio provides a syllabus which lists authors to read, recommending that one begin with and return periodically to the most important of all, Homer.[17] Further evidence comes from Plato, who indicated what steps to take (within the context of *paideia*) to ensure that one did not 'fall behind others in experience', and Epictetus, who described how students bristled at the exposure of gaps in their understanding.[18]

This sense of inadequacy could also be engendered or aggravated by the invective of others. Demosthenes, in court with his accuser Aeschines, charges him with not really being an educated man but

---

[14] O'Brien, *Introductory Thanksgivings*, p. 135.

[15] T. Y. Mullins, 'Disclosure: A Literary Form in the New Testament', *NovT* 7 (1964), 50.

[16] W. Wuellner, 'Greek Rhetoric and Pauline Argumentation', in W. R. Schoedel and R. L. Wilken (eds.), *Early Christian Literature and the Classical Intellectual Tradition: in Honorem Robert M. Grant* (Paris: Beauchesne, 1979), p. 185.

[17] *Or.* 18.1–2. J. W. Cohen, *Dio Chrysostom*, LCL, vol. II, p. 209 suggests 'he failed to get rhetorical training in his youth' and notes that Dio's list is not dissimilar to that of Dionysius of Halicarnassus and Quintilian. On Homer's importance see pp. 77–80.

[18] Plato, *The Republic*, 53c; Epictetus, *Discourse*, I.8.10.

'one of those who made stupid pretensions to culture' and who 'falls short': such people disgust everybody when they open their mouths but fail to make the desired impression.[19] Isocrates similarly describes the Lacedaemonians who have 'fallen behind' in *paideia* – in contrast to the Athenians who excel as either μαθηταί or διδάσκαλοι.[20] The verbatim comparison (συζήτησις) recorded in Philo shows how readily the sophists drew attention to the inadequacies of their opponents, 'the so-called lovers of virtue' who trailed behind as 'almost without exception obscure' individuals, 'easily looked down on', people of 'mean estate'. The sophists by contrast measured their own successful life by its trappings.[21]

Already in 1 Corinthians 1.5–7 Paul introduces this notion of inferiority to the discussion. The verb ὑστερεῖν in verse 7 undergirds Paul's emphasis on the sufficiency of the *charismata* which Christ has bestowed on them to counter the feeling of inadequacy reflected in the non-biblical sources cited above which was shared by members of the Corinthian church.[22]

In what ways did the Corinthians feel deficient? When Paul assures the congregation that they have actually been enriched in Christ in every way, he makes a specific reference to their problem by adding immediately ἐν παντὶ λόγῳ καὶ πάσῃ γνώσει . . . ὥστε ὑμᾶς μὴ ὑστερεῖσθαι ἐν μηδενὶ χαρίσματι (verses 5,7). The terms λόγος and γνῶσις were used subsequently by opponents to disparage Paul's own rhetorical ability (2 Cor. 11.6) as were other terms found in 1 Corinthians 1–4, in retaliation for his attack on the sophistic tradition.[23] The two terms do not appear together elsewhere in 1 Corinthians; however the issue of λόγος is discussed in 1 Corinthians 1.10–4.31, where it refers to eloquence.[24]

---

[19] *De Corona*, 128.   [20] *Panathenaicus*, 209.
[21] *Det.* 34, and discussion p. 108.
[22] G. D. Fee, *The First Epistle to the Corinthians* (Grand Rapids: Eerdmans, 1987), p. 41, suggests that the Corinthians 'come short either in comparison with others or normal expectations of Christians who have the Spirit'. The former is to be preferred in the light of the inferiority engendered by the sophistic movement.
[23] See pp. 219–21 for a discussion of the way in which the terms could be used by Paul either of himself and/or the church in 1 Cor. 1–4 and then be taken up by his opponents against him in 2 Cor. 10–13.
[24] 1 Cor. 1.17,18; 2.1,4,13; 4.19,20. Conzelmann, *Corinthians*, p. 27 translates λόγος as 'eloquence'. The term γνῶσις is restricted elsewhere to the discussion of food offered to idols and the issue of spiritual gifts,1 Cor. 8.1,7,10,11; and 12.8; 13.2 8; 14.6. He believes that in 1 Cor. 1.5 both terms must be left 'in indefiniteness'. K. Grayston, 'Not with a Rod', *ET* 88 (1976), 13–16, suggests rather improbably that the two terms reflect a division between those who insisted on λόγος as remembered instructions of Jesus in ch. 14 and those who were drawn to γνῶσις

The encouragement some ancient authors occasionally gave to the rhetorically untrained to speak and not be intimidated by those with training is not unlike that which Paul offers here.[25] Does Paul's own positive experience after being overawed in Corinth also lie behind his prodding the Corinthians to speak without feeling inferior? According to A. D. Litfin, Paul in this section affirms that God initiates both the calling and the enabling of the church in Christ, but he incorrectly assumes that these opening verses contain no evidence of serious problems in the church.[26] On the contrary, even as he thanks God Paul alludes to what troubles him, namely the Corinthian sense of inadequacy concerning rhetorical ability (λόγος).[27] If Paul did not use rhetoric in his preaching (1 Cor. 2.1–5), then no rank and file Corinthian Christian should feel precluded from speaking either in the church (1 Cor. 12–14) or in sharing the Christian message with outsiders.

The idolatry of sophistic imitation: 1 Corinthians 1.10–17a

Paul turns from the issue of inferiority to problems created by zealous adherence to teachers. Various suggestions have been made concerning the nexus between ἔρις (verse 11) and verses 13–17, with their reference to division, baptism and crucifixion. Some suggest that the mystery cults, characterised by special relationships between the baptised and the baptiser, provide the background.[28] Others explain the problem as the corruption of the natural affinity between the preacher and individual converts.[29] Best, in seeking to understand the issues in 1.13–17 and Paul's discussion in 1.18ff.,

---

in ch. 5–8. Others see the former term referring to the 'form' and the latter to the 'content'. O'Brien, *Introductory Thanksgivings*, p. 118. H. D. Betz, *Der Apostel Paulus und die sokratische Tradition: eine exegetische Untersuchung zu seiner 'Apologie' 2 Korinther 10–13* (Tübingen: J. C. B. Mohr (Paul Siebeck), 1972), p. 59 sees the terms in 2 Cor. 11.6 as part of the ongoing debate between philosophers and sophists. The term γνῶσις in 1 Cor. 1.5 may mean 'knowledge' relating to how one should live and act as a person.

25 See the citation from Philodemus on p. 214 and Paul's problem in Acts 18.9–11.
26 Litfin, *St Paul's Theology of Proclamation: an Investigation of 1 Corinthians 1–4 and Greco-Roman Rhetoric*, SNTS 79 (Cambridge: Cambridge University Press, 1994), pp. 179–80.
27 Paul returns to this theme in 4.6–21, see pp. 196–201.
28 J. Héring, *The Second Epistle of Paul to the Corinthians*, English translation (London: Epworth Press, 1967), p. 7.
29 A. Chapple, 'Local Leadership in the Pauline Churches: Theological and Social Factors in its Development: A Study based on 1 Thessalonians, I Corinthians, and Philippians', PhD dissertation, University of Durham (1984), pp. 318–19.

expresses the difficulty NT scholars face: 'Surely . . . there must have been some other factor, unknown to us, which led him to introduce baptism; probably something in the nature of the division in Corinth will have related to it.'[30]

We have explained the Corinthians' intense response to Paul and others as a conformity to the sophistic environment and its commitment to and zeal for a particular teacher.[31] Just as one enrolled in the school of a sophist or became a zealous follower and admirer at public declamations, so the newly baptised received instruction from their Christian teacher. Where household baptisms occurred, the entry of a teacher into that social unit had its cultural precedent in the sophistic movement.[32] It seems reasonable therefore to explain this nexus of leaders, parties and baptism as another result of the sophistic mind-set of Corinth.

But though this might explain the background, the issue of baptism *per se* does not fully account for Paul's argument. He not only dismisses the idea that Christ can be divided but then, negatively, links himself with both crucifixion and baptism in the name of Jesus – μὴ Παῦλος ἐσταυρώθη ὑπὲρ ὑμῶν ἤ εἰς τὸ ὄνομα Παύλου ἐβαπτίσθητε (verse 13). None can claim to have been baptised in the name of Paul.[33] J. Munck suggests that Paul criticises converts who have put 'the teachers they invoke – he mentions himself as an example (1.13) – in the place of Christ';[34] that is, following teachers with blind loyalty had unwittingly resulted in the messengers of the crucified Messiah occupying the Messiah's rightful place in the church. Paul responds with three questions which parade the folly of this unthinking cultural response to their teachers (verse 13).[35] Thus Paul redirects the confession of the

---

[30] Best, 'The Power and the Wisdom of God', pp. 12–13.
[31] See pp. 140–1, 170–3.
[32] See R. F. Hock, *The Social Context of Paul's Ministry Tentmaking and Apostleship* (Philadelphia: Fortress Press, 1980), pp. 53–4, and evidence assembled by S. K. Stowers, 'Social Status, Public Speaking and Private Teaching: the Circumstances of Paul's Preaching Activity', *Novt* 26 (1984), 66 and n. 40.
[33] Baptising was not the ministry he was sent to perform in Corinth: 'Christ did not send me to baptise' (verse 17a). Paul minimises its significance.
[34] J. Munck, '1 Thess. 1.9–10 and the Missionary Preaching of Paul: Textual Exegesis and Hermeneutic Reflexions', *NTS* 9 (1962–3), 105.
[35] Paul elsewhere heaps up questions as part of his method of argument in 'rhetorical' sections; see 1 Cor. 9 for fifteen questions and 2 Cor. 11 for four. For a brief discussion of 1 Cor. 1.13 see W. Wuellner, 'Paul as Pastor: The Function of Rhetorical Questions in First Corinthians', in A. Vanhoye (ed.) *L'Apôtre Paul: Personnalité, Style et Conception du Ministère* (Leuven: Leuven University Press,

sophistic–minded Christians to declare that their new allegiance amounts to nothing more than loyalty to formerly honoured gods. They may well have been acquainted with Corinthian confessions of belonging to Aphrodite, Apollo and Dionysos (τᾶς ᾿Αφροδίτας ἐμι, ᾿Απέλλονος ἰμί and Διονύσου).[36] By transferring their affirmation of loyalty from the sophistic to the pagan religious sphere Paul delivered a stunning rebuke, for they would never have imagined that their party slogans amounted to this.

These verses, then, form more than a mere 'shaming section' in Paul's argument[37] – and declaring that 'it can only be viewed as a sardonic rebuke of the Corinthians' proclivity to personality-centred ἔριδες' does not expose the issues at stake.[38] A sophistic understanding of the Corinthian Christians' exclusive relationship to individual teachers amounted to idolatry even though they adhered to those who were Christians.

Sophistic boasting: 1 Corinthians 1.17b–31

In 1 Corinthians 1.17b–31 Paul judges the boasting of the sophistic tradition, concluding with a scriptural prohibition against all boasting (verse 31), for it is incongruous with his message and commission. He declares that he was not sent to baptise, but to preach the gospel, οὐκ ἐν σοφίᾳ λόγου, ἵνα μὴ κενωθῇ ὁ σταυρὸς τοῦ Χριστοῦ. Litfin rightly argues that the issue here is not the theological content of Paul's preaching, but 'the form or manner of

---

1986), pp. 68–9, where he uses the phrase 'rhetorical questions' to refer to 'new' rhetoric and not to 'ancient' rhetoric.

[36] J. H. Kent, *Corinth: Inscriptions 1926–1960* (Princeton: American School of Classical Studies at Athens, 1966), VIII/III, no. 3; and C. Roebuck, *The Asklepieion and Lerna*, Corinth XIV (Princeton: American School of Classical Studies at Athens, 1951), no. 1, fig. 4; and N. Bookidis and R. S. Stroud, *Demeter and Persephone in Ancient Corinth*, American Excavations in Old Corinth, Corinth Notes 2 (Princeton: American School of Classical Studies at Athens, 1987), p. 27. It could be that there was a 'Christ' party who saw the party slogans as idolatrous and determined that their only loyalty was to the Messiah himself, and therefore they were better than the others, cf. 1 Cor. 4.23. P. Vielhauer, *Geschichte der urchristlichen Literatur: Einleitung in das Neue Testament, die Apokryphen und die Apostolischen Väter* (Berlin: Walter de Gruyter, 1975), pp. 135–7, has argued that this slogan is a rhetorical formulation by Paul in order to expose the foolishness of the Corinthians' party slogans.

[37] Wuellner, 'Greek Rhetoric', p. 185.

[38] Litfin, *St Paul's Theology of Proclamation*, p. 186. He does not identify it as having arisen from the sophistic tradition, yet in the following verses 17–31 he sees it as a judgement passed on Paul's preaching drawn from the canons of Graeco–Roman rhetoric.

preaching', with οὐκ ἐν σοφίᾳ λόγου governing the argument that follows.[39] The phrase here means 'without rhetorical skill'.[40] The reason Paul gives for eschewing this rhetorical method of presentation is that it actually 'empties' (κενοῦν) the cross of its essential message (verse 17c).[41] How could this occur? Evidence from Philo indicates that rhetorical methods often overshadowed the message as a means to persuade the audience. Audiences surrendered their critical faculties to the techniques of the sophists.[42] Epictetus likewise bespeaks the elevation of eloquence and rhetorical ability over content.[43] Paul came to Corinth determined to present not simply Jesus as the Messiah, but 'him crucified'. He did not aim to persuade his audience of the truth of this message by the use of the three *pisteis* in rhetoric, namely ἦθος, πάθος and ἀπόδειξις. His reasons for it are clearly spelt out in 1 Corinthians 2.1–5: he does not wish their πίστις to rest in human wisdom but ἐν δυνάμει θεοῦ. As in 2.4 and 2.5, so also in 1.18 Paul adapts the rhetorical term δύναμις with respect to λόγος to indicate where the true 'eloquence' or the 'power' of persuasion of the preached message resided.[44] In both passages it rested with God through the crucified Messiah, and not with the rhetorical technique of Paul or any other evangelist. Because rhetorical techniques clouded content he declared them unsuitable. Attention would be diverted from the message of the crucified God as Paul or Apollos as orators themselves become the focal point.

Not only eloquence poses a threat to the gospel. Paul also argues, by citing two OT passages, that God intended to destroy the wisdom of the wise, since it had not been the means by which He had come to be known. Who the wise and prudent were was outlined by Paul in 1.20ff., namely σοφός, γραμματεύς, ὁ συζητητὴς τοῦ αἰῶνος τούτου ('the debater of the age'). But to whom do these terms refer? H. A. W. Meyer thought σοφός was

---

[39] *Ibid.*, p. 188, n. 29. He argues that the phrase ἐν σοφίᾳ λόγου reaches back not only to εὐαγγελίζεσθαι, but to ἀπέστειλεν, citing as support both Conzelmann, *Corinthians*, p. 37, and J. Weiss, *Der erste Korintherbriefe* (reprinted Göttingen: Vandenhoeck & Ruprecht, 1977), p. 22.

[40] C. K. Barrett, *The First Epistle to the Corinthians* (London: A. & C. Black, 1971), p. 49; Litfin, *St Paul's Theology of Proclamation*, pp. 188–92; Fee, *The First Epistle to the Corinthians*, p. 64, n. 79.

[41] Litfin, *St Paul's Theology of Proclamation*, p. 189 believes that 'this clause encapsulates much of the theme of the section 1.18–2.5'.

[42] See pp. 91–4 for a discussion of the sophists as 'magicians'.

[43] See pp. 123–4.   [44] For discussion see pp. 158–9.

generic, γραμματεύς referred to Jewish scribes and συζητητής to the Greek sophists. He suggested that ὁ συζητητής described those engaged in sophistic disputes, citing in support Xenophon's observation that συζήτησις was in vogue among the sophists.[45] E. A. Judge and others agree that the last term refers to orators or sophists.[46] It has also been suggested that the first two terms merely cling to the OT citations, the third being Paul's real concern in Corinth.[47] Another proposal is that the first two refer to Greek and Jewish teachers with the third then comprehensively covering both cultures.[48] Alternatively an exclusively Jewish referent has been claimed for all three words by reason of the OT citations in verses 19 and 20.[49] But the immediate context includes the Jewish demand for signs and the Greek search for wisdom, so that it may be difficult to claim one ethnic identity for the three terms. Some maintain that the first two refer to the knowledge of learned men and the third to their activity in seeking to convince others that their knowledge is true while others teach falsehood. Finally, and because of this diversity of opinion, some commentators have simply regarded them as a general reference to wise men, scholars and disputants.[50]

The important question is whether subsequent discussion throws any light on 'the debater of this age'. If so, it would not only resolve

[45] H. A. W. Meyer, *Critical and Exegetical Handbook to the Epistles to the Corinthians*, English translation (Edinburgh: T. & T. Clark, 1892), vol. i, p. 39.

[46] E. A. Judge, 'The Reaction Against Classical Education in the New Testament', *Journal of Christian Education Paper 77* (1983), 11, who believes the three terms refer to three main contemporary types of tertiary scholars, and Héring, *The Second Epistle of Paul to the Corinthians*, p. 12, who identifies the third term as 'sophist'.

[47] C. J. Ellicott, *St Paul's First Epistle to the Corinthians with a Critical and Grammatical Commentary* (London: Longmans, Green & Co., 1887), p. 22.

[48] A. Plummer and A. Robertson, *A Critical and Exegetical Commentary on the First Epistle of St Paul to the Corinthians* (Edinburgh: T. & T. Clark, 1914), pp. 19–20 citing Acts 6.9, 9.29, 28, 29 for Jewish 'disputers'.

[49] For a summary of this discussion and a critique see J. Munck, 'The Church without Factions', in *Paul and the Salvation of Mankind* (London: SCM Press, 1959), pp. 144–8; and more recently, K. Müller, '1 Kor.1.18-25. Die eschatologisch-kritische Funktion der Verkundigung des Kreuzes', *BZ* 10 (1966), 251–72; and W. Wuellner, 'The Sociological Implications of 1 Corinthians 1.26-31 Reconsidered', in E. A. Livingstone (ed.), *Studia Evangelica*, vol. vi (Berlin: Akademie-Verlag, 1974), pp. 666–72, and 'Ursprung und Verwendung der σοφός, δυνατός, εὐγενής-Formel in 1 Kor. 1.26', in C. K. Barrett et al. (eds.), *Donum Gentilicium: New Testament Studies in Honour of David Daube* (Oxford: Oxford University Press, 1977), pp. 165–84.

[50] Barrett, *The First Epistle to the Corinthians*, p. 53, and Best, 'The Power and the Wisdom of God', p. 21.

the uncertainty for commentators, but more importantly, it would further explain Paul's criticism of the sophistic tradition (assuming verses 20–31 are united in dealing with this issue). It will be argued that just as the σοφός and γραμματεύς are discussed in verses 20–25, so the activity of the sophists and orators as the debaters of this age is reflected in the argument in verses 26–31.

Munck has already demonstrated that the terms mentioned in verse 26, σοφοί, δυνατοί and εὐγενεῖς, were used of those instructed by the sophists, and that the σοφοί are the sophists whose parents are δυνατοί and εὐγενεῖς. He drew his evidence from the early third-century works of Philostratus, *Lives of the Sophists* and of Diogenes Laertius.[51] The recent work of G. W. Bowersock and E. L. Bowie firmly establishes that this is *the* social class from which the sophists came.[52]

Surveying the use of these terms by first-century authors quickly reveals that they are commonly applied to the ruling class of eastern cities. Thus, in an essay on 'How to tell a flatterer from a friend', Plutarch says that ὁ σοφός could at the same time be described as πλούσιος, καλός, εὐγενής, βασιλεύς and the rich man as a ῥήτωρ καὶ ποιητής. These were obviously terms which epitomised social status; and those to whom they were applied would have been flattered.[53]

Dio Chrysostom, Philo and Plutarch all discuss εὐγένεια.[54] Dio

---

51 Munck, 'The Church without Factions', p. 161, n. 2 for evidence. His position was not adopted by Wuellner, 'The Sociological Implications', pp. 666–72, who argued on grammatical grounds that the terms referred to the three gifts of God to mankind in Genesis 1. This was further supported on the grounds of the alleged homily genre of 1 Cor. 1–3, and the fact that the terms do not appear together in non-biblical literary sources. For the fascinating history of interpretation of verses 26–9 see K. Schreiner, 'Sur biblischen Legitimation des Adels: Auslegungeschichtliche Studien zu 1 Kor.1.26-29', *ZKG* 85 (1975), 317–57, from Irenaeus to the present, who argues that previous interpreters had read their own situation into the text. He adopts the position that Paul was challenging the prevailing notion that slaves were τὰ μὴ ὄντα to which Christ gave a new dignity. *Contra* Dio, *Or.* 15.29–32 and Philo, *Det.* 33–4; and G. Theissen's argument, *The Social Setting of Pauline Christianity: Essays on Corinth* (Philadelphia: Fortress Press, 1982), pp. 71–2.

52 See G. W. Bowersock, 'The Cities of the Sophists', in *Greek Sophists in the Roman Empire* (Oxford: Clarendon Press, 1969), ch. 2 esp. pp. 21–9 on the sophists as the 'well-born', their use of the money, their intellect, influence and social eminence; also E. L. Bowie, 'The Importance of the Sophists', *Yale Classical Studies* 27 (1982) 29–59.

53 'How to tell a Flatterer from a Friend', *Moralia*, 58e.

54 For earlier interest see for example G. B. Walsh, 'The Rhetoric of Birthright and Race in Euripides *Ion*', *Hermes* 106 (1978), 310.

observes: 'The descendants of families of ancient wealth were called "well-born" by a certain class.' This class he calls 'ignorant', contrasting their popular use of the term with that of philosophers. These families also distinguish between 'the noble' (γενναῖοι), and 'the well-born' (εὐγενεῖς), on the one hand and 'the free-born' on the other. In addition, Dio objects to the misuse of another set of categories, namely 'ignoble' (ἀγενεῖς) and 'mean' (ταπεινοί) which were used of certain strata of society.[55]

Philo notes that some in his own day sing the praises of ΄εὐγένεια as the greatest of gifts and [so] deserve the strongest censure. This is because they think that those who have generations of wealth, and fame behind them are εὐγενεῖς.' His contemporaries won praise by their 'silver, gold, both honours and offices' and 'good condition and beauty of body', and used 'ignoble' as a term of reproach. Philo denounced those who spring from great houses, who 'boast and glory' in the splendour of their race.[56]

Plutarch, in a fragment of a larger work, 'Concerning good birth', says that it is but 'ancient wealth' and 'ancient reputation'. He calls it 'a gift of uncertain fortune' (τύχη) and exposes it so that all may see 'that this inflated name of good birth hangs on two alien pegs'.[57] While all these authors denounce εὐγένεια in one form or another, it remains clear that the term referred to a powerful group in first-century society who possessed 'old money' and great prestige.

There is little need to argue that the term οἱ δυνατοί had long referred to the rulers of cities. Thucydides provides many instances of such use – sometimes in contrast with ὁ δῆμος and other times with οἱ ἀδύνατοι. Of particular interest is his description of Cylon as εὐγενής τε καὶ δυνατός.[58] A. Sänger, depending heavily on Josephus, observes that οἱ δυνατοί derived their status from wealth,

---

55 Dio, *Or.* 15.29–32; see also 31.74, 47.14, 52.16, and Plutarch, who uses the same two terms for the 'ignoble' and 'mean', *Lives, Pericles*, 24.4–5. See also *P.Oxy.* 33, ιν. lines 15–16, v. lines 3,5,7,9 (late second century AD) for the use of εὐγένεια and ἀγένεια, where Appianus speaks of his nobility and his rights, of being well-born and a gymnasiarch, and ironically of the emperor as ὁ ἀγενής.
56 Philo, *De virtutibus*, in which he devotes a subsection to Περὶ εὐγενείας, 187–226.
57 For the text see *Fragments*, 139–40.
58 Eg. 1.89.3, 102.2. For a reference to Cylon see 1.126.3, and the rulers and the ἀδύνατοι 1.141.6 as a term used by Thucydides in preference to οἱ ὀλίγοι. For discussion A. Lintott, *Violence, Civil Strife and Revolution in the Classical City* (London: Croom Helm, 1982), pp. 92–4.

and that this ancient wealth and reputation was an ingredient of the 'well-born'.[59]

It was Isocrates who from an earlier period had argued that the men who were 'superior and pre-eminent' in the history of Athens were not only 'well-born' and of 'reputation', but were also noted for their wisdom and eloquence. If one wanted to learn how the greatness and glory of Athens was achieved, Isocrates suggests, ask of one of its leaders, 'What was his birth?' and 'What was the character of his education?'[60] Little, moreover, had changed by the time of the Roman empire: the assemblies of the cities still elected magistrates whose qualifications for office included a property requirement. In essence, they were nominated because they were 'well-to-do' (εὔπορος).[61] They had enjoyed that form of education available only to the rich, that is, the well born.[62] The assemblies' concern was unchanged: to elect 'members of the local ruling class, men of good family and property'.[63] Based on this wealth of literary evidence we can conclude that 1 Corinthians 1.26 refers to the ruling class of Corinth from which orators and sophists came. Furthermore, the catalogue of Corinthian inscriptions clearly shows that orators contributed to the political life of the city and would have been regarded as among the δυνατοί, εὐγενεῖς and the σοφοί.[64]

---

[59] A. Sänger, 'Die δυνατοί in 1 Kor.1.26', *ZNW* 76 (1985), 285–91.

[60] Isocrates, *Antidosis*, 308. J. A. Davis, *Wisdom and Spirit: An Investigation of 1 Corinthians 1.18-3.20 against the Background of Jewish Sapiential Tradition in the Greco–Roman Period* (Lanham, NY and London: University Press of America, 1984), p. 76, notes that the Pauline trilogy of terms is not found in exactly that formulation elsewhere, citing the investigation by J. M. Gibbs, 'Wisdom, Power and Wellbeing', in E. A. Livingstone (ed.), *Papers on Paul and Other New Testament Authors*, Studia Biblica 1978, 3 (Sheffield: Sheffield Academic Press, 1980), pp. 119–55, which does not examine any Graeco–Roman sources. Synonyms are clearly located in this passage in Isocrates, for example.

[61] E.g. *BGU* 18, line 13 (AD 169).

[62] For the statue and inscription erected by the 'well-born pupils' of Lollianus, the second-century AD sophist of Athens, see G. Kaibel, *Epigrammata Graeca ex lapidibus collecta* (Berlin: 1878), no. 877.

[63] P. A. Brunt, 'The Romanization of the Local Ruling Classes in the Roman Empire', in D. M. Pippidi (ed.), *Assimilation et résistance à la culture gréco–romaine dans le monde ancien: Travaux du VIᵉ Congrès International d'Etudes Classiques* (Paris: 'Belles Lettres', 1976), pp. 161, 164, 166.

[64] Kent, *Corinth*, no. 226, where the orator undertook the costly liturgy of the President of the Games on three occasions; no. 264, where the orator was a member of the Panhellenion; and no. 307, where the orator was a Helladarch and priest. R. MacMullen, *Roman Social Relations 50 BC to AD 284* (London and New Haven: Yale University Press, 1974), p. 107, notes that 'great power as a speaker, style and taste in one's address' were required by men of standing in the

We may add to this evidence an actual sophistic debate (συζήτησις) from the first century which develops an argument strikingly similar to that of Paul in 1 Corinthians 1.26–31. The extant verbatim report of this debate contains much boasting about status and indicates that external evidence of success functioned as a μάρτυς. Sophists exploited a contemporary interpretation of the Platonic view of the senses as the soul's allies to show that their acquisition of 'wealth and fame and honours and offices and everything else of that sort' enabled them to enjoy what nature intended.[65] They thus provided a list of the trappings of their success, supplementing wealth with a claim they were ἔνδοξοι and πλούσιοι. Their 'fame and honours and office' show that they were ἡγεμόνες, ἐπαινούμενοι, τιμώμενοι, whilst the words 'everything else of that sort' further testify to their success. In a demeaning σύγκρισις the sophists aligned these terms with a set of antonyms which bore 'witness of the life' of their opponents, the 'so-called lovers of virtue'.

Sophists	Opponents
ἔνδοξοι	ἄδοξοι,
πλούσιοι	εὐκαταφρόνητοι
ἡγεμόνες	ταπεινοί
ἐπαινούμενοι	τῶν ἀναγκαίων ἐνδεεῖς
τιμώμενοι	ὑπηκόων καὶ δούλων ἀτιμότεροι
ὑγιεινοί	ῥυποῶντες
πίονες	ὠχροί
ἐρρωμένοι	κατεσκελευμένοι
ἁβροδίαιτοι	λιμόν ὑπ' ἀστρίας ἐμβλέποντι
θρυπτόμενοι	νοσερώτατοι
πόνον οὐκ εἰδότες	
ἡδοναῖς συζῶντες	μελετῶντες ἀποθνῄσκειν

city. See also *SEG*, XVIII, no. 137 for a third-century AD Corinthian orator who was 'first among orators, pre-eminent as *agonothetes*, having acquired glory in every public office', cited in T. B. Savage, *Power through Weakness: Paul's Understanding of the Christian Ministry in 2 Corinthians*, SNTS 86 (Cambridge: Cambridge University Press, 1996), p. 47, n. 194.

[65] Philo, *Det.* 33–4 and discussion pp. 107–9. Cf. also Diogenes Laertius, 206: 'he too had the sophist's off-handed boastfulness' (ἀπὸ τοῦ στόματος καύχησιν τὴν σοφιστικήν).

Clearly these sophists were among the well born and the powerful, and would have paraded their education as proof of wisdom.[66] Paul in 1 Corinthians 1.26–8 uses a similar set of antonyms to show God's work contrasted with Fortune's blessing.[67]

Status in secular Corinth	God's calling
σοφοί	τὰ μωρὰ τοῦ κόσμου
δυνατοί	τὰ ἀσθενῆ τοῦ κόσμου
εὐγενεῖς	τὰ ἀγενῆ τοῦ κόσμου
	τὰ ἐξουθενημένα
	τὰ μὴ ὄντα[68]

God has, in the words of the Magnificat, 'put down the mighty from their seat and exalted the humble and meek'.

While the Greeks seek wisdom and the Jews ask for a sign, the debaters of this age boast that their lifestyle testifies to the class to which they belong, namely the wise, the powerful and the well-born. God, however, has put to shame οἱ σοφοί by choosing those whom they themselves describe as τὰ μωρὰ τοῦ κόσμου (verse 27b); τὰ ἰσχυρά by choosing those described as τὰ ἀσθενῆ (verse 27c); and τὰ ὄντα by choosing τὰ ἀγενῆ τοῦ κόσμου, καὶ τὰ ἐξουθενημένα, τὰ μὴ ὄντα.[69]

Paul argues that God has chosen to humble all, including the sophists, for a purpose: so that no flesh might boast before Him (verse 28b). This He did by eviscerating any claim to secular wisdom which could commend them or bring any to the true knowledge of God (verse 21).

According to Paul, God had called few from the class to which the sophists belonged – though they would have certainly

---

[66] *Det.* 32–4.

[67] Paul here is engaging in ἐναντιότης, arguments from opposites within the same species, Quintilian IX.3.90. This is what the sophists in Philo's *Det.* 32–4 were doing. See especially #32, *contra* N. Schneider, *Die rhetorische Eigenart der paulinischen Antithese* (Tübingen: J. C. B. Mohr (Paul Siebeck), 1970), who, after surveying discussion of antithesis in the handbooks, comes to a conclusion that Paul derives this method from his Jewish background. It is one of the four methods of rhetorical *amplificatio* and Paul makes good use of it here and in 1 Cor. 4.6–13.

[68] 1 Cor. 1.27–8 and on the use of the neuter to emphasise the attribute of the person see *BDF* #138(1).

[69] For the evidence of the antithesis between τὰ μὴ ὄντα and εὐγενεῖς see Theissen, *Social Setting*, pp. 71–2.

considered themselves worthy of the privilege. Upon those who were 'easy to look down on' (εὐκαταφρόνητοι, to quote the sophists in Philo's *Det.* 34), God had actually bestowed an all-sufficient status in Christ, namely σοφία τοῦ θεοῦ . . . δικαιοσύνη τε καὶ ἁγιασμὸς καὶ ἀπολύτρωσις (verse 30). Thus, whilst Aristotle recorded that men said, 'By Fortune, Τυχή, I am a man of noble birth, wealth and power',[70] Paul could affirm that by an act of God in Christ the Corinthian Christians had a lasting status conferred upon them, even though there were many whose secular status was the antithesis to that of the wise, the powerful and the well born.

'Therefore', Paul adds, 'as it is written, "Let him who boasts, boast of the Lord"' (verse 31). This is an apt and compelling citation concerning status from Jeremiah 9.23–4a.

> Let not the wise man boast of his wisdom,
> Let not the mighty man boast of his might,
> Let not the rich man boast of his riches,
> But let him who boasts, boast of this,
> that he knows and understands Me.

The boasting about the μάρτυς of life reflected in the social class of verse 26, as well as the arrogance displayed by Alexandrian sophists in Philo's *Det.* 34, was proscribed by this text.

What is implicit in the reference to ὁ συζητητής (verse 20) thus becomes explicit in verses 26–31 as Paul sustains his assault on sophistic boasting. In 1 Corinthians 1.26–31 Paul does not simply record God's shaming of the Corinthian sophists' boastful μάρτυς – an argument from a successful life – to support his *apologia* that God has overthrown wisdom as the grounds upon which he can be known (1.19). He cites without further comment at this stage the universal proscription from the OT that the only legitimate boasting is that which glories in the Lord's accomplishments.[71]

---

[70] *Rhetoric*, II.12.2.
[71] In light of the above discussion, the attempt by J. A. Davis, *Wisdom and Spirit*, p. 81, to place the discussion of 1 Cor. 1.18–3.20 against the background of later sapiential Judaism does not succeed and calls into question his overall enterprise.

**The sophist/disciple boasting and imitation reversed:
1 Corinthians 3.18–23**

Secular Corinth, however, held no monopoly on boasting, as Paul's subsequent discussion shows. In 3.18–23 Paul warns the σοφὸς ἐν ὑμῖν ἐν τῷ αἰῶνι τούτῳ who boast ἐν ἀνθρώπῳ in the church against self-deception. He commands 'the not many wise' to become foolish in order to become wise, for the wisdom of this world is foolishness in God's eyes. The proof of this lies in the two OT citations, Job 5.13 and Psalm 94.11: 'He catches the wise in their craftiness' and 'The Lord knows that the thoughts of the wise are futile' (verses 19–20). Paul's conclusion is ὥστε μηδεὶς καυχάσθω ἐν ἀνθρώποις (verse 21a). This injunction confronts the boasting of the few Corinthian Christians who were regarded as wise by secular Corinth's standards and who, as Christians, continued boasting about their secular teachers.

Paul, however, is also concerned that it is inappropriate for the Corinthians to boast of their Christian teachers, as confirmed by the following verses. In verse 21b Paul affirms πάντα γὰρ ὑμῶν ἐστιν and then explains himself: 'whether Paul or Apollos or Peter or the world or life or death or the present or the future', πάντα ὑμῶν. He then adds in verse 23: 'You belong to Christ.' The church members do not belong to Paul or Apollos or Peter: Paul, Apollos and Peter actually belong to them.

Paul radically reverses the μαθητής/σοφιστής perception by which the congregation measured its relationship to the teachers, for the secular Corinthian precedent was totally inappropriate in the church. While sophistic Corinth may have affirmed ἐγὼ εἰμι . . ., and the Corinthian church did the same of its teachers, Paul is in effect stating, Παῦλος ἐστιν ὑμῶν. So within the Christian church 'the sophist' belongs to the μαθηταί. The ministry of the Christian teacher is to be seen in functional and not status terms, as Paul indicates in 1 Corinthians 3.5 with the use of 'what' (τί) rather than 'who' (τίς). It has been observed that 1 Corinthians 3.18–23 'sums up the entire argument beginning in 1.18'.[72] This passage clearly rejects the Corinthian affirmations of loyalty in 1.12 and is the culmination of the argument spanning 1.10–3.23.

---

[72] Betz, 'Rhetoric and Theology', in A. Vanhoye (ed.), *L'Apôtre Paul*, p. 39. However, the reason given by him is not convincing for he discusses it under the issue of 'knowledge' and makes no reference to the issue of the inversion of the sophist/disciple relationship.

The irony of Paul's 'covert allusion', boasting, status and true imitation: 1 Corinthians 4.6ff.

In 1 Corinthians 4.6ff. Paul again addresses Corinthian boasting in their teachers.[73] This is linked with being 'puffed up' on behalf of Paul against Apollos and vice versa (verse 6). Previous discussion makes it clear that the disciples of sophists were engaged in ἔρις and ζῆλος and that the term 'puffed up' aptly epitomises the competitive spirit which existed.[74]

In verse 6 Paul indicates that he is making use of λόγος ἐσχηματισμένος, that is, the rhetorical device called 'a covert allusion', ταῦτα δὲ ἀδελφοί μετεσχημάτισα εἰς ἐμαυτὸν καὶ Ἀπολλῶν δι' ὑμᾶς. In order to appreciate the significance of Paul's shaming the church for imbibing aspects of the sophistic tradition one must understand the device and how he uses it in 1 Corinthians 4.[75]

Rhetoricians made use of the covert allusion for a number of

---

[73] Various suggestions have been made as to the significance of 1 Cor. 4.6–13. J. McHugh, 'Present and Future in the Life of the Community: 1 Cor. 4.6–13 in the Context of 1 Cor. 4.6–21', in L. de Lorenzi (ed.), *Paolo: A Una Chiesa Divisa* pp. 181–2, argues that Paul here is using irony, accusing the Corinthians of thinking that they have already entered into the kingdom because of the references to being already full, rich and acting like kings. Munck, 'The Church without Factions', p. 165, also argues for an eschatological thrust. P. Marshall, *Enmity in Corinth: Social Conventions in Paul's Relations with the Corinthians* (Tübingen: J. C. B. Mohr (Paul Siebeck), 1987), pp. 181, 194–207, believes that Paul is using ὕβρις, 'the traditional idea of excess', to discredit the behaviour of his enemies, adopting 'the shameful figure of the socially humiliated person' by using the 'rhetoric of status'. Fee, *The First Epistle to the Corinthians*, p. 165, sees this as the application of the theology of the cross in 1.18–2.16 to the Christian life. Barrett, *The First Epistle to the Corinthians*, p. 105, suggests that Paul uses irony to deflate their exaggerated view of their teachers. This is also seen as a personal application of the preceding discussion of 3.5–4.5 with an exposition of the pastoral office aimed to rebuke the inflated glorying of his readers, Plummer and Robertson, *1 Corinthians*, pp. 79–80. It is said to be Paul's answer to a slogan cited in 4.6 that the lack of 'wisdom, power and honour is part of the lot that God assigned to the suffering apostles', N. A. Dahl, 'The Church in Corinth', in *Studies in Paul: Theology for the Early Christian Mission* (Minneapolis: Augsburg Publishing House, 1977), pp. 54–5. W. Schmithals, *Gnosticism in Corinth*, English translation (Nashville: Abingdon Press, 1971), p. 180, says it identifies a clear theme of 'the rejection of the arrogant self-consciousness of the Gnostics'.
[74] See pp. 173–5.
[75] B. Fiore, '"Covert Allusion" in 1 Corinthians 1–4', *CBQ* 47 (1985), 88–90. He was not the first to observe this fact. F. H. Colson, 'Μετεσχημάτισα 1 Cor. iv 6', *JTS* 17 (1916), 379–84. Marshall, *Enmity in Corinth*, pp. 181–207, did not take into account the use of this important rhetorical device which Paul actually names in his extended discussion of this passage.

reasons. They did so when they wished to speak in an indirect way. They may have wished to say one thing obliquely and yet pursue something else in practice, or to say the opposite to what they were actually doing. It could also be used to speak one's mind (λεχθήσεσθαι παρρησίας ἔνδειξιν) but to forestall audience distress by including some ameliorating information. The device was particularly helpful for the sake of 'decency' (εὐπρέπεια), to maintain the safety of the speaker, or out of deference to the status of the persons addressed (δι' ἀξίωσιν τῶν προσώπων). Such persons could include a noble or honoured citizen, a general, a ruler, an entire city or even a country.[76] The covert allusion could usually be identified by the use of irony. Dionysius of Halicarnassus said, 'In short, the figure of irony is generally a sign of figured speech, σχῆμα ἐσχηματισμένων', and subsequent discussion by Paul shows that he certainly mingled irony with the rhetorical device.[77]

How did Paul use this device? B. Fiore expresses surprise that Paul, in using λόγος ἐσχηματισμένος in 4.6, actually draws the Corinthians' attention to the fact. He suggests that the apostle 'thereby negates the covertness of the rhetorical form' and makes 'explicit censures'. 'Whatever good is to be gained through oblique references would seem to be lost in the ironical characterisation of the Corinthians in 4.7–8.'[78] He is not sure why Paul has done this and suggests that '*perhaps* pastoral demands of the community in crisis can explain his abandonment of the rhetorical restraint of a lecture hall or judicial forum'.[79] The key to understanding him, however, lies in assessing the proportions as Paul mingles irony with this rhetorical device,[80] for he ironically uncovers his covert allusion in the following section in order to advance his case.

Paul begins in 1 Corinthians 4 with ameliorating words, building on the encouragement of 3.21–4.2. As has been noted, he reaffirms their enrichment in Christ (1 Cor. 3.21–3, cf. 1.5) before moving

---

[76] Fiore, '"Covert Allusion" in 1 Corinthians 1–4', 90–1 and sources cited.
[77] Cited by *ibid.*, 90. K. A. Plank, *Paul and the Irony of Affliction*, SBL Semeia Studies (Atlanta: Scholars Press, 1987), pp. 33–70, discusses 'the rhetorical situation' in 1 Cor. 1–4 predominantly through the lens of modern, not ancient, rhetoric. He makes no reference to recent literature on ancient rhetoric, and the primary focus is on 1 Cor. 4.9–13.
[78] Fiore, '"Covert Allusion" in 1 Corinthians 1–4', 95.
[79] *Ibid.*, 96.
[80] Fee, *The First Epistle to the Corinthians*, p. 167, n. 10, who feels that Fiore's essay is 'seriously marred by its failure to recognise the apologetic element in chap. 4'.

on. He then tells the Corinthians that they need to regard both Apollos and Paul in non-status functional terms (4.1ff.), and rebukes them for usurping the role of the divine judge when they dare to assess his ministry. He concludes with a call to judge nothing prematurely (verses 3–5). The ταῦτα of verse 6 may well refer to the immediately preceding section and its words of encouragement. Paul says that he has applied these things for their benefit so that they will not go beyond the things that have been written (verse 6a).[81] At this point, however, a marked change takes over when Paul refers to what they have been doing (εἷς ὑπὲρ τοῦ ἑνὸς φυσιοῦσθε κατὰ τοῦ ἑτέρου, verse 6c). Three penetrating questions follow: τίς γὰρ σε διακρίνει ('For who made you a judge?');[82] τί δὲ ἔχεις ὃ οὐκ ἔλαβες and the supplementary question εἰ δὲ καὶ ἔλαβες, τί καυχᾶσαι ὡς μὴ λαβώ (verse 7). These questions vigorously rebuke the Corinthians for comparing Paul and Apollos, and for boasting as if gifts originated from themselves.

In the next verse Paul declares ironically that the Corinthians ἤδη κεκορεσμένοι, ἤδη ἐπλουτήσατε, ἤδη ἐβασιλεύσατε.

1 Corinthians 4.8	Sophists' boasting
ἤδη κεκορεσμένοι,	ὑγιεινοί κτλ
ἤδη ἐπλουτήσατε,	πλούσιοι, ἔνδοξοι
ἤδη ἐβασιλεύσατε	ἡγεμόνες κτλ[83]

These terms find a ready echo in the sophists' boasting. Paul adds, again with irony, that he wishes they would act according to their status in Christ and behave like kings, so that he could share their status with them.[84] He notes how God had put the apostles to shame: 'For I think that God has exhibited us apostles as last of all, like men sentenced to death; for we have become a spectacle to the world, to angels and to men' (verse 9).

---

[81] *Ibid.*, pp. 167–9, for a summary of the discussion relating to this section of the verse.

[82] This makes the best sense of the question. The use of γάρ certainly connects it to the previous activity of verse 6c. διακρίνω carries the concept of deciding, hence the suggestion of arbitrator – a theme discussed in 4.3–5. Cf. Marshall, *Enmity in Corinth*, p. 205, and Fee, *The First Epistle to the Corinthians*, p. 171, n. 30, who renders it as 'Who concedes you any superiority?' following *BAGD* #205.

[83] Philo, *Det.* 33–4.

[84] On the use of the term 'king' for flattery see p. 189. For a full discussion of this and other terms used here by Paul see J. T. Fitzgerald, *Cracks in an Earthen Vessel: An Examination of the Catalogues of Hardships in the Corinthian Correspondence*, SBL Dissertation Series 99 (Atlanta: Scholars Press, 1988), pp. 135–7.

Ironically, in the next verse Paul wrests away the high-status terminology of the elite of secular Corinth introduced in 1 Corinthians 1.26 and applies it to the Christians' status in Christ: but *you* are wise in Christ (ὑμεῖς δὲ φρόνιμοι ἐν Χριστῷ = οἱ σοφοί) ... but *you* are strong (ὑμεῖς δὲ ἰσχυροί = οἱ δυνατοί) ... but *you* are glorious (ὑμεῖς ἔνδοξοι = οἱ εὐγενεῖς).[85] He also takes over the terminology of low status of the Corinthian Christians in 1.27–8, τὰ μωρὰ τοῦ κόσμου, τὰ ἀσθενῆ τοῦ κόσμου, τὰ ἀγενῆ τοῦ κόσμου and τὰ ἐξουθενημένα and τὰ μὴ ὄντα, and applies it to the apostolic teachers in 1 Corinthians 4.10, describing them as μώροί, ἀσθενεῖς, ἄτιμοι.[86]

Status in Corinth		God's calling	Apostolic status
1.26	4.10	1.27–8	4.10
Secular	in Christ	Secular	in the world
σοφοί	φρόνιμοι	τὰ μωρὰ τοῦ κόσμου	μωροί
δυνατοί	ἰσχυροί	τὰ ἀσθενῆ τοῦ κόσμου	ἀσθενεῖς
εὐγενεῖς	ἔνδοξοι	τὰ ἀγενῆ τοῦ κόσμου	ἄτιμοι
		τὰ ἐξουθενημένα	
		τὰ μὴ ὄντα[87]	

In addition terms of ignominy describe the apostles: 'To the present hour we hunger and thirst, we are ill-clad and buffeted and homeless, and we labour working with our own hands.[88] We have become, and are now the refuse of the world, the off-scouring of all things' (verses 11–13).[89]

Paul assures them that he uses irony to admonish and not shame them, for he says that his relationship to them is not as that of a

---

85 Theissen, *Social Setting*, p. 72, rightly sees these terms sociologically as a modification of 1 Cor. 1.26, as does Conzelmann, *1 Corinthians*, p. 89. Fee, *The First Epistle to the Corinthians*, p. 176, n. 57, notes that Theissen does not discuss the irony of the passage.

86 See Philo, *Som.* I, 155, where he actually uses ἰσχυροί and δυνατοί in this passage as synonyms, and ἀσθενεῖς as an antonym.

87 See Sänger, 'Die δυνατοί in 1 Kor.1.26', p. 288.

88 Philo, *Det.* 33, where the sophists boasted that their hands had not known labour, πόνον οὐκ εἰδότες.

89 R. Hodgson, 'Paul, the Apostle and First Century Tribulation Lists', *ZNW* 74 (1983), 59–80, esp. p. 65, where he suggests that 4.10–13 is didactic rather than apologetic and autobiographical. He does not take into account the rhetorical forms of the whole passage with its irony. Fitzgerald, *Cracks in an Earthen Vessel*, p. 147, who notes its use, has not connected the passage with the reversal of status strategy of Paul in 1 Cor. 1.26–8.

παιδαγωγός to the sons of a household, but that of a father in Christ (verses 14–15).[90] They are exhorted to imitate him (Παρακάλω οὖν ὑμᾶς μιμηταί, verses 14–17).[91] The full weight of irony is to be seen in these verses, for whilst Plato disparaged the sophists as 'imitators of realities', Paul ironically summons the Corinthians with their sophistic orientation to an altogether different form of imitation.[92] They must not, like the disciples of a sophist, model themselves on their teacher's mannerisms and techniques of rhetoric. Instead they ought to emulate the apostles of the crucified Messiah with their low status and suffering – and the ignominy which that brings before the sophistic milieu of Corinth. This imitation, called his 'ways in Christ' (verse 17), bears no resemblance to that of the sophistic tradition.

In verses 18–21 Paul concludes his discussion of the sophistic problem with a reference to those who have become 'puffed up' in the face of his delayed return to Corinth. These 'certain people' (τινες), already arrogant, have grown even more so with the church's request for Apollos to return. Verses 18–19a suggest that the supporters of the only other genuine candidate for the Corinthian church's loyalty, Apollos, are interested in him because of his δύναμις and λόγος. The tradition of the sophist's μαθηταί was to imitate their sophist.[93] Given that Apollos was a man of powerful eloquence (ἀνὴρ λόγιος, δυνατός) with regard to the scriptures, who engaged in dialogue εὐτόνως and demonstrated his convictions through the scriptures (Acts 18.24, 28), the fact that some preferred Apollos is not altogether unexpected.

But Paul declares that when he arrives DV his concern will not be in the 'eloquence' (λόγος) of the puffed-up, but their power (ἀλλὰ τὴν δύναμιν), because the kingdom of God is not ἐν λόγῳ ἀλλ' ἐν δυνάμει. The juxtaposition of these two important

---

90 N. H. Young, 'Paidagogos: The Social Setting of a Pauline Metaphor', *NovT* 29 (1987), 169–70, on Paul as their 'progenitor into the gospel' and not a 'postnatal appointee'.

91 *Contra* B. Sanders, 'Imitating Paul: 1 Cor. 4.16', *HTR* 74 (1981), 353–63, who doubts that 4.16 invites the church to imitate Paul's sufferings in verses 9–13. On the recommended use of μίμησις as a device 'which serves to excite the gentler emotions' see Quintilian, IX.2.58.

92 *The Sophist*, 235a.

93 Cf. Philostratus, *Lives of the Sophists*, 586: 'I will undertake to imitate them [the sophists and their style], and will reproduce extempore the style of every one of them . . . as for Herodes, the prince of eloquence, I should be thankful if I could mimic him'.

rhetorical terms resembles Philo's complaint against the sophists. While they are competent as speakers, yet they prove themselves to be impotent in living.[94] Here, as in 1 Corinthians 2.4–5, Paul is not averse to taking a key rhetorical term, δύναμις, and relating it not to rhetoric but to the kingdom of God. He warns that choices concerning his coming will be determined by the Corinthians: he can come with a rod or with love in a spirit of gentleness (verse 21).

Conclusion

Some suggest that Paul in his development of 1 Corinthians has demonstrated his own rhetorical sophistication. But that Paul consciously structured the letter along the lines of an oration is uncertain; and those who think he did disagree on the details.[95] His ability to do so is not in doubt,[96] but if he had, he would have exposed himself to the charge of engaging in what he condemns, given his critique of the sophistic movement and his parody of the rhetorical form in 4.6ff.[97]

More certain is that Paul inverts a basic sophistic perception by declaring that in the church the teacher belongs to the disciples rather than vice versa, as was the case in the secular world of Corinth. He also overturns the notion of imitating a teacher's mannerisms and techniques, instead challenging the disciples of the crucified Messiah to emulate his position of ignominy. Finally, a critique of the sophistic tradition emerges based on its inappropri-

---

[94] For Philo's discussion see pp. 85–9.
[95] Wuellner, 'Greek Rhetoric', p. 184. He has argued that 1 Cor. 1–4 consists of an *exordium* 1.4–9; followed by the main theme 1.10; a shaming section 1.11–18; followed by the first major 'digression' 1.19–3.20; a brief *peroratio* 3.21–3 and then in ch. 4 what could have readily followed 1.18, pp. 179–86. He has drawn attention to the existence of what was called a *digressio* in the rhetorical handbooks and noted that 1.19–3.20 justified the use of such a device. M. Bünker, *Briefformular und rhetorische Disposition im 1 Korintherbrief*, Göttinger Theologische Arbeiten 28 (Göttingen: Vanderhoeck & Ruprecht, 1983), pp. 53–8, however, argues for *exordium* 1.10–17; *narratio* 1.18–2.16 (2.1–5 *digressio*); *probatio* 3.1–17; *refutatio* 4.1–13; *peroratio* 4.14–21. See L. L. Welborn, 'A Conciliatory Principle in 1 Cor. 4.6', *NovT* 29.4 (1987), 340, who believes, 'It goes without saying that there are many things in 1 Cor. 1–4 which have no counterpart in ancient rhetoric ... Yet ... we may conclude that Paul's use of a particular rhetorical form was clear to his readers'. He proceeds to discuss the genre as a συμβουλευτικὸς λόγος περὶ ὁμόνοιας but only to explain the meaning of 1 Cor. 4.6, 'not to go beyond the things that have been written'.
[96] For further discussion see p. 217.
[97] See pp. 207–8 on Paul's letters.

ateness as an essential qualification for church leadership. The censure of Christian admiration for rhetorical skill permeates Paul's *apologia*, both as he defends his own *modus operandi* and as he formulates definitions of Christian leadership and discipleship.

10

PAUL AMONG THE CHRISTIAN SOPHISTS

Introduction

Paul's critique of the sophistic tradition appears to have angered at least some in the Corinthian congregation, including those deemed wise by the standards of this age (1 Cor. 3.18). They, along with others, had become 'puffed up' because Paul was unable to return to Corinth at the time of writing (1 Cor. 4.18–19). The congregation, in spite of its characteristic loyalty to former teachers, had been persuaded to seek the return of the rhetorically accomplished Apollos. But Apollos refused their request (1 Cor. 16.12). 2 Corinthians 10–13 suggests that as a result, itinerant teachers with similar training in rhetoric were recruited to instruct the congregation.[1] These teachers, who now had access to Paul's assessment of the sophistic tradition in 1 Corinthians 1–4, sought to undermine his devastating apostolic critique of it. By borrowing key rhetorical categories from that critique they mounted a major attack against him by highlighting Paul's inherent deficiencies as a public speaker in order to justify their own ministry in the church and to repulse any attempts by Paul to re-establish the authority lost during the humiliating visit to Corinth which followed the writing of 1 Corinthians.[2] Some of their actual comments are recorded by Paul

---

[1] *Contra* C. K. Barrett, 'Christianity at Corinth' in *Essays on Paul* (London: SCM Press, 1982), p. 14, who has argued that the problems in 2 Cor. are not related to those in 1 Cor.; and D. Georgi, *The Opponents of Paul in Second Corinthians*, English translation (Edinburgh: T. & T. Clark, 1987), p. 317, where the adversaries in 1 Cor. were Gnostics and those in 2 Cor. were shaped by Hellenistic Jewish apologetics.

[2] For the most recent review of the evidence of his visits and the sequence of letters which adheres to the canonical order of 1 Cor. and 2 Cor. 10–13 (even when the thesis of two or more letters in 2 Cor. is adopted) see J. M. Gilchrist, 'Paul and the Corinthians: the Sequence of Letters and Visits', *JSNT* 34 (1988), 47–69.

in 2 Corinthians 10.10 and 11.6, together with the allegation of duplicity in Paul's handling of money (2 Cor. 12. 16–18).

The first section of this chapter, 'The assessment of Paul as orator and debater', analyses the critique of Paul in 2 Corinthians 10–13. The remainder of the chapter, 'Paul's assessment of the Christian sophists', examines Paul's remarks concerning not only the sophistic tradition *per se*, but also its Christian exponents in the Corinthian church.

The sophistic assessment of Paul as orator and debater: 2 Corinthians 10.10, 11.6, 12.16

While the background of Paul's opponents in 2 Corinthians has been the subject of considerable discussion,[3] our concern is with their assessment of his performance in 2 Corinthians 10.10 and 11.6. They claimed that he was 'unpresentable' in appearance as a public speaker (ἡ παρουσία τοῦ σώματος ἀσθενής), and that by contemporary canons of speaking he was 'inarticulate' (ὁ λόγος ἐξουθενημένος, 10.10). He was only a layman in oratory (ἰδιώτης ἐν τῷ λόγῳ, 11.6) who used underhand methods to obtain financial support for his ministry (12.14–18).

Paul as an orator: 2 Corinthians 10.10

The disparity between Paul's letters, described as βαρεῖαι καὶ ἰσχυραί, and his actual 'bodily presence' and 'contemptible speech' provided the impetus for his opponents' criticism in 2 Corinthians 10.10.[4] This disparity elicited comment, 'They are saying' (ὅτι . . . φησίν), from his opponents and solidified his image as an unpresentable and inarticulate public speaker in a city highly conscious of rhetorical prowess.[5]

---

[3] For a summary see J. J. Gunther, *St Paul's Opponents and Their Background: A Study of Apocalyptic and Jewish Sectarian Teaching*, Supp. *NovT* xxxv (Leiden: E. J. Brill, 1973), p. 1; E. Earle Ellis, 'Paul and his Opponents', in *Prophecy and Hermeneutic in Early Christianity* (Tübingen: J. C. B. Mohr (Paul Siebeck), 1978), ch. 6, and more recently R. P. Martin, *2 Corinthians* (Waco: Word, 1986), pp. 336–42.
[4] See Martin, *2 Corinthians*, p. 311 for the argument that Paul has opponents in mind. 2 Cor. 10.10 is regarded as an actual report of what his adversaries said of him. See also Aristides *Or.* 33.4, 'They say that I do wrong because I do not declaim frequently . . . This is their charge.'
[5] On the importance of presenting oneself well in the secular world see pp. 116–17.

Writing versus extempore orators

2 Corinthians 10.10 presupposes a dichotomy, observed by his opponents, between Paul's letters on the one hand and his personal presence and public speech on the other. This verse reflects a continuing debate among the sophists over written versus extempore oratory,[6] an argument begun in the fourth century BC.[7] An excellent example of this debate is found in the exchanges between Alcidamas and Isocrates.[8]

Alcidamas, in his work *On the Writers of Written Discourse or On the Sophists*, conceded that sophists who engaged in literary rhetoric or written speeches might be able to write well. There was, however, no guarantee that the clever writer could speak acceptably extempore. If he tried, he would suffer 'mental embarrassment, wanderings and confusion' (#9,16). He may be able to write 'with extreme care, rhythmically connecting phrases, perfecting style', but when compelled to speak extempore 'in every respect he makes an unfavourable impression, and differs not a whit from the voiceless' (ἰσχνός, #16a).[9] Indeed, 'through lack of a ready presence of mind he is quite unable to handle his material fluently or winningly' (#16b). Alcidamas believed that written discourses should not be called real speeches (λόγοι δίκαιοι) because they are 'wraiths, semblances and imitations' (#27–8). He further insisted that extempore speakers held a greater influence over their audience because of their spontaneity than those who delivered written

---

[6] H. L. Hudson-Williams, 'Political Speeches in Athens', *CQ* (n.s.) 45 (1951), 68–73, and more recently N. O'Sullivan 'Written and Spoken in the First Sophistic', in I. Worthington (ed.) *Voice into Text: Orality and Literacy in Ancient Greece* (Leiden: Brill, 1996), ch. 7.

[7] For example, Philodemus discussed the inability of eminent writers to speak presentably in public and the steps some took to rectify this problem; see pp. 208–10.

[8] On the orations of Isocrates see *LCL*, vol. II. On Alcidamas see L. Radermacher, 'Alcidamas', in *Artium scriptores: Reste der voraristotelischen Rhetorik* (Wien: Rudolfe M. Rohrer, 1951), no. 15, English translation by La Rue Van Hook, 'Alcidamas versus Isocrates: The Spoken versus the Written Word', *CW* 12 (1918), 91–4. For discussion see S. Wilcox, 'Isocrates' Fellow-Rhetoricians', *AJP* 66 (1945), 171–86; G. A. Kennedy, *The Art of Persuasion in Greece* (Princeton: Princeton University Press, 1963), pp. 176–7; and most recently A. Hardie, *Statius and the Silvae: Poets, Patrons and Epideixis in the Graeco–Roman World* (Liverpool: Francis Cairns, 1983), pp. 78–81.

[9] For the rendering of ἰσχνόν 'plain style' see the discussion by Quintilian, XII.10.58 of this as one of three styles of speaking 'The first is termed the plain (or ἰσχνόν), the second grand and forcible (or ἁδρόν), and the third either intermediate or florid'.

speeches (#22). The writings of Alcidamas and Aristotle testify to
the fact that in courts of law and in assembly both written and
extempore speeches were allowed.[10] Alcidamas, however, opposed
forensic orators engaged in 'speech writing' (λογογραφία) and
deliberative orators dependent on a manuscript.[11] Therefore he
formulated an especially sharp distinction between written discourse and extempore oratory. The exponents of the former were
bound to fail in the latter, although, according to Alcidamas, the
extempore orator could readily engage in the former.[12] A much
later observer noted in the *Scholia* of Aristides – ὁ ῥήτωρ μᾶλλον
ὁρώμενος πείθει, ἥπερ διὰ γραμμάτων.[13]

Alcidamas' work responded to attacks found in Isocrates' discourse *Against the Sophists* (391 BC). The latter was written as he
commenced a career as a teacher of rhetoric, having spent 403–392
BC as a speech writer (λογογράφος) for Athenian law courts.
Among those he attacked were the teachers of rhetoric who
advertised that they could fashion all who followed their instruction
into eloquent orators. Isocrates opposed extempore speech and,
although the antithetical position he adopted was related in some
ways to his background and his inability to speak in public, he also
believed that 'oratory is only good if it has the qualities of fitness
for the occasion, propriety of style, and originality of treatment'.[14]
He disapproved of those who taught deliberative oratory because
they promised to make orators of students regardless of natural
ability and experience (#9–10).

This dichotomy in rhetoric was firmly established in Isocrates'
time as his polemical work, *The Antidosis*, written many years later,
was to show. The predominant emphasis on declamation in education among orators in the first century AD demonstrates further the
primacy of extempore speech over written speeches,[15] an emphasis
reflected in 2 Corinthians 10.10. Dio Chrysostom reiterated the
common opinion when he said 'he who utters his thoughts aloud is
more nearly in the mood of a man addressing an audience than one
who writes . . . it contributes more to your habit of readiness'.[16]

[10] Wilcox, 'Isocrates' fellow-rhetoricians', 181–2, n. 32 citing Aristotle, 1180b–81a.
[11] *Alcidamas*, 13–14, cf. Plutarch, *Lives, Demosthenes*, XI.
[12] *Alcidamas*, 6.
[13] W. Windorf, *Aristides*, 191.3 (Leipzig, 1829), vol. III, p. 606.
[14] *Against the Sophists*, 9–10, 13.   [15] See pp. 21–3.
[16] Dio, 'On Training for Public Speaking', *Or.* 11.18; Philostratus, *Lives of the Sophists*, 583; Plutarch, *Lives, Demosthenes*, VIII.

Paul's letters: 2 Corinthians 10.10a

When Paul's opponents said in verse 10a that his letters were βαρύς, what did they mean?[17] C. Forbes argues that it expressed righteous indignation. He notes, citing in support the second-century AD work of Hermogenes, that the word itself refers to a technique used by orators who felt themselves badly treated or maligned.[18] The problem with this interpretation is that while Paul may have used the technique to refute his opponents, can the opponents actually say that Paul's letters are full of *righteous* indignation?

There is another possible explanation. Lucian notes the injunction given to the rhetorician that he is to throw away his endless loquacity, antithesis, balanced clauses, periods, foreign phrases and 'everything else that makes speech βαρύς'.[19] The word is used here of various rhetorical techniques outlined in the first part of his sentence, not of a particular one bearing that name. In this instance the idea is 'impressive'. It has been noted that the other term, ἰσχυρός, is a description of stylistic qualities: 'forcefulness, strength and vigour'.[20] If this interpretation is correct then Paul's detractors are asserting that from a distance Paul can write impressive and persuasive letters in the rhetorical style – not unlike those rhetoricians Alcidamas discusses in such pejorative terms. Did Paul's

---

[17] Various opinions have been expressed. Martin, *2 Corinthians*, p. 311: 'impressive and forceful' like the rest of his letters; A. J. Dewey, 'A Matter of Honor: A Social–Historical Analysis of 2 Corinthians 10' *HTR* 78 (1985), 213: 'assertion of authority'; R. Bultmann, *The Second Letter to the Corinthians*, English translation (Minneapolis: Augsburg Publishing House, 1985), p. 190: 'admonitions'; H. D. Betz, *Der Apostel Paulus und die sokratische Tradition: eine exegetische Untersuchung zu seiner 'Apologie' 2 Korinther 10–13* (Tübingen: J. C. B. Mohr (Paul Siebeck), 1972), p. 44: 'pretentious and impressive' (he argues that the reference is to the letters' claims which are indeed impressive); A. Plummer, *A Critical and Exegetical Commentary on the Second Epistle of St Paul to the Corinthians*, (Edinburgh: T. & T. Clark, 1915), p. 282: 'tyrannical and violent'; P. Marshall, *Enmity in Corinth: Social Conventions in Paul's Relations with the Corinthians* (Tübingen: J. C. B. Mohr (Paul Siebeck), 1987), pp. 385–6: 'impressive'.

[18] See C. Forbes, 'Comparison, Self-praise and Irony: Paul's Boasting and Conventions of Hellenistic Rhetoric', *NTS* 32 (1968), 16 and his discussion of βαρύς as the appropriate response of a speaker who had been badly treated. For the literary evidence, citing Hermogenes, *On Rhetorical Forms*, 2.viii see pp. 12–13. For a similar discussion see Aristides, Περὶ βαρύτητος #448. Marshall, *Enmity in Corinth*, p. 387, suggests that βαρύς refers to the 'grand style' in rhetoric.

[19] *The Dialogue of the Dead*, 373.

[20] Marshall, *Enmity in Corinth*, p. 386, citing Dionysius of Halicarnassus, *Thucydides*, 54.

detractors say, 'He might well argue that in his coming to, and conduct in, Corinth he is anti-sophist (1 Cor. 2.1–5) but look at the letters he has written'? Clearly some in the church suspect Paul of operating in a secular fashion (κατὰ σάρκα περιπατούμενος, 2 Cor. 10.2–3), and now level against him the very charge he had voiced against them in 1 Corinthians 3.3, namely, κατὰ ἄνθρωπον περιπατούμενοι.[21] Could Paul defend himself if, having forcefully denounced the use of rhetorical devices in preaching, his own letters betrayed their use?[22] Did his letters conform to the very tradition which he had proscribed for the Corinthians in 1 Corinthians?

Rhetorical ὑπόκρισις

If Paul aimed to πείθειν διὰ γραμμάτων, to borrow a phrase from *The Scholia of Aristides*, then how did he measure up when it came to public speaking? His opponents of course insisted that 'his bodily presence was weak and his speech was of no account', reflecting their assessment of his rhetorical delivery (ὑπόκρισις). D. A. Russell has shown that 'delivery' along with 'histrionic technique' were of supreme importance in declamation.[23] Philodemus, the Epicurean writer of the first century BC, in *On Rhetoric*, devotes a section of this discourse to delivery and discusses its use by ancient sophists as well as his contemporaries.[24] His evidence is extremely illuminating and complements the material from the second century AD onwards which undergirds Russell's conclusions.

Philodemus observes that delivery has risen to pre-eminence in his own day – though its significance to the ancients should not be

---

[21] See p. 172.
[22] For a discussion of earlier letters and rhetorical structure (especially with regard to 1 and 2 Thessalonians) see R. Jewett, 'The Rhetoric of the Thessalonian Letters', in *The Thessalonian Correspondence: Pauline Rhetoric and Millenarian Piety* (Philadelphia: Fortress Press, 1986), ch. 5; for alternative readings of the same letters see G. S. Holland, *The Tradition that You Received from Us: 2 Thessalonians in the Pauline Tradition* (Tübingen: J. C. B. Mohr (Paul Siebeck), 1988); and F. W. Hughes, *Early Christian Rhetoric and 2 Thessalonians* (Sheffield: Sheffield Academic Press, 1988).
[23] D. A. Russell, *Greek Declamation* (Cambridge: Cambridge University Press, 1983), p. 82.
[24] S. Sudhaus, *Philodemi volumina rhetorica* (Leipzig, 1892), cited by volume with pagination, fragment and lines and the page of English translation by H. M. Hubbell, 'The Rhetorica of Philodemus', *The Connecticut Academy of Arts and Sciences* 23 (1920); for citation 'On delivery' see I.193, XI–XVIII, 300–1.

underestimated. He notes that for Athenaeus it was the most important element of rhetoric. Isocrates, he adds, refrained from public appearances because he lacked ability in this regard, and his orations were criticised for being 'hard to deliver in public'. Demosthenes said that delivery was 'the first thing in oratory, and the second and the third', yet he was criticised because of 'the loudness and shrillness of his own voice' as well as for being 'too theatrical and not simple and noble in his delivery'. Philodemus seems to have held that most of the ancient sophists were judged to have exhibited poor delivery.[25]

Philodemus concedes, however, that the sophists of his own day have improved on the delivery of their predecessors thanks to the attention that delivery now receives in their classrooms. But even this is mixed praise; he thinks the development 'a product of recent foolishness' for it results in the sophistic claim that they alone have formulated 'an art of delivery'. Philodemus does not deny this boast, but wishes it known that the poets and prose writers also have a theory of delivery even if it is not codified.[26]

The importance of delivery for declaimers is that, when successful, it makes them appear 'dignified and noble'. Philodemus does not denigrate a good delivery, because it 'lends dignity to the speaker, secures the attention of the audience and sways their emotions'. However, to his mind the sophists maintained no monopoly in this area because delivery involves 'a natural and unconscious bodily expression of the emotions'. It depends on 'natural endowment, beauty of voice, grace of body and self-possession'. The sophists, on the other hand, magnified the artistry of rhetoric because of delivery, and then claimed its superiority over philosophy.[27] The disproportionate attention given to delivery in Philodemus' day remained a hallmark of rhetoric in the first century AD.

After rejecting the art of delivery as developed by the sophists, Philodemus outlines his own position. Delivery depends on 'natural endowments and melody, sublimity, tones and breadth of voice and

---

[25] *On Rhetoric*, I.193, XI; I.197, XVI; I.200, XVIII; pp. 300–1. F. Solmsen, 'The Aristotelian Tradition in Ancient Rhetoric', *AJP* 62 (1941), 45–6, notes that there was considerable attention given to ὑπόκρισις. Theophrastus first theorised on 'delivery' and Aristotle subsequently suggested that in dealing with the topic special attention be paid to voice and its modulation.

[26] *On Rhetoric*, I.198. XVII; p. 301.

[27] *Ibid.*, I.194. XIII; I.196. XIV; I.199–200. XVII–XVIII; pp. 300–1.

both the dignity and proportion of face, hand and the rest of the body'. The emphasis on 'singing' may reflect another aspect of more amateurish oratorical delivery, for, Philodemus notes, 'Some who have acquired a rhythmical style from these schools [of sophists] have become considerably more pleasing in the *demos* and the *ecclesia*.'[28] He discusses elsewhere the aid 'charm' (ἐπίχαρις) gives to 'deliberative speaking in the assembly' and 'the pleading of forensic causes'.[29] This also falls under the heading of delivery. Philodemus thus shows the importance attached to ὑπόκρισις both in the past and in his own day. His discussion illuminates the grounds upon which public speakers would have been judged both in his own day and in the first century AD, namely whether they were good or poor on delivery.

A more positive attitude towards delivery comes from Quintilian, a near-contemporary of Paul. He too notes the emphasis given it by Demosthenes, and with reference to Cicero's discussion, and observes that both voice and physical appearance are included under this rubric. In Quintilian's estimation, good delivery is thus 'hampered by incurable impediments of speech . . . physical uncouthness may be such that no art can remedy it, while a weak voice is incompatible with first-rate excellence in delivery' (XI.3.12–13). He also discusses at great length body gestures and adornment.[30]

Another aspect of ὑπόκρισις is discussed in Dio Chrysostom. He insists that Diogenes associated with Antisthenes not so much because he approved of the man but because he derived pleasure from his words. Thus Dio contrasted the man with his words, and noted that the former was the weaker.[31] This common distinction between bodily presence and λόγοι means that Antisthenes' performance as a public speaker would have been overshadowed by flaws in his physical appearance. Demosthenes, in the face of such criteria, hired an actor to help him with his delivery.[32] Philodemus records that Isocrates refrained from public speaking, whilst Dionysius of Halicarnassus explains why: he lacked 'the first and most important quality of a public speaker', namely he failed to exhibit 'self-confidence and a strong voice'.[33] Isocrates thus falls into that

---

[28] *Ibid.*, 1.195. XIV; p. 301, II.252. XLVIII; p. 355.
[29] *Ibid.*, 1.195. XIII; p. 300.
[30] Quintilian, XI.3.1, 6, 7, 12, 13, 65–149.   [31] *Or.* 8.1–2.
[32] Plutarch, *Lives, Demosthenes*, XI.
[33] Philodemus, *On Rhetoric*, I.195, XVI, p. 301; Dionysius of Halicarnassus, *The Critical Essays*; *Isocrates*, 1.

group of non-performing orators whom Alcidamas calls 'voice-less'.[34] Demosthenes even turned the standard expectations into a weapon when he disparagingly claimed that Aeschines went to law to display his oratory and his vocal prowess, but when diction (λόγος) and quality of voice (ὁ τόνος τῆς φωνῆς) failed him, he turned to pandering to public sympathies. ὑπόκρισις played no part in his success.[35] But victory without ὑπόκρισις was rare.[36]

Paul's ὑπόκρισις: 2 Corinthians 10.10

H. D. Betz opines that the discussion in 10.10 can be epitomised under the term σχῆμα, which in the Cynic tradition related to outward appearance. In support of this he cites Lucian's 'Lover of Lies' 34, as a parallel to Paul's being ἀσθενής. Lucian describes Pancrates as 'wonderfully learned', familiar with all σοφία καὶ παιδεία. His friend, Arignotus, is surprised because he identifies him as speaking 'imperfect Greek', as 'flat-nosed with protruding lips and thinnish legs'.[37] By the canons of delivery both his speech and appearance would be judged inadequate for public oratory. Arignotus clearly associates ὑπόκρισις with its rhetorical connotations and not the Cynic concept of σχῆμα as Betz suggests.[38] It has already been noted that in his search for examples in Epictetus, Betz overlooked the significance of the discourse entitled 'On

---

[34] *Alcidimas*, 16. See also #15 where written orators are described as being as inexperienced as laymen in the faculty of speaking, having 'less voice' than a layman.

[35] Demosthenes, *De corona*, 280.   [36] Quintilian XI.3.12–13, cited on p. 210.

[37] *Der Apostel Paulus*, pp. 45, 53–4; 'Rhetoric and Theology', in A. Vanhoye (ed.), *L'Apôtre Paul: Personnalité, Style et Conception du Ministère* (Leuven: Leuven University Press, 1986), p. 41. Lucian does not use the term σχῆμα. Betz' choice of σχῆμα as the issue being discussed in 2 Cor. 10.10 falls short because σχῆμα has to do with personal appearance only, *Der Apostel Paulus*, p. 45; 'Rhetoric and Theology', p. 41. See Dio Chrysostom, Περὶ τοῦ σχήματος, *Or.* 72 for a helpful discussion of the meaning of σχῆμα. It is no synonym for ὑπόκρισις, a term defined by Philodemus in relation to rhetoric.

[38] V. P. Furnish, *II Corinthians*, The Anchor Bible (Garden City, NY: Doubleday, 1984), p. 468, has suggested that Epictetus III.22.86–9 resembles 10.10b, that Epictetus argues that if a Cynic hopes to carry the day with his teaching, then he must be able to say, 'Look, both I and my body are witnesses of this.' However, Epictetus discusses a Cynic who is 'consumptive . . . pale and thin'. He alone commends his message who extols the virtues of the plain and simple lifestyle; this requires a person whose body is a μαρτυρία of the truth of Cynic philosophy. While it would be possible to describe the physical appearance of this debilitated Cynic as ἀσθενής, this is not what the term means in the sophistic movement as Lucian shows.

personal adornment' (Περὶ καλλωπισμοῦ).[39] The student of rhetoric from Corinth who comes to Epictetus reflects in his dress and appearance his understanding of what was expected of an orator, and at the end of the discourse Epictetus delivers his most telling blow by calling the student 'ugly' because of his lack of traditional virtues.[40]

The judgement of Paul's opponents that 'his bodily presence was weak' was rendered according to the canons of rhetoric. It meant that his presence constituted such a liability as to all but guarantee his failure as an effective public orator.[41] He elicited no murmur of approval when audiences first saw him – as did the sophist whom Philostratus so admired.[42] The traditional description of Paul would justify the dissatisfaction felt by his detractors.[43] Paul's speech fared no better, for they describe his λόγος as ἐξουθενη-μένος (verse 10b).[44] This deficiency precluded him entering the public arena or even taking steps to overcome the problem.[45] The use of the perfect participle may suggest that the problem could not be remedied. The attention of the Corinthian congregation had been drawn to the fact that Paul's speech in effect amounted to 'nothing' by opponents who appear to have attacked him on this point to show up his inconsistency. In the light of the *apologia* concerning his coming (1 Cor. 2.3) his enemies could argue that his activity was governed not by theological considerations but by his own deficiencies as a public speaker. To be sure, such weaknesses

---

[39] Betz, *Der Apostel Paulus*, pp. 53–4.   [40] Epictetus, III.1.41–2 cf. 1.6.

[41] For the preoccupation of orators with outward appearance see the discussion in Epictetus pp. 116–17.

[42] Philostratus, *Lives of the Sophists*, 572. The Athenians thought his appearance and clothes so exquisite that before he spoke a word 'a low buzz of approval went around as a tribute to his perfect elegance'. Cf. also #571, #581.

[43] *Acts of Paul and Thecla* records that 'Paul was a man little of stature, bald-headed, with crooked legs, well-born, with eye-brows meeting and a long nose.' See *Acta Apostolorum Apocrypha*, I, 237.

[44] Furnish, *II Corinthians*, p. 468, translates it as 'contemptible' of Paul's manner and style; Martin, *2 Corinthians*, p. 313, 'contempt and scorn', arguing that his rhetorical ability was non-existent; Bultmann, *The Second Letter to the Corinthians*, p. 190, thinks it a term of reproach, εὐκαταφρόνητος parallel to ἀσθενής in 1 Cor. 1.28; C. K. Barrett, *The Second Epistle to the Corinthians*, (London: A. & C. Black, 1973), p. 261, 'contemptible' with reference to the fact that Paul could tie himself up in grammatical knots (of which Barrett sees 2 Cor. 10.1–10 an example); J. P. Meyer, *Ministers of Christ: A Commentary on the Second Epistle to the Corinthians* (Milwaukee: Northwestern Publishing House, 1963), p. 237, 'disdain'; Plummer, *2 Corinthians*, p. 283, 'not worth listening to', cf. Rom. 14.3,10.

[45] See pp. 210–11 and also Plutarch, *Lives, Demosthenes*, XI.

had blocked great orators of the past from entering the public arena. It has already been argued that Paul's opponents appear to have used the language of 1 Corinthians 3.4 against him in 2 Corinthians 10.2–3, which is further evidence that they rejected Paul's theological defence of his *modus operandi* in 1 Corinthians 2.1–5. They attributed his 'failure' instead to a lack of ὑπόκρισις.

The above discussion implies that the sophists' preference for extempore oratory over the written form, and their preoccupation with declamation, control their judgement against Paul in 10.10b.[46] The pejorative terms used by his opponents are strong evidence that he has been assessed as a public speaker by the canon of ὑπόκρισις, and has been found wanting.

Paul as a debater: 2 Corinthians 11.6

Paul records εἰ δὲ καὶ ἰδιώτης τῷ λόγῳ, ἀλλ' οὐ τῇ γνώσει, ἀλλ' ἐν παντὶ φανερώσαντες ἐν πᾶσιν εἰς ὑμᾶς (11.6).[47] This verse appears alongside his contention that he is in no way inferior to the 'super-apostles' mentioned in the previous verse. Verse 6a reiterates an evaluation of Paul,[48] but requires that we address three questions. (1) What does the term ἰδιώτης signify when linked with τῷ λόγῳ? (2) What is to be made of the strong adversative statement which follows? (3) How does the final adversative comment relate to the previous statements?

ἰδιώτης τῷ λόγῳ

What does ἰδιώτης τῳ λόγῳ mean in a rhetorical context? Philodemus indicates that two features distinguish the layman, philosopher and dialectician from the rhetorician or sophist. First, the former group does not 'display their speeches rhetorically' and second, they do not follow 'the received form' of sophistic speakers. He cites as an example the ignoble tricks of the forensic rhetorician

---

[46] Dewey, 'A Matter of Honor', 213, suggests that the problem is that respect commanded by claims of apostolic authority (verses 9–10a) was not sustained by his physical appearance and rhetorical performance (verse 10b). But that the problem has another cause is plain, for he (along with his appearance, etc.) was already known by many in the congregation.

[47] For a summary of views expressed on the meaning of this text by R. Bultmann, E. Käsemann, H. D. Betz, J. Munck and S. H. Travis, see Martin, *2 Corinthians*, p. 343.

[48] Furnish, *II Corinthians*, p. 505.

whose δύναμις dominated his presentation. Without it the orator would appear 'modest' in court and thereby 'forfeit that peace of life and solidarity of character which contributes most to his success' – a reference to the rhetor's extravagant lifestyle.[49] Philodemus then encourages the ἰδιώτης and other non-orators not to be ashamed if they cannot produce the second distinguishing mark, namely forms of speech used in forensic and deliberative oratory. A jury finds 'even stammering' by a layman more persuasive than the forms used by the orator, which, in his opinion, aim only to mislead. The classical virtues (ἀνδρεία, δικαιοσύνη, and σωφρο-σύνη) influence the jury more than forms of rhetorical speech. The 'non-orators' may indeed possess some knowledge of rhetoric, but they have abandoned ἀπάτη in their practice of it.[50] Philodemus thus condemns sophistic rhetoric – by which he means the efforts of those who deliver panegyric orations and declamations, and compose written works – for such sophists perform in schools and lecture rooms, leaving it to others to function in the forum and the *ecclesia*. Those who do engage in real conflict, unlike the pretenders, do so without depending on ἀπάτη.[51]

As already noted, Philo of Alexandria labels as ἰδιώτης not only those who have never been instructed in rhetoric, but also 'those who are beginning to learn, those making progress and those who have reached perfection'. He has already distinguished between σοφιστής, ἰδιώτης, and men in general in *Agr.* 143.[52] We saw that he applies the term not only to students of rhetoric, but even to graduates of the sophists' schools. The opposite of ἰδιώτης for Philo was τεχνίτης or ἀσκητής, not σοφιστής, for the ἀσκητής practised virtue, unlike the sophist.[53]

Isocrates applies the term ἰδιώτης to those who have been trained in a school of rhetoric but have become neither orators nor teachers of rhetoric. He records 'from all our schools only two or three students turn out to be real champions [in the contests of oratory], the rest retiring from their studies into private life, ἰδιώτας'.[54] As the editor noted, 'private' is 'distinguished from the professional life of public orators and teachers

---

49 Philodemus 2.134. v, 306: literally 'display his speeches rhetorically or according to the received form of the sophists'; and see 2.139. xi, 307.
50 'Deceit', 'trickery', 'fraud'. For a discussion of ἀπάτη in Philo and his use of this Platonic category see pp. 91–2.
51 Philodemus, ii.136, vi.139, xi; p. 307.   52 See *Agr.* 159–60.
53 See p. 106 for discussion.   54 Isocrates, *Antidosis*, 201. Cf. 204 .

of oratory'.[55] Isocrates notes that those trained in oratory but preferring to live in private have by reason of their training become 'keener judges and more prudent counsellors' – it would be wrong to assume that they did not play a role in the affairs of the city.[56]

Epictetus includes in the term tax gatherers, orators and procurators by way of contrast with philosophers.[57] Alcidamas and Aristides use the term in their discussion of orators and sophists to refer to laymen untrained in rhetoric.[58] Because of this range of usage, context must be the primary determinant of meaning.

Paul as ἰδιώτης τῷ λόγῳ

Did ἰδιώτης τῷ λόγῳ in 2 Corinthians 11.6 signify the same for Paul's opponents as for Philodemus, Philo of Alexandria and Isocrates or for Epictetus, Alcidamas and Aristides? G. A. Kennedy says that 'it basically denotes a private person, not a professional', but cites no evidence to support this interpretation of verse 6a.[59] The answer can be determined by an analysis of the whole of verse 6, and in the light of that a comparison can also be made with the findings on 10:10.

11.6b presents the strong adversative statement: 'but certainly not in knowledge'.[60] γνῶσις is widely held to mean either spiritual knowledge or the gospel.[61] J. P. Meyer, however, suggests that Paul means his own expertise in forensic rhetoric. He concludes after a short survey of Acts 24 that Luke's presentation of Paul's performance before Felix suggests he possessed skill in this type of rhetoric – although he rejected as unsuitable for the gospel the rhetorical stance of his opponents in 2 Corinthians 2.14 and 2

---

[55] G. Norlin, *Isocrates*, LCL, II. p. 301, n. b.

[56] Isocrates, *Antidosis*, 204.

[57] *Discourses* III.7.1, xvi.13 and *Encheiridion*, 29. In other occurrences he warns against having social intercourse with laymen, III.16.3, 6, 7, 9, 10, and see *Encheiridion*, 33 and 17 where the reference is to 'a private citizen' in contrast to an official.

[58] Alcidamas, 1,4,15; Aristides, *Or.* 51.29.

[59] G. A. Kennedy, *New Testament Interpretation through Rhetorical Criticism* (Chapel Hill: University of North Carolina Press, 1984), p. 95.

[60] On the classical use of ἀλλά in the apodosis after εἰ which means 'yet' or 'certainly' or 'at least' see BDF #448(5).

[61] Bultmann, *The Second Letter to the Corinthians*, p. 204; Martin, *2 Corinthians*, p. 343; Plummer, *2 Corinthians*, p. 300; Furnish, *II Corinthians*, p. 490; cf. Betz, *Der Apostel Paulus*, p. 59, where he believes it refers to 'content' as compared with 'form'.

Corinthians 4.2.[62] Could Paul, although usually not wishing to make a rhetorical display, rely on forensic rhetoric if the need arose? Certainly an examination of Paul's facility in his confrontation with Tertullus as reported by Luke in Acts 24 suggests this was so.[63]

Does the remainder of verse 6 uphold this reading? With another strong adversative Paul affirms ἀλλ' ἐν παντὶ φανερώσαντες ἐν πᾶσιν εἰς ὑμᾶς (verse 6c). The textual variants betray the difficulty of this phrase – leading R. Bultmann to describe the clause as 'scarcely intelligible'.[64] He does note, however, along with other commentators, that the object of the verb must be αὐτήν, referring to γνώσει in verse 6b.[65] Does this mean that Paul on occasion used his knowledge of forensic rhetoric for the benefit of the Corinthians? Favouring this proposition is the rhetorical flourish Paul makes with ἐν παντί . . . ἐν πᾶσιν. This resembles Acts 24.3, where Tertullus says in his *exordium*, πάντῃ τε καὶ πανταχοῦ, which is generally accepted as a rhetorical comment.[66] If Paul can point to the manifestation of his forensic knowledge, could it be that there were occasions on which he used it to defend himself in court, hence the reference in verse 6c? According to Luke, Paul was prepared to defend himself before Gallio, although circumstances rendered that unnecessary (Acts 18.14). More significant still is his telling use of rhetorical devices such as the covert allusion in 1 Corinthians 4.6ff. Of his rhetorical skill J. P. Meyer concludes: 'The Corinthians knew this not from hearsay but from personal experience.'[67]

---

62   Meyer, *Ministers of Christ*, pp. 254–7. On the use of the Lucan portrait of Paul see my 'Favorinus' and my concluding remarks in B. W. Winter and A. D. Clarke (eds.), *The Book of Acts in its Ancient Literary Setting*, The Book of Acts in its First-Century Setting (Grand Rapids and Carlisle: Eerdmans and Paternoster, 1993), pp. 196–205, and 'The Importance of the *Captatio Benevolentiae* in the Speeches of Tertullus and Paul in Acts 24:1–21', *JTS* ns 42 (1991).
63   See my 'The Importance of the *Captatio Benevolentiae*', 505–31, for a discussion of Paul's expertise in forensic rhetoric.
64   Bultmann, *The Second Letter to the Corinthians*, p. 204, for a discussion of variants; cf. Martin, *2 Corinthians*, p. 343, who argues that the text as cited above should stand.
65   On the use of paronomasia by orators see *BDF* #448(1) and C. G. Wilke, *Die neutestamentliche Rhetoric. Ein Seitenstuck zur Grammatik des neutestamentlichen Sprachidioms* (Dresden and Leipzig, 1843), pp. 413–5. For the use of πᾶς in the *exordia* of the forensic petitions see *P.Fouad* 26, line 32; *P.Ryl.* 114, line 45; and *P.Oxy.* 2131, line 17, and my discussion in 'The Role of the *Captatio Benevolentiae*', 508–12.
66   Meyer, *Ministers of Christ*, p. 257. For examples of such rhetorical flourishes see *BDF* #488 (1).
67   Meyer, *Ministers of Christ*, p. 257.

Paul could also follow rhetorical forms in his letters.[68] H. D. Betz has argued for Galatians' rhetorical structure, as have others for the Thessalonian letters.[69] Both Paul and Philo use rhetorical forms for the purpose at hand.[70] Paul would not present his gospel rhetorically for reasons carefully spelt out already in 1 Corinthians 2.1–5, but felt free to employ accepted rhetorical forms in his writings. It thus appears that, to borrow a notion from Philodemus, Paul felt compelled to renounce not rhetoric itself but the deceit (ἀπάτη) which all too often accompanied its spoken manifestation, especially of the sophists.[71]

2 Corinthians 10.10 runs parallel to 11.6. While in the former a contrast is drawn between Paul's writing and his public face as a speaker, in the latter a dichotomy occurs between Paul's capacity as an orator and his knowledge of rhetoric. A corresponding division exists in 1 Corinthians 2.1–5 where Paul displays a knowledge of the three traditional proofs on the one hand, and, on the other, explicitly states that his preaching stance forms part of a strategy which benefits those who responded positively to his message (1 Cor. 2.4–5).

The critique of Paul's opponents in 10.10 and 11.6 is consistent with autobiographical details found in 1 Corinthians 2.3, namely that his visit to Corinth was marked by fear, trembling and much weakness. He suffered from a presentation which fell short of the quality expected of a public orator or sophist who aimed to persuade a first-century Corinthian audience. This attracted his

---

[68] *Contra* A. Lynch, 'Pauline Rhetoric: 1 Corinthians 1.10–4.21', MA dissertation, University of North Carolina (1981), p. 46, who concludes 'Moreover, if 1.17 contains a confession of a lack of rhetorical ability on the part of the apostle this section of the letter is ironically the most blatant display of rhetorical ability in the entire letter.' But we do not deny Pauline rhetorical ability with respect to writing. The point is that he renounced the use of 'grand style' in preaching.

[69] H. D. Betz, *Galatians*, (Philadelphia: Fortress Press, 1969). For a modification of Betz' thesis see R. G. Hall, 'The Rhetorical Outline of Galatians: A Reconsideration', *JBL* 106.2 (1987), 277–87, where he argues for a deliberative rather than a judicial form. G. W. Hansen, *Abraham in Galatians: Epistolary and Rhetorical Contexts* (Sheffield: Sheffield Academic Press, 1985), pp. 2,16–21,61–84, has explored the issue more fully and produced significant modifications to Betz' position, and P. H. Kern, 'Rhetoric, Scholarship and Galatians: Assessing an Approach to Paul's Epistle', PhD dissertation, University of Sheffield (1994), has given detailed reasons why Galatians was not written in conformity with Graeco-Roman rhetoric. See also n. 22.

[70] For discussion see previous note and D. T. Runia, 'Philo's *De Aeternitate Mundi*: the Problem of its Interpretation', *Vigiliae Christianae* 35 (1981), 130.

[71] *On Rhetoric*, 2.134.v, 307. Cf. Paul's comment on δόλος in 2 Cor. 12.16.

opponents' attention because it was an irreparable deficiency. How could Paul expect to exercise a continuing speaking role in the church when preaching standards had risen dramatically subsequent to his departure, most especially through exposure to Apollos? In the eyes of the Corinthians Paul may well represent Alcidamas' man whose abilities allowed for a well-crafted written discourse, yet rendered him 'inarticulate' in extempore rhetorical speech. The meaning of the term as defined by Philodemus, Philo of Alexandria and Isocrates reflected the reality of Paul's educational status – trained in rhetoric but not living the professional life of a public orator and teacher, even though he engaged in public proclamation and private instruction.

Paul's finances: 2 Corinthians 12.16

Someone had suggested to the church that though Paul himself had not openly sought financial gain, he had actually tricked the Corinthians into supporting him. In 2 Corinthians 12.16 he notes that on his third visit he would not be a financial burden. He then raises what is obviously a charge brought against him: 'but being crafty (πανοῦργος), I caught you with guile (δόλος)'.[72] In the following verse he cross-examines them about the allegation that he had taken financial advantage of them. Had Titus and the unnamed disciple who accompanied him taken advantage of them? No, they had not; in fact all three employed the same policy.

That first-century sophists hungered for money was a perennial allegation.[73] Paul has previously defended his financial policy (1 Cor. 9) precisely because some in Corinth have actually challenged him on the matter (9.3).

2 Corinthians 12.14–18 suggests that while Paul's detractors could not refute his defence based on the evidence, they now allege that he has surreptitiously provided the means by which others can collect money for him. To have financial intermediaries was not without precedent. Isocrates drew attention to the practice in his own day, noting that fees for instruction in a sophist's school were deposited with a third party. He maintained that such a procedure rendered hypocritical the sophists' claim to inculcate ἀρετή in their pupils.[74]

---

[72] Martin, *2 Corinthians*, pp. 445–6. See Betz, *Der Apostel Paulus*, p. 104, for the use of the word. Philo, *Post.* 101, uses it with reference to the sophists.
[73] See pp. 28, 49 and 95–7.   [74] *Against the Sophists*, 5–6.

The conduct of his financial affairs in 1 Corinthians 9 may have sounded admirable given Paul's lofty theory of a self-supporting apostolic ministry, but there were some who insisted that it did not bear close scrutiny (2 Cor. 12.14–18). Perhaps, they seem to have suggested, some of the money was not really destined for the poor in Jerusalem. This was despite the care Paul took to avoid giving the wrong impression.[75]

The opponents' use of 1 Corinthians against Paul

It has also become clear that Paul's opponents selected concepts and terms from his critique of the sophistic movement in 1 Corinthians 1–4 and 9 and used them to discredit him before the church. Bultmann has rightly paralleled Paul's ἀσθενής in 2 Corinthians 10.10 with τὰ ἐξουθενημένα ... τὰ μὴ ὄντα of 1 Corinthians 1.28.[76]

The ἰσχυρός-ἀσθενής language of 1 Corinthians 4.10 has been carefully exploited in 2 Corinthians 10.10. The dichotomy to which Paul referred in 1 Corinthians 1.26 between the Corinthians' secular status and their Christian status, and which he used in 1 Corinthians 4.10 in relation to himself and the church, was now used against Paul in order to contrast his deficiencies as a public orator with his obvious writing ability as a rhetorician.

His λόγος καὶ κήρυγμα, which 1 Corinthians 2.4 had affirmed was not in ἐν πειθοῖς σοφίας λόγοις, is now exploited by opponents who remind the Corinthians that Paul's λόγος is that of an ἰδιώτης (2 Cor. 11.6). While Paul could say in 1 Corinthians 1.5–7 that the Corinthians did not lag behind in eloquence and knowledge, had he not proven himself deficient in λόγοι and κατὰ πρόσωπον μὲν ταπεινὸς ἐν ὑμῖν (2 Cor. 10.1,11.6)?[77]

Paul may have denigrated the συζητητὴς τοῦ αἰῶνος τούτου in

---

[75] 1 Cor. 16.3–4. Cf. K. F. Nickle, *The Collection: A Study of Paul's Strategy*, SBT 48 (London: SCM Press, 1966), pp. 82–5, for a discussion of the great care taken to ensure that those who handled the half-shekel tax of Diaspora Jews could not pilfer or be accused of pilfering it on the way to or in Jerusalem. A. J. Malherbe, *Paul and the Popular Philosophers* (Minneapolis: Fortress Press, 1989), p. 115, states that he was charged with acting 'with guile by enriching himself by means of the collection for Jerusalem'.

[76] Bultmann, *The Second Letter to the Corinthians*, p. 190, and on this term see p. 193; cf. p. 108.

[77] Martin, *2 Corinthians*, p. 342, notes that 2 Cor. 11.5 with the use of ὑστερεῖν contains an innuendo cast at Paul.

1 Corinthians 1.20, but how did he himself perform? Was he not a persistent failure when it came to ὑπόκρισις (2 Cor. 10.10)? Was not his *apologia* in 1 Corinthians 2.1–5 a masterful theological rationalisation of his self-evident weak, trembling and inadequate performance as a public speaker in Corinth?

Paul had accused the Corinthian congregation of behaving in a secular fashion by evaluating Christian teachers according to sophistic standards (κατὰ ἄνθρωπον περιπατούμενοι). He further-more added pejorative terms to highlight their immature conduct (1 Cor. 3.1–4). Now his detractors accused him of precisely the same conduct in 2 Corinthians 10.2. He was κατὰ πρόσωπον μὲν ταπεινὸς ἐν ὑμῖν and bold when away but was in effect κατὰ σάρκα περιπατούμενος (2 Cor. 10.1).[78] They chose to highlight his deficiencies by drawing attention to the discrepancies between his poor performance as a public speaker when in Corinth and the very 'weighty and strong letters' he wrote when absent (2 Cor. 10.1ff.).[79]

J. Harrison has made the very unlikely suggestion that 1 Cor-inthians 1–4 and 2 Corinthians 10–13 may form one letter because of nine parallel thoughts he finds within the two passages.[80] The reconstruction offered above does not follow Harrison in arguing for parallel thought, but rather recognises the use by Paul's enemies of his criticisms in order to undermine his influence on the Corinthian church.

The evidence reveals that Paul's *modus operandi* is being judged by sophistic categories (2 Cor. 10.10, 11.6 and 12.14–18). Further-more, the assault was framed in the light of his own critique of the sophistic tradition in 1 Corinthians 1–4. Whatever remains unknown about these opponents of Paul in 2 Corinthians, this

---

[78] Malherbe, *Paul and the Popular Philosophers*, p. 116 suggests that the reference is to Paul's 'mean, inconsistent, underhanded, conniving conduct' connecting the imagery of verses 1–2 with 'the rigorist Cynics who have confidence in the armor of the gods' in verses 3–6; but argues that Paul appropriates a 'self-sufficient, self-confident Stoic' image. The term ταπεινός was one of social shame, cited by the sophists in Philo in their abuse of the virtue-seekers (*Det.* 32). The imagery would in that case be simply sophistic and not Cynic.

[79] *Contra* M. Jones, *St Paul as Orator: A Critical, Historical and Explanatory Commentary on the Speeches of St Paul* (London: Hodder and Stoughton, 1910), p. 1, where the definition of an orator by which Paul is assessed revolves around one's 'power to produce striking effects, and [the] marvellous facility of adapting himself to every class of hearer and to every variety of condition'. His analysis, however, is restricted to speeches in Acts.

[80] J. Harrison, 'St Paul's Letters to the Corinthians', *ET* 77 (1966), 285–6. Not all his parallels are appropriate, nor does he demonstrate his unlikely thesis that 1 Cor. 1–4 and 2 Cor. 10–13 were written at the same time.

much is certain: they were trained in the Greek rhetorical tradition. Others have followed separate paths to the conclusion that Paul's accusers were sophists.[81] The objection that since these Christians were Jews they could not be sophists poses no problem, for Philo, his nephew and others were Jews trained in Greek *paideia*.[82] The sophists could have argued convincingly that if the secular ἐκκλησία of Corinth demanded of speakers a facility in oratory, then the ἐκκλησία τοῦ Θεοῦ in the same city should flourish with teachers of no less ability. Paul clearly lacked the necessary prowess.

Paul's assessment of the Christian sophists: 2 Corinthians 10–13

Paul calls his opponents in 2 Corinthians 10–13 'ignorant' and 'fools' because they engaged in σύγκρισις and boasted about their achievements. To the Corinthians he discloses that he intends to do all in his power to undermine the false claim that they work on the same terms as he does (11.12). 2 Corinthians 10–13 contains his attempt to do so. God promised to destroy the wisdom of the wise and bring to nothing the reasoning of the clever so that men could know him (1 Cor. 1.19, 21); it appears that Paul saw himself engaged in a similar demolition work against strongholds of entrenched arguments, λογισμοί, and proud obstacles to the knowledge of God in the congregation.[83] This included his opponents (2 Cor. 10.4–5).

Substantial discussion of καύχημα and its cognates in 2 Corinthians 10–13 underpins Paul's argument.[84] This is not unex-

---

[81] Betz, *Der Apostel Paulus*, pp. 29–30, sees in 11.6 a contrast reflecting the argument between sophists and philosophers. See also S. H. Travers, 'Paul's Boasting in 2 Corinthians 10–12', *Studia Evangelica* 6 (1973), 528, 531, n. 5; M. E. Thrall, 'Super-apostles, Servants of Christ, and Servants of Satan', *JSNT* 6 (1980), 47; and P. W. Barnett, 'Opposition in Corinth', *JSNT* 22 (1984), 15, where he observes the opponents' skill in Greek rhetoric.

[82] For the most recent discussion see M. Hengel, 'Greek Education and Literature in Jewish Palestine', in *The 'Hellenization' of Judaea in the First Century after Christ*, English translation (London: SCM Press, 1990), ch. 3.

[83] Used by Aristotle as a term for 'reasoning', but here used in a pejorative sense.

[84] 2 Cor. 10.8, 13, 15–6, 17; 11.10, 12, 16–18, 21, 30; 12.1, 5, 6, 9, 11. As C. K. Barrett, 'Boasting (καυχᾶσθαι κτλ.) in the Pauline Epistles', in A. Vanhoye (ed.), *L'Apôtre Paul*, p. 362, points out, of its fifty-five occurrences, thirty-nine are in 1 and 2 Cor. For the most recent studies on the use of the term see B. A. Dowdy, 'The Meaning of KAUCHASTHAI in the New Testament', PhD dissertation, Vanderbilt University (1955), esp. 168, where he argues (unconvincingly) for a transition in the meaning of the term from a pejorative to a noble one in both

pected, for sophistic boasting was the thread which had bound together subsidiary issues as Paul's critique of the sophistic tradition in 1 Corinthians 1–4 unfolded.[85] Now Paul would employ the same standard to appraise the proponents of the sophistic tradition. As the previous section of this chapter has shown, the Corinthian church had already passed judgement on him (2 Cor. 10–13).[86] Secondary literature on 2 Corinthians 10–13 has overlooked the sophistic context in which the antithetical use of καύχημα takes on particular significance.[87] We have already encountered the problem of καύχημα in 1 Corinthians 1.26–8 and 4.8–13, and the similarities between the Alexandrian and Corinthian sophistic traditions concerning boasting in status and achievement have been shown to be striking.[88] We now turn to the dual questions: how did Paul's opponents boast?, and in what did they boast?

Sophistic boasting

In voicing their criticism of Paul's lack of ὑπόκρισις (2 Cor. 10.10) his opponents would have called attention to their own strengths in this regard, for they surely would not have offered such a biting attack if they themselves had been κατὰ πρόσωπον ταπεινός (10.1).[89] Not only had the opponents unfairly contrasted his past ministry with the one he currently conducted via his letters, thereby drawing attention to his unsuitability for further ministry in

---

Judaism and Christianity; and J. S. Bosch, *'Gloriarse' segun San Pablo: Sentido y teología de καυχάομαι* (Rome: Biblical Institute Press, 1970) which is primarily a word study. It is deficient in that it fails to observe that those who boasted were unlikely to have used the term to describe what they were doing. See R. Ansoul, 'The Self-Estimate of the Apostle Paul Contained in II Corinthians 10 and 11', PhD dissertation, Macquarie University (1978), p. 3, for epigraphic evidence of boasting of achievements without using καύχημα. The handbooks on rhetoric taught a student how to engage in subtle boasting, see Forbes, 'Comparison, Self-praise and Irony', 7.

[85] See our previous chapter.

[86] This conclusion does not endorse the view of Betz, *Der Apostel Paulus*, whose thesis is that Paul had been tried *in absentia* by a congregational 'court'.

[87] C. H. Dodd, 'The Mind of Paul: a Psychological Approach', *BJRL* 17 (1933), 91–105, proposed that the term was not only used paradoxically by Paul, but that it had a psychological dimension. When Paul recognised his limitations (12.8–10) he was liberated from them. W. Schmithals, *Gnosticism in Corinth*, English translation (Nashville: Abingdon Press, 1971), p. 178, argues unconvincingly on the issue of boasting that Paul 'apparently understands the reproaches of the Gnostics only as a disputing of his apostolic authority, without seeing through the mythological basis of this disputing or even missing such a basis'.

[88] See pp. 190–1.   [89] Marshall, *Enmity in Corinth*, pp. 329–30.

Corinth (10.1–10), but they had also offered an internal σύγκρισις of their achievements based on ὑπόκρισις:[90] 'Not that we have the effrontery[91] to measure or compare ourselves with some of those who commend themselves but (ἀλλὰ) when they themselves measure themselves by one another (ἐν ἑαυτοῖς ἑαυτοὺς μετροῦντες) and compare themselves with themselves (καὶ συγκρίνουντες ἑαυτοὺς ἑαυτοῖς), they are without understanding' (10.12).[92] They were judging (ἐγκρῖναι) or comparing (συγκρῖναι) their achievements among themselves, so that self-promotion came at the expense of one's colleagues in the congregation (10.12).[93] They thus indulged, like Philo's sophists, in a rhetorical σύγκρισις, only it was amongst themselves rather than against a common opponent.

Despite their skill in ὑπόκρισις Paul considers his opponents ignorant because they indulge in this rhetorical activity of 'measuring and comparing'. Regardless of its acceptance as a standard rhetorical convention and its place in the handbooks, to measure one's activities against a colleague's was a highly subjective and foolish endeavour.[94] It lacked objectivity and ultimately amounted to nothing more than self-praise in pursuit of praise from others. Like the sophists in Epictetus, they solicited the praise of their audience.[95] But for Paul, only the Lord's approval could render a person δόκιμος (10.18). Once more he invokes Jeremiah 9.24 against boasting. Just as he depended upon these words to convey divine displeasure with the boasting and status pretensions of the sophistic tradition in 1 Corinthians 1.31 (within his unfolding critique of 1 Cor. 1–4) so too in 2 Corinthians 10.17 he relies on the Jeremiah prohibition to combat 'measuring and comparing': 'Let him who boasts, boast in the Lord.' It is not the one who

---

[90] See Forbes, 'Comparison, Self-praise and Irony', 2–8, for a survey of evidence. See also Marshall, *Enmity in Corinth*, p. 329.

[91] The word τολμᾶν was used for the debate between philosophers and sophists, Betz, *Der Apostel Paulus*, pp. 67–9.

[92] The absurdity of what they are doing is clearly brought out with the repeated use of 'themselves'.

[93] It is clear that ἔρις and ζῆλος are still present (2 Cor. 12.20), and it cannot be between Paul and Apollos at this stage. A good example of the nature of this comparison can be seen in *P.Oxy.* 2190, where Didymus declares that he will care for his students better than any other sophist in Alexandria.

[94] See Forbes, 'Comparison, Self-praise and Irony', 2–8.

[95] ἐπαίνεσον με. When Epictetus asks, 'What do you mean by "praise"?', the response is 'Cry to me "Bravo!" or "Marvellous!"' (although such praise would not have been quite so blatant in the church), Epictetus, III.23.23–4. For discussion of this passage see p. 123.

commends himself who is accepted, but the one whom the Lord commends (2 Cor. 10.17–18). Can the Lord commend those in Corinth who, in their 'boastful mission', have gone beyond 'the limit' (1 Cor. 1.29, 2 Cor. 11.12)?

Secondly, in what did Paul's opponents boast? As has already been noted, the sophists' grounds for boasting were their πλοῦτος, δόξα, τιμή and ἀρχή which they expressed in terms of their achievements and the accompanying lifestyle.[96] According to Paul, his opponents were actually claiming credit for 'other men's labours' performed 'in another's field', that is, the founding apostle's (2 Cor. 11, 15–16). With this assertion that he will not engage in this sort of conduct, designating it boasting εἰς τὰ ἄμετρα, Paul makes it plain that his ministry has divinely fixed boundaries.[97] Surely (note the use of the strong adversative ἀλλά) if there can be any legitimate boasting, it must be within the parameters fixed by God (κατὰ τὸ μέτρον τοῦ κανόνος). They would include Paul's Corinthian ministry (verse 14). He repeats that he will 'not boast beyond limit' (εἰς τὰ ἄμετρα καυχώμενοι) in the labours of other men (verse 15), but he hopes to preach in the regions beyond Corinth 'without boasting of work already done in another's field' (verse 16). The opponents are stealing Paul's δόξα for themselves while denigrating him and his achievements – though by divine standards they have done nothing worthy of boasting.

Paul's 'sophistic' boasting

Paul discusses the work which he has undertaken 'in his own field' by taking upon himself his opponents' mantle of boasting in ch. 11,[98] requesting that they 'bear with me in a little foolishness'. The passage which follows has rightly been described as 'an ironic

---

[96] Philo, *Det.* 33–4. See pp. 107–9.
[97] On the discussion of κανών see E. A. Judge, 'The Regional *kanon* for Requisitioned Transport', *New Docs* 1 (1976), 36–45, Marshall, *Enmity in Corinth*, pp. 367–71.
[98] A. Friedrichsen, 'Zum Stil des paulinischen Peristasenkatalogs 2 Kor. 11.23ff', and 'Peristasenkatalogs und *res gestae* nachtrag zu 2 Kor. 11.23ff', *Symbolae Osloenses* (1929) 25–9, 78–82, who had argued the unlikely possibility that Paul's boasting was meant to be a parody of the *Res Gestae* of Augustus, cited in T. B. Savage, *Power through Weakness: Paul's Understanding of the Christian Ministry in 2 Corinthians* SNTS 86 (Cambridge: Cambridge University Press, 1996), p. 63, n. 37. See also E. A. Judge, 'Paul's Boasting in Relation to Contemporary Professional Practice', *Australian Biblical Review* 16 (1968), 37–50; Forbes, 'Comparison, Self-praise and Irony', 16–22.

parody of self-praise and comparison of his opponents', 'a σύγ-κρισις style counter-attack' (11.1–12.10).[99] The irony is that Paul does not wear the wise man's cloak but the fool's, an indirect but no less obvious comment on his opponents. In so structuring his argument he makes it patently clear to the Corinthians that he speaks not κατὰ κυρίον but in foolishness (11.17). Nevertheless, he feels that he must speak out, for his opponents boast κατὰ σάρκα, and therefore he too will boast (11.18). The Corinthians must have recognised that Paul was linking the 'measuring and comparing' of his boastful, ignorant opponents in 10.12 with the many who boast 'according to the flesh' in 11.18. This becomes sharper still, for, having said that he would not dare to do what others have done (10.12), he himself now does it 'as a fool': 'In whatever any one dares to boast – I am speaking as a fool' (τολμῶ κἀγώ, 11.21b). Then he clarifies this (ἐν ᾧ) by discussing his own credentials and achievements in his κανών. It is clear from 11.22ff. that Paul is catching his opponents at their own game in order to secure their indictment before the congregation.

In tabulating his credentials and achievements, Paul initially must have sounded like any sophist who proves his life is a witness (μάρτυς ὁ βίος).[100] By Jewish standards he was among the εὐγενεῖς (verse 23). As regards his work 'in his field' he succinctly affirms his superior performance over that of his opponents, but then adds, because he is engaging in a σύγκρισις, 'I am talking irrationally'.[101] This comment was intended as a direct assault on the sophistic convention of comparison. The long list of Paul's achievements turns out, ironically, to be a catalogue of his afflictions and deprivations (11.23–7). The long list of churches established by Paul (a sure sign of his apostolic success) is missing, dismissed with the statement, 'And, apart from other things, there is the daily pressure of my anxiety for all the churches' (11.28).[102] Paul's

---

[99] Forbes, 'Comparison, Self-praise and Irony', 16–7. It may well have been that the thought of μετασχηματίζειν of these false apostles persuaded him to adopt the disguise of his opponents and actually indulge in boasting. For the use of this term for a 'covert allusion' see discussion on pp. 196–7.

[100] For discussion of Philo, *Det.* 33 see pp. 107–8 and 1 Cor. 1.26–8, pp. 193–4.

[101] παραφρονέω, 'talking in an irrational manner'.

[102] R. Hodgson, 'Paul, the Apostle and First Century Tribulation Lists', *ZNW* 74 (1983), 79–80, where he compares Arrian's *History of Alexander and Indica*, 2.233–5, Plutarch *Lives*, 327a and *Moralia* 498e, in his interest in the history of religious background to the Pauline list. He states that Paul speaks of διακονία for τύχη, but whether it can be argued that Paul would 'substitute' the former for

boasting throughout this passage (11.23–9) relates not to his successes, but to his vulnerability and lack of status as he travelled from city to city. When held up to the canons of weakness Paul says, 'Who is weak?' 'Am I not also weak?' (verse 30).

Paul declares that if it was necessary to boast (καυχᾶσθαι δεῖ), then he would do so, but it would be of his own weaknesses – a statement affirmed by an oath rarely heard in Paul (11.30–1). His reason for swearing 'that the God and Father of the Lord Jesus knows that I do not lie' was to eliminate the possibility, which would have almost certainly occurred to the Corinthians, that Paul was engaging in a recognised form of inverted boasting, that is, 'self-deprecation'.[103]

An interesting addendum to Paul's list of tribulations is the only event with a specific geographical location (11.32–3). The Damascus incident demonstrates yet again Paul's weakness and lack of heroism. Had he been recognised as a person of status and come to the city as a sophist, he would have received deferential treatment. As it was, his account shows that he faced nothing but humiliation, for being lowered over the wall would have been the ultimate sign of failure for a sophist.[104] Noteworthy sophists were met outside the city walls and escorted by the city fathers and young men of good birth. Paul, in fleeing over the wall under cover of night, resembles more an undesirable alien than a sought-after foreign sophist destined for citizenship and the honours of the council.[105]

As Marshall observes, Paul boasts only of 'events forced on him by necessity, apparent failures, imprisonments by legal authorities, humiliations', of things which 'marked him off as a man of shame'. If he was the superior servant of Christ, then a list of his finest deeds would have been expected.[106] But no such list is

the latter begs a number of questions, not least whether the events actually happened.
[103] Forbes, 'Comparison, Self-praise and Irony', 11, for evidence of this convention.
[104] *Contra* Travers, 'Paul's Boasting in 2 Corinthians 10–12', 530; Forbes, 'Comparison, Self-praise and Irony', 20–1, that the reference is to the antithesis to *corona muralis* for the soldier first up the wall into a besieged city referred to in *Livy*, 28.48.5. Martin, *2 Corinthians*, pp. 384–5 rejects this view and believes that it is connected to 10.4–5 with its allusion to *Prov.* 21.22, where the wise man 'scales the cities of the mighty and brings down the strongholds in which the godless trust' as an example of Paul's flight from Damascus in his life of weakness as against the exploits of the wise.
[105] For evidence of the reception of a noted sophist coming to a city see p. 149.
[106] Marshall, *Enmity in Corinth*, pp. 352–3.

forthcoming. Even as the 1 Corinthians 4.10–13 'tribulation' list had a polemical thrust aimed at the pretensions of the Corinthian Christians, so too the tribulation list of 2 Corinthians opposes the arrogance of his opponents.[107]

In 12.1–10 Paul boasts about another area of ministry which, surprisingly, reveals his weakness: visions. Paul, in the beginning of his discussion of his revelations, reminds the Corinthians that he boasts not because it is profitable, but only because it has become necessary (12.1). To prove conclusively that nothing is gained by boasting he argues that it was precisely that which for others might have become the greatest claim to spiritual power, namely visionary experiences, which stopped him from exalting himself after the fashion of the super-apostles (10.1).[108]

As C. Forbes succinctly concludes, 'they . . . boast of qualities which they do not have. Paul will not even boast of those he does possess.'[109] Paul's reason emerged from his humiliating experience, the thorn in the flesh, which brought him a word from God. God's grace would be sufficient for him amidst the trials of his ministry because God's 'power is perfected in weakness'. This revelation persuaded Paul to rejoice in his tribulations, for his strength, he now saw, lay at the point of his weakness (verses 7–10). The same truth also held for the Messiah who was crucified in weakness and yet lives through the power of God. His ministers are 'weak in him' but likewise live through the power of God with respect to the Christian community (εἰς ὑμᾶς, 13.4).

Paul argues ironically that he has been forced by the Corinthians to boast because they failed to do it for him. What should they boast about? 'For I was not at all inferior to these superlative apostles, even though I am nothing' (εἰ καὶ οὐδέν εἰμι, 12.11).

What was Paul hoping to achieve in 11.16ff.? It was his stated aim in 11.12 to undermine the claim of those who sought recognition as missionaries or apostles of comparable status. How did he do this? Forbes observes that 'Paul is admitting comparability here only "as a fool", due to the fact that certain "fools" in Corinth had been indulging in comparisons. He wishes to satirise their pretensions by use of the same form: in his view there is no such

---

[107] See p. 199.
[108] A. T. Lincoln, 'Paul the Visionary: The Setting and Significance of the Rapture to Paradise in II Corinthians 12.1–10', *NTS* 25 (1979), 218.
[109] Forbes, 'Comparison, Self-praise and Irony', 21.

comparability.'[110] He has sought to demonstrate that the teachers were in reality fools, their claims to wisdom notwithstanding. While disclaiming any intention of engaging in a *synkrisis* with his opponent, 10.12a, Paul 'ironically conceded the exaggerations and misrepresentations of his opponents, only to refute them' in 10.12bff.[111]

In the end, Paul's evaluation of his sophistic opponents with their σαρκικὴ σοφία (noted already in 2 Cor. 1.12) is clearly in keeping with his critique of the sophistic tradition in 1 Corinthians 1–4 and 9. The earlier critique was enunciated well before the appearance of sophistic teachers in the Corinthian church in 2 Corinthians. Here now were not just congregational members who were wise by the standards of this age but rhetorically trained teachers who refused to join in becoming fools in order to become wise as Christians.

Conclusion

This chapter has argued that the dispute in Corinth did not pit an untrained rhetorician against sophistic Christian leaders in Corinth. Paul demonstrated substantial rhetorical skills in his struggle against opponents in 2 Corinthians 10–13. His strategy was, however, controlled by an all-encompassing theological interpretation of weakness which was erected upon the paradigm of the Messiah crucified in weakness but now reigning by the power of God (13.4). This was replicated in Paul's own weakness, for his ministry was also empowered by the same divine power – to the benefit of the Corinthian congregation (2 Cor. 12.7–9, 13.4).

Likewise Paul took over boasting from the sophistic teachers with their technique of σύγκρισις by which they commended themselves in order to generate adulation. Boasting, like weakness, was interpreted in the light of Paul's soteriological understanding of the crucified Messiah. There was henceforth to be no boasting in σαρκικὴ σοφία. The attempt to import this improper activity into the Corinthian church met with Paul's firm resolve to undermine its

---

[110] *Ibid.*, 18.

[111] See ch. 2, n. 43 for the similar ironical use by Dio of the traditional encomium of Alexandria in order to contrast the beauty of the environs of the city with the lack of ἀρετή of the Alexandrians, *Or.* 32.39. Forbes, 'Comparison, Self-praise and Irony', 16, has argued that Paul is using εἰρωνεία and βαρύτης here along the lines suggested by Hermogenes.

proponents with *all* the powers of persuasion at his disposal. One could now only boast in the Lord, as Jeremiah 9.23–4 had affirmed.

Kennedy finds in Paul's argument two kinds of rhetoric, 'the radical (basically sacred) rhetoric of authority and the rhetoric of rational argumentation which was perceived as more worldly', and two kinds of boldness, 'the humble' variety of 10.1 (related to the Lord's authority) and the 'worldly' boldness of ch. 11.[112] The best treatment, however, of Paul's boasting from the standpoint of rhetorical forms comes from Forbes, who combines the discovery of rhetorical devices with an evaluation of their use in 2 Corinthians 10–13.[113] While substantial work has been done on the structure of the 'fool's speech' in 2 Corinthians 11.22–12.11,[114] the final word on the form of 2 Corinthians 10–13 has perhaps not yet been written.[115]

This chapter has maintained a narrow focus on (1) the sophistic reaction to Paul's critique of their tradition in 1 Corinthians 1–4 and 9, and (2) his reply in 2 Corinthians 10–13. What has emerged in this remarkable exchange is a spirited defence by Paul following the personal attack launched by his sophistic opponents. Having had his own critique used against him, he shows that he is not bereft of rhetorical skill as he turns their techniques against them. If they used σύγκρισις against him, he too could use it to great effect – though he did not in any way share their delusion that human commendation was ultimately important.

[112] Kennedy, *New Testament Interpretation through Rhetorical Criticism*, pp. 93–6.
[113] Forbes, 'Comparison, Self-praise and Irony'.
[114] J. Weiss, 'Beiträge zur Paulinischen Rhetorik', in *Theologischen Studien B. Weiss* (Göttingen: Vandenhoeck & Ruprecht, 1897), pp. 185–7, late last century initiated the discussion, basing his work on Demosthenes and Cicero. For a summary of the discussion see Martin, *2 Corinthians*, pp. 357–62. M. M. DiCicco, *Paul's Use of Ethos, Pathos, and Logos in 2 Corinthians 10–13*, Mellen Biblical Studies Series 31 (Lewiston, NY: Mellen Biblical Press, 1995), suggests that the three traditional proofs have moulded Paul's discussion in 2 Cor. 10–13. If it is correct that Paul rejects these persuasive techniques in his evangelism in Corinth (1 Cor. 2:1–5) as has been argued here, it is inexplicable why he would make such full use of them in a later letter to the Corinthians without again calling into question his integrity.
[115] A precedent in the δημηγορία form may well exist, for which the letters of Demosthenes are perhaps an example. Its aim was to persuade the People 'to come to the aid of the distressed', and respond to the request in order to benefit their city. Such an examination is beyond the purview of this discussion, see J. A. Goldstein, *The Letters of Demosthenes* (New York and London: Columbia University Press, 1968), esp. ch. 6–8, citing 133. Betz, *Der Apostel Paulus*, p. 43 has suggested the possibility of the genre reflected in Plato's *Symposium*.

Like the Israelites who asked, when confronted with Saul's prophetic activity, 'Is Saul among the prophets?' (1 Samuel 10.11) so the Corinthians asked of his first-century namesake, 'Is Paul among the sophists?' That he failed as a 'public' orator when judged by the canons of the first-century sophistic tradition with its emphasis on extempore declamation meant that he was excluded from the circle of virtuoso orators in Corinth who attracted a large public following. This discussion has shown, however, that Paul overcame any oratorical limitations with epistolary argumentation which, with his distinct λογισμοί, could conquer the rhetorical devices of his adversaries. Aristides was to claim in the following century that, 'Alone of all the Greeks whom we know, we did not engage in oratory for wealth, reputation, honour, marriage, power of acquisition.' Paul could also make a similar rejection, although unlike Aristides, who wrote 'But for me oratory means everything' , the former renounced its use as the appropriate medium for the message.[116]

A great deal of heartache and anguish had occurred since Paul, in the face of ἔρις and ζῆλος, first exhorted the Corinthians to unity and tranquillity (1 Cor. 1.11ff.). For all that, 2 Corinthians 12.20 shows little progress, with ἔρις, ζῆλος, θυμοί, ἐριθεῖαι, καταλαλιαί, ψιθυρισμοί, φυσιώσεις, and ἀκαταστασίαι still present and aggravated by the sophistic Christian teachers. Paul says that he may yet come to Corinth and find to his dismay that the dislocation persists. However skilled Paul may be among the sophists, his ultimate concern as a spokesman for the Messiah and a steward of the mysteries of God is to build up the Christian ἐκκλησία. Demolition of his opponents has unfortunately become a prerequisite to that aim (1 Cor. 4.1; 2 Cor. 10.4–5, 8).

E. A. Judge, whose groundbreaking 1969 essay alerted NT scholars to the manner in which this conflict was carried out, concluded his discussion with the observation that 'Paul's struggle [in 2 Corinthians 10–13 was] with rhetorically trained opponents for the support of his rhetorically fastidious converts',[117] a fastidiousness well attested in secular Corinth. Part II of this book substantiates his judgement.

---

[116] *Or.* 33.19–20 and 1 Cor. 1.17, 2.4 .

[117] Judge, 'Paul's Boasting', 48 and again 'The Reaction against Classical Education in the New Testament', *Journal of Christian Education Paper 77* (1983), 13: 'his rivals were performing in the church at Corinth as professional rhetoricians or sophists'.

11

CONCLUSIONS

The first-century sophistic movement

The character of the sophistic movements in the early Roman Empire in Alexandria and Corinth has emerged from Greek, Jewish and Christian sources of the first and early second centuries AD. Interest in early first-century Greek rhetoricians has tended to focus on Rome, where large numbers gravitated from the East.[1] While some conclude that as a result of this migration, Alexandria's stock of sophists was depleted in the first century, our evidence indicates otherwise.[2] In the days of Philo and Dio Chrysostom the sophistic movement was thriving in that city.

Philo's corpus has yielded a rich vein of information on the early first-century sophists. If non-literary sources have created the impression that declamation on historic themes dominated school activities, Philo's evidence corrects this by showing that philosophical debate and declamations on cardinal virtues also constituted an important part of their activities.[3] Plato's objections to the sophistic movement remained valid in Philo's day, and provided him with a bulwark against it and its proponents. A clear picture of the debating and declaiming activities of the sophists emerges from various places in Philo's corpus. In addition there is a unique first-century verbatim account of the philosophical defence of the

---

[1] For a full list see C. Bornecque, *Les Déclamations et les déclamateurs d'après Sénèque le père* (reprinted Hildesheim: Georg Olms Verlag, 1967); and D. A. Russell's discussion, *Greek Declamation* (Cambridge: Cambridge University Press, 1983), pp. 8–9; and G. A. Kennedy, *The Art of Rhetoric in the Roman World* (Princeton: Princeton University Press, 1972), pp. 336–77.

[2] P. M. Fraser, *Ptolemaic Alexandria*, 2nd edn (Oxford Clarendon Press, 1972), vol. I, p. 810; E. G. Turner, 'Oxyrhynchus and Rome', *HSCP* 79 (1975), 5; G. W. Bowersock, *Greek Sophists in the Roman Empire* (Oxford: Clarendon Press, 1969), pp. 20–1.

[3] See pp. 86–7; cf. pp. 31–2.

sophistic lifestyle with its lack of practical interest in the traditional teaching specialisation of the sophists, namely civic virtues.[4] Dio's Alexandrian oration reveals the orators and sophists at work in Alexandrian *politeia*, usurping what he considers the traditional role of the philosophers.

P.Oxy. 2190 is another invaluable source, portraying the sophists from a student's perspective as they impinged upon his somewhat hedonistic activities in Alexandria. This is our only extant source which discusses the movement from the perspective of a student of rhetoric who laboured under difficulties some of which were self-imposed. The Alexandrian sources, when taken as a whole, provide a good deal of insight into the sophistic movement under the Julio–Claudian and the Flavian emperors.

Epictetus' discussion with a student of rhetoric from Corinth reveals the opportunities in store in *politeia* for a successful orator in that city and also helps illuminate the concept of 'bodily presence' used in 2 Corinthians 10.10. The same author also discusses the activities of sophists, especially declamations. Epictetus has long been neglected in secondary literature on rhetoric in the first and early second century.[5] However, information from his corpus enhances our understanding of the sophistic tradition, supplementing the evidence of Dio Chrysostom and Plutarch. The latter recorded the activities of the sophists at the Isthmian Games, particularly the highly competitive spirit engendered between themselves and amongst their pupils. Plutarch also confirms their social status and exalted position in the life of Corinth.

From the sophistic side, Favorinus and Herodes Atticus reveal the wealth of praise potentially available to foreign sophists in Corinth. They also testify to the honours bestowed by 'the Council and the People' upon orators who won their favour and, in the case of the former, how fickle the Corinthians could be in withdrawing it and overthrowing his statue.

The Pauline letters to Corinth also contain information which is not found elsewhere on the first-century sophistic movement. It is possible to trace the impact of the sophistic movement on a newly emerged gathering, ἡ ἐκκλησία τοῦ θεοῦ, with the initial anti-

---

[4] M. Untersteiner, *The Sophists*, English translation (Oxford: Blackwell, 1954), p. xv.

[5] E.g. R. Volkmann, *Die Rhetorik der Griechen und Römer in systematischer übersicht* (reprinted Hildesheim: Georg Olms Verlag, 1963); Kennedy, *The Art of Rhetoric*.

sophistic coming of Paul, the subsequent relationship of converts with himself and other teachers wrongly conceptualised as that of a disciple with his sophist. There is the apostle's evaluation of the sophistic tradition; the recruiting of teachers by the Corinthians who endorsed that tradition possibly because the powerful orator, Apollos, did not return as invited; the sophistic critique of Paul as rhetorician and debater by those teachers; and finally the denunciation by Paul of those who believed that such qualifications were an ideal or even a prerequisite for an adequate teaching ministry in Corinth.

With hindsight one might consider it almost inevitable that there would be sophistic inroads into the church's perception of preachers, given the role of teachers as public speakers in secular Corinth. Paul suggested to the Corinthians in 1 Corinthians 3.1 that the problem was nascent even while he was with them. He did not underestimate it, adopting as he did a radical stance at the commencement of his ministry with a *modus operandi* which was consciously anti-sophistic. He aimed thereby to distance himself from any possible identification with that movement. Renouncing the use of 'the persuasive words of wisdom' in his preaching, trusting in God's power alone, and deciding to work with his own hands so as not to hinder that proclamation, were the necessary steps to take in sophistic Corinth in Paul's estimate (1 Cor. 2.5 and ch. 9). That still did not prevent problems from taking root after he left, especially with the arrival of the rhetorically gifted Apollos. In fact, Apollos' and Paul's difficult decision would provide the ammunition used against the latter, as our study of 2 Corinthians 10–13 has shown.

As contemporaries, Philo and Paul provide important and unexpected sources of information on the sophistic movement in the first century. In fact, they fill a crucial gap in our understanding of the first sixty years of the movement in the East, for we have no other extensive sources in this period in the East.[6]

---

[6] See Kennedy's *The Art of Rhetoric*, covering 300 BC–AD 300. He discusses Dionysius of Halicarnassus, Caecilius of Calacte and 'Longinus', all of whom came from the East but lived in Rome in the Augustan age. He begins his work on 'the Age of the Sophists', ch. 7, with Dio Chrysostom, and proceeds with Aelius Aristides, Lucian, Fronto and Gellius. It is clear that the full survey of Philo of Alexandria's evidence should occupy as much space as, if not more, than that given to two others who were Jews, Caecilius of Calacte and 'Longinus', cf. pp. 371, 451–2 with 339, 335, 364–9, 370–1, 502, 555, 618 and 280, 341, 353, 368–76, 451–2, 459, 464, 521 devoted to the latter two. In his discussion of

G. W. Bowersock's conclusion that 'The Second (or New) Sophistic is a culmination, not a sudden burst or fad' finds confirmatory evidence from both Alexandria and Corinth.[7] The Second Sophistic was in bud at the beginning of the first century AD and as far as the evidence exists, it came to bloom with at least two major spurts in its growth. While it remains difficult to determine precisely why it gained such impetus, we can point to the increased financial incentives for forensic orators during the reign of Claudius. The disruption of relationships between the philosophers and certain emperors had the effect of favouring orators and sophists during Vespasian's day which resulted in the latter group being exempted from taxes and liturgies. They were exploited to the full as the rescript of Domitian shows.

What can be said with certainty is that in Alexandria and Corinth there was a high-profile sophistic movement in the first century which differed little if at all from the later description of it by Philostratus in his *Lives of the Sophists*. That must cause scholars to ponder again the beginning and growth of that very powerful movement in the early empire which came to be designated as the 'Second Sophistic'. Philostratus, born *c.* AD 170, records that Nicetes in Nero's Principate broke new ground in his oratory, which he seems to suggest epitomised the nature of the Second Sophistic and thus heralded its 'modern' beginning in the first century.[8] However, Philo's evidence points to an even earlier date.

Philo's and Paul's sophistic opponents

Among Philo's opponents were the Alexandrian sophists, to whom he referred on numerous occasions.[9] It has also been shown that 1 Corinthians deals with the inroads of the sophistic tradition in the church and 2 Corinthians 10–13 with the impact of sophistic Jewish Christian teachers. The common view that the issues raised

---

'Christian Rhetoric' there is a passing reference to the NT, 129–32, which he evaluated in his subsequent treatment of the topic, where there is a very slender treatment of 1 Cor. 1–4, and 2 Cor. 10–13, *New Testament Interpretation through Rhetorical Criticism* (Chapel Hill: University of North Carolina Press, 1984), pp. 24–5 and 92–5, and Acts 24, 136.
[7] *Greek Sophists*, p. 9.   [8] Philostratus, *Lives of the Sophists*, 511–12.
[9] He used the term 'sophist' in its technical sense, see ch. 3. Another group within the Jewish community with whom he was at variance were the 'literalists'. See M. J. Shroyer, 'Alexandrian Jewish Literalists', *JBL* 55 (1936), 261–84.

by opponents in 1 Corinthians differed from those in 2 Corinthians 10–13 needs revision.[10] There were those in 1 Corinthians 3.18 who were οἱ σοφοὶ ἐν τῷ αἰῶνι τούτῳ. They were the same as those whom Paul described in 1 Corinthians 4.19 as being 'puffed up' because he could not return immediately. Paul notes that they were eloquent but lacked Christian δύναμις. There also appears to be a link between these particular people and those invited as alternative ἄνδρες λόγιοι after the refusal of Apollos to return to Corinth, and the subsequent problems which these sophistic teachers of 2 Corinthians created for the church's founding apostle.

In this book the nature of the divisions has been traced to a sophistic and not a theological source. This means that the conclusions of J. Munck on 1 Corinthians 1–4 were essentially correct. His primary concern in 'The Church without Factions' was, however, to refute the long-standing influential conclusions of F. C. Baur's Pauline/Petrine dichotomy which, according to Baur, manifested itself in the conflict situations in the Corinthian church.[11] The aim here has been not only to document the evidence needed to substantiate Munck's sophistic thesis, but to seek to explain why Paul so vigorously opposed a sophistic model of church leadership.[12]

Whatever one may say of Paul's opponents in 2 Corinthians, the group must have been Jewish in origin but also well trained in Greek rhetoric. As Hellenophiles, they would have propounded the view that such elitist training was the ideal or even an essential prerequisite for the high teaching or preaching office of the church, especially in Gentile areas.[13] A similar virus had infected Judaism

---

[10] E.g. C. K. Barrett, 'Paul's Opponents in 2 Corinthians', in *Essays on Paul* (London: SCM Press, 1982), ch. 4. For a survey of opinion on the 'false apostles' see R. P. Martin, *2 Corinthians* (Waco: Word, 1986), pp. 336–41.

[11] J. Munck, 'The Church without Factions', in *Paul and the Salvation of Mankind* (London: SCM Press, 1959).

[12] *Ibid.*

[13] The development of leadership in the Pauline churches, especially in Corinth, cannot be sufficiently dealt with by recourse to the Weber dichotomy of charismatic versus hierarchical leadership, without first giving due weight to the nature of the elitist leadership in secular society with its essential requirement of rhetorical training. For recent discussions which proceed along the sociological constructs without reference to this crucial social background, see B. Holmberg, *Paul and Power: The Structure of Authority in the Primitive Church as Reflected in the Pauline Epistles*, English translation (Philadelphia: Fortress Press, 1980), and A. Chapple, 'Local Leadership in the Pauline Churches: Theological and Social Factors in its Development: A Study based on 1 Thessalonians, 1 Corinthians, and Philippians', PhD dissertation, University of Durham (1984). Since these

so that Philo felt obliged to issue a warning and to attempt to cure those who had already succumbed to it. Philo indicates that there were fellow Jews who pursued *paideia* not for virtue's sake but 'with no higher motive than parading their superiority, or from desire of office under our rulers'.[14] Both men were locked in what they deemed a religious struggle with the sophists and their traditions in the first century. The philosophers were therefore not alone in opposing the sophists.

The sophistic versus the Gnostic thesis

A passing reference was made to Gnosticism in our preface. The subsequent exploration of an alternative thesis has been fully justified in light of the Alexandrian evidence. If there was any relationship between Gnosticism and the Philonic corpus, it has been argued that it was in terms of the latter borrowing from the former.[15]

W. Schmithals' thesis of the Gnostic background as the key which illuminates the Corinthian texts has not secured a general consensus among recent major commentators.[16] Furthermore, it has been argued that first-century evidence of Gnosticism which is coterminous with, or prior to NT letters, is absent.[17] The weight of opinion has moved away from a Gnostic thesis.[18] The sophistic thesis is preferable to even a modified form of the latter, namely incipient Gnosticism.

   words were originally written the gap has been made good by A. D. Clarke, *Secular and Christian Leadership in Corinth: A Socio-Historical and Exegetical Study of 1 Corinthians 1–6* (Leiden: E. J. Brill, 1993).
14 *Legat.* III.167.
15 See D. T. Runia, *Philo and the Timaeus of Plato* (Leiden: E. J. Brill, 1986), p. 588; B. A. Pearson, 'Philo, Gnosis and the New Testament', in A. H. B. Logan and A. J. M. Wedderburn (eds.), *The New Testament and Gnosis: Essays in Honour of Robert McLachlan Wilson* (Edinburgh: T. & T. Clark, 1983), p. 340: 'Philo cannot be described as a "Gnostic" . . . Philo is not dependent upon or influenced by Gnosticism . . . Philo is an important source for some of the Hellenistic elements borrowed by the Gnostics'; and E. Schürer, *The History of the Jewish People in the Age of Jesus Christ*, 2nd edn (Edinburgh: T. & T. Clark, 1987), vol. III.2, p. 889, where others including 'the Gnostics . . . drew from Philo, to greater or lesser degrees, directly or indirectly, consciously or unconsciously'.
16 H. Conzelmann, G. Fee, R. P. Martin, V. P. Furnish and F. Lang, *Die Briefe an die Korinther* (Göttingen: Vandenhoeck & Ruprecht, 1986).
17 See E. M. Yamauchi, *Pre-Christian Gnosticism: A Survey of the Proposed Evidences*, 2nd edn (Grand Rapids: Baker Book House, 1983), p. 186.
18 Yamauchi, 'Pre-Christian Gnosticism Reconsidered a Decade Later', in *ibid.*, ch. 12.

Even if evidence for the existence of incipient Gnosticism was found in the first century in Alexandria and Corinth, it would still be necessary to explain the presence in Philo's corpus of numerous references to sophists which were used by him in a technical sense and not as a pejorative comment on others. The same holds true for the Corinthian epistles where 'the debaters of this age' are mentioned and rhetorical terminology and argumentation are used of and against them in 1 Corinthians 1–4 and 9 and 2 Corinthians 10–13.

Philo's chief opponents were the Alexandrian sophists. That has been substantiated both from a careful analysis of the term and his critique of and debates with the sophists. In our introduction we laid down criteria the fulfilment of which was felt to demonstrate a sophistic background in the Corinthian church. It was stated there that the presence of sophists in secular Corinth could not *per se* constitute proof that this was the issue in the church. It had to be demonstrated that the ἔρις and ζῆλος of which Paul complains in 1 Corinthians 1.11, 3.3 were clearly related to the sophistic movement; that his *modus operandi* in Corinth had been formulated in the light of sophistic conventions in 1 Corinthians 2.1–5 and 1 Corinthians 9;[19] that he offered a substantial critique of the sophistic movement in 1 Corinthians 1–4; that his own ministry had been subsequently critiqued in 2 Corinthians 10–13 by those trained in Greek rhetoric; and that in answering his opponents in 2 Corinthians 10–13, he did so in categories which showed that he was arguing with Christian sophistic teachers in the church. It is suggested that these criteria have been satisfied. Paul's opponents in 1 Corinthians 1–4 and 2 Corinthians 10–13 were adherents to the sophistic tradition.

Philo, Paul and rhetoric

Both Philo and Paul reveal their debt to Greek rhetoric. In the case of the former, this clearly emerges not only from his personal testimony, but also in numerous passages from his corpus. It is also seen in his debates with his nephew and his leading role in the Jewish embassy to Gaius. It has been noted that he was never tied

---

[19] For Paul's discussion of a similar context that determined his *modus operandi* in another city see my 'The Entries and Ethics of Orators and Paul (1 Thessalonians 2:1-12)', *Tyn.B.* 44.1 (1993), 55–74.

to the rhetorical forms he used but moulded them to suit his own purposes, thereby signifying his mastery of rhetorical techniques.

This study has also helped to unlock a little further the enigmatic issue of Paul's rhetorical education. E. A. Judge remarks: 'To have been brought up in Tarsus need not have committed Paul to a full rhetorical education, let alone a philosophical one, while being brought up in Jerusalem need not have excluded him from at least a general acquaintance with the Greek cultural tradition.'[20] C. Forbes has subsequently canvassed this issue in the light of Paul's use of rhetorical methods in 2 Corinthians. Having established Paul's deployment of rhetorical skills, Forbes has weighed up the alternatives. Either Paul acquired them during his preaching career or secured them in his formal education in Greek *paideia*, 'at least to the level of the *grammatici*, or the rhetorical school'.[21] Forbes favours the latter route on the grounds of the use of rhetorical conventions which Paul had so skilfully mastered, a fact demonstrated in 1 Corinthians 1–4 and 2 Corinthians 10–13.[22] His conclusions could be further supported depending on the weight attached to the forensic knowledge and ability displayed by Luke's presentation of Paul. His knowledge of the limits of evidence coupled with his expert defence against the forensic orator Tertullus before the Roman governor (Acts 24),[23] and his use of the little

---

[20] E. A. Judge, 'St Paul and Classical Society', *Jahrbuch für Antike und Christentum* 15 (1972), 29, assumes wrongly, 'Half of Gamaliel's pupils are said to have been trained in the wisdom of the Greeks', for the reference is to the Gamaliel II. However, the inroads of Greek rhetoric in Jerusalem can rightly be assumed. S. E. Johnson, 'Tarsus and the Apostle Paul', *Lexington Theological Quarterly* 15.4 (1980), 105–13, argues that Paul's education was in Tarsus, while W. C. van Unnik, *Tarsus or Jerusalem: The City of Paul's Youth*, English translation (London: Epworth Press, 1962), assembles linguistic evidence in support of the view that Jerusalem was the place of Paul's upbringing and education. See also Forbes, 'Comparison, Self-praise and Irony', 22–4 and n. 97.

[21] C. Forbes, 'Comparison, Self-praise and Irony: Paul's Boasting and Conventions of Hellenistic Rhetoric', *NTS* 32 (1986), 24.

[22] There is, of course, evidence that those who felt their deficiencies in this area could gain such skills later in life. Dio Chrysostom provides an interesting list of prescribed reading for such a situation, see p. 182, but it seems unlikely that this was how Paul obtained his prowess.

[23] See my 'The Importance of the *Captatio Benevolentiae* in the Speeches of Tertullus and Paul in Acts 24:1–21', *JTS* (n.s.) 42 (1991), 524–5, and also my 'Official Proceedings and Forensic Speeches in Acts 24-26', in B. W. Winter and A. D. Clarke (eds.), *The Book of Acts in its Ancient Literary Setting, The Book of Acts in its First Century Setting* (Grand Rapids and Carlisle: Eerdmans and Paternoster, 1993), ch. 11. For a discussion of Paul's legal training see also T. Lyall, 'Paul', in *Slaves, Citizens, Sons: Legal Metaphors in the Epistles* (Grand Rapids: Zondervan, 1984), Appendix 5.

known right of appeal to Caesar all point to Paul's training in oratory.[24] His designation as ἰδιώτης in 2 Corinthians 11.6 must therefore be understood as a reference to a non–professional, that is, a non-practising speaker and writer who was nevertheless trained in oratory.[25] Acts 24 does record that he could operate as a forensic orator for his own defence as he pitted his skills against Tertullus. His quick response before Festus in appealing to the emperor in the light of Jewish moves would also cast him in a similar role to that of Tertullus for the readers of Acts. While Philo too would have seen himself as an ἰδιώτης, he did act as an orator on at least one recorded occasion with the embassy to Gaius. The educated man in the first century could turn his rhetorical skills to good effect in defence of his cause whether it be in the secular ἐκκλησία, on embassies or before the courts.

When it came to the public presentation of Paul's message, he not only rejected 'the grand style' of rhetoric, but also the persuasive techniques which invigorated Greek rhetoric (1 Cor. 2.1–5). The comments of his opponents in 2 Corinthians 10.10 have established how others saw his 'bodily presence' and his 'inadequate' λόγοι. Paul's account in 1 Corinthians 2.1–5 and that of his adversaries in 2 Corinthians 10.10 and 11.6, present a composite picture. That he could have used 'the grand style' when speaking publicly is not problematical: that he chose not to when preaching is explicable for theological reasons he gives (1 Cor. 2.5).

Given Paul's rhetorical training, there is naturally evidence of its fruits to be found in his writings, as would have been the case with any person who underwent such instruction in the early empire. The training would leave an indelible mark on the composition of letters. Philo also demonstrates the same to be true in his writings. He, like Paul, could make use of appropriate forms of presentation and organisation of material learnt from youth.[26] That Philo and

---

[24] Acts 25.1. Unlike his Jewish adversaries, Paul did not have to be lectured by the successor of Felix that Roman law required the accusers to face their accused before sentence could be passed. On Paul's knowledge of the law see P. Garnsey, *Social Status and Legal Privilege in the Roman Empire* (Oxford: Clarendon Press, 1970), p. 76, concerning the move by Paul to appeal to Caesar as the exercising of 'a little-used, if not virtually obsolete prerogative of provincial [Roman] citizens to choose between courts and seek to have their case referred to Rome'; and on Paul's move see his more technical discussion, 'The *Lex Julia* and Appeal under the Empire', *JRS* 56 (1966), 185–6.

[25] See pp. 211–13 for discussion.

[26] For Philo see D. T. Runia, 'Philo's *De Aeternitate Mundi*: the Problem of its

Paul should adopt, yet not slavishly follow, rhetorical forms by adapting them, suggests that they could be well and truly at home with them.

These findings have implications for recent NT studies, some of which make wholesale use of rhetorical handbooks in the analysis of the *dispositio*, that is, the rhetorical structure of NT letters and Paul's use of rhetorical devices. Some studies do not appear to be sufficiently discriminating. They work on the assumption that Paul made full use of all 'the tricks of the trade' recommended in those rhetorical handbooks which the sophists used with such consummate skill. Discussions need to be carefully filtered through the composite picture of Paul and rhetoric and his rejection of the 'grand style' which was so widely admired in his own day.

In endeavouring to locate Paul on the first century rhetorical 'map', it should be noted that it had an unusual feature. Like its forerunners, it did have a specific location for rhetoric as the basis for primary through to tertiary education. In another place on the map, literary works reflect the fruits of such education as do forensic rhetoric and speeches in the secular ἐκκλησία or before governors and emperors. The map of Paul's and Philo's day however looked different from former ones because of the dominant space now occupied by declamations. It must be noted that neither of these men produced these demonstration pieces for the purpose of displaying rhetorical prowess as the sophists did. They were pursuing loftier goals. To cite Philo, they did not engage 'in shadow boxing', as many of the sophists did with their declamations, but in actual contests where great issues were at stake for their hearers or readers.[27] The first-century map had changed and it was so preoccupied with declamation that it had substantially redrawn some of the contours.

Rhetorical studies often proceed without sufficient awareness of the fact that Paul rejected 'the grand style' for preaching because he judged it to be a medium that was counter-productive to his intention to gain converts whose faith rested not in the wisdom of men but in the power of God (1 Cor. 2.5). When we look at other literary evidence we can see that he also avoided the wide use of complex rhetorical devices in his communications with the Chris-

Interpretation', *Vigiliae Christianae* 35 (1981), 138, and for Paul see p. 208, n. 22, and pp. 196–201.
27 See Philo, *Det.* 41.

tian community. Where he did use such a device, for example, the covert allusion, his ironic exposure of its contents would quickly become clear to the Corinthians as he completed his discussion (1 Corinthians 4.6). He could undeniably exploit rhetorical forms in his letters. Indeed his prowess was even conceded by his opponents (2 Cor. 10.10).[28]

In spite of the fact that Paul was capable of using rhetoric, the Corinthian church was apparently united in their preference for the rhetorically accomplished speaker, Apollos, on whom they rested their hopes for the future advancement of the Christian community in this prestigious Roman colony (1 Cor. 16.12). Their choice of the 'speaking' Apollos over the 'writing' Paul reflects a long-standing preference that goes back to the days of Isocrates. As this study has shown, it certainly reflects the spirit of the age of the early Roman Empire, for the public orator was clearly in the ascendancy. The Christians' rationalisation of their choice of Apollos and, then subsequently, speakers trained in rhetoric is explicable. It was to be the first-hand experience of Favorinus that not only the Corinthian men but also their 'women and children' would gather any day to listen to a fine orator.[29] Apollos was all that. Paul was not.

Philo and Paul – towards a comparison

These two Hellenised Jews adopted notably similar approaches to the sophistic movement, for both were committed to Scripture as the canon whereby the movement could be assessed for their readers.

Philo believed that the experience of characters from 'The Books of Moses' provided the paradigm for his evaluation of the sophists and the conflict they inevitably created. It is also important to note that Philo's discussion of the sophistic tradition was but part of a pioneering attempt to bring together the OT and philosophy, that

---

[28] *Contra* H. D. Betz, 'Rhetoric and Theology', in A. Vanhoye (ed.), *L'Apôtre Paul, Personnalité, Style et Conception du Ministère* (Leuven: Leuven University Press, 1986), pp. 43, 47, who suggests that it was the rhetoric of self-examination of the moral philosophers and not the rhetoric of persuasion which Paul favoured. He does argue convincingly that the 'fool's speech' of 2 Cor. 11 enabled Paul 'to demonstrate to the Corinthians that if he wanted he could conform to the standards prescribed by his critics, but that for good reasons he would not. In his wildly foolish self-parody Paul does, without actually doing, what he himself judges to be inappropriate.' Paul does go on to boast, but it is in his weaknesses, given the word of the Lord concerning power made perfect in weakness, 2 Cor. 11:30, 12.8–10.

[29] Dio Chrysostom, *Or*. 37.33.

is, he sought to exegete the OT in the light of those philosophical traditions which he perceived as being most closely allied to it. Thus the key to understanding Philo's discussion of the sophistic tradition in Alexandria is found in Plato's critique of it interpreted through 'The Books of Moses'.[30]

Paul likewise turned to the OT to evaluate the sophists and their movement in Corinth. He offers, in contrast to Philo, no allegorical or sophistic treatment of characters such as Hagar and Sarah (although elsewhere Paul does treat these two persons allegorically, Gal. 4.21–31). Paul's command 'not to go beyond the things that are written' (1 Cor. 4.6) depends on citations from Isaiah 29.14, Psalm 33.10, Job 5.13, Psalm 94.11 and Jeremiah 9.23–4. These were the parameters which ought to determine the Corinthians' conduct, evaluation and response to the sophistic tradition. For Paul the boasting by sophists, who were clearly 'the debaters of this age', had been overthrown by God whom they had failed to know despite their wisdom, for He could only be known through the cross of Christ. Thus the key for Paul's evaluation of their activity is the OT prophets and wisdom writers interpreted through the work of Christ, in comparison with Philo's use of the Pentateuch interpreted through largely Platonic categories.[31]

In both 1 Corinthians 1–4 and 2 Corinthians 10–13 Paul relies on Jeremiah 9.22–4, where the boasting of the wise, the powerful and the rich had been proscribed. That trilogy of terms in Jeremiah, along with its alternative exhortation 'to boast in the Lord', established for Paul the important nexus with the sophists of Corinth in much the same way that the 'magicians' in Moses and Plato had for Philo. The wise, the well-born and the powerful epitomised the class from which the sophists came and which the latter helped perpetuate through an elitist educational system which emphasised the art of rhetoric. Given that the great sin of the sophistic movement was its boasting – a weakness manifest in the record of the Alexandrian sophists in Philo's *Det.* 32–4 and reflected in the status terminology used in 1 Corinthians 1.26–8 and

---

[30] Runia, *Philo and the Timaeus*, pp. 446–7, and it was this methodological tool which marked 'a pivotal point in the history of thought'. See p. 111.

[31] For a recent comparison of the two writers based on an exegetical technique called 'charismatic exegesis' which was coined for the purpose of the essay, see S. K. Wan, 'Charismatic Exegesis: Philo and Paul Compared', *SPA* 6 (1994), 54–82. Much fruitful work could be done taking into account the variety of exegetical techniques available to, and used by, these two versatile authors in order to deal with the many situations to which they responded.

4.8,10–13 – Paul made the Jeremiah prohibition against boasting about wisdom, status and achievement a primary text in his critique of the Corinthian sophistic movement.

Both Philo and Paul also used their training in rhetoric to overthrow the rhetorical devices of the sophists. Philo insisted that only those who were trained in rhetoric were capable of engaging the sophists in debate; and he led the way as he showed others how this could be done (*Det.* 35, 41). But he also added that only training in rhetoric coupled with virtuous living could defeat the sophists.

Paul, with the ironical use of the antithetical status comments on the sophists and his innovative treatment of the rhetorical device of 'covert' allusion in 1 Corinthians 4.6ff., demonstrated the foolishness of boasting by those who had been called to the *imitatio Christi*. In 2 Corinthians 10–13 he took this a step further as he used irony to refute the boasting of his sophistic opponents in the church, and to rebuff their attempts to promote themselves as teachers on an equal footing with the genuine apostles.

Athens and Jerusalem, the Academy and the church

This study has shown that Athens had indeed a great deal to do with Jerusalem in this formative period for Judaism, and the Academy had certainly disturbed the concord of the church through the sophistic movement and its promoters in Corinth – to answer Tertullian's well-known question.[32] In the judgement of these two Hellenised Jews, it was extremely dangerous for Alexandrian Jews and Corinthian Christians to marry their religious traditions to the sophistic spirit of their age because of ideological difficulties and the consequences for their communities. Had the question been asked in Philo and Paul's day, as Tertullian did in his when he boasted, 'Where is there any likeness . . . between the disciples of Greece and heaven?', sadly for them neither could have answered categorically that there was none.[33] It was to remedy such a deficiency that both authors wrote.

---

[32] 'What has Athens to do with Jerusalem, or the Academy with the concord of the Church?', *De praescr. Haereticorum*, 7.

[33] *Apol.*, 46. On the use of the term οἱ Ἕλληνες to refer to the students of the sophists see Philostratus, *Lives of the Sophists*, 518, 571, 600 and discussion in the glossary of rhetorical terms provided by W. C. Wright, *Philostratus and Eunapius*, LCL, p. 569.

In what sense were Philo and Paul among the sophists? While secular Alexandria and Corinth adored the sophists and their tradition, inside the Christian community of the important Roman colony of Corinth Paul would not do so. Rather he insisted for the sake of their spiritual health that converts should not do so, either. Philo was no less adamant with respect to his community and condemned those fellow Alexandrian Jews who embraced *paideia* simply to boast of their wisdom or secure social or political advancement in the important Roman province of Egypt. Although both had participated in the Greek *paideia* on which the sophistic movement thrived, and were 'among the sophists' in first-century Alexandria and Corinth, for the most fundamental of theological reasons neither could ever be one of them.

APPENDIX P. OXY 2190

C. H. Roberts was the original editor of the text which required considerable restoration of the first nineteen lines of the left-hand side of the first column, *P.Oxy.* 2190, XVIII, 145–7. Some alternative readings of the papyrus were proposed by M. David, B. A. van Groningen and E. Kiessling (eds.), *Berichtigungsliste der Griechischen Papyruskunden aus Ägypten*, (Leiden: E. J. Brill, 1964) vol. IV, p. 63. E. G. Turner 'Oxyrhynchus and Rome', *HSCP*, 79 (1975), 7–9, nn. 17–25, weighed such suggestions and commented further on the text. J. Rea, 'A Student's Letter to His Father: P.Oxy. XVIII 2190 Revised', *ZPE* 99 (1993), 75–88, recently presented a substantial revision of the text. His reconstruction of the first column of the papyrus where it diverges from Roberts is reproduced under each line of the main text. While there are differences between these two leading papyrologists the discussion in chapter 1 is not materially affected. The only exception is in lines 10–11, where Roberts' reconstruction suggests that the young student has smashed up his father's chariot. I incline more to Rea's reconstruction which makes a reference to the fact that he regards the teachers of Alexandria as 'trash'.

Rea helpfully points to evidence that φιλόλογος was a term used in funerary inscriptions for brilliant young men who died before they fulfilled their potential, and could be used of members of the Alexandrian Museum. His view that the word is not a personal name, 'Philologos', as suggested by Roberts, is accepted but his translation of the term as 'tutor' is not. It is suggested that word would be best rendered 'scholar', that is, 'For now in my search for a scholar', line 7, and 'since the scholar whose classes they used to attend has died', line 25. The student is clearly searching for someone whom he could emulate and would see a sophist as such a person. His problem is that he has been unable to secure entry into a school run by someone of sufficient stature. Rea's rendering of καθηγητής as 'teacher' is rejected as is his translation of φιλόλογος in lines 7 and 25 as 'tutor'. φιλόλογος does not convey the duties understood in the first century of a tutor whose *ad hoc* role is explained in part of the letter itself. (See pp. 29–30)

? Νεῖλος Θ]έωνι τῶι κυρίωι πατρὶ
πλεῖστα]   χαίρειν
τῆς μὲν παρούσ]ης ἀθυμίας ἀπήλλαξας 'ἡμᾶς' δηλώσας ὡς
ἐστί σοι ἀδιά]φορα τὰ γενόμενα περὶ τοῦ θεάτρου.
ἐγὼ μὲν οὖν φ]θάσας καταπλεῦσαι τυχεῖν λαμπρῶν   5
ἤλπιζον δὲ φ]
.........ἄξιό]ν τι τῆς προθυμίας ἔπρα[ξ]α. νῦν
ἀγαθῶν, καὶ τί ἀ]ντι
γὰρ ἐπιζητῶ]ν φιλόλογον καὶ Χαιρήμονα τὸν καθηγητὴν καὶ Δίδυμον τὸν τοῦ Ἀριστοκλέο[υς], παρ᾿ οἷς
ἐλπὶς ἦν καὶ ἐμ]έ τι κατορθῶσαι, οὐκέτι ἐν τῆι πόλει
εὗρον, ἀλλὰ τ]ὰ ἅρματα {παρ᾿} οἷς τῆι εὐθείαι ὁδῶι χρὴ   10
εὗρον, ἀλλὰ κα]θάρματα
ἀνελθεῖν πρόχθ]ες διεφθορόσι <ὡς> καὶ πρότερόν σοι ἔγρα-
σάμενοι οἱ πλείον]ες
ψα.........]ἔγραψα τοῖς περὶ Φιλόξενον ἐπι-
ψα, καθάπερ καὶ]
τρεπτέον τὸ πρᾶ]γμα καὶ ὑπ᾿ ἐκείνων τῶι εὐδοκιμοῦν-
σκέψασθαι τὸ πρᾶ]
τι.....ὥστ᾿ ἐ]μὲ παραιτησάμενον Θέωνα εὐθὺς
τι συνεστάθην, ὃ κ]αὶ
καθηγητοῦ τυγχάνε]ιν κ[α]ὐτὸς κατεγνωκὼς αὐτοῦ   15
ἀπεδοκίμασας ο]ἵ[ο]ν
.........ὡς ἀμ]ελῶς ἔ[χ]οντος τὴν ἕξιν. μεταδόν-
ὡς ἐνδεῆ παντ]
τος δέ μου Φι]λοξένωι τὴν σὴν γνώμην τὰ αὐτὰ μὲν
ἐπήνει...α]ὐτὴν μόνην τὴν τὼν σοφιστῶν ἀ-
ἐφρόνει, διὰ τα]
πορ[ία]ν συνπαθεῖν τῆι π[ό]λει φάσκων, καταπλε[ύσο]ν-
τα δὲ τὸν Δί{δι}δυμον, ὡς ἔ[ο]ικεν, φίλον ὄντα αὐτῶι καὶ   20
σχολὴν ἔχοντα, ἔλεγεν ἐπιμελήσεσθαι τῶν ἄλ-
λων μᾶλλον καὶ τοὺς τοῦ Ἀπολλωνίου τοῦ {του} Ἡρώ-
δου παραβαλε[ῖ]ν ἔπειθεν αὐτῶι· καὐτοὶ γὰρ με[τ]ὰ τούτου δεξ[ι]ώτερον καθηγητὴν ἕως τοῦ νῦν ἐπιζητ[ο]ῦ-

δεινότερον[1]
σ[ι]ν ἀπαθανόντος φιλολόγου ὦι παρέβαλλον εὐ-		25
ξάμενο[ς] δ᾽ ἄν ἔγωγε εἴπερ ἀξίους λόγου καθηγητὰς
εὗρον μηδὲ ἐξ ἀπόπτου Δίδυμον ἰδεῖν, τοῦτο αὐτὸ ἀθυμῶ ὅτι ἔδοξεν εἰς σύγκρισιν τοῖς ἄλλο[ις]
ἔρχεσθαι οὗτος ὃς ἐπὶ τῆς χώρας καθηγεῖτο.
τοῦτο οὖν εἰδὼς ὅτι πλὴν τοῦ μάτην μισθοὺς πλείονας		30
τελεῖν ἀπὸ καθηγητοῦ οὐδὲν ὄφελος, ἀλλὰ ἀπ᾽ ἐμαυτοῦ
ἔχω. τάχεως ὅ τι ἐάν σοι δοκῆι γράψον.
ἔχω δὲ
τὸν Δίδυμον, ὡς καὶ φιλόξενος λέγει, ἀεί μοι πρ[οσ]ευ-
καιροῦντα καὶ πᾶν ὅτι δύναται παρεχόμενον, [ἔτι δὲ]
τῶν ἐπιδεικνυμένων ἀκροώμενος, ὧν ἐστὶν ὁ Πο-		35
σεδώνιος τάχα θεῶν θελόντων καλῶς πράξομαι.
ἡ δ᾽ ἐπὶ τούτοις ἀθυμία ἐστιν ἡ ὀλιγωρεῖν τοῦ σώματος
ἡμᾶς ἀναγκάζουσα, ὡς οὐδ᾽ ἐπιμελεῖσθαι δέον αὐτῶν
[τ]οὺς μήπω πράσσοντας καὶ μάλιστα ὅτε οὐ[δ]ὲ οἱ
χαλκὸν εἰσφέροντες εἰσίν· τότε μὲν γὰρ πρὸς ἡμέρας		40
χρήσιμος Ἡρακλᾶς, κακὸς κακῶς, ὀβόλους ἐπ[ε]ισ-
έφερεν, νῦν δὲ ἅμα τῷ δεθῆναι ὑπὸ Ἰσιδώρου, ὥσ[π]ερ
ἦν ἄξιον, ἔφυγεν καὶ ἀνῆλθεν, ὡς δοκῶ, πρὸς σέ· ὃν
εὖ ἴσθι μηδ᾽ ἂν ὀκνήσοντά σοί ποτε ἐπιβουλεῦσαι.
οὐ γὰρ ᾐσχύνετο πρὸ πάντων μετὰ χαρᾶς τὰ περὶ τοῦ		45
θεάτρου ἐν τῆι πόλει φημίζων καὶ λαλῶν τα ψεύ-
δη ἃ οὐδ᾽ ἂν κατήγορος εἴποι καὶ ταῦτα μηδὲν ἄξιον αὐτοῦ πάσχων ἀλλὰ λελυμένος καὶ ὡς ἐλεύθε-
ρος πάντα ποιῶν. ἀλλ᾽ ὅμως δύνῃ εἰ μὴ πέμπεις αὐ-
τὸν παραδοῦναί γε τέκονι, ἀκούω γὰρ ὅτι νεάκι-		50
σκος δύο δραχάμας τῆς ἡμέρας ποιεῖ, ἢ συνζεῦ-
ξον αὐτὸν ἄλλωι ἔργωι ὅθεν πλείονα χαλκὸν λή-
ψεται ἵνα τὸ μισθάριον αὐτοῦ συλλεγόμενον
πέμπηται ἡμεῖν διὰ χρόνου. οἶδας γὰρ ὅτι καὶ ὁ Δι-
ογᾶς γράμματα μανθάνει. ἐν ὧι τὸν μεικρὸν πέμ-		55
πεις, πλατύτερον ἐν οἰκίαι ἰδιωτικῆι τόπον ὀψόμεθα·
ἵνα γὰρ γειτνιευσῶμεν Διονυσίωι ἐν μεικρῶι λείαν
τόπωι γεγόναμεν. ἐκομισάμεθα τὸν κοίκα α᾽[κ]ρι-
ἀσφα-
[βῶ]ς ὅσα ἔγραψας ἔχοντα καὶ τὰ ἄγγη σὺν τῶι ἡμικαδίωι
[λῶ]ς
ἐν οἷς εὕρομεν ἀντὶ χοέων ι η κ β̄· καὶ ὧν ἔγραψας ἔπεμ-		60

---

[1] Roberts reads 'cleverer', while Rea's 'more stylish' is also possible.

ψα μετ' ἐπιστολῆς ἑκάστωι ἡμικάδιον τοῦ ὁλοφάκου.
τὰ ἕξ μέ(τρα) ἔλαβον καὶ κῶον ὄζους πληρὲς καὶ ταριχηρὰ
κρέα ρκς καὶ τὰ ἐν τῶι κάδωι καὶ τὰ ὀπτα λ.
ἔρρωσο. Χοιὰκ δ.

Verso (along the fibres)

]ἐθει Νείλου.   65

Translation

Neilus to Theon, his lord and father, very many greetings . . .
You have released me from my present despondency by making it
plain that the business about the theatre was a matter of indiffer-
ence to you. For my part, I've lost no time in sailing down stream
to find distinguished . . . and I have achieved something in return
for my eagerness. I was looking for a scholar (φιλόλογος) and
Chaeremon the tutor (καθηγητής) and Didymus the son of Aristocles as I thought that with them I too might still meet with
success, but found them no longer in the city, but (only) trash, in
whose hands most pupils have taken the straight road to having
their talent spoiled.[2]
I have written to Philoxenus and his friends telling them that
they, too, must leave the matter in the hands of the esteemed . . . so
that I, after rejecting Theon, may find a teacher as soon as possible,
for I myself formed a bad opinion of him . . . as possessing a
completely inadequate training. When I informed Philoxenus of
your view he began to be of the same opinion, saying that it was on
account of a shortage of sophists (σοφιστής) . . . was in the same
condition as the city, but he said that Didymus, who, it appears, is
a friend of his and has a school (σχολή), would be sailing down
and would take more care than the others. He persuaded the sons
of Apollonius son of Herodes to go to enrol [in the school of
Didymus].
And after this they, too, together with Philoxenus, have been

---

[2] Rea's reconstruction of lines 10–11 is accepted, ἀλλὰ καθ]άρματα παρ' οἷς τῆι
εὐθείαι ὁδῶι χρη[σάμεοι οἱ πλείο]νες διεφθορόσι, 'but (only) trash, in whose
hands most pupils have taken the straight road to having their talent spoiled'. It is
more plausible that Roberts' which read 'and the chariots in which the direct
journey up to them has to be made were smashed up', ἀλλὰ τ]ὰ ἅρματα {παρ'} οἷς
τῆι ἐθείαι ὁδῶι χρὴ ἀνελθεῖν πρόχθ]ες διεφθορόσι.

searching until now for a more stylish tutor (καθηγητής) since the scholar (φιλόλογος), to whom they used to go, has died. As for myself, if only I had found some decent teacher (καθηγητής), I would pray never to set eyes on Didymus, even from a distance – what makes me despair is that this fellow who used to be a mere provincial sees fit to compete with the rest.

However, knowing as I do that apart from paying useless and excessive fees there is no good to be had from a tutor (καθηγητής), I am depending on myself. If you have any opinions on the matter, write to me soon. As Philoxenus also says, I have Didymus always ready to spend his time on me and do everything to help within his capabilities, and by hearing the orators declaiming, of whom Posidonius is one, I shall, with the help of the gods do well for myself.

The cause of my despondency about this, which is making me neglect my health, is that those who have not yet succeeded ought not to concern themselves with these matters, especially when there are none who are bringing in any money. For at that time the useful Heraclas – curse him! – used daily to contribute some obols, but now, what with his being imprisoned by Isidorus, as he deserved, he's escaped and gone back, I think, to you. Be assured that he would never hesitate to intrigue against you, for, of all things, he felt no shame at gleefully spreading reports in the city about the incident in the theatre and telling lies such as would not come even from the mouth of an accuser and that too when, so far from suffering what he deserves, he's been released and behaves in every respect like a free man. All the same, if you are not sending him back, you could at any rate hand him over to a carpenter – for I'm told that a young fellow makes two drachmas a day – or put him to some other employment at which he'll earn more money; his wages can then be collected and in due course sent to us, for you know that Diogas, too, is studying. While you are sending the little one, we will look about for more spacious rooms in a private house; for in order to be near to Dionysius we've been living in rooms much too small. We received the basket containing exactly the articles you mentioned and the vessels together with the half-*cadus* jar in which we found 22 *choes* instead of 18. To each of the people of whom you wrote I have sent a half-*cadua* of lentils accompanied by a letter. I have received the six measures and a full *coion* of vinegar and 126 lbs. of salted meat and contents of the *cadus* and the 30 baked loaves. Farewell. Choiak 4.

BIBLIOGRAPHY

Alexandre, M. 'La Culture profane chez Philon', in R. Arnaldez, C. Mondésert and J. Pouilloux (eds.), *Philon d'Alexandrie*, Paris: Editions du Cerf, 1967, pp. 108–127.

'The Art of Periodic Composition in Philo of Alexandria', in D. T. Runia, D. M. Hay and D. Winston (eds.), *Heirs of the Septuagint: Philo, Hellenistic Judaism and Early Christianity, Festschrift for Earle Hilgert*, The Studia Philonica Annual 3 (1991), pp. 135–50.

Anderson, G. *Philostratus: Biography and Belles Lettres in the Third Century A.D.*, London: Croom Helm, 1986.

'The *Pepaideumenos* in Action: Sophists and their Outlook in the Early Empire', *ANRW* II.33.1 (1989), 79–208.

The Second Sophistic: A Cultural Phenomenon in the Roman Empire, London and New York: Routledge, 1993.

Anderson, R. D. *Ancient Rhetorical Theory and Paul*, Kampen: Kok, 1996.

Ansoul, R. 'The Self-Estimate of the Apostle Paul Contained in II Corinthians 10 and 11', PhD dissertation, Macquarie University, 1978.

Arnim, H. von. *Leben und Werke des Dio von Prusa*, Berlin, 1898.

Banks, R. ' "Walking" as a Metaphor of the Christian Life: The Origins of a Significant Pauline Usage', in E. W. Conrad and E. G. Newing (eds.), *Perspectives on Language and Text: Essays and Poems in Honour of Francis I. Andersen on his Sixtieth Birthday July 28, 1985*, Winona Lake: Eisenbrauns, 1987, pp. 303–13.

Barigazzi, A. *Favorino di Arelate: Opera*, Florence: Lelice Le Monnier, 1966.

Barnes, E. J. 'Petronius, Philo and Stoic Rhetoric', *Latomus* 32 (1973), 787–98.

Barnett, P. W. 'Opposition in Corinth', *JSNT* 22 (1984), 3–17.

Barraclough, R. 'Philo's Politics: Roman Rule and Hellenistic Judaism', *ANRW*, II.21.1 (1983), 417–533.

Barrett, C. K. *The First Epistle to the Corinthians*, London: A. & C. Black, 1971.

The Second Epistle to the Corinthians, London: A. & C. Black, 1973.

'Paul's Opponents in 2 Corinthians', in *Essays on Paul*, London: SCM Press, 1982, ch. 4.

'Christianity at Corinth', in *Essays on Paul*, London: SCM Press, 1982, ch. 1.

'Boasting (καυχᾶσθαι κτλ.) in the Pauline Epistles', in A. Vanhoye (ed.), *L'Apôtre Paul: Personnalité, Style et Conception du Ministère*, Leuven: Leuven University Press, 1986, pp. 362–8.

Barrow, R. H. *Plutarch and his Times*, London: Chatto & Windus, 1967.

Barry, W. D. 'Aristocrats, Orators and the Mob: Dio Chrysostom and the World of the Alexandrians', *Historia* 42 (1993), 82–103.

Barton, G. A. 'Some Influences of Apollos in the New Testament', *JBL*, 43 (1924), 207–9.

Bastianini, G. 'Lista dei Prefetti d'Egitto dal 30ᵃ al 299ᴾ', *ZPE*, 17 (1975), 262–388.

Baur, F. C. *Paul, the Apostle of Jesus Christ, His Life and Work, His Epistles and His Doctrine*, English translation, London and Edinburgh: Williams and Norgate, 1876, vol. i.

Behr, C. A. *P. Aelius Aristides: The Complete Works*, Leiden: E. J. Brill, 1981, vol. ii.

Bekker, I. *Anecdota Graeca*, Berlin, 1819.

Bengio, A. 'La Dialectique de Dieu et de l'homme chez Platon et Philon d'Alexandrie: une approche du concept d'ἀρετή chez Philon', PhD dissertation, University of Paris, 1971.

Benner, M. *The Emperor Says: Studies in the Rhetorical Style in Edicts of the Early Empire*, Studia Graeca et Latina Gothoburgensia, vol. xxxiii, Göteborg: Acta Universitatis Gothoburgensis, 1975.

Best, E. 'The Power and the Wisdom of God', in L. de Lorenzi (ed.), *Paolo: A Una Chiesa Divisa (1 Co 1–4)*, Rome: Abbazia di S. Paolo, 1980, pp. 9–39.

Betz, H. D. *Galatians*, Philadelphia: Fortress Press, 1969.

Der Apostel Paulus und die sokratische Tradition: eine exegetische Untersuchung zu seiner 'Apologie' 2 Korinther 10–13, Tübingen: J. C. B. Mohr (Paul Siebeck), 1972.

'Rhetoric and Theology', in A. Vanhoye (ed.), *L'Apôtre Paul: Personnalité, Style et Conception du Ministère*, Leuven: Leuven University Press, 1986, pp. 16–48.

Billings, T. H. *The Platonism of Philo Judaeus*, Chicago: University of Chicago Press, 1919.

Bjerkelund, C. J. *Parakalō: Form, Funktion und Sinn der parakalō-Sätze in den paulinischen Briefen*, Oslo: Universitetsforlaget, 1967.

Black, E. 'Plato's View of Rhetoric', in K. V. Erickson (ed.), *Plato: True and Sophistic Rhetoric*, Amsterdam: Rodopi, 1979, pp. 171–91.

Blunt, P. A. 'The Administrators of Egypt', *JRS* 65 (1975), 124–47.

'Princeps and Equites', *JRS* 73 (1983), 61–6.

Bokser, B. M. *Philo's Description of Jewish Practices*, Berkeley: The Center for Hermeneutical Studies in Hellenistic and Modern Culture, 1977.

Bonner, S. F. *Roman Declamation in the Late Republic and Early Empire*, Liverpool: University Press of Liverpool, 1949.

Bookidis, N. and Stroud, R. S. *Demeter and Persephone in Ancient Corinth*, American Excavations in Old Corinth, Corinth Notes 2, Princeton: American School of Classical Studies at Athens, 1987.

Booth, A. D. 'Elementary and Secondary Education in the Roman Empire', *Florilegium* 3 (1981), 1–20.

'Litterator', *Hermes* 109 (1981), 371–8.
'The Appearance of the Schola Grammatici', *Hermes* 106 (1978), 117–25.
Bordes, J. *Politeia dans la pensée grecque jusqu'à Aristote*, Paris: 'Belles Lettres', 1982.
Borgen, P. *Bread from Heaven: An Exegetical Study of the Concept of Manna in the Gospel of John and the Writings of Philo*, Leiden: E. J. Brill, 1965.
'Philo of Alexandria: A Critical and Synthetical Survey of Research since World War II', *ANRW* II.21 (1984), 98–154.
Borgen, P. and Skarsten, R. '*Quaestiones et Solutiones*: Some Observations on the Form of Philo's Exegesis', *SP* 4 (1976–7), 1–15.
Bornecque, H. *Les Déclamations et les déclamateurs d'après Sénèque le père*, reprinted Hildesheim: Georg Olms Verlag, 1967.
Bornkamm, G. 'The Missionary Stance of Paul in 1 Corinthians 9 and in Acts', in L. E. Keck and J. L. Martin (eds.), *Studies in Luke–Acts: Essays Presented in Honour of Paul Schubert*, Nashville: Abingdon Press, 1966, pp. 167–89.
Borthwick, E. K. 'Dio Chrysostom on the Mob at Alexandria', *CR* (n.s.) 22 (1972), 1–3.
Bosch, J. S. *'Gloriarse' segun San Pablo: Sentido y teología de καυχάομαι*, Rome: Biblical Institute Press, 1970.
Bowersock, G. W. 'A New Inscription of Arrian', *GRBS* 8 (1967), 279–80.
Greek Sophists in the Roman Empire, Oxford: Clarendon Press, 1969.
(ed.), *Approaches to the Second Sophistic*, University Park, Pennsylvania: American Philological Association, 1974.
Bowie, E. L. 'Greeks and their Past in the Second Sophistic', *Past and Present* 46 (1970), 3–41.
'The Importance of the Sophists', *Yale Classical Studies* 27 (1982), 29–59.
Brandstätter, C. 'De notium πολιτικός et σοφιστής usu rhetorico', *Leipzig Stud. z. Class. Phil.* 15 (1894), 215–28.
Bréhier, E. *Les Idées philosophiques et religieuses de Philon d'Alexandrie*, Paris: Boivin et Cie, 1925.
Bruce, F. F. *Commentary on the Book of Acts*, 3rd edn, Edinburgh: Marshall, Morgan and Scott, 1962.
New Testament History, New York: Doubleday, 1971.
Men and Movements in the Primitive Church, Exeter: Paternoster Press, 1979.
Brunt, P. A. 'The Romanization of the Local Ruling Classes in the Roman Empire', in D. M. Pippidi (ed.), *Assimilation et résistance à la culture gréco-romaine dans le monde ancien: Travaux du VIe Congrès International d'Etudes Classique,* Paris: 'Belles Lettres', 1976, pp. 161–73.
'The Administrators of Egypt', *JRS* 65 (1975), 124–47.
Bultmann, R. *The Second Letter to the Corinthians*, English translation, Minneapolis: Augsburg Publishing House, 1985.
Bünker, M. *Briefformular und rhetorische Disposition im 1 Korintherbrief*, Göttinger Theologische Arbeiten 28, Göttingen: Vandenhoeck & Ruprecht, 1983.

Buxton, R. G. A. *Persuasion in Greek Tragedy: A Study of peitho*, Cambridge: Cambridge University Press, 1982.

Caplan, H. 'The Decay of Eloquence at Rome in the First Century', in D. C. Bryant, B. Hewitt, K. R. Wallace and H. A. Wichelns (eds.), *Studies in Speech and Drama in Honor of Alexander M. Drummond*, New York: Cornell University Press, 1944, pp. 295–325.

Carson, D. A. 'Pauline Inconsistency', *The Churchman* 100 (1986), 6–45.

Chadwick, H. 'All things to all men (I Cor. xi.22)', *NTS* 1 (1954–5), 261–75.

'St. Paul and Philo of Alexandria', *BJRL*, 48.2 (1966), 286–307.

Chapple, A. 'Local Leadership in the Pauline Churches: Theological and Social Factors in its Development: A Study based on 1 Thessalonians, 1 Corinthians, and Philippians', PhD dissertation, University of Durham, 1984.

Charlesworth, M. P. 'Providentia and Aeternitas', *HTR* 29 (1936), 107–32.

Clarke, A. D. *Secular and Christian Leadership in Corinth: A Socio-Historical and Exegetical Study of 1 Corinthians 1–6*, Leiden: E. J. Brill, 1993.

Clarke, M. L. *Higher Education in the Ancient World*, London: Routledge and Kegan Paul, 1971.

Rhetoric at Rome: A Historical Survey, London: Cohen & West, 1953.

Classen, C. J. 'Aristotle's Picture of the Sophists', in *The Sophists and their Legacy: Proceedings of the Fourth International Colloquium on Ancient Philosophy, Hermes* 44 (1978), 7–24.

Coby, P. 'The Education of a Sophist: Aspects of Plato's *Protagoras*', *Interpretation* 10 (1982), 139–58.

Colson, F. H. 'Μετεσχημάτισα 1 Cor. iv 6', *JTS* 17 (1916), 379–84.

'Philo on Education', *JTS*, 18 (1917), 151–62.

Conley, T. *'General Education' in Philo of Alexandria*, Hermeneutical Studies in Hellenistic and Modern Culture, no. 15, Berkeley: Center for Hermeneutical Studies in Hellenistic and Modern Culture, 1975.

Philo's Rhetoric: Studies in Style, Composition and Exegesis, Center for Hermeneutical Studies Monograph Series no. 1, Berkeley: Center for Hermeneutical Studies in Hellenistic and Modern Culture, 1987.

'Philo's Use of *topoi*', in D. Winston and J. Dillon (eds.), *Two Treatises of Philo of Alexandria: a Commentary of De Gigantibus and Quod Deus Sit Immutabilis*, Brown Judaic Studies, no. 25, Chico: Scholars Press, 1983, pp. 155–78.

'Philo's Rhetoric: Argumentation and Style', *ANRW* II.21.1 (1984), 343–71.

Conybeare, F. C. *Philo about the Contemplative Life*, Oxford: Clarendon Press, 1895.

Conzelmann, H. *The First Epistle to the Corinthians*, English translation, Philadelphia: Fortress Press, 1975.

Cosgrove, C. H. 'Arguing like a Mere Human Being: Galatians 3.15–18 in Rhetorical Perspective', *NTS* 34.4 (1988), 536–49.

Court, J. D. 'Some Aspects of Rank and Status in Epictetus: Development of a Methodology', MA dissertation, Macquarie University, 1986.

Crook, J. A. *Legal Advocacy in the Roman World*, London: Duckworth, 1995.

Dahl, N. A. 'Paul and the Church in Corinth in 1 Cor. 1.10–4.21', in W. F. Farmer et al. (eds.), *Christian History and Interpretation: Studies Presented to John Knox*, Cambridge: Cambridge University Press, 1967, ch. 15.

'The Church in Corinth', in *Studies in Paul: Theology for the Early Christian Mission*, Minneapolis: Augsburg Publishing House, 1977.

Danker, F. W. *Benefactor: Epigraphic Study of a Graeco–Roman and New Testament Semantic Field*, St Louis: Clayton Publishing House, 1982.

Darrow, F. S. 'The History of Corinth from Mummius to Herodes Atticus', PhD dissertation, Harvard University, 1906.

David, M. et al. *Berichtigungsliste der Griechischen Papyruskunden aus Ägypten*, Leiden: E. J. Brill, 1964, vol. IV.

Davis, J. A. *Wisdom and Spirit: An Investigation of 1 Corinthians 1.18–3.20 against the Background of Jewish Sapiential Tradition in the Greco–Roman Period*, Lanham and London: University Press of America, 1984.

Deissmann, A. *Light from the Ancient East: The New Testament Illustrated by Recently Discovered Texts of the Graeco–Roman World*, English translation, reprinted Grand Rapids: Baker Book House, 1978.

Delling, G. and Maser, R. 'Bibliographie zur Jüdische-Hellenistischen und Intertestamentarischen Literatur 1900–1970', in *Texte und Untersuchungen*, 106, Berlin: Akademie Verlag, 1975, pp. 56–80.

Desideri, P. *Dione di Prusa: un intellettuale greco nell'Impero Romano*, Biblioteca di Cultura Contemporanea, vol. CXXXV, Messina: Casa Editrice G. d'Anna, 1978.

Dewey, A. J. 'A Matter of Honor: A Social–Historical Analysis of 2 Corinthians 10', *HTR* 78 (1985), 209–17.

De Witt, N. E. 'Organization and Procedure in Epicurean Groups', *CP* 31 (1936), 205–11.

DiCicco, M. M. *Paul's Use of Ethos, Pathos, and Logos in 2 Corinthians 10–13*, Mellen Biblical Studies Series 31, Lewiston, NY: Mellen Biblical Press, 1995.

Diels, H. & Kranz, W. *Die Fragmente der Vorsokratiker*, Berlin: Weidmann, 1974, vol. I.

Dillon, J. *The Middle Platonists: A Study of Platonism 80 B.C. to A.D. 220*, London: Duckworth, 1977.

Dittberner, A. 'Who is Apollos and Who is Paul?', *The Bible Today* 71 (1974), 1549–52.

Dodd, C. H. 'The Mind of Paul: a Psychological Approach', *BJRL* 17 (1933), 91–105.

Dorjahn, A. P. 'Apollonius Dyscolus on Homer', *CP* 25 (1930), 282–4.

'Philodemus on Homer', *CJ* 26 (1931), 457–8.

Dorrie, H. 'Zur Methodik antiker Exegese', *ZNW* 65 (1974), 121–38.

Dowdy, B. A. 'The Meaning of KAUCHASTHAI in the New Testament', PhD dissertation, Vanderbilt University, 1955.

Drabkin, I. E. 'On Medical Education in Greece and Rome', *Bulletin of the History of Medicine* 15 (1944), 333–51.

Drummond, J. *Philo Judaeus: or the Jewish-Alexandrian Philosophy in its Development and Completion*, London and Edinburgh: Williams & Norgate, 1888.

Dudley, R. H. *A History of Cynicism from Diogenes to the 6th Century A.D.*, London: Methuen, 1937.

Dungan, D. L. *The Sayings of Jesus in the Churches of Paul*, Philadelphia: Fortress Press, 1971.

Earnesti, J. C. G. *Lexicon technologiae graecorum rhetoricae*, reprinted Hildesheim: Georg Olms Verlag, 1962.

Edwards, W. M. 'DIALOGOS, DIATRIBH MELETH', in J. N. Powell and F. A. Barber (eds.), *New Chapters in the History of Greek Literature, Second Series*, Oxford: Clarendon Press, 1929, pp. 188–224.

Ellicott, C. J. *St. Paul's First Epistle to the Corinthians with a Critical and Grammatical Commentary*, London: Longmans, Green & Co., 1887.

Elliott, J. K. 'The Use of ἕτερος in the New Testament', *ZNW* 70 (1969), 140–1.

Ellis, E. Earle 'Paul and his Opponents', in *Prophecy and Hermeneutic in Early Christianity*, Tübingen: J. C. B. Mohr (Paul Siebeck), 1978, ch. 6.

Fairweather, J. *Seneca the Elder*, Cambridge: Cambridge University Press, 1981.

Fee, G. D. *The First Epistle to the Corinthians*, Grand Rapids: Eerdmans, 1987.

Feldman, L. H. *Scholarship on Philo and Josephus*, New York: Yeshiva University, 1963.

'The Orthodoxy of the Jews in Hellenistic Egypt', *JSS* 22 (1960), 215–37.

Ferguson, J. *The Religions of the Roman Empire*, London: Thames & Hudson, 1970.

Fiore, B. '"Covert Allusion" in 1 Corinthians 1–4', *CBQ* 47 (1985), 85–102.

Fischel, H. A. *Rabbinic Literature and Greco–Roman Philosophy: A Study of Epicurea and Rhetoric in early Midrashic Writings*, Studia Post-Biblica, 31, Leiden: E. J. Brill, 1973.

Fitzgerald, J. T. *Cracks in an Earthen Vessel: An Examination of the Catalogues of Hardships in the Corinthian Correspondence*, SBL Dissertation Series, 99, Atlanta: Scholars Press, 1988.

Forbes, C. 'Comparison, Self-praise and Irony: Paul's Boasting and Conventions of Hellenistic Rhetoric', *NTS* 32 (1986), 1–30.

Forbes, C. A. 'Education and Training of Slaves in Antiquity', *TAPA*, 86 (1955), 321–60.

Foster, S. 'A Note on the "Note" of J. Schwartz', *SP* 4 (1976–7), 25–32.

Fraser, P. M. *Ptolemaic Alexandria*, 2nd edn, Oxford: Clarendon Press, 1972, vol. I.

Friedrichsen, A. 'Zum Stil des paulinischen Peristasenkatalogs 2 Kor. 11.23ff', *Symbolae Osloenses* (1929), 25–9.

'Peristasenkatalogs und *res gestae* nachtrag zu 2 Kor. 11.23ff', *Symbolae Osloenses* (1929), 78–82.

Furnish, V. P. *II Corinthians*, The Anchor Bible, New York: Doubleday, 1984.

Garnsey, P. 'The *Lex Julia* and Appeal under the Empire', *JRS* 56 (1966), 167–89.

Social Status and Legal Privilege in the Roman Empire, Oxford: Clarendon Press, 1970.

Geagan, D. J. 'Notes on the Agonistic Institutions of Roman Corinth', *GRBS* 9 (1968), 69–80.

Gebhard, E. R. 'The Isthmian Games and the Sanctuary of Poseidon in the Early Empire', in T. E. Gregory (ed.), *The Corinthia in the Roman Period, JRA Supp. 8* (1994), pp. 78–94.

Geoltrain, P. G. 'Le Traité de la *Vie Contemplative* de Philon d'Alexandrie', *Semitica* 10 (1960), 5–67.

Georgi, D. *The Opponents of Paul in Second Corinthians*, English translation, Edinburgh: T. & T. Clark, 1987.

Gibbs, J. M. 'Wisdom, Power and Wellbeing', in E. A. Livingstone (ed.), *Papers on Paul and Other New Testament Authors*, Studia Biblica 1978, vol. III, Sheffield: Sheffield Academic Press, 1980, pp. 119–55.

Gilchrist, J. M. 'Paul and the Corinthians: the Sequence of Letters and Visits', *JSNT* 34 (1988), 47–69.

Gleason, M. W. *Making Men: Sophists and Self-Presentation in Ancient Rome*, Princeton: Princeton University Press, 1995.

Glucker, J. *Antiochus and the Late Academy*, Hypomnemata, vol. LVI, Göttingen: Vandenhoeck & Ruprecht, 1978.

Goldstein, J. 'Jewish Acceptance and Rejection of Hellenism', in E. P. Sanders (ed.), *Jewish and Christian Self-Definition: Aspects of Judaism in the Graeco–Roman Period*, London: SCM Press, 1981, vol. II, ch. 4.

Goldstein, J. A. *The Letters of Demosthenes*, New York and London: Columbia University Press, 1968.

Goodenough, E. R. *Jurisprudence of the Jewish Courts in Egypt*, New Haven: Yale University Press, 1929.

Goodheart, H. L. and Goodenough, E. R. *A General Bibliography of Philo*, New Haven: Yale University Press, 1938.

Graindor, P. *Un milliardaire antique: Herodes Atticus et sa famille*, Cairo, MISR, 1930.

Grayston, K. 'Not with a Rod', *ET* 88 (1976), 13–16.

Gruen, E. S. 'Philosophy, Rhetoric and Roman Anxieties', in *Studies in Greek Culture and Roman Policy*, Leiden: E. J. Brill, 1990, ch. v.

Grundmann, W. 'Die nepioi in der urchristlichen Parenese', *NTS* 5 (1958–9), 190–205.

Gunther, J. J. *St Paul's Opponents and Their Background: A Study of Apocalyptic and Jewish Sectarian Teaching*, Supp. *NovT*, vol. XXXV, Leiden: E. J. Brill, 1973.

Gusmani, R. 'I nomi greci in -ω', *RIL* 96 (1962), 399–412.

Guthrie, W. K. C. *The Sophists*, Cambridge: Cambridge University Press, 1971.

Gwyn Griffiths, J. 'Allegory in Greece and Egypt', *Journal of Egyptian Archaeology* 53 (1967), 79–102.

Hadas-Lebel, M. *De Providentia I et II: Les oeuvres de Philon d'Alexandrie*, 35, Paris: Editions du Cerf, 1973.

Haenchen, E. *The Acts of the Apostles: a Commentary*, English translation, Oxford: Blackwell, 1971.

Hall, F. W. *A Companion to Classical Texts*, Oxford: Clarendon Press, 1913.

Hall, R. G. 'The Rhetorical Outline of Galatians: A Reconsideration', *JBL* 106.2 (1987), 277–87.

Halleway, E. 'Biblical Midrash and Homeric Exegesis', *Tarbiz* 31 (1959), 157.

Hamerton-Kelly, R. G. 'Some Techniques of Compositon in Philo's Allegorical Commentary with Special Reference to *De Agricultura*: A Study in Hellenistic Midrash', in R. Hamerton-Kelly and R. Scroggs (eds.), *Jews, Greeks and Christians: Religious Cultures in Late Antiquity. Essays in Honor of William David Davies*, Leiden: E. J. Brill, 1976, pp. 45–56.

Hands, A. R. *Charities and Social Aid in Greece and Rome*, London: Thames and Hudson, 1968.

Hansen, G. W. *Abraham in Galatians: Epistolary and Rhetorical Contexts*, Sheffield: Sheffield Academic Press, 1985.

Hanson, A. E. 'Memorandum and Speech of an Advocate', *ZPE* 8 (1971), 15–27.

Hanson, R. P. C. *The Acts in the Revised Standard Version with Introduction and Commentary*, Oxford: Clarendon Press, 1967.

Hardie, A. *Statius and the Silvae: Poets, Patrons and Epideixis in the Graeco–Roman World*, Liverpool: Francis Cairns, 1983.

Harmon, A. M. 'The Poet κᾱτ' ἐξοχήν', *CP* 18 (1923), 35–47.

Harris, B. F. 'Bithynia: Roman Sovereignty and the Survival of Hellenism', *ANRW* II.7.1 (1980), 857–901.

'Dio of Prusa: A Survey of Recent Works', *ANRW* II, 33.5 (1991), 3853–81.

Harris, H. A. *Trivium, Greek Athletics and the Jews*, Cardiff: University of Wales Press, 1976.

Harrison, A. R. W. *The Law of Athens: Family and Property*, Oxford: Clarendon Press, 1968.

Harrison, J. 'St Paul's Letters to the Corinthians', *ET* 77 (1966), 285–6.

Hartman, L. 'Some Remarks on 1 Cor. 2.1–5', *Svensk Exegetisk Årsbok* 39 (1974), 109–20.

Heinemann, I. *Philons griechische und jüdische Bildung*, Breslau: Marcus, 1932.

Hengel, M. *Judaism and Hellenism: Studies in their Encounter during the Early Hellenistic Period*, English translation, London: SCM Press, 1974.

Jews, Greeks and Barbarians: Aspects of the Hellenization of Judaism in the Pre-Christian Period, English translation, London: SCM Press, 1988.

The 'Hellenization' of Judaea in the First Century after Christ, English translation, London: SCM Press, 1990.

Henrichs, A. 'Vespasian's Visit to Alexandria', *ZPE* 3 (1968), 51–80.

Henry, A. S. 'Seats in Theatre and Stadium, Statues and Painted Portraits', in *Honours and Privileges in Athenian Decrees: The Principle Formulae of Athenian Honorary Decrees*, Hildesheim and New York: Georg Olms, 1983, ch. x.

Héring, J. *The First Epistle of Saint Paul to the Corinthians*, English translation, London: Epworth Press, 1962.

The Second Epistle of Saint Paul to the Corinthians, English translation, London: Epworth Press, 1967.

Herrmann, L. 'Apollos', *RSR* 50 (1976), 330–6.

Hilgert, E. 'Bibliographia Philoniana 1935–1981', *ANRW* ii.21.1 (1984), 47–97.

Hock, R. F. *The Social Context of Paul's Ministry: Tentmaking and Apostleship*, Philadelphia: Fortress Press, 1980.

Hock, R. F. and O'Neil, E. N. *The Chreia in Ancient Rhetoric*, vol. i, *The Progymnasmata*, Atlanta: Scholars Press, 1986.

Hodgson, R. 'Paul the Apostle and First Century Tribulation Lists', *ZNW* 74 (1983), 59–80.

Hoistad, R. *Cynic Hero and Cynic King*, Uppsala: Bloms, 1948.

Holland, G. S. *The Tradition that You Received from Us: 2 Thessalonians in the Pauline Tradition*, Tübingen: J. C. B. Mohr (Paul Siebeck), 1988.

Holmberg, B. *Paul and Power: The Structure of Authority in the Primitive Church as Reflected in the Pauline Epistles*, English translation, Philadelphia: Fortress Press, 1980.

Hooker, M. D. 'Hard Sayings', *Theology* 69 (1966), 19–22.

Horne, C. M. 'The Power of Paul's Preaching', *Bulletin of the Evangelical Society* 8 (1965), 111–16.

Horsley, G. H. R. 'The Purple Trade and the Status of Lydia of Thyatira', *New Docs.* 2 (1982), 25–32.

Horsley, R. A. 'Wisdom of Word and Words of Wisdom', *CBQ* 39 (1977), 224–39.

Householder Jr., F. W. *Literary Quotation and Allusion in Lucian*, New York: King's Crown Press, 1941.

Hubbell, H.M. 'The Rhetorica of Philodemus', *The Connecticut Academy of Arts and Sciences* 23 (1920), 243–382.

Hudson-Williams, H. L. 'Political Speeches in Athens, *CQ* (n.s.) 45 (1951), 68–73.

Hughes, F. W. 'The Rhetoric of Letters', in *Early Christian Rhetoric and 2 Thessalonians*, Sheffield: Sheffield Academic Press, 1989, ch. 2.

Hunter, A. M. 'Apollos the Alexandrian', in J. R. McKay and J. F. Miller (eds.), *Biblical Studies: Essays in Honour of William Barclay*, London: Collins, 1976, pp. 147–56.

Hurd Jr., J. C. *The Origin of 1 Corinthians*, London: SPCK, 1965.

Hyldahl, N. 'Den korintiske situation – en skitse', *Dansk Teologisk Tidsskrift*, 40 (1977), 18–30.

Ibrahim, M. H. 'The Study of Homer in Graeco–Roman Education', Ἀθηνα 76 (1976–7), 187–95.

Ὁ ἑλληνορώμαικη παιδεία ἐν Αἰγυωπτώ, Athens: Myrtidi, 1972.

Jewett, R. *The Thessalonian Correspondence: Pauline Rhetoric and Millenarian Piety*, Philadelphia: Fortress Press, 1986.

Johnson, S. E. 'Tarsus and the Apostle Paul', *Lexington Theological Quarterly* 15.4 (1980), 105–13.

Jones, C. P. 'Towards a Chronology of Plutarch', *JRS* 65 (1966), 72–3.

'The Date of Dio of Prusa's Alexandrian Oration', *Historia* 22 (1973), 302–9.

'The Reliability of Philostratus', in G. W. Bowersock (ed.), *Approaches to the Second Sophistic*, University Park, Pennsylvania: American Philological Association, 1974, pp. 11–16.

The Roman World of Dio Chrysostom, Cambridge, Mass. and London: Harvard University Press, 1978.

Plutarch and Rome, Oxford: Clarendon Press, 1971.

Jones, M. *St Paul as Orator: A Critical, Historical and Explanatory Commentary on the Speeches of St Paul*, London: Hodder and Stoughton, 1910.

Judge, E. A. 'The Early Christians as a Scholastic Community: Part II', *Journal of Religious History* 1 (1960), 125–37.

'The Origin of the Church at Rome: A New Solution', *RTR* 25 (1966), 81–94.

'Paul's Boasting in Relation to Contemporary Professional Practice', *Australian Biblical Review* 16 (1968), 37–50.

'St Paul and Classical Society', *Jahrbuch für Antike und Christentum* 15 (1972), 19–36.

'St Paul and Socrates', *Interchange* 13 (1973), 106–16.

'The Regional *Kanon* for Requisitioned Transport', *New Docs* 1 (1976), 36–45.

Rank and Status in the World of the Caesars and St Paul, Christchurch: University of Canterbury Publications, 1982.

'The Reaction against Classical Education in the New Testament', *Journal of Christian Education Paper* 77 (1983), 7–14.

'Cultural Conformity and Innovation in Paul: Some Clues from Contemporary Documents', *Tyn.B.* 35 (1984), 3–24.

Kaibel, G. *Epigrammata Graeca ex lapidibus collecta*, Berlin, 1878.

Kant, L. H. 'Jewish Inscriptions in Greek and Latin', *ANRW* II.20.2 (1987), 671–713.

Käsemann, E. 'A Pauline Version of the "Amor Fati"', in *New Testament Questions of Today*, English translation, London: SCM Press, 1969.

Kasher, A. *The Jews in Hellenistic and Roman Egypt: the Struggle for Equal Rights*, Tübingen: J. C. B. Mohr (Paul Siebeck), 1985.

Kaster, R. A. 'Notes on "Primary" and "Secondary" Schools in Late Antiquity', *TAPA* 113 (1983), 323–46.

Keil, B. *Aelius Aristides*, Berlin, 1898.

Kelly, W. G. 'Rhetoric as Seduction', in K. V. Erickson (ed.), *Plato: True and Sophistic Rhetoric*, Amsterdam: Rodopi, 1979, pp. 313–23.

Kennedy, G. A. *The Art of Persuasion in Greece*, Princeton: Princeton University Press, 1963.

The Art of Rhetoric in the Roman World, Princeton: Princeton University Press, 1972.

'The Sophists as Declaimers', in G. W. Bowersock (ed.), *Approaches to the Second Sophistic*, University Park, Pennsylvania: American Philological Association, 1974, pp. 17–22.

Classical Rhetoric and its Christian and Secular Tradition from Ancient to Modern Times, London: Croom Helm, 1980.

Greek Rhetoric under Christian Emperors, Princeton: Princeton University Press, 1983.

New Testament Interpretation through Rhetorical Criticism, Chapel Hill: University of North Carolina Press, 1984.

A New History of Classical Rhetoric, Princeton: Princeton University Press, 1994.

Kent, J. H. *Corinth: Inscriptions 1926–1960*, Princeton: American School of Classical Studies at Athens, 1966.

Kerferd, G. B. 'The First Greek Sophist?', *CR* 64 (1950), 8–10.

The Sophistic Movement, Cambridge: Cambridge University Press, 1981.

Kern, P. H. 'Rhetoric, Scholarship and Galatians: Assessing an Approach to Paul's Epistle', PhD dissertation, University of Sheffield, 1994.

Kindstrand, J. F. 'The Date of Dio of Prusa's Alexandrian Oration – A Reply', *Historica* 27 (1978), 378–83.

Kroll, W. "Εν ἤθει' in R. Stark and P. Steinmetz (eds.), *Rhetorika: Schriften zur aristotelischen und hellenistischen Rhetorik*, Hildesheim: Georg Olms Verlag, 1968, ch. 13.

Lampe, P. 'Theological Wisdom and the "Word about the Cross": The Rhetorical Scheme in 1 Corinthians 1–4', *Interpretation* 44.2 (1990), 117–31.

Lang, F. *Die Briefe an die Korinther*, Göttingen: Vandenhoeck & Ruprecht, 1986.

Lanham, R. A. *A Handlist of Rhetorical Terms*, Berkeley and London: University of California Press, 1968.

Lebram, J. C. H. 'Eine stoische Auslegung von *Ex.* 3.2 bei Philo', in *Das Institutum Judaicum der Universität Tübingen in der Jahren 1971–2*, Tübingen: J. C. B. Mohr (Paul Siebeck), 1972, p. 31.

Leopold, J. 'Philo's Knowledge of Rhetorical Theory', in D. Winston and J. Dillon (eds.), *Two Treatises of Philo of Alexandria: a Commentary of De Gigantibus and Quod Deus Sit Immutabilis*, Brown Judaic Studies, no. 25, Chico: Scholars Press, 1983, pp. 129–36.

'Rhetoric and Allegory', in D. Winston and J. Dillon (eds.), *Two Treatises of Philo of Alexandria: a Commentary of De Gigantibus and Quod Deus Sit Immutabilis*, Brown Judaic Studies, no. 25, Chico: Scholars Press, 1983, pp. 155–70.

Levick, B. *Tiberius the Politician*, London: Thames & Hudson, 1976.

Lewis, N. and Reinhold, M. *Roman Civilization. Sourcebook II: The Empire*, New York: Columbia University Press, 1966.

Lightfoot, J. B. *Notes on Epistles of St Paul from Unpublished Commentaries*, London: MacMillan, 1895.

Lim, T. H. 'Not in Persuasive Words of Wisdom, but in Demonstration of the Spirit and Power', *NovT* 29.2 (1987), 137–49.

Lincoln, A. T. 'Paul the Visionary: The Setting and Significance of the Rapture to Paradise in II Corinthians 12.1–10', *NTS* 25 (1979), 204–20.

Lintott, A. *Violence, Civil Strife and Revolution in the Classical City*, London: Croom Helm, 1982.

Litfin, A. D. *St Paul's Theology of Proclamation: an Investigation of 1 Corinthians 1–4 and Greco–Roman Rhetoric*, SNTS Monograph Series 79, Cambridge: Cambridge University Press, 1994.

Ljungman, H. *Pistis: A Study of its Presuppositions and its Meaning in Pauline Use*, Acta, 64, Lund: Gleerup, 1964.

Lösch, S. 'Die Dankesrede de Tertullus: Apg. 24.1–4', *Theologische Quartalschrift* 112 (1931), 295–319.

Lyall, T. 'Paul', in *Slaves, Citizens, Sons: Legal Metaphors in the Epistles*, Grand Rapids: Zondervan, 1984, Appendix 5.

Lynch, A. 'Pauline Rhetoric: 1 Corinthians 1.10–4.21', MA dissertation, University of North Carolina, 1981.

Mack, B. L. 'Decoding the Scripture: Philo and the Rules of Rhetoric', unpublished paper from the *Philo Seminar*, Canterbury, August 1983, 1–44.

MacMullen, R. *Roman Social Relations 50 BC to AD 284*, London and New Haven: Yale University Press, 1974.

Malherbe, A. J. 'Gentle as a Nurse: The Cynic Background of 1 Thess 2', *NovT* 12 (1970), 203–17.

Social Aspects of Early Christianity, Baton Rouge: Louisiana State University Press, 1977.

The Cynic Epistles, Missoula: Scholars Press, 1977.

Paul and the Popular Philosophers, Minneapolis: Fortress Press, 1989.

Mansfeld, J. 'Philosophy in the Service of Scripture: Philo's Exegetical Strategies', in J. M. Dillon and A. A. Long (eds.), *The Question of 'Eclecticism': Studies in Late Greek Philosophy*, Berkeley: University of California Press, 1988, ch. 3.

Marcus, R. 'An Armenian–Greek Index to Philo's *Questiones* and *De Vita Contemplativa*', *Journal of the American Oriental Society* 53 (1933), 251–82.

'Recent Literature on Philo', in S. W. Baron and A. Marx (eds.), *Jewish Studies in Memory of George A. Kohut*, New York: The Alexander Kohut Memorial Foundation, 1935, pp. 463–91.

Marrou, H. I. *A History of Education in Antiquity*, English translation, London: Sheed & Ward, 1956.

Marshall, I. H. *The Acts of the Apostles: an Introduction and Commentary*, Leicester: Inter-Varsity Press, 1980.

Marshall, P. *Enmity in Corinth: Social Conventions in Paul's Relations with the Corinthians*, Tübingen: J. C. B. Mohr (Paul Siebeck), 1987.

Marten, J. R. 'Inscriptions at Corinth', *Hesperia* 46 (1977), 178–98.

Martin, J. *Antike Rhetorik: Technik und Methode*, Munich: C. H. Beck'sche Verlag, 1974.

Martin, R. P. *2 Corinthians*, Waco: Word, 1986.

Mason, H. J. *Greek Terms for Roman Institutions: a Lexicon and Analysis*, *ASP* 13, Toronto: A. M. Hakkert, 1974.

Mayer, R. 'Geschichtserfahrung und Schriftauslegung: Zur Hermeneutik des frühen Judentums', in O. Loretz and W. Strolz (eds.), *Die hermeneutische Frage in der Theologie*, Freiburg: Editiones Herder, 1968.

McCant, J. W. 'Paul's Thorn of Rejected Apostleship', *NTS* 34.4 (1988), 550–72.

McCrum, M. and Woodhead, A. G. *Select Documents of the Principates of the Flavian Emperors*, Cambridge: Cambridge University Press, 1961.

McHugh, J. 'Present and Future in the Life of the Community: 1 Cor. 4.6–13 in the Context of 1 Cor. 4.6–21', in L. de Lorenzi (ed.), *Paolo: A Una Chiesa Divisa (1 Co. 1–4)*, Rome: Abbazia di S. Paolo, 1980, pp. 177–208.

Meeks, W. A. *The First Urban Christians: The Social World of the Apostle Paul*, New Haven and London: Yale University Press, 1983.

Mendelson, A. 'Encyclical Education in Philo of Alexandria', PhD dissertation, University of Chicago, 1971.
    Secular Education in Philo of Alexandria, Cincinnati: Hebrew Union College Press, 1982.

Meyer, H. A. W. *Critical and Exegetical Handbook to the Epistles to the Corinthians*, English translation, Edinburgh: T. & T. Clark, 1892, vol. I.

Meyer, J. P. *Ministers of Christ: a Commentary on the Second Epistle to the Corinthians*, Milwaukee: Northwestern Publishing House, 1963.

Michel, M. A. 'Quelques aspects de la rhétorique chez Philon', in R. Arnaldez, C. Mondésert and J. Pouilloux (eds.), *Philon d'Alexandrie*, Paris: Editions du Cerf, 1967, pp. 81–103.

Millar, F. 'Epictetus and the Imperial Court', *JRS* 55 (1965), 141–60.
    The Emperor in the Roman World (31 B.C.–A.D. 337), London: Duckworth, 1977.
    'Empire and City, Augustus to Julian: Obligations, Excuses and Status', *JRS* 73 (1983), 76–96.

Mitchell, M. *Paul and the Rhetoric of Reconciliation: An Exegetical Investigation of the Language and Composition of 1 Corinthians*, Tübingen: J. C. B. Mohr (Paul Siebeck), 1991.

Moles, J. L. 'The Career and Conversion of Dio Chrysostom', *JRS* 68 (1978), 79–100.

Momigiliano, A. 'Review and Discussion', *JRS* 40 (1950), 146–53.

Montford, J. F. 'The Arts: Greek Music in the Papyri and Inscriptions', in J. U. Powell and E. A. Barber (eds.), *New Chapters in the History of Greek Literature*, Oxford: Clarendon Press, 1929, pp. 146–83.

Morrison, J. S. 'An Introductory Chapter in the History of Greek Education', *Durham University Journal* 12 (1949), 55–63.

Mortley, R. J. 'Plato and the Sophistic Heritage of Protagoras', *Eranos* 67 (1969), 24–32.
    'The Past in Clement of Alexandria: A Study of an Attempt to define Christianity in Socio-Cultural Terms', in E. P. Sanders (ed.), *The Shaping of Christianity in the Second and Third Centuries, Jewish and Christian Self-Definition*, Philadelphia: Fortress Press, 1980, vol. I, ch. 12.

Müller, K. '1 Kor. 1.18–25. Die eschatologisch-kritische Funktion der Verkundigung des Krauzes', *BZ* 10 (1966), 246–72.

Mullins, T. Y. 'Disclosure: a Literary Form in the New Testament', *NovT* 7 (1964), 44–50.

Munck, J. 'Menigheden uden Partier', *Dansk Teologisk Tidsskrift* 15 (1952), 215–233; English translation, 'The Church without Factions', in *Paul and the Salvation of Mankind*, London: SCM Press, 1959, ch. 5.

'1 Thess.1.9–10 and the Missionary Preaching of Paul: Textual Exegesis and Hermeneutic Reflexions', *NTS* 9 (1962–3), 95–110.

Murphy-O'Connor, J. *St Paul's Corinth: Texts and Archaeology*, Wilmington: Glazier, 1983.

Mussies, G. *Dio Chrysostom and the New Testament*, Leiden: E. J. Brill, 1972.

Myres, S. J. *Homer and His Critics*, London: Routledge and Kegan Paul, 1958.

Neyrey, J. 'The Forensic Defence Speech and Paul's Trial Speeches in Acts 22–26: Form and Function', in C. H. Talbert (ed.), *Luke–Acts: New Perspectives from the Society of Biblical Literature*, New York: Crossroads, 1984.

Nickle, K. F. *The Collection: a Study of Paul's Strategy*, SBT, no. 48, London: SCM Press, 1966.

'A Parenthetical Apologia: 1 Cor. 9.1–3', *Currents in Theology and Mission*, 1. 2 (1974), 68–70.

Nikiprowetzky, V. *Le Commentaire de l'écriture chez Philon d'Alexandrie*, Leiden: E. J. Brill, 1977.

North, H. F. 'Canons and Hierarchies of the Cardinal Virtues in Greek and Latin Literature', in L. Wallach (ed.), *The Classical Tradition: Literary and Historical Studies in Honor of Harry Caplan*, New York: Cornell University Press, 1966, pp. 165–83.

Nutton, V. 'Two Notes on Immunities: Digest 27, 1, 6, 10 and 11', *JRS* 74 (1984), 52–63.

O'Brien, P. T. *Introductory Thanksgivings in the Letters of Paul*, Supp. *NovT* 44, Leiden: E. J. Brill, 1977.

Oke, C. C. 'Paul's Method not a Demonstration but an Exhibition of the Spirit', *ET* 47 (1955–6), 35–6.

Ollrog, W. *Paulus und seine Mitarbeiter: Untersuchungen zu Theorie und Praxis der paulinschen Mission*, Wissenschaftliche Monographien zum Alten und Neuen Testament, 20, Neukirchen-Vlwyn: Neukirchener Verlag, 1979.

Orth, E. *Logios*, Leipzig: Norske, 1926.

O'Sullivan, N. 'Written and Spoken in the First Sophistic', in I. Worthington (ed.), *Voice into Text: Orality and Literacy in Ancient Greece*, Leiden: Brill, 1996, ch. 7.

Pack, R. A. *The Greek and Latin Literary Texts from Greco–Roman Egypt*, 2nd edn, Ann Arbor: University of Michigan Press, 1972.

Painter, J. 'Paul and the pneumatikoiv at Corinth', in M. D. Hooker and S. G. Wilson (eds.), *Paul and Paulinism: Essays in Honour of C. K. Barrett*, London: SPCK, 1982, ch. 19.

Parkes, E. P. *The Roman Rhetorical Schools as a Preparation for the Courts under the Early Empire*, The Johns Hopkins University Studies in Historical and Political Science, 63.2, Baltimore: Johns Hopkins Press, 1945.

Pearson, B. A. 'Philo, Gnosis and the New Testament', in A. H. B. Logan and A. J. M. Wedderburn (eds.), *The New Testament and Gnosis: Essays in Honour of Robert McLachlan Wilson*, Edinburgh: T. & T. Clark, 1983, pp. 77–84.
'Philo and Gnosticism', *ANRW* II.21.1 (1984), 295–342.
Pépin, J. 'Remarques sur la théorie de l'exégèse allégorique chez Philon', in R. Arnaldez, C. Mondésert and J. Pouilloux (eds.), *Philon d'Alexandrie*, Paris, Editions du Cerf, 1967, pp. 131–68.
Peters, F. E. *The Harvest of Hellenism*, New York: Simon and Schuster, 1970.
Petit, F. *Quaestiones in Genesim et in Exodum: Fragmenta graeca*, Paris, Editions du Cerf, 1978.
Phillipson, C. *The International Law and Custom of Ancient Greece and Rome*, 2 vols., London: MacMillan, 1911.
Plank, K.A. *Paul and the Irony of Affliction*, SBL Semeia Studies, Atlanta: Scholars Press, 1987.
Plummer, A. and Robertson, A. *A Critical and Exegetical Commentary on the First Epistle of St Paul to the Corinthians*, Edinburgh: T. & T. Clark, 1914.
Plummer, A. *A Critical and Exegetical Commentary on the Second Epistle of St Paul to the Corinthians*, Edinburgh: T. & T. Clark, 1915.
Pogoloff, S. M. *Logos and Sophia: The Rhetorical Situation of 1 Corinthians*, SBL Dissertation Series 134, Atlanta: Scholars Press, 1992.
Préaux, C. 'Lettres privées grecques d'Egypte relatives à l'éducation', *Revue Belge de Philologie et d'Histoire* 8 (1929), 757–800.
Prelaker, D. H. 'Apollos und die Johannesjunger in Act 18.24–19.6', *ZNW* 30 (1931), 301–4.
Radermacher, L. 'Alcidamas', in *Artium scriptores: Reste der voraristotelischen Rhetorik*, Wien: Rudolfe M. Rohrer, 1951.
Radice, R. and Runia, D. T. *Philo of Alexandria: An Annotated Bibliography 1937–1986*, Leiden: E. J. Brill, 1988.
Ramage, E. S. *Urbanitas: Ancient Sophistication and Refinement*, Norman University of Oklahoma Press, 1973.
Rankin, D. H. *Sophists, Socrates and Cynics*, London: Croom Helm, 1983.
Rea, J. 'A Student's Letter to His Father: *P.Oxy.* XVIII 2190 Revised', *ZPE* 99 (1993), 75–88.
The Oxyrhynchus Papyri, London: Egyptian Exploration Society, 1988, vol. LV.
Reinhold, M. *The History of Purple as a Status Symbol in Antiquity*, Collection Latomus, 116, Brussels: Revue d'études latines, 1970.
Reinmuth, O. W. 'The Edict of Tiberius Julius Alexander', *TAPA* 65 (1934), 248–59.
Reneham, R. *Greek Textual Criticism: A Reader*, Loeb Classical Monograph, Cambridge, Mass.: Harvard University Press, 1969.
Rhys Roberts, W. 'Caecilius of Calacte: A Contribution to the History of Greek Literary Criticism', *AJP* 18 (1897), 302–12.
'The Literary Circle of Dionysius of Halicarnassus', *CR* 14 (1900).
Roberts, C. H. 'The Greek Papyri', in J. R. Harris (ed.), *The Legacy of Egypt*, 2nd edn, Oxford: Clarendon Press, 1971.

Robins, R. H. *Ancient and Mediaeval Grammatical Theory in Europe*, London: G. Bell & Sons, 1951.

Robinson, A. T. 'Apollos the Gifted', *Biblical Review* 6 (1921), 380–3.

Robinson, J. A. T. *The Body: A Study in Pauline Theology*, SBT, no. 6, London: SCM Press, 1952.

Roebuck, C. *The Asklepieion and Lerna*, Corinth *XIV*, Princeton: American School of Classical Studies at Athens, 1951.

Romilly, J. de *Magic and Rhetoric in Ancient Greece*, Cambridge, Mass. and London: Harvard University Press, 1975.

Rosaeg, N. A. 'Paul's Rhetorical Arsenal and 1 Corinthians 1–4', *Jian Dao* 3 (1995), 51–75.

Rowe, C. J. *Plato*, Brighton: Harvester, 1984.

Rudolph, K. *Gnosis: The Nature and History of an Ancient Religion*, English translation, Edinburgh: T. & T. Clark, 1983.

Runia, D. T. 'Philo's *De Aeternitate Mundi:* the Problem of its Interpretation', *Vigiliae Christianae* 35 (1981), 105–51.

Philo of Alexandria and the Timaeus of Plato, Leiden: E. J. Brill, 1986.

Runia, D. T. and Radice, R. *Philo of Alexandria: An Annotated Bibliography 1937–1986*, Leiden: E.J. Brill, 1988.

Russell, D. A. *Plutarch*, London: Duckworth, 1972.

Greek Declamation, Cambridge: Cambridge University Press, 1983.

Russell, D. A. and Wilson, N. G. *Menander Rhetor*, Oxford: Clarendon Press, 1981.

Samuel, D. M. *Rhetorical Papyrus in the Yale Collection*, PhD dissertation, Yale University, 1964.

Sandbach, F. H. *The Stoics*, London: Chatto & Windus, 1975.

Sanders, B. 'Imitating Paul: 1 Cor. 4.16', *HTR* 74 (1981), 353–63.

Sandmel, S. 'Confrontation of Greek and Jewish Ethics: Philo, *De Decalogo*', in D. J. Silver (ed.), *Judaism and Ethics*, New York: Ktav Publishing House, 1970, vol. I, pp. 61–76.

Philo's Place in Judaism: A Study of Conceptions of Abraham in Jewish Literature, New York: Ktav Publishing House, 1971.

'Virtue and Reward in Philo', in J. L. Crenshaw and J. T. Willis (eds.), *Essays in Old Testament Ethics: J. P. Hyatt in Memoriam*, New York: Ktav Publishing House, 1974, pp. 217–23.

Philo of Alexandria: an Introduction, Oxford and New York: Oxford University Press, 1979.

'Philo Judaeus: an Introduction of the Man, his Writings, and his Significance', *ANRW* II.21.1 (1984), 3–46.

Sänger, A. 'Die δυνατοί in 1 Kor. 1.26', *ZNW* 76 (1985), 285–91.

Savage, T. B. *Power through Weakness: Paul's Understanding of the Christian Ministry in 2 Corinthians*, SNTS Monograph Series 86, Cambridge: Cambridge University Press, 1996.

Schiller, A. A. *Roman Law: Mechanisms of Development*, The Hague: Mouton, 1978.

Schmithals, W. *Gnosticism in Corinth*, English translation, Nashville: Abingdon Press, 1971.

'Die Korintherbriefe als Briefsammlung', *ZNW* 63 (1972), 263–88.

Schnackenburg, R. 'Christian Adulthood according to the Apostle Paul', *CBQ* 25 (1965), 334–70.

Schneider, N. *Die rhetorische Eigenart der paulinischen Antithese*, Tübingen: J. C. B. Mohr (Paul Siebeck), 1970.

Schreiber, A. *Die Gemeinde in Korinth: Versuch einer gruppendynamischen Betrachtung der Entwicklung der Gemeinde von Korinth auf der Basis des ersten Korintherbriefes*, Münster: Aschendorff, 1977.

Schreiner, K. 'Sur biblischen Legitimation des Adels: Auslegungeschichtliche Studien zu 1 Kor. 1.26–29', *ZKG* 85 (1975), 317–57.

Schümacher, R. *Der Alexandriner Apollos, Eine exegetische Studie*, Munich: 1916.

Schürer, E. *The History of the Jewish People in the Age of Jesus Christ*, 2nd edn, Edinburgh: T. & T. Clark, vols. II, III.1, III.2, 1979–87.

Schwartz, J. 'L'Egypte de Philon', in R. Arnaldez, C. Mondésert and J. Pouilloux (eds.), *Philon d'Alexandrie*, Paris: Editions du Cerf, 1967, pp. 35–45.

'Note sur la famille de Philon d'Alexandrie', *Annuaire de l'Institut de Philologie et d'Histoire Orientales et Slaves,* Université Libre de Bruxelles, 13 (1953), 591–602.

Sherwin-White, A. N. *Roman Society and Roman Law in the New Testament*, Oxford: Clarendon Press, 1963.

Shroyer, M. J. 'Alexandrian Jewish Literalists', *JBL* 55 (1936), 261–84.

Sider, R. D. *Ancient Rhetoric and the Art of Tertullian*, Oxford: Oxford University Press, 1971.

Skarsten, R. '*Quaestiones et Solutiones* – Some Observations on the Form of Philo's Exegesis', *SP* 4 (1976–7), 1–15.

Sly, D. I. *Philo's Alexandria*, London and New York: Routledge, 1996.

Smallwood, E. M. *Philonis Alexandrini: Legatio ad Gaium*, Leiden: E. J. Brill, 1961.

Smith, R. W. *The Art of Rhetoric in Alexandria: its Theory and Practice in the Ancient World*, The Hague: Martinus Nijhoff, 1974.

Solmsen, F. 'Aristotle and Cicero on the Orator's Playing on Feelings', *CP* 33 (1938), 393–4.

'The Aristotelian Tradition in Ancient Rhetoric', *AJP* 62 (1941), 35–50.

Sprague, R. K. *Plato's Use of Fallacy: a Study of the Euthydemus and Some Other Dialogues*, London: Routledge & Kegan Paul, 1962.

Stanton, G. R. 'Sophists and Philosophers: Problems of Classification', *AJP* 94.4 (1973), 304–6.

Steinthal, H. *Geschichte der Sprachwissenschaft bei den Griechen und Römern*, Berlin, 1891, vol. II.

Stephens, S. A. *Yale Papyri in the Beinecke Rare Book And Manuscript Library II, ASP*, 24, Chico: Scholars Press, 1985.

Stowers, S. K. *The Diatribe and Paul's Letter to the Romans*, SBL Dissertation Series, 57, Chico: Scholars Press, 1981.

'Social Status, Public Speaking and Private Teaching: The Circumstances of Paul's Preaching Activity', *NovT* 26 (1984), 59–82.

Sudhaus, S. *Philodemi volumina rhetorica*, Leipzig, 1892.

Sumney, J. L. *Identifying Paul's Opponents: the Question of Method in 2 Corinthians*, Sheffield: Sheffield Academic Press, 1990.

Süss, W. *Ethos*, Leipzig: Teubner, 1910.

Szarmach, M. 'Les Discours Diogeniens de Dion', *Eos* (1977), 77–90.

Tabor, A. J. D. *Things Unutterable: Paul's Ascent to Paradise in its Greco–Roman, Judaic and Early Christian Contexts*, Lanham: University Press of America, 1986.

Taubenschlag, R. 'The Legal Profession in Greco–Roman Egypt', in *Festschrift Fritz Schulz*, Weimar: Hermann Böhlaus Nachfolger, 1951, vol. II, pp. 189–91.

Taylor, J. *The Declamations of Quintilian, Being an Exercitation or Praxis upon His XII Books, Concerning the Institution of the Orator*, London, 1686.

Tcherikover, V. A. *Hellenistic Civilization and the Jews*, Philadelphia: Jewish Publication Society of America, 1961.

Tcherikover, V. A. and Fuks, A. (eds.) *Corpus Papyrorum Judaicarum*, Cambridge, Mass.: Harvard University Press, 1957.

Terian, A. 'A Critical Introduction to Philo's Dialogues', *ANRW* II.21.1 (1984), 272–94.

Philonis Alexandrini De Animalibus: the Armenian Text with an Introduction, Translation, and Commentary, Studies in Hellenistic Judaism, no. 1, Chico: Scholars Press, 1981.

Theissen, G. *The Social Setting of Pauline Christianity: Essays on Corinth*, English translation, Philadelphia: Fortress Press, 1982, ch. 2.

Psychological Aspects of Pauline Theology, English translation, Edinburgh: T. & T. Clark, 1987.

Thomas, G. S. R. 'The Origin of the Church at Rome: a New Solution', *RTR* 25 (1966), 81–94.

Thomas, J. D. 'L. Peducaeus Col(nus), Praefectus Aegypti', *ZPE* 21 (1976), 153–6.

Thrall, M. E. 'Super-apostles, Servants of Christ, and Servants of Satan', *JSNT* 6 (1980), 42–57.

Thusing, W. ' "Milch" und "feste Speise" (1 Kor. 3.1ff und Hebr. 5.11–6.3) Elementarkatechese und theologische Vertifung in neutestamentlicher Sicht', *Triere Theologische Zeitschrift* 76 (1976), 233–46.

Tobin, T. H. *The Creation of Man: Philo and the History of Interpretation*, CBQ Monograph Series, 14, Washington: Catholic Biblical Association, 1983.

Travers, S. H. 'Paul's Boasting in 2 Corinthians 10–12', *Studia Evangelica* 6 (1973), 527–32.

Turner, E. G. 'Oxyrhynchus and Rome', *HSCP* 79 (1975), 1–24.

'TIBERIVS IVLIUS ALEXANDER', *JRS* 44 (1954), 54–64.

van Unnik, W. C. *Tarsus or Jerusalem: The City of Paul's Youth*, English translation, London: Epworth Press, 1962.

Untersteiner, M. *The Sophists*, English translation, Oxford: Blackwell, 1954.

van der Valk, M. 'The Homeric Quotations or the Indirect Tradition of the Homeric Text', in *Researches on the Text and Scholia of the Iliad*, Leiden: E. J. Brill, 1963, Part 2, pp. 64–369.

Van Hook, La Rue. 'Alcidamas versus Isocrates: The Spoken versus the Written Word', *CW* 12 (1918), 91–4.

Vielhauer, P. *Geschichte der urchristlichen Literatur: Einleitung in das Neue Testament, die Apokryphen und die Apostolischen Väter*, Berlin: Walter de Gruyter, 1975.

Volkmann, R. *Die Rhetorik der Griechen und Römer in systematischer übersicht*, reprinted Hildesheim: Georg Olms Verlag, 1963.

Wacholder, V. B. C. *Eupolemus: A Study of Judaeo–Greek Literature*, New York: Hebrew Union College, 1974.

Wagner, W. H. 'Philo and Paideia', *Cithera* 10 (1971), 53–64.

Walden, J. W. H. *Universities of Ancient Greece*, London: Routledge, 1912.

Walsh, G. B. 'The Rhetoric of Birthright and Race in Euripides *Ion*', *Hermes* 106 (1978), 301–15.

Wan, S. K. 'Charismatic Exegesis: Philo and Paul Compared', *SPA* 6 (1994), 54–82.

Warfield, B. B. 'Paul's Buffeting of His Body', *ET* 31 (1919–20), 520–2.

Warnach, W. 'Selbtliebe und Gottesliebe im Denken Philons von Alexandrien', in H. Feld and J. Nolte (eds.), *Wort Gottes in der Zeit: Festschrift Hermann Schelkle*, Düsseldorf: Patmos, 1973, pp. 198–214.

Watson, A. 'Vespasian: Adsertor Libertatis Publicae', *CR* (n.s.) 23 (1973), 127–8.

Watson, D. F. 'The New Testament and Greco–Roman Rhetoric: a Bibliography', *JETS* 31.4 (1988), 465–72.

Weiss, J. 'Beiträge zur Paulinischen Rhetorik', in *Theologischen Studien B. Weiss*, Göttingen: Vandenhoeck & Ruprecht, 1897, pp. 165–247.

Der erste Korintherbriefe, reprinted Göttingen: Vandenhoeck & Ruprecht, 1977.

Welborn, L. L. 'On the Discord in Corinth: 1 Corinthians 1–4 and Ancient Politics', *JBL* 106.1 (1987), 85–111.

'A Conciliatory Principle in 1 Cor. 4.6', *NovT* 29.4 (1987), 320–46.

Westermann, A. *Vitae Decem Oratorum*, 1833.

Wheelock, F. H. (ed.) *Quintilian as Educator*, New York: Twayne Publishers, 1974.

White, J. L. 'Epistolary Formulas and Clichés in Greek Papyrus Letters', *SBL Seminar Papers* 2 (1978), 289–319.

Wilamowitz-Moellendorff, U. von. 'Asianismus und Atticismus', *Hermes* 35 (1900), 1–52.

Wilcox, S. 'Isocrates' Fellow-Rhetoricians', *AJP* 66 (1945), 171–86.

Wilke, C. G. *Die neutestamentliche Rhetoric. Ein Seitenstuck zur Grammatik des neutestamentlichen Sprachidioms*, Dresden and Leipzig, 1843.

Wilkens, U. *Weisheit und Torheit*, Tübingen: J. C. B. Mohr (Paul Siebeck), 1979.

Wilmes, E. 'Beiträge zur Alexandrinerede (*Or.* 32) des Dion Chrysostomos', PhD dissertation, University of Bonn, 1978.

Windorf, W. *Aristides*, Leipzig, 1829.

Winston, D. 'Philo's Ethical Theory', *ANRW* II.21.1 (1984), 372–416.

Winston, D. and Dillon, J. (eds.) *Two Treatises of Philo of Alexandria: A Commentary of De Gigantibus and Quod Deus Sit Immutabilis*, Brown Judaic Studies 25, Chico: Scholars Press, 1983.

Winter, B. W. 'Apollos as *aner logios*: A Problem for the Corinthian

Church and Paul', unpublished paper at the conference on the Graeco–Roman Cultural Setting of the Corinthian Correspondence, Macquarie University, Sydney, July, 1982.

' "If a man does not wish to work . . ." A Cultural and Historical Setting for 2 Thessalonians 3.6–16', *Tyn.B.* 40.2 (1989), 303–15.

'The Public Honouring of Christian Benefactors: Romans 13.3 and 1 Peter 2.14–15', *JSNT* 33 (1988), 87–103.

'The Importance of the *Captatio Benevolentiae* in the Speeches of Tertullus and Paul in Acts 24:1–-21', *JTS* (n.s.) 42 (1991), 505–31.

'The Messiah as the Tutor: the Meaning of καυηγητής in Matthew 23:10', *Tyn. B.* 42.1 (1991), 152–7.

'The Entries and Ethics of Orators and Paul (1 Thessalonians 2:1–12)', *Tyn. B.* 44.1 (1993), 55–74.

'Favorinus', in B. W. Winter and A. D. Clarke (eds.), *The Book of Acts in its Ancient Literary Setting, The Book of Acts in its First-Century Setting*, Grand Rapids and Carlisle: Eerdmans and Paternoster, 1993, pp. 196–205.

'Official Proceedings and Forensic Speeches in Acts 24–26', in B. W. Winter and A. D. Clarke (eds.), *The Book of Acts in its Ancient Literary Setting, The Book of Acts in its First Century Setting*, Grand Rapids and Carlisle: Eerdmans and Paternoster, 1993, ch. 11.

Seek the Welfare of the City: Christians as Benefactors and Citizens, Early Christians in the Graeco–World, Grand Rapids and Carlisle: Eerdmans and Paternoster, 1994.

'*Christentum und Antike*: Acts and Paul's *Corpus* as Ancient History', in T. W. Hillard, R. A. Kearsley, C. E. V. Nixon and A. Nobbs (eds.), *Ancient History in a Modern University*, Grand Rapids: Eerdmans, 1997, Vol. II, pp. 549–59.

Winterbottom, M. *Roman Declamation: Extracts with Commentary*, Bristol: Bristol Classical Press, 1980.

'Declamation, Greek and Latin', in A. Ceresa-Gastaldo (ed.), *Ars Rhetorica: Antica e Nuova*, Genova: Istituto de Filologia Classica e Medievale, 1983, pp. 67–76.

The Minor Declamations Ascribed to Quintilian, Texte und Kommentar, vol. XIII, Berlin and New York: Walter de Gruyter, 1984.

Wischnitzer, M. 'Notes to a History of the Jewish Guilds', *HUCA* 23.2 (1952), 246–53.

Wiseman, J. 'Corinth and Rome I', *ANRW* II.7.1 (1979), 438–548.

Wisse, J. *Ethos and Pathos from Aristotle to Cicero*, Amsterdam: Hakkert, 1989.

Wolfson, H. A. *Philo: Foundations of Religious Philosophy in Judaism, Christianity and Islam*, 2 vols., Cambridge, Mass.: Harvard University Press, 1962.

Woodhead, A. G. *Select Documents of the Principates of the Flavian Emperors*, Cambridge: Cambridge University Press, 1961.

Woodside, M. St. A. 'Vespasian's Patronage of Education and the Arts', *TAPA* 73 (1942), 123–9.

Wuellner, W. 'Haggadic Homily Genre in 1 Corinthians 1–3', *JBL* 89 (1970), 201.

'The Sociological Implications of 1 Corinthians 1.26–31 Reconsidered', in E. A. Livingstone (ed.), *Studia Evangelica*, vol. VI, Berlin: Akademie-Verlag, 1974, pp. 666–72.

'Ursprung und Verwendung der σοφός, δυγατός, ευγενής-Formel in 1 Kor.1.26', in C. K. Barrett, E. Bammel and W. D. Davies (eds.), *Donum Gentilicium: New Testament Studies in Honour of David Daube*, Oxford: Oxford University Press, 1977, pp. 165–84.

'Greek Rhetoric and Pauline Argumentation', in W. R. Schoedel and R. L. Wilken (eds.), *Early Christian Literature and the Classical Intellectual Tradition: in Honorem Robert M. Grant*, Paris: Beauchesne, 1979, pp. 177–88.

'Paul as Pastor: The Function of Rhetorical Questions in First Corinthians', in A. Vanhoye (ed.), *L'Apôtre Paul: Personnalité, Style et Conception du Ministère*, Leuven: Leuven University Press, 1986, pp. 49–77.

Yamauchi, E. M. *Pre-Christian Gnosticism: a Survey of the Proposed Evidences*, 2nd edn, Grand Rapids: Baker Book House, 1983.

Young, N. H. 'Paidagogos: The Social Setting of a Pauline Metaphor', *NovT* 29 (1987), 150–76.

Zeyl, D. 'Socratic Virtue and Happiness', *Archiv für Geschichte der Philosophie* 64 (1982), 225–37.

SUBJECT INDEX

INDEX OF NON-LITERARY SOURCES

INDEX OF LITERARY SOURCES

AUTHOR INDEX

Deils, H. 80
Deissmann, A. 156
Desideri, P. 40, 43, 47, 56–7, 126
DiCicco, M. M. 229
Dillon, J. 106
Dittberner, A. 175
Dodd, C. H. 222
Dorjahn, A. P. 78
Dorrie, H. 80
Dowdy, B. A. 221
Drummond, J. 6, 62
Dudley, R. H. 44
Dungan, D. L. 165

Earnesti, J. C. G. 84
Edwards, W. M. 32
Ellicott, C. J. 188
Elliott, J. K. 174
Ellis, E. Earle 181, 204

Fairweather, J. 122
Fee, G. D. 11, 156–7, 183, 196–8, 236
Feldman, L. H. 96, 176
Fiore, B. 196–7
Fischel, H. A. 61, 67
Fitzgerald, J. T. 198–9
Forbes, C. 37, 42, 51, 158, 207, 222–9, 238
Forbes, C. A. 24
Foster, S. 109
Fraser, P. M. 2, 20, 231
Friedrichsen, A. 224
Furnish, V. P. 211–13

Garnsey, P. 239
Geagan, D. J. 120
Gebhard, E. R. 127
Geoltrain, P. G. 77
Georgi, D. 203
Gibbs, J. M. 191
Gilchrist, J. M. 203
Gleason, M. W. 4, 132
Glucker, J. 25, 27–8, 38, 58
Goldstein, J. 97, 229
Goldstein, J. A. 133, 229
Goodenough, E. R. 60
Goodheart, H. L. 60
Graindor, P. 137
Grayston, K. 183
Grundmann, J. J. 172
Gunther, J. J. 204
Guthrie, W. K. C. 4

Hadas-Lebel, M. 103
Hall, F. W. 41

Hall, R. G. 217
Halleway, F. E. 80
Hands, A. R. 162
Hansen, G. W. 217
Hardie, A. 205
Harmon, A. M. 78
Harris, B. F. 40, 47, 126, 152
Harris, H. A. 60
Harrison, J. 220
Hartman, L. 148
Heinemann, I. 61
Hengel, M. 97, 221
Henrichs, A. 42
Henry, A. S. 133
Héring, J. 159, 184
Hock, R. F. 21, 148, 169, 185
Hodgson, R. 199, 225
Hoistad, R. 47
Holland, G. S. 208
Holmberg, B. 235
Hooker, M. D. 172
Horne, C. M. 147
Horsley, G. H. R. 38
Householder Jr., F. W. 78, 79
Hudson-Williams, H. L. 205
Hughes, F. W. 146, 208
Hunter, A. M. 175
Hurd Jr., J. C. 145
Hyldahl, N. 175

Ibrahim, M. H. 26, 79

Jacoby, F. 33
Jewett, R. 208
Johnson, S. E. 238
Jones, C. P. 1, 4, 7, 9, 40–5, 47, 51–4, 56–8, 64, 114–15, 126, 132, 134, 141, 152
Jones, M. 220
Judge, E. A. xi, 12, 19, 34, 37, 148, 156, 160, 188, 224, 230, 238

Kaibel, G. 137, 191
Kasher, A. 175
Käsemann, E. 167
Kaster, R. A. 20, 27
Kelly, W. G. 83, 92
Kennedy, G. W. 6, 8, 21–2, 31–3, 53, 61, 76, 110–11, 116, 125, 133, 153–4, 205, 215, 229, 231–4
Kent, J. H. 114, 120, 138–9, 142, 162, 186, 191
Kerferd, G. B. 4, 31, 49, 93, 95, 96, 164, 173